The Social Organization
of Schooling

The Social Organization of Schooling

Larry V. Hedges and Barbara Schneider, Editors

Russell Sage Foundation ◆ New York

The Russell Sage Foundation

The Russell Sage Foundation, one of the oldest of America's general purpose foundations, was established in 1907 by Mrs. Margaret Olivia Sage for "the improvement of social and living conditions in the United States." The Foundation seeks to fulfill this mandate by fostering the development and dissemination of knowledge about the country's political, social, and economic problems. While the Foundation endeavors to assure the accuracy and objectivity of each book it publishes, the conclusions and interpretations in Russell Sage Foundation publications are those of the authors and not of the Foundation, its Trustees, or its staff. Publication by Russell Sage, therefore, does not imply Foundation endorsement.

Library of Congress Cataloging-in-Publication Data

The social organization of schooling / edited by Larry V. Hedges and Barbara Schneider.
        p.   cm.
  Includes bibliographical references and index.
  ISBN 0-87154-340-0
     1. Schools—United States—Sociological aspects.   2. Educational sociology.
  3. School management and organization—United States.   I. Hedges, Larry V.
  II. Schneider, Barbara L.

  LC191.4.S653 2005
  306.43'2—dc22   2004061462

The paper used in this publication meets the minimum requirements of American National Standard for Information Sciences—Permanence of Paper for Printed Library Materials. ANSI Z39.48-1992.

Text design by Suzanne Nichols.

RUSSELL SAGE FOUNDATION
112 East 64th Street, New York, New York 10021
10 9 8 7 6 5 4 3 2 1

Contents

CONTRIBUTORS   vii

ACKNOWLEDGMENTS   ix

FOREWORD
Larry V. Hedges and Barbara Schneider   xi

Introduction   THE SOCIAL ORGANIZATION OF SCHOOLS
Barbara Schneider   1

PART I   THE RELATIONSHIP BETWEEN SOCIOLOGY AND THE
STUDY OF EDUCATION   13

Chapter 1   A SOCIOLOGICAL AGENDA FOR RESEARCH
ON EDUCATION
Charles E. Bidwell   15

Chapter 2   ECOSYSTEMS AND THE STRUCTURING
OF ORGANIZATIONS
W. Richard Scott   37

PART II   TEACHING AS A PROFESSION   49

Chapter 3   TEACHING AND THE COMPETENCE OF OCCUPATIONS
Robert Dreeben   51

Chapter 4   THE PROSPECTS FOR TEACHING AS A PROFESSION
Susan Moore Johnson   72

Chapter 5   THE ANOMALY OF EDUCATIONAL ORGANIZATIONS AND
THE STUDY OF ORGANIZATIONAL CONTROL
Richard M. Ingersoll   91

Chapter 6   PROFESSIONAL COMMUNITY BY DESIGN: BUILDING
SOCIAL CAPITAL THROUGH TEACHER
PROFESSIONAL DEVELOPMENT
Adam Gamoran, Ramona Gunter, and Tona Williams   111

PART III   THE MICROSOCIOLOGY OF SCHOOLS
AND CLASSROOMS   127

Chapter 7   THE NORMATIVE CULTURE OF A SCHOOL AND
STUDENT SOCIALIZATION
Maureen T. Hallinan   129

Chapter 8   WHY WORK WHEN YOU CAN PLAY? DYNAMICS OF FORMAL
AND INFORMAL ORGANIZATION IN CLASSROOMS
Daniel A. McFarland   147

Chapter 9   SCHOOL ORGANIZATION, CURRICULAR STRUCTURE, AND
THE DISTRIBUTION AND EFFECTS OF INSTRUCTION FOR
TENTH-GRADE SCIENCE
Robert A. Petrin   175

Chapter 10   SUBGROUPS AS MESO-LEVEL ENTITIES IN THE SOCIAL
ORGANIZATION OF SCHOOLS
Kenneth A. Frank and Yong Zhao   200

PART IV   CHANGE IN SOCIAL ORGANIZATIONS   225

Chapter 11   THE CROSS-NATIONAL CONTEXT OF THE GENDER GAP IN
MATH AND SCIENCE
Catherine Riegle-Crumb   227

Chapter 12   ORGANIZATIONAL COUPLING, CONTROL, AND CHANGE:
THE ROLE OF HIGHER-ORDER MODELS OF CONTROL IN
EDUCATIONAL REFORM
Christopher B. Swanson   244

Chapter 13   ACHIEVEMENT AND EQUITY
Chandra Muller and Kathryn S. Schiller   270

Chapter 14   SCHOOL TRANSITION PROGRAMS IN ORGANIZATIONAL
CONTEXT: PROBLEMS OF RECRUITMENT, COORDINATION,
AND INTEGRATION
Kathryn S. Schiller   284

Chapter 15   MOBILIZING COMMUNITY RESOURCES TO REFORM
FAILING SCHOOLS
Lori Diane Hill   301

REFERENCES   321

INDEX   357

Contributors

LARRY V. HEDGES is Stella M. Rowley Distinguished Service Professor in the Departments of Sociology and Psychology and Harris Graduate School of Public Policy Studies at the University of Chicago.

BARBARA SCHNEIDER is professor in the Departments of Sociology and Human Development and codirector of the Sloan Working Families Center at the University of Chicago and NORC.

CHARLES E. BIDWELL is William Claude Reavis Professor Emeritus in the Departments of Sociology and Education at the University of Chicago.

ROBERT DREEBEN is professor emeritus in the Department of Education and the College at the University of Chicago.

KENNETH A. FRANK is associate professor in the College of Education at Michigan State University.

ADAM GAMORAN is professor of sociology and educational policy studies and director of the Wisconsin Center for Education Research at the University of Wisconsin at Madison.

RAMONA GUNTER is research assistant in educational policy studies at the University of Wisconsin at Madison.

MAUREEN T. HALLINAN is William P. and Hazel B. White Professor in the Department of Sociology and director of the Center for Research on Educational Opportunity at the University of Notre Dame.

LORI DIANE HILL is assistant professor in the School of Education and the Center for Afroamerican and African Studies at the University of Michigan.

RICHARD M. INGERSOLL is associate professor in the Department of Sociology and Graduate School of Education at the University of Pennsylvania.

SUSAN MOORE JOHNSON is Carl H. Pforzheimer, Jr. Professor of Teaching and Learning in the Graduate School of Education at Harvard University.

DANIEL A. MCFARLAND is assistant professor in the School of Education at Stanford University.

CHANDRA MULLER is associate professor in the Department of Sociology at the University of Texas at Austin.

ROBERT A. PETRIN is a graduate student in the Department of Sociology at the University of Chicago.

CATHERINE RIEGLE-CRUMB is postdoctoral fellow in the Population Research Center at the University of Texas at Austin.

KATHRYN S. SCHILLER is assistant professor in the Department of Education Administration and Policy Studies at the University of Albany, State University of New York.

W. RICHARD SCOTT is professor emeritus in the Department of Sociology at Stanford University.

CHRISTOPHER B. SWANSON is senior research associate in the Education Policy Center at the Urban Institute.

TONA WILLIAMS is project assistant in the Wisconsin Center for Education Research at the University of Wisconsin at Madison.

YONG ZHAO is professor in the College of Education and director of the Center of Technology and Teaching at Michigan State University.

Acknowledgments

The completion of this volume rests on the work of many talented and committed individuals. Professor Robert Dreeben generously offered suggestive insights into several chapters. The editing for all of the chapters was undertaken by Lisa Hoogstra, Holly Sexton, Ann Owens, Allison Atteberry, Monica Li, Richard Striano, Page Lessy, Nora Broege, Maureen Marshall, and Paul Hanselman. Paul Hanselman and Ann Owens also helped in the formatting of the equations, tables, and figures. Page Lessy oversaw the process of contacting authors, preparing manuscript copy, and checking references. Jason Labate and Ann Owens had responsibility for the overall management and organization of the papers, including fiscal oversight.

Many of the papers were originally delivered at a conference honoring Charles E. Bidwell, which was generously supported by the National Opinion Research Center and the University of Chicago Department of Sociology. We would especially like to thank Craig Coelen, president of NORC, and Andrew Abbott, who was the chair of the Sociology Department, for their financial and organizational assistance. Kathleen Parks (NORC vice president for research), Isabel Garcia, Gail Spann, and Adelle Hinojosa helped in arranging support and logistics for the event. Jennifer Hanis-Martin, Elizabeth Greenbaum, and Surella Seelig were particularly helpful in making the conference a memorable occasion.

Finally, we thank the Russell Sage Foundation and Suzanne Nichols for support for this volume.

Foreword

The study of schools as social systems is at a new and challenging crossroad. Scholars have suggested that the turn of the century marked a propitious time to reassess not only the structure but the function of our nation's educational system, particularly in light of decades of institutional reforms and the movement of many more high school students into postsecondary education. The increasing privatization of education, the growing use of technology, and an increasing emphasis on school accountability and teacher and student performance are substantially changing the landscape of American schooling. What seems to be lacking is a sound theoretical understanding of how our educational system is working and how it is changing.

In 1965 Charles E. Bidwell wrote "The School as a Formal Organization," which appeared in James G. March's *Handbook of Organizations*. This essay, which described the field of the sociology of education, substantially altered the approach that scholars used to analyze schools as social systems. The comprehensive analytic framework, absent to that point, that Bidwell brought to the study of schooling infused the sociology of education with theoretical form and carefully chosen examples. Willard Waller (1932), decades earlier, had described in detail the lives of American schoolteachers, their students, and students' families. Bidwell's chapter was important not just because he described what people do in schools, but because his characterization of the relationships among them and the larger society was conceptually innovative and empirically directive. He delineated power relations, networks, and functional definitions of pedagogy as mechanisms within social systems that could be identified, measured, and analyzed in order to learn how to improve the effectiveness of schooling, not only for students but also for teachers and administrators.

This volume was inspired by the work of Charles E. Bidwell, who is regarded as one of the principal theorists in the field of sociology of education. His 1965 piece set out a framework that enabled analysts to bring to large-scale education studies, as well as to smaller case studies, a more complex vision of the school as a social system. Nearly forty years later it seems timely to rethink some of Bidwell's ideas, especially since his work emphasized the social aspect of schooling, which is often overlooked in education studies that focus primarily on academic achievement. Building on his early work and his more recent investigations of teacher networks, this volume takes a forward look at some of the major questions that sociological studies of schools are tackling both theoretically and empirically.

Researchers from fields such as organization theory, education, and sociology, with varying methodological approaches, have contributed to this book. Their

chapters are intended to provide new frameworks for understanding and analyzing many of the challenges facing education today in the areas of teacher professionalism, student social and academic engagement in learning, and organizational reforms such as standards-based instruction and systemwide accountability
measures. The scholars who contributed to this volume include both the well established and those who are just beginning their careers. We deliberately assembled this talented group of individuals to uniquely represent the expertise of those
steeped in the literature and the creativity of those who will shape the field in the
future.

Larry V. Hedges and Barbara Schneider
The University of Chicago, 2004

Introduction

The Social Organization of Schools

Barbara Schneider

T he sociology of education continues to thrive as a field of study. Researchers, particularly those interested in educational reform, have increasingly come to recognize the importance of understanding the social context of schooling and how it affects the actions and attitudes of those who are involved in it. Whether concerned with implementing a new mathematics curriculum or adopting legislation for teacher accountability, researchers are confronted with identifying the mechanisms that can stimulate and sustain change in individuals and institutions. To identify these mechanisms, investigators typically begin by developing deep conceptions of the social context and how it operates. Relying on theories and knowledge of social systems that are time- and place-dependent, sociologists of education continue to examine the conditions that drive changes in organizations, instruction, curricula, and learning. The fifteen chapters in this volume describe how the social context of education is defined and functions today and spell out the implications of these conceptions for school reform, standards, and teacher and student accountability.

The authors in this volume forge explicit links between social context and mechanisms for change in the social structure of classrooms and schools and the consequences of those links for instruction and student learning. Several of the chapters include empirical analyses that draw on new or existing datasets; others are extended essays that highlight developments in organization theory, teacher professionalism, and social norms and the socialization of children in schools.

The chapters are organized into four thematic parts: the relationship between sociology and the study of education, teaching as a profession, the microsociology of schools and classrooms, and change in social organizations. In linking the past with the present, the authors were asked to address variations on the following questions: How has organization theory influenced the study of schools as social organizations? What properties characterize the social organization of schools? What types of experiences shape teachers and distinguish them from other professionals? How can the teaching profession become more professional? How are values and normative commitments formed, and how do they influence teacher and student actions? How do interpersonal relationships among students, teachers, and parents affect organizational learning in schools and students' cognitive and social outcomes? And finally, what are some of the mechanisms that can bring about change in classrooms and schools and improve academic performance?

THE RELATIONSHIP BETWEEN SOCIOLOGY AND THE STUDY OF EDUCATION

Focusing primarily on the conceptualization of schools as social systems, part I highlights the unique organizational properties of schools and the dynamic relational transactions that occur within them. In chapter 1, Charles Bidwell analyzes the relationship between the discipline of sociology and the study of education, reviewing the areas on which researchers have focused their attention, the types of problems that are being examined today, and the areas in which investigators should direct their attention in the future. Tracing the major themes in the sociology of education over the past hundred years, Bidwell argues that most sociologists and organization theorists from the 1900s to the 1950s looked at the administrative structure of the educational system, often ignoring the internal workings of the school and its place in the local community. He believes that researchers today tend to be too specialized in their approaches to educational problems and rarely understand the relationships between instructional changes in classrooms and evolving societal changes at both the national and global levels. Research can help to explain the institutional dynamics of schools by focusing on the academic and social events that students experience in classrooms and by relating these to changes in the formal organization and curricular structure of schools. Bidwell challenges conventional ideas about what drives educational change, placing a renewed emphasis on the short-term internal workings of the classroom and their effect on larger institutional changes. Working from the inside out, he underscores the importance of studying student and teacher interactions longitudinally and the effect of these interactions on teachers' and students' behaviors and attitudes.

Analysis of the microsocial dynamics of the school and classroom and socialization outcomes has a relatively long history in the sociology of education. Bidwell acknowledges the organizational concepts of classrooms identified in the work of Robert Dreeben (1970), Rebecca Barr and Dreeben (1983), Maureen Hallinan and Aage Sørenson (1983), and Adam Gamoran (1987) but criticizes investigators for failing to give adequate attention to what is taught and how teachers function in the classroom and school. By conceptualizing the classroom or school as a social system, we can see more clearly how state and national educational reforms are mediated through the power structure and activities of local actors, including teachers and students.

The conceptual underpinnings of Bidwell's proposal for a research agenda are discussed in part by W. Richard Scott in chapter 2. Scott describes how Bidwell and his colleague John Kasarda theorized the profound ways in which organizations are shaped by their environments. Beginning with reviews of earlier studies that examined the environment of organizations as relatively formal and static and centered on organizational structure, rules, and norms, Scott asserts that Bidwell and Kasarda recognized the importance of the institutional environment but went on to employ ecological theory to study organizational processes. In contrast to other ecological scholars who examined the populations of similar organizations competing for similar resources, Bidwell and Kasarda were concerned with a specific organization and the individuals within it. Organizations, according to Bidwell and Kasarda, consist of individuals whose activities are directed at the exchange and transformation of resources. Scott argues that Bidwell and Kasarda's perspective is "relational" in its conception. They see organizations not as independent entities but rather as interdependent with the environments in which they exist. Bidwell and Kasarda's perspective focuses not on the rules and formalized structure of the organization but on the relationships and actions of the shifting collections of individuals within it.

Scott's description of Bidwell and Kasarda's model, which stresses the importance of process over entity, and structuring over structure, complements Bidwell's recommendations for a new research agenda for schools. In his conclusion, Scott maintains that organizations are evolving into more interdependent systems that interact with and are affected by their social context and that are penetrated by their participants and changeable in their boundaries. These ideas echo those of Bidwell, who contends that researchers need to study both the interrelationships among the individuals in schools and the schools' relationship to society.

TEACHING AS A PROFESSION

Underscoring the argument made by Bidwell in chapter 1 that the work and the workplace of teachers lie at the core of what sociologists need to consider more thoughtfully in their studies of education, part II examines the teaching profession. Three of the chapters address the question of what constitutes the "work" of teachers, the challenges of identifying the competencies of teaching in contrast to other occupations, the reasons why teaching has failed to be considered a profession, and the complexities and uncertainties that are inherent in the practice of teaching. The last chapter in this section turns to the workplace to discuss how a designed professional community of teachers can overcome some of the problems identified earlier and form strong social relationships that support change and improvements in teaching.

Robert Dreeben in chapter 3 raises the question of whether teaching is practiced with efficacy. To assess efficacy, he uses Philip Selznick's (1957, 50) idea of an organization's "distinctive competence to do a *kind* of thing," and within this frame he substitutes "occupation" for organization. Concentrating on the role of competence in an occupation—that is, the availability and employment of practical knowledge within a particular field—Dreeben argues that competence is the key concept missing in attempts to professionalize teaching. He compares competence in teaching to competence in law, engineering, and copy machine repair.

Teaching is the stepchild among occupational studies, according to Dreeben; lacking the political cachet of other types of jobs or careers, such as musician or physician, it has received limited systematic attention from sociologists. Describing what teachers do is difficult; conceptualizing what they do is even more difficult. Teachers work independently and have few opportunities to interact with their colleagues. The problems they face in their classrooms are usually particular and immediate, and the nature and difficulty of those problems depend on school level and student population. The occupation has little status, and teachers often have to ward off public criticism, which, while often not directed at them specifically, tends to question the legitimacy of the profession.

Dreeben takes issue with the notion of a single route to professionalism, arguing that occupations have different historical trajectories and that the meaning of professionalism differs depending on the occupation under consideration and its history. The training for becoming a teacher and the language used to describe the technical knowledge of teachers are nebulous and do not necessarily have the same meaning from one teacher to another. This lack of common meaning is related to how rarely the work of teachers is observed. Because their work is unobserved and their actions are often unrecorded, the work of teachers receives limited attention among researchers and in the teacher preparation curriculum of new recruits. As Bidwell suggests, and Dreeben underscores, what teachers do needs to be observed, analyzed, and published so that a codified knowledge about teaching as work could be generated and accumulated.

In chapter 4, Susan Moore Johnson further explores the status of teaching as a profession, connecting the impression of teachers as second-rate professionals to recent policy reports. Prior to the 1950s, teaching was seen as short-term, itinerant, and uncredentialed work taken by men as an interim step to a better job or by women who remained spinsters or taught for a short time before marrying and having children. Following the baby boom, when the demand for teachers increased, societal conditions did little to enhance the reputation of teaching. Teaching was viewed as akin to child care, subject to public funding and scrutiny, and based on a weak and contested knowledge base. Following the publication of *A Nation at Risk* in the 1980s (National Commission on Excellence in Education 1983), educators and policymakers increasingly came to view enhancing the professionalism of teachers as important to school improvement.

In her chapter, Johnson explains how teachers' lack of autonomy was held to be a major deterrent to improving practice. Emphasizing the importance of autonomy for teachers, the national report *A Nation Prepared: Teachers for the Twenty-first Century* recommended that teachers hold a bachelor's degree in the arts and sciences as a prerequisite for the study of teaching and a master's degree in teaching. A series of consortia were established to transform teaching, one of which advocated replacing teacher education courses with standards, a position that influenced the creation of the National Board for Professional Standards. Peer review of classroom performance by master or lead teachers and a greater voice for teachers in school policy decisionmaking were other reforms initiated to improve teacher professionalism. Some of these reforms have prevailed, while others, according to Johnson, have been less than successful. What reformers failed to recognize was the influence of societal changes, such as demographic shifts in the teaching force and limitations on state funding, on attempts to improve teacher professionalism.

In chapter 5, Richard Ingersoll evaluates the "loose-coupling perspective" often used to characterize the organization of schools. Ingersoll notes that schools, like other organizations, have a formal hierarchy, a specialized division of labor, and a formal structure of rules and regulations. Some observers have argued that a bureaucratic structure, with its formal rules and sanctions, is not the most effective mechanism for exercising organizational control and accountability, especially in schools. Asserting that schools have more control and coordination than some analysts have assumed, Ingersoll closely examines the decisions, issues, and activities associated with the work of teachers in schools.

Consistent with Bidwell, Ingersoll asserts that teacher actions are largely determined by the social context of their schools. Cohesion and cooperation among the faculty, communication among the staff and with the parents and students, and curricular coherence are shaped in part by the teachers but also by the administrators who work in schools. These conditions are not necessarily imposed externally but rather occur through teachers' daily interactions with others. Examinations of the social organization of teachers' work reveal that the classroom is not a separate, inviolate zone of teacher autonomy. Rather the work of teachers is subject to considerable direct control and constraint by those with whom they interact.

In chapter 6, Adam Gamoran, Ramona Gunter, and Tona Williams use intensive case studies to demonstrate how a school district has promoted a professional community among its staff. In the Bidwell tradition, Gamoran and his colleagues have turned their attention inside the schools to examine the activities of teachers and determine the extent to which successful educational reforms are influenced by strong collegial ties focused on teaching and learning. The authors claim that relational ties help to establish a professional community in which teachers exhibit shared values, focus collectively on student learning, collaborate, engage in reflective conversations about student learning, and share their practices with one another. These ideas, which place the social psychological aspects of relationships among teachers and students at the core of school change, permeate not only chapter 6 but also many of the other chapters in this volume. Attending to the social psychological often requires that investigators use a variety of methods, some of which include social network analysis and in-depth observations and case studies.

Part of a larger study, the analysis presented in chapter 6 relies on information from a small elementary school district that draws students from both a midsized city and a suburb. Over the course of several years the investigators observed twenty-six professional development workshops, interviewed sixty-one teachers and fifteen administrators, and surveyed over two hundred classroom mathematics and science teachers in four elementary schools. Using a variety of analytic methods, including social network analyses and more standard forms of multivariate analysis, Gamoran and his colleagues show how a professional community can evolve and be sustained.

Monthly professional development activities, in which student work was collaboratively reviewed, helped to encourage a common technical vocabulary, information sharing, trust, and norms and expectations about student performance. The relationships among the teachers asking for help seemed to function in much the same way as those among the teachers interacting within high school departments in Bidwell's research. Teachers in elementary schools are more likely to ask for help from teachers who are in the same grade level, just as teachers in high schools are more likely to interact with those in the same subject area. With respect to changing instructional practice, teachers who are highly engaged in fostering student thinking, delivering challenging content, and promoting an "equitable classroom community" tend to learn from a wide range of colleagues, whereas teachers who participate less in these types of activities learn mainly from those more involved in them than they are. Gamoran and his colleagues conclude that while these results are from only one district, it does appear that a stronger professional community can develop in this setting, though it may not be replicable in other places. Results seem to suggest that educational reforms, particularly those that are teacher-centered, may be more sustainable when activated and reinforced at the local level.

THE MICROSOCIOLOGY OF SCHOOLS AND CLASSROOMS

As Scott indicates in chapter 2, social network theory is one of the most understudied areas in research on organizations, yet it is also one of the fastest growing. The chapters in part III either employ formal social network analysis or intensively examine the relational ties between individuals to demonstrate how social norms are shaped and reinforced among teachers and students. In chapter 7, Maureen Hallinan examines the social psychological processes that link school context to student socialization. The chapter begins by discussing the origin and dimensions of the normative culture of a school, which consists of the set of norms, values, and meanings that are endorsed by the significant members of a school community. A school's normative culture typically has three components: the norms governing students' academic performance, social participation, and moral behavior. These three components differ within and across schools, often reflecting the values of the teachers, administrators, and parents of the students they serve. Hallinan draws on several intensive studies of schools to illustrate the variety of normative cultures in U.S. public and private schools.

How school norms are transmitted to the students and how students respond is the second major theme of this chapter. Academic norms are communicated primarily through the curriculum, the organization of instruction, school admissions policies, written documents, verbal exchanges, rewards and punishments, and role modeling. Social participation and moral behaviors are also influenced by these factors. In the instance of social participation, social service activities, community involvement, and participation in extracurricular programs are also key components in developing norms. A student's response to the school's normative culture depends in part on that student's intellectual, social, and psychological needs. One school may meet a student's intellectual and psychological needs better than another school. When a student enters a new school, teachers and peers become a referent group for the student to reflect on his or her own goals and objectives and determine how to attain them. If the intellectual challenges and social relationships students experience in school fail to meet their developmental needs, they are likely to resist school norms and risk becoming alienated from their school. However, students who are motivated to comply with the rules and regulations of their school are more likely to cooperate in the learning process, be accountable for their actions, and assume responsibilities as adults.

Daniel McFarland's and Robert Petrin's chapters both investigate relational ties. In chapter 8, McFarland focuses on student networks and the influence of status, popularity, and academic performance on student participation in class. In chapter 9, Petrin explores the relationships between teacher instructional techniques and student engagement and learning in science classes. Both chapters place the dynamics of classroom interaction at the heart of their analyses; however, rather than using formal network analysis, both authors use multilevel modeling to take into account the nested qualities of educational systems. McFarland models students within classrooms; Petrin studies students within courses within schools.

Using classroom observations, surveys, and school records of tenth- and twelfth-graders in two schools, McFarland studies student participation and status within classrooms. Answering the question "What makes some classes and students more academically and/or sociably vocal than others?" McFarland finds that some classes are more vocal than others because the students are given more opportunities to interact with one another through group work and discussion. Some students are more vocal than others because they have social standing among their classmates and their physical attractiveness affords them legitimacy in activities identified as work and play. Academic status appears to have relevance in classroom academic activities but not in other domains. Popular students appear to be at the center of interactions in classrooms.

Over the course of the academic year, work activities tend to include more play activities. Students eventually socialize during classroom activities even if the tasks required by the teachers do not encourage or promote it. Sociability in classrooms, if left undirected and unmanaged, can undermine task requirements and inhibit and dissuade students from becoming involved in classroom activities. Based on these findings, McFarland calls for research on how the social organization of peer groups in classrooms influences group cohesion, motivation, and interest in work and play in school activities and how and why the relationship between academic and social status in peer groups varies across students' schooling careers.

In the next chapter, Robert Petrin is also concerned with characterizing the experiences of high school students. Instead of using a peer group approach, he adopts an organizational framework and applies recent advances in comparative statistical methods to the analysis of instructional resources in schools. Drawing on the organizational and Opportunity to Learn paradigms, Petrin argues that high school courses represent positions in the curricula that are essentially "contexts within contexts" embodying teachers' goals and mandates, school academic and professional environments, and the distribution of various material and human capital resources within schools. In examining different tenth-grade science courses, Petrin assumed that instructional resources would vary across courses within schools and that these variations would be linked to student learning and engagement, once students' prior ability and other background characteristics had been taken into account. These assumptions regarding science courses were predicated in part on his prior research on mathematics courses, where he found that teacher-centered instruction was more likely to occur in geometry versus algebra classes and that when teachers used this instructional approach, students were more likely to be engaged and to have higher rates of learning.

Analyses are based on data from the National Educational Longitudinal Study of 1988 to 1994 (NELS:88–94). Petrin begins by identifying four tenth-grade science curricular positions (earth and environmental science, biology, chemistry, and physics) and constructs separate measures of student instructional experiences for each position simultaneously to determine whether they vary in systematic ways within the science curriculum. Recognizing that instructional practices are not only shaped by course content and the academic and demographic characteristics of students allocated to courses, he then examines the influence of school resources and classroom constraints on instructional experiences and student outcomes. His findings show that instructional experiences have sizable effects on student engagement and achievement in tenth-grade biology and chemistry, even after school resources, classroom constraints, teacher goals, professional beliefs, and student background characteristics are taken into account. Instruction that is teacher-centered, student-centered, or some combination of the two varies in effectiveness among students. Petrin suggests that researchers need to pay attention to students' experiences across all positions in the curriculum instead of focusing attention on either remedial or advanced courses. The distribution and effects of instruction within and between schools, he argues, are social facts that should inform subsequent theory and research on teaching, school organization, and curricular reform.

In chapter 10, Kenneth Frank and Yong Zhao use formal social network analysis to study the implementation of computer technology over time among a group of teachers and administrators in an elementary school. They then verify these findings from the elementary school with a second cross-sectional dataset that includes several hundred teachers and administrators in nineteen elementary schools. Underlying Frank and Zhao's research is the assumption that school actors, like members of most other social systems, organize themselves into formal units and subgroups in which relations, or ties, are concentrated. Specifically, the authors look at how interactions affect beliefs and behaviors, how identifying the structuring of interactions helps us to understand organizational decisionmaking, and what conditions influence the formation of subgroups within schools.

Focusing on technological innovations, they find that school actors' talk about technology affects their use of it. Talk about computer technology and curriculum is concentrated in subgroups as well as in grade levels. However, technology talk is slightly more likely to transcend the formal or organizational boundaries of grade level than is curricular talk. Finally, technology talk anticipates the formation of collegial ties, indicating that informal structures are responsive to a school's attempts to implement innovations.

CHANGE IN SOCIAL ORGANIZATIONS

Part IV concentrates on different educational reforms and their effect on existing models of organizational control at the global, national, state, and local levels. Bidwell points out in chapter 1 that one approach to understanding social change is through a globalization paradigm. He notes that while this perspective is partially compelling, it tends not to examine local situations, or at least not exhaustively. He argues that focusing on the specifications of the local mechanisms that undergird social change may provide stronger evidence of educational diffusion. Chapter 11 provides an example of how such local practices within a global frame can be studied. Catherine Riegle-Crumb examines how girls' and boys' academic performance in mathematics and science is influenced by opportunities for participation in the home, labor force, and government in various countries. Her analyses are based on two international datasets, the United Nations Women's Indicators and Statistics Database—which allows for the study of gender stratification across forty countries and includes measures of fertility rates, availability of legal abortion, and rates of participation in both the labor force and government—and the Third International Mathematics and Science Survey.

Her results show that in countries where women have higher levels of government representation, there are smaller gender gaps in mathematics and science achievement among students in middle school. Additionally, in countries where women have greater domestic freedom and participate more in the labor force, girls are more similar to boys in terms of favorable mathematics and science attitudes. Riegle-Crumb demonstrates how systems of national gender inequality are maintained by the connections between perceived opportunities and real outcomes. Her evidence suggests the presence of a vicious cycle whereby gender stratification in one generation is passed on to the next, creating a "dysfunctional inheritance of gender roles." It is this process that is reified globally.

Moving to the national and state levels, Christopher Swanson focuses in chapter 12 on two reform strategies that have received national attention—standards-based reforms and accountability-based reforms—and examines the extent to which states have adopted educational policies consistent with these reforms. The data for his study were obtained from state-level information published by the Council of Chief State School Officers, and the analysis employs a statistical approach known as item response theory (IRT).

His results show a lack of fit between the enactment of professional standards and standards-based reform, suggesting that standards-based reform, as it is practiced, appears to embody a narrow process-oriented model of organizational change rather than a more integrated combination of factors that encompass both teacher practice and curricular content. Among those states that enacted standards-based reforms, adoption typically began by establishing what students were expected to know, moved to defining the levels of mastery students were expected to exhibit with respect to content, and then attempted to align statewide testing programs with the content, using innovative assessment techniques. Although nearly all states that have adopted standards-based reforms developed curricular frameworks, fewer states have adopted performance indicators, and only a very limited number have implemented innovative assessment programs.

With respect to accountability standards, states show considerable overlap: that is, if they have adopted graduation requirements, they are also likely to have adopted assessment programs and accountability systems. These results suggest that individual policies can be viewed as largely interchangeable rather than as interdependent reforms. Levels of accountability vary across the fifty states, and the southeastern states appear to be at the vanguard of this reform movement. States with a culture of strong local control in education tend to have the lowest levels of state-led policies in the areas of standards-based or accountability reforms.

Swanson's results, which are based on two distinct approaches to educational reform, reveal that coherent reform strategies are being pursued systematically across states that share certain characteristics, such as local versus greater state control of educational policies. Researchers' explanations of prior unsuccessful educational initiatives often center on the structural fragmentation of the educational system. In contrast, policy analysts have tended to blame the failures of reforms on their design characteristics. Swanson argues that these two factors do not operate independently of one another. The loosely coupled character often attributed to movements for change in education may be the product of complex structural and governance relationships.

Chapter 13 also is concerned with state policies, in this case, variation in testing policies and its relationship to opportunities to learn, measured by course-taking in mathematics. This chapter by Chandra Muller and Kathryn Schiller examines the effects of states' strategies for raising standards and enacting accountability standards for students' academic progress on increasing enrollment in higher-level mathematics courses among students of different backgrounds and abilities. Using data from two nationally stratified longitudinal datasets—one on students, the National Education Longitudinal Study of 1988 to 1992, and the other on high schools, the National Longitudinal Study of Schools—the authors find that state policies are likely to have mixed effects on students' course-taking. With respect to standards, state policies have a small effect on students' mathematics course-taking in high school. The authors explain that this finding is not surprising given that the courses students take in high school are influenced by many other factors, such as school policies regarding class schedules and course prerequisites and student abilities and interests.

Increasing school accountability for student test performance seems to increase students' opportunities for learning, and holding schools accountable for students' learning appears to encourage more course-taking in mathematics. On average, students tend to accumulate more mathematics during their schooling careers irrespective of the level at which they were placed as freshmen, when accountability measures are in place. However, the effect is strongest for students who took higher-level courses as freshmen. The link between freshmen course placements and accumulated course credit is stronger in states for which test performance was linked to school consequences, suggesting that formal organizational structures such as accountability measures can have consequences. However, their effects are not uniform across all student populations. State policies such as accountability measures can create complex systems that have positive benefits for everyone. But raising the floor does not necessarily give students at the bottom an extra boost that moves them closer to having educational opportunities similar to those of students who are already advantaged.

One educational problem that most young people face is the transition from elementary school to middle school or high school. The structure of the schooling system in the United States, which has most adolescents moving from their elementary or middle school into a new and more complex institution, the high school, occurs at the same time that most young people are in the developmental throes of adolescence. Marked by physical changes, growing independence and social interest, and increasing cognitive development, the transition for many teenagers to often large, competitive, impersonal high schools can be personally and intellectually difficult. In chapter 14, Kathryn Schiller takes a school-level approach and examines three different high school transition programs to learn how institutional type and geographic location are related to the type of program that is adopted. Analyzing data from the National Education Longitudinal Study of 1988 to 1992, she finds that the average number of transition programs tends to be similar across high schools. However, private schools use significantly fewer programs, and magnet schools have significantly more programs. Location also appears to matter: urban schools use more programs compared to suburban and rural schools.

Differentiating among the types of programs, Schiller finds that public neighborhood schools and choice schools (not magnets) have similar programs that emphasize efforts to coordinate with their feeder schools but give limited attention to activities that facilitate students' integration into their new schools. Magnet and vocational schools have similar programs but tend to place less emphasis on coordination programs and more on activities that involve parents. Catholic and private schools tend to emphasize the use of intensive programs in which middle school students visit high school classes and "big brother and big sister buddy programs" that link them with high school students. Following Bidwell (1965), Schiller emphasizes that the types of programs high schools adopt are shaped by their environments and by the potential problems they have in recruiting members and obtaining resources. Private schools that rely on parent support are more likely to institute programs that might be too organizationally demanding in large public high schools. In small closed communities with few feeder schools, where most students move to high school with their friends, students and parents are less likely to require intensive knowledge of high school practices. The need for information is likely to be different for students attending magnet schools, where the student population and school practices are likely to be dissimilar from their feeder schools.

In the last chapter, Lori Diane Hill provides an in-depth case study that shows how a school community collaborative is using a citywide reform policy to re-create itself as a more viable educational institution. Schools in communities characterized by high concentrations of poverty and high degrees of social isolation are disproportionately affected by the current crisis in public education. One approach that community leaders have taken is to try to ensure that youth in their communities have access to quality educational institutions. Hill focuses on how one grassroots organization, the Vernon Collaborative, successfully acquired more resources and facilitated urban school reform within its community.

Framing her argument using social capital theory and linking it to social trust, Hill shows how the activities of the collaborative redefined the expectations and obligations of the members of the school community and set the high school on a new path of reconstitution. Vernon High School was at one time the center of a thriving, racially segregated, but economically heterogeneous neighborhood. Over the years the high school, once seen as a place to receive a good education, came to be seen by the residents and the school system as failing. Alumni of Vernon High School and other community organizers decided that something dramatic had to be done to change the course of education at the school. They organized themselves into a collaborative that focused on reform in the classrooms. Relying on her observations and interviews, Hill describes how the collaborative worked with the teachers and students in an attempt to mobilize internal and external resources and channel them into the school. The idea that one of the most promising strategies for reforming urban schools is having local communities take an active role has been a key aspect of school reform for decades. However, what form that involvement should take has been unclear. This chapter describes a new model for community engagement that holds promise for moving reform forward.

The reciprocal relationships that link individual, institution, and context are the focus of the fifteen chapters in this volume. As Bidwell argues, the work of sociologists of education is increasingly distinguished by efforts to understand, measure, and determine the effects of social context, whether in the classroom, the high school department, the school, the community, or the government. Without considering social context, it is unlikely that scholars or policymakers will be able to design and implement reforms that result in significant societal change.

Part I

The Relationship Between Sociology and the Study of Education

Chapter 1

A Sociological Agenda for Research on Education

Charles E. Bidwell

The long history of intellectual exchange between the discipline of sociology and the study of education has been fruitful for both of the partners. In this chapter, I review where we have been in this exchange and then consider where we are now and where we might go next. The research agenda that I propose addresses two underanalyzed problems: the global diffusion of the organizational forms and curricula that characterize national systems of education and the microsociology of schools.

My discussion of each is based on four premises. First, our main analytical task in the sociology of education, as in all of social science, is to explain change in social organization and in socially organized behavior. Second, to explain change of this kind we must discover the mechanisms that initiate and sustain the change process (see Hedström and Swedberg 1998). Third, these mechanisms always consist of the behavior of individual or corporate actors. Fourth, these mechanisms therefore will be discovered, whatever the level of social aggregation under analysis, by examining local events, that is, events that are particular to a time and place.

WHERE WE HAVE BEEN

When they lectured and wrote about education, Émile Durkheim and Max Weber prefigured two principal theoretical strands that have characterized the exchange between sociological and educational scholarship. Durkheim, the onetime professor of pedagogy lecturing on moral education (Durkheim 1925/1961), systematically analyzed the ways in which social participation socializes children, specifying the mechanisms for socialization found in classroom social organization. Later, lecturing on the history of education in France (Durkheim 1938/1977), he offered an essentially political analysis of institutional formation to account for the development of secondary and higher education from the beginnings of the University of Paris forward.

Weber's discussion of education at various points in *Economy and Society* (Weber 1921/1978) provides both a long-term and a short-term framework for understanding how education takes the form it does from time to time and place to place. His long-term analysis anchors forms of education within orders of belief and corresponding orders of domination, so that over the long sweep of history the organization and content of schooling change as societies move from charismatic, through traditional, to rational-legal modes of thought and authority. His short-term analysis echoes Durkheim on the development of education in France. It centers on politics, finding in the national mass politics of turn-of-the-twentieth-century Western Europe and America the mechanisms that drive change in educational organization, curricula, and access as schooling moves from traditional and aristocratic forms to rational and bureaucratic ones.

Schools and Schoolteachers

The apparent disjuncture in the organization of contemporary American school districts between elaborated administrative superstructures and relatively simple pedagogical infrastructures challenged Weber's (1921/1978, 1006–12) depiction of bureaucracy as a rational construction intended to deal efficiently with the complexities of collective enterprise. Subsequent sociological theories of formal organization have been derived substantially from attempts to understand this disjuncture. They are rooted in particular in the work of James March and Johan Olsen (1976) on "garbage can" decisionmaking, of Karl Weick (1976) on loose coupling, and the subsequent neo-institutional theories of organizational form (Meyer and Rowan 1977; Powell and DiMaggio 1991).

When American sociology was coming of age in the 1920s, Willard Waller was collecting diaries and other personal documents from rural schoolteachers. These documents provided the data for *The Sociology of Teaching* (1932). In this classic volume, Waller treated the high school as a social system that was fully open to its local environment. There the social order of the classroom and school arose from antagonistic interaction between administrators, teachers, and students, shaped substantially by the local institutionalization of the school as a "museum of virtue."

As the sociology of education grew and prospered in the years following World War II, Waller's holistic conception of school and community virtually disappeared from view.[1] The field had become the beneficiary of a growing governmental and popular concern for equity in access to schooling and a concomitant turn to social science to ground public policy (Dreeben 1994). As the field grew, it differentiated. James Coleman's *The Adolescent Society* (1961a) began an enduring line of work on the life of students in school centered on ways in which their location in the formal and informal elements of school social organization affects their academic achievement and subsequent life chances.

This body of work itself branched. One branch has treated relationships between a school's normative climate and individual students' achievement. Some of these studies have measured "climate" as no more than an aggregation of the dispositions of individual students or teachers, or in other ways as a correlate of school-level properties (see, for example, Brookover et al. 1979; McDill and Rigsby

1973; Rutter et al. 1979; Wilson 1959). Others have considered climate to be a function of more microlevel aspects of school social organization, usually limited to peer relationships (see, for example, Campbell and Alexander 1965; Coleman 1961b).[2]

The other branch has come to dominate empirical work in the sociology of education. It is the study of curricular differentiation—how placement in elementary school ability groups and high school tracks affects students' achievement (on ability grouping, see, for example, Barr and Dreeben 1983, and on tracking, see Oakes, Gamoran, and Page 1992).

A second line of work has been slower to appear. Treating the school as a workplace for faculty, this research considers how the formal and informal organization of teachers' work provides, or fails to provide, resources of social capital that they can use to deal with everyday problems of teaching. Dan Lortie (1969, 1975) and Robert Dreeben (1973) opened this field. It since has engaged several investigators (for example, Bidwell and Yasumoto 1999; McLaughlin and Talbert 2001; Rowan 1990b; Siskin 1994; Yasumoto, Uekawa, and Bidwell 2001).

Intersecting with commentary on the weak professionalization of the American teaching force (Dreeben 1996; Herbst 1989b), this body of work, like Waller, depicts American schoolteachers situated in a work environment that contains often irreconcilable demands. That is, teachers in American public schools are said to be vulnerable to local pressures about what and how to teach and to recurrent waves of pedagogical innovation. For this reason, these commentaries conclude, teachers must depend primarily on local colleagues for help in resolving the dilemmas that these conflicts create and on these same colleagues and, even more, their students for social support as they go about their daily work. Brian Rowan (1990b) provides the most trenchant analysis of the conflicting elements of teachers' work environments, and Lortie (1969, 1975) and Dreeben (1968) the most compelling accounts of teachers' dependence on the goodwill and approbation of their students.

Education in Society

The study of education as an institution in society, begun with such force by Durkheim and Weber, also has been slow to develop. Not until 1984 did another major statement about the formation of national systems of education appear— Margaret Archer's (1979) magisterial treatment of the emergence of education in Britain, France, and Russia. Like Durkheim and Weber, Archer treats the institutionalization of systems of education as a consequence of the interest-driven action of powerful collective actors.

This tradition, however, has not continued. Rising neo-institutional theory soon informed research on the global spread of forms of education that occurred in the surge of nation-building following the Second World War. This body of work has come to dominate research on education in nation-states. Neo-institutional theory has replaced politics and power as mechanisms of institutionalization with sociocultural and cognitive mechanisms. These mechanisms include the formation and diffusion of national systems as expressions of the global diffusion of a template of beliefs about what modern nations look like and what their schools and curricula look like (Meyer and Hannan 1979; Meyer, Kamens, and Benavot 1992).

WHERE WE ARE NOW

Specialization in scholarship has its benefits, principal among them the possibility of depth and refinement in the conceptualization of the phenomenon that is under the specialist's microscope. However, it also has costs. Those costs arise in particular from failures of understanding when the phenomenon is part of a larger system of events, so that the phenomenon can be understood fully only by including its principal relationships to other parts of the system. The current state of sociological scholarship on education seems to me to be paying rather substantial costs of specialization. This is true of work on schools in society and of work on the lives of teachers and students in the social orders of schools.

The Institution of Education

Local events should be of prime concern to sociologists who are interested in education as an institution in societies. Analyses of the diffusion of education conducted by John Meyer and his colleagues (Meyer and Hannan 1979; Meyer, Kamens, and Benavot 1992) conclude that the diffusion process has produced a worldwide convergence in both the organizational forms and the curricular substance of national educational systems. In these analyses, the systems tend to converge on a conception of educational modernity that itself has diffused to inform in a compelling way national elites and other makers of educational policy in emerging no less than in extant nation-states.

This analysis is consonant with the growing literature that treats globalization—that is, the emergence of economic and political interdependence and convergent beliefs about the nature and conditions of modern life—as perhaps the current master trend of social change. However, two of the major students of globalization, Saskia Sassen (2001) and Janet Abu-Lughod (1999), agree about the continuing importance of the local in the midst of the apparent homogenization of world societies. They argue that integration into the global economy has significant consequences that are particular to place.

This way of thinking about global trends in social and economic change is particularly important because it begins to specify the mechanisms that produce these trends. The trends themselves, after all, are simply descriptions of principal directions of change in the attributes of localities. To say that the observed worldwide diffusion of certain structural and substantive forms of education can be attributed to another pattern of diffusion, the diffusion of conceptions of modern statehood and schools, is in fact more an effort to explain one process by another than an attempt to provide a satisfactory account of the mechanisms involved.

Explanation of this kind begs the prime analytical question of cause, that is, the specification of mechanisms (on the process-mechanism distinction, see Hedström and Swedberg 1998). John Meyer and his collaborators are well aware of the importance of this specification (see, for example, Meyer and Hannan 1979), but they do not explore it in depth. More recently, Francisco Ramirez (1997) and Colette Chabbott and Ramirez (2000) have addressed the issue of mechanism with more precision. In particular, they have proposed that international agencies and non-governmental organizations provide economic incentives that drive developing nations toward a common standard of statehood, including a common standard of educational provision. This explanation is cogent, but undoubtedly partial. Moreover, the issue of the local consequences of involvement in a global pattern of educational diffusion remains to be addressed.

Randall Collins (2000) reminds us that the model of education that is spreading worldwide is the outcome of social processes of relatively recent origin. Collins discusses the development of the modern university, but his argument has a broader application to the development of education in societies. He proposes that the university in its modern form emerged in a context of bureaucratization and professionalization that has created markets for credentials and the concomitant training and examining that are required for credentials to be earned. As the mechanisms that have motivated both of these processes, he proposes the action of groups of professionals, officials, and teachers pursuing interests in power, wealth, or status. In this way, he argues, the modern university took shape in the context of the thoroughgoing bureaucratization of nineteenth- and early-twentieth-century European and American societies.

The reader could easily quarrel with some of the particulars of Collins's account and might be skeptical about his underlying theoretical argument. What I wish to underscore is his meta-theoretical approach, namely, his concern with process, with identifying the mechanisms that drive the process and, most notably, with specifying these mechanisms as constituted of specific events in specific societies and times. The theory may be general, but its evaluation is local.

Another facet of Collins's argument is instructive. He proposes that education has its own institutionalizing impact on societies by shaping social stratification. In contrast to Pierre Bourdieu's stress on educational systems as reflections of social stratification (see, for example, Bourdieu and Passeron 1977), Collins (2000, 214) asserts that "we . . . go through a lengthy process of acquiring . . . degrees that determine what jobs we can get because of . . . changes in school organization that started in the Christian Middle Ages and have recently spread around most of the world. . . . [World societies'] distinctive forms of social stratification have been created by their forms of education."

Sassen's (2001) depiction of global cities has a similar focus on local processes of institutionalization. She asks about the impact of integration into the global economy on a city's social and economic organization. She predicts, for example, growing gaps in income between social strata brought about by a waning middle class, the decline of mass consumption as a component of the local economy, and the rise of a cosmopolitan style of life characterizing a newly dominant professional class.

In addition, both Sassen (2001) and Abu-Lughod (1999) ask how local urban histories, demography, political and social organization, and culture give particular shape to the local impact of integration into the global economy. This same question must be asked about the interplay of the local and global in the formation and development of national educational systems.[3]

Teaching in the Schools

At present, we construct models of students' academic achievement that effectively exclude teachers from an active role in the achievement process. Doing so, we make an implicit assumption that what students learn arises primarily from their own capabilities and motives and their consequent capacities to exploit their exposure to instruction. What this instruction consists of—in particular, what the teacher's acts contribute to the process—is left substantially unspecified.

For example, the Sørenson and Hallinan (1977) model of opportunities to learn, one of the most precisely specified representations of the academic achievement process, treats achievement as a function of students' ability, their motivation, and a term for "quality of instruction" that is not disaggregated. Other research on the school as context for academic achievement presents models that treat the context in less aggregate terms. However, they center either on the school or the classroom as a stock of resources, including such resources as teachers' formal preparation, verbal ability, gender, or race (see, for example, Coleman et al. 1966), or on the amount or content of what is taught, excluding how the teacher and students interact (see, for example, Barr and Dreeben 1983).

It is time to bring the teacher—in particular, the teacher who is in the act of teaching—back in, simply because the content of what is taught takes form and has its effects largely as a function of the way it is taught. Moreover, such teacher attributes as verbal fluency or race have their effects primarily through what the teacher does in interaction with students, including both formal instruction and less formal student-teacher exchanges.

Dan Lortie (1969, 1975) depicts teachers working in substantial isolation from their colleagues, which he treats as a function of a mechanical division of instructional labor. His analysis has become the standard reference. Of course, teachers do not act altogether independently or autonomously. How they conduct their classes and how they interact with students are to a considerable degree consequences of formal organizational regulation. Richard Ingersoll (2003, this volume) shows how administrative and other regulative structures in schools affect teachers' procedural compliance and their commitment to their work and their schools. Other research on the social organization of the faculty workplace, in both elementary and high schools, suggests that colleague interaction, in particular informal ties, can influence substantially the way a faculty does its work (Bidwell and Yasumoto 1999; Bryk, Lee, and Holland 1993; Johnson 1990; McLaughlin and Talbert 2001; Siskin 1994).

Teaching is fairly described as weakly professionalized (Dreeben 1996; Herbst

1989b). In this volume, Robert Dreeben posits the systematic demonstration of competence in difficult situations as a key condition of professionalization. He argues that schoolteaching has not met this condition. Similarly, Susan Moore Johnson (this volume) documents a history of failures to professionalize the teaching occupation. Teachers' occupational organizations are not impotent. Rather, having followed the path of unionization, these organizations come into play with respect to the extrinsic conditions of teachers' work, not its pedagogical substance. If one accepts two propositions, that the teaching occupation has only marginally codified the substance of teaching and that it lacks effective means of occupational control over the conduct of its members, then an analysis of the work of teachers must center on local events in schools and school districts.

WHERE SHALL WE GO? APPLYING A THEORY OF INSTITUTIONALIZATION

In this volume, Richard Scott calls our attention to Mustafa Emirbayer's (1997) distinction between "entities" and "processes." He reminds us that for much of its history, the sociology of organizations generally, and of schools in particular, has treated their structures in static terms, as constituted of independent entities, rather than in dynamic terms, as interrelated in ongoing processes of structural production and reproduction.

In contemporary neo-institutional research on the global diffusion of education, the receiving nation-states, the termini of the diffusion process, are treated as entities. They are passive rather than dynamic recipients of the master myth of educational modernity and its organizational and curricular specification. By contrast, Durkheim, Weber, and Archer take as the fundamental question understanding the interactions of changes in societies and changes in their systems of education.

Most of the empirical literature on schooling also is couched in the terms of social statics. When schooling is treated as status attainment, it is only the individual student who changes—who, for example, learns, gains tastes, develops motives, and forms aspirations. These changes take place in the context of the unchanging school environment, an entity. The possibility that changing students and changing environments interact is not addressed.

Applying a theory of institutionalization can shed new light on the causal mechanisms involved in the emergence and change of national systems of education and in the process of schooling in individual schools. The most useful theory is a political theory that was given early, but relatively full, expression by William Graham Sumner (1906), and later in essentially the same terms by Arthur Stinchcombe (1968). Sumner's theory contains two key propositions. First, social institutions come into being through the action of powerful groups in pursuit of their own interests, whether ideal or material. Second, however powerful the actors who make such attempts, institutionalization cannot occur in the absence of fit with the moral, social, organizational, and material conditions in its immediate environment. That is, institutional formation is subject to the discipline of environmental selection (on these and related points, see Bidwell 2001).

These two propositions are about the creation and early stabilization of institutions. To these, add Philip Selznick's (1949, 1957) proposition that institutions are creators of value, that is, once they come into being, participation in the institutionalized world that they create tends to become a good in itself. The valorization of institutions adds to their stability. So, for example, in his study of the Tennessee Valley Authority (TVA), Selznick argues that by grounding the occupational and, by extension, personal identities of its staff, the TVA was valorized so that their efforts were directed substantially toward maintaining the organizational status quo. These classic propositions on institutionalization provide a theoretical frame with wide applicability to the study of social change. I consider their application first to research on the global diffusion of education and second to studies of the institutional dynamics of schools.

Studying the Dynamics of Global Diffusion and National Systems

For research on the global diffusion of education, there are two key questions. First, how do local events in specific societies constitute the mechanisms that drive the emergence and stabilization of national systems of education, that is, how they are organized and what they teach? Second, what are the consequences of these organizational forms and curricula for other social institutions?[4] These questions should be explored in detailed studies of both historical and contemporary societies. What is required at this point are not the sweeping, multi-society comparisons that have been the hallmark of research on the global spread of education, but rather case studies that rely on fine-grained archival, observational, and interview data. As studies of this kind accumulate, they can provide a more secure base for comparative analyses that then could ground generalizing inferences about the dynamics of global educational institutionalization.

With respect to the first of the questions, local events as mechanisms, the conception of institutionalization as a political process leads the sociologist to ask, as Margaret Archer (1984) asked: Which are the powerful groups? On what is their power based? What is the nature of their interests, both ideal and material, in the provision of education? What actions do they take? And what are the consequences for how the educational system is organized and its curriculum composed?

Such studies inevitably will focus on the interests and actions of elites, but they need not and should not be confined to elite groups, nor need or should they be confined to actors within the society under study. Because national systems are governmental systems, governments, parties, and professional educators each may supply powerful, interested actors on the educational scene. The very global spread of education indicates the potential importance of international organizations as interested and potent actors. This aspect of investigations, like Weber's (1921/1978) and then Archer's (1979), almost certainly will deal centrally with matters of access to schooling of different levels and curricular substance and thus with the consequences of the institutionalization of educational systems for social stratification.

The postulate of environmental selection raises an additional set of questions. The current findings on the worldwide spread of educational forms and curricula (Meyer, Kamens, and Benavot 1992) indicate a massive convergence across national boundaries. However, in the absence of detailed local information, it is difficult to say how much these findings mask local variation and whether variation of this kind is superficial or substantial. The question of environmental selection centers in part on the degree to which material resources constrain the form and scope of educational provision and in part on local beliefs and customs as they are expressed in popular demand. Here individually less powerful actors—individuals and households—become in the aggregate potent sources of both opportunity for and constraint on the emergence and expansion of particular levels and kinds of education (Craig 1981).

I can put this point differently by proposing that for educational forms or curricula to persist they must express a society's core values and the norms that govern the conduct of its members. Some local variation in the content of curricula, for example, may derive from the particular interests of the powerful, such as political elites' use of courses in national literatures as tools of national building. However, it remains to be seen whether local variation in the structure of access to different levels of schooling or in the kinds of education provided, inter alia, is minor variation around a common theme of global convergence or whether it indicates a more profound interaction of global trends and strong local political and cultural forces (see Fourcade-Gourinchas and Babb 2002).

With respect to the second question, consequences for other social institutions, I already have noted the possibility of effects on social stratification, and they are the most obvious and the most sociologically important. Consider further Collins's (2000) proposition that the institutionalization of formal sequences of training, examining, and concomitant credentialing forms principal occupational categories. This proposition needs comparative investigation, built upon detailed case studies of historical and contemporary societies.

Collins's proposition is based on the cogent premise that the credential is a resource that occupational groups can use to control access to membership and employment. In the classic accounts of this use of credentials, the active agents of restriction are the occupational groups themselves. They attempt to gain a place in the university curriculum and control the content and evaluation standards used therein (see, for example, Hughes 1958; Larson 1977).

However, Collins advocates a more active role for education in the creation of social stratification. His argument suggests that when universities, or, more properly, such powerful actors as faculties, academic organizations, and foundations, develop new, practically applicable, curricular fields, they alter the opportunity structure for the collective mobility of occupations. New fields may be created in the academy for many reasons, including the differentiation of knowledge, the ambition of academic entrepreneurs, and the demographic overexpansion of university specialties relative to student demand (Ben-David and Collins 1966; Parsons and Platt 1973).

When Collins's proposition is evaluated, the results very likely will show that there are active roles for both academic and occupational groups. This research should push on into the analysis of consequences for the resulting systems of stratification (for example, the numbers and relative size of identifiable social strata), the substantive bases for the formation of these strata (for example, control of information versus material wealth), and the consequent distribution of individual life chances.

However, consequences for social stratification are not the only institution-changing effects of educational institutionalization that are worth studying. How expansion and other changes in educational provision affect national, political, and economic development has been a vexed research topic for some time, with unclear findings (see, for example, McGinn 1980). To a considerable extent, the difficulty lies in ambiguity about the conceptualization of national development, a topic that lies beyond the purview of this chapter. Another difficulty has been created by failures to specify the attributes of educational systems that are implicated in specific forms of national development.

To date, the bulk of the work in this area has been limited to three issues: the formation of human capital as it affects labor force participation, the role of higher education in technical knowledge creation, and consequences for technological innovation and the reach and flexibility of the economy (see, for example, McGinn 1980). There may be merit in broadening the scope of inquiry. Particular promise may reside, for example, in efforts to show how participation in varying amounts and kinds of schooling contributes to the formation of a sense of national identity among youth and affects the capacity of youth in varying social and economic circumstances to participate in civil society.

Finally, there is the question of the valorization of institutions. Within the frame of local history, the course of institutional change in national systems can be analyzed as an outcome of the relative power and interests of the principal actors on the educational scene and of environmental opportunity and constraint. Nevertheless, the possibility that institutions may become objects of value for the persons who participate in them cautions us not to overlook the degree to which these participants, including the faculties of universities and schools and their professional organizations, are invested in organizational maintenance.

Institutional valorization has particular interest with respect to the stabilization of national educational systems and the degree to which they are able to adapt to major environmental changes. Consider, for example, that during the latter half of the nineteenth century the schools and universities of Britain—and, to a degree, of France—were much slower than those of Germany and the United States to respond to the demand for instruction in science and other technologically relevant subject matters that was generated by rampant industrialization. A strong case can be made that these differences derived substantially from variation in the investment of elites in the traditional liberal curriculum, interacting with variation in the competitiveness of the educational systems. If so, these cross-national differences were rooted in the distinctive historical development of each national society (Ben-David 1977/1992; Clark 1983).

Value-based interest in the welfare of educational systems and their component organizations has complex roots in both material interests and belief in the intrinsic value of one or another variety of schooling. Such interests were, for example, a prime motivation of professional educators in the urban systems of the United States during early-twentieth-century conflicts over the nature and scope of vocational education (Katznelson and Weir 1985; Peterson 1985).

The slowness of British education to adapt to technological and economic change, despite the dramatic challenge of the Crystal Palace Exposition, can be attributed in part to the value that members of the English aristocracy and gentry placed on a classical curriculum. Weber's (1921/1978) discussion of the transformation of the educational systems of Europe during the early years of the last century is similar. He stresses the value placed on classical studies by aristocratic families, set over against the interest of an expanding and increasingly powerful bourgeoisie in education that would prepare their offspring for work in commerce and the professions.

Studying the Institutional Dynamics of Schools

Two lines of research can help us understand the institutional dynamics of schools. One would focus on the microsociology of schools, situating events in classrooms within the social organizational context of the school and examining these events as processes through which students achieve academically and are otherwise socialized. The other would address the formal organization of schools and school districts, identifying mechanisms of structural and curricular stabilization and change. I discuss the former in some detail and consider the latter more briefly, chiefly to show how short-term events within schools may affect longer-term processes in the institutionalization of schools as organizations.

STUDYING THE MICROSOCIOLOGY OF SCHOOLS   Research on the microsociology of schools should focus on the classroom because it is the place where teaching takes place and a prime location where, in other ways, school life socializes students. The classroom is highly permeable to its immediate social environment, the most significant components of which are the networks of ties among teachers and among students. Without losing its focus on this immediate environment, this research should be designed to take into account administrative leadership, in particular formal and informal ties between administrators and teachers, and the broader environment of local community interests and actors and organizational and governmental policy and regulation.

Events in classrooms should be analyzed under the twin premises that they are consequences of the demographic and institutionalized setting in which they take place and that they stimulate teachers' efforts to alter institutionalized structures or ways of doing the school's work. Classroom events can be analyzed as a function of the power and the ideal and material interests of teachers and students, of their normative investment in the school, and of opportunities for and constraints on their action. These opportunities and constraints are created most immediately in the classroom's organizational and local community environments, which are themselves a matter of power and interests, in particular the power and interests of administrators and parents. Less directly, they derive from the more global environment of public policy, involving the power and interests of the actors who make or influence these policies.

An ambitious study would situate the classroom in the context of both faculty and student social organization, treating the school holistically as a social system open to its environment but with its own peculiar culture and social order. In the same vein, it should not neglect the formal organization of the curriculum. Despite evidence that curricular stratification is decreasing in American schools (Lucas 1999), Robert Petrin (this volume) provides evidence that students' positions in the differentiated curricular structures of American high schools have significant consequences for how they are taught and for their academic engagement and achievement. One wants to know how distinct curricular structures distribute variation in classroom processes and intersect faculty and student social organization. A more modest study could begin by analyzing relationships between social processes in the classroom and either the faculty or the student social organizational context.

Whatever the scope of the study, the array of measured student outcomes should increase. Achievement in school and later in the labor force and aspirations for these two kinds of achievement have been virtually the only schooling outcomes that have gained sociological attention for the past half-century. This narrow focus is no surprise. Public policy centers on equity in attainment and on the formation and efficient use of human capital, while achievement test scores, occupational prestige scores, and earnings streams can be used as dependent variables in survey analyses (Bidwell 1999; Dreeben 1994).

That the socializing effects of schools are much broader is something that we know perfectly well but have ignored. These effects encompass the formation of values and normative commitments and motives, predispositions, and tastes that are not limited to schooling and work but undergird the wide range of social participation. They also include skills in interpersonal relationships and knowledge that is not formally in the curriculum but nevertheless a part of the informal learning that takes place in schools. This informal learning includes understandings of the nature of authority and of appropriate relationships to authority, understandings of the nature of formal organizations and how to conduct oneself as member or client, and understandings of the polity and of the responsibilities of citizenship.

Not since Dreeben's (1968) theoretical work on norm learning in school and the neo-Marxist accounts of schooling as social reproduction (Bowles and Gintis 1976; Katz 1968) has sociological attention, either theoretical or empirical, been paid in any systematic way to these outcomes and their sources in schooling. In this volume, Maureen Hallinan gives close attention to the noncognitive outcomes of schooling and opens the question of how the distinctive cultures of schools social-ize students to produce these outcomes. To my mind, the formation of achieve-ment motivation, a socioemotional counterpart to the formation of human capital, and preparation for participation in the polity and in the civil society are of the greatest import for widening the research agenda on schooling.

Research on Classroom Events and Student Social Organization   Daniel McFar-land (2001, 2004, this volume) has made a promising start in the analysis of rela-tionships between the microsociology of the classroom and the social organization of student life, linking these relationships to variation in, and students' resistance to, instruction. Building in large part on studies of classroom interaction as dis-course (Mehan 1980), of interaction framing (Snow 1986), and of classroom task structures (Bossert 1979; Stodolsky 1988), McFarland made detailed observations over sustained periods of time of verbal interaction between students and teachers and among the students in high school classrooms. His work is an analysis of the microsocial mechanisms involved in the production of student cooperation or re-sistance in teacher-assigned classroom tasks. It shows how vulnerable the class-room social order is to the roles that students enact elsewhere in the school. These roles, for example, in athletics or prestige-awarding extracurricular activities, pro-vide students with power that they can use in the classroom to initiate and sustain episodes of collaboration in or opposition to what the teacher tries to accomplish.

It also shows that different task structures—for example, lecturing by compar-ison with small-group work—provide different opportunities for interacting stu-dents to breach the task-oriented frame of work that the teacher has induced. In this way, they deflect the class from the direction the teacher has in view and pro-vide opportunities for more active collective student resistance to the teacher's intentions.

These characteristics of classroom social order—the interplay of task structures, student roles, and the incidence of student resistance—undoubtedly provide sig-nificant mechanisms in the production of both levels and directions of student ef-fort and thus of levels and directions of student achievement. This line of research should be extended so that the incidence and severity of student resistance are treated as intervening between socially ordered classroom events and academic achievement and achievement motivation. It would be promising as well to inves-tigate consequences for non-academic aspects of socialization that are likely to be affected by participation in classrooms characterized by differing degrees of col-lective compliance with their formally authoritative regimes.

Research on Classroom Events and Faculty Social Organization   Because of the relatively enclosed nature of classrooms, with the one-teacher class still the domi-nant pattern, this research should investigate nonroutine classroom events and the ways in which teachers respond to them. Teachers usually solve the everyday problems that occur in classrooms as a result of day-to-day fluctuations in stu-dents' engagement and performance by drawing on their own instructional reper-toires. However, when they must deal with larger, secular changes—for example, changes in students' preparation, tastes, motivation, or classroom conduct—the repertoire may not suffice. These changes may be sudden (for example, as a consequence of changes in attendance boundaries) or incremental (for example, as a consequence of slow, but steady population succession in a school's community).

In either case, such changes are likely to affect an entire faculty, or a large portion of it, and may stimulate organizational learning by the affected teachers. At this point it is of interest to ask, in James March's (1991) language, about a faculty's collective capacity to exploit the methods that its members have fixed on as successful, to explore alternatives to methods that have proven unsuccessful, and then to test the alternatives and exploit the more successful of these alternatives. Nonroutine changes in student cohorts that enter a school and its classrooms may stimulate teachers to exploit the more effective established ways of teaching and to explore still more effective alternatives to these subject matters or methods. Whether a faculty has the social capital required for organizational learning takes us directly into the social organization of relationships among faculty colleagues.[5]

Studying Faculty Social Organization and Student Classroom Resistance   To illustrate what might be done to probe relationships between a faculty's social capital, organizational learning, and outcomes for students, I sketch the conceptualization and touch on the design of a study that, like McFarland's work, is concerned with effects on students' classroom resistance. I have chosen this illustration in part because of its complementarity to McFarland's research and in part because resistance is implicated not only in learning subject matter but also more broadly in students' socialization. Episodes of engagement and resistance provide opportunities for achievement motives to be induced, raised, and lowered. These episodes also provide opportunities for students to learn about the nature of power, about legitimate authority, and about compliance and legitimate and illegitimate refusals to comply.

How teachers respond to nonroutine change can be treated as a function of their collective capacity as a faculty to set a new process of local pedagogical institutionalization in motion. This capacity, in turn, can be treated as a function of: their power, that is, how much autonomy and how much social capital they have for organizational learning; their interests, that is, the degree to which they are professionally committed to locally effective instruction; and the degree to which they value the existing local pedagogical order. Their collective capacity is a function also of environmental selection, that is, the degree to which existing and alternative ways to teach accord with administrative preferences, school and district policies, and local community demand.

Consider first the analysis of faculty social organization. Here the literature is contradictory, so that the proposed research program must probe systematically into the principal dimensions of variation in teachers' colleague relationships and the sources of this variation. Lortie (1975) found that the public school teachers he studied, given their isolation from colleagues, turned mainly to their students for the social support that sustained them in their roles, becoming vulnerable to students' demands, in particular their expectations about how much effort to expend on schoolwork. His finding is consistent with other work in which teachers are depicted as primarily subject to the impersonal discipline of bureaucratic regulation and routine (Shedd and Bacharach 1991).[6]

If teachers are vulnerable to students' demands concerning levels and directions of effort, they presumably are forced into classroom compromises that weaken the standards that they would prefer to hold for their students. This proposition (Cusick 1983; Powell, Farrar, and Cohen 1985) harkens back to Waller (1932) on the school class as a social order of student-teacher antagonism, worked out in an inexorable "battle of the requirements."

However, when Rowan (1990b) considered the substance of teachers' work, he found that schoolteachers are confronted by multiple and often conflicting demands by parents and students, coupled with the increasing rigors of external accountability-based policies. Consequently, he argued, they turn to one another for both technical assistance and social support in the face of these vexing conditions of work. His reasoning, like that of the growing literature on teacher interaction and community in elementary and high schools, is consistent with the more general proposition that people find it necessary to make sense of formally organized work lives and that they turn to colleagues in the effort to do so (Weick 2001). The school workplace presumably is no exception.

In the high school, this sense-making context is likely to be the subject-matter department (McLaughlin and Talbert 2001; Siskin 1994; Johnson 1990). Some studies of the high school workplace suggest that such colleague interaction may extend to the formation and maintenance of fundamental orientations to the ends and methods of teaching (Bidwell and Yasumoto 1999), at times with palpable consequences for students' academic achievement (Yasumoto, Uekawa, and Bidwell 2001).

Studies of the elementary school workplace also document conditions under which colleague communities may form. The formal division of labor again appears as an important constraint on the formation of these relationships (for example, colleague interaction bounded by school grades). So does the action of the school principal, with their formation a substantial function of the principal's efforts to build communal relationships among teachers (McPherson 1972).

However, Ingersoll (2003, this volume) urges caution, arguing that in such critical areas of classroom life as curriculum and student discipline, teachers' autonomy is severely restricted by formal school and district policies and regulations. He suggests that teachers' autonomy, with the exception of relatively minor matters of classroom conduct, is largely illusory.

Resolving these contradictory arguments and findings requires systematic investigation across school levels. This research must identify the conditions under which teachers form colleague networks of varying structure (for example, networks that vary in degrees of density and centrality and in levels of subgroup differentiation), varying content (for example, pedagogical doctrines and methods of maintaining classroom discipline), and varying levels of consensus. The intensity and scope of district-level bureaucratization, the degree to which curricular and disciplinary decisionmaking is centralized, and the leadership style of the principal are obvious candidates for this phase of the research.

From the literature on social networks and on the social organizational context of organizational learning, we can derive testable propositions about the consequences of faculty social organization for students' academic resistance and engagement. These propositions center on relationships between the form of teachers' egocentric networks of colleague ties and, first, their individual power in the classroom and, second, their collective capacity to identify and solve pedagogical problems that are presented by nonroutine compositional change in the flows of students to their schools and classrooms. In this volume, Adam Gamoran, Ramona Gunter, and Tona Williams analyze the conditions that foster problem-solving collaboration among teachers, while Kenneth Frank and Yong Zhao show how collaborative exchanges between elementary school teachers can aid in the productive adaptation of innovations.

It follows from Lortie's proposition that the sparser and less cohesive a teacher's egocentric colleague network, the more dependent that teacher is likely to be on students for esteem and other social rewards in the classroom. Therefore, given McFarland's findings, students' classroom resistance should be higher and disruptions of the teacher's instructional strategies and tactics more numerous the sparser and less cohesive the teacher's ties to colleagues.

Teaching that is well adapted to the classroom situation, no less than modest levels of student resistance and classroom disruption, should promote the rates at which students learn and the likelihood that they will acquire positive achievement motives. Therefore, another promising line of inquiry would probe the consequences of the structure of colleague networks and the behavior-generating mechanisms that it provides for the local institutionalization of teachers' instructional methods, that is, the consequences for their stability and adaptation to the exigencies of local classroom situations. This research requires the specification of both the microstructural and related environmental conditions and the social psychological mechanisms involved in the local institutionalization of practice.

The three classic propositions about institutionalization specify conditions under which this local institutionalization is likely. First, teachers' collective beliefs about their teaching should gain stability and thus resist change when they are initiated by such powerful actors as respected principals, senior teachers, or other teachers in central positions in the colleague network. Second, the beliefs must survive environmental selection, and third, they must acquire local value.

In the absence of codified standards of teaching performance, the discipline of environmental selection is a discipline of perceived success. When groups of teachers believe that they have worked out successful ways of teaching, or at least when they have not encountered strong evidence that they are unsuccessful, their way of working becomes an accomplishment of collective sense-making. Therefore, these ways of teaching become objects of value, anchoring the identity of the colleague group and the loyalty of its members.

It follows that when teacher networks are dense and their constituent ties are strong and positive, how teachers teach should stabilize and become resistant to change. In dense networks, information channels are overlapping and thus redundant and consensus building. In cohesive networks, the teacher group has the social capital for effective social control. Under these structural conditions, teachers can learn with relative ease about what their colleagues think is the best way to teach, so that, when these beliefs tend to converge, a simple tipping point mechanism should increase the consensus. Efficient diffusion mechanisms of communication and interpersonal influence, coupled with individuals' desire to maintain a good local pedagogical reputation, in particular a reputation for pedagogical trustworthiness, should lead to a parallel convergence of classroom practice. Both the consensus and uniformity of practice should be reinforced by self-fulfilling pedagogical expectations in which teachers' belief in the efficacy of a given set of practices creates both selective perception of effectiveness and consistent, effortful use of the believed-in ways of teaching (for a more general discussion of these "situational" mechanisms, see Hedström and Swedberg 1998, 17–23).

Because schools, like all formal organizations, depend on procedural stability, when instructional methods are viable, a substantial degree of instructional stability is essential to the survival and academic productivity of schools. However, schools, like all organizations, must also have the capacity for organizational learning if they are to remain productive. Teachers must be able to adapt institutionalized ways of teaching to the day-to-day problems that they confront in the classroom, including those created by students' resistance. They must also have the ability to adapt to problems of larger scale, such as those that derive from substantial change in the preparation or interests of the students they teach—exploitation and exploration in March's (1991) words.

When teachers' networks are cohesive, they also are likely to have strong boundaries, with sparse external ties that provide channels of information through which the exploration of alternatives can take place. Moreover, the local institutionalization of ways of teaching, by virtue of the value attached to them, should reduce the likelihood of such bridging ties and the willingness of teachers in the network to entertain either the possibility of diminished success or of reasonable alternatives to current procedure.

Ronald Burt (1992, 2004) studied business firms and research and development organizations characterized by individual competitiveness and entrepreneurialism. There he found that the rates at which alternative ways of working are explored and at which this information is exploited are functions of low redundancy in the structure of ties and a relatively high incidence of ties that link work groups to external sources of information. However, relationships within school faculties are rarely ordered according to competitiveness, and schools provide few and weak formal incentives for pedagogical entrepreneurialism, given seniority-based compensation and an essentially unstratified division of faculty labor.

Research into organizational learning in the faculty setting should probe for the microstructural conditions that favor an effective balance between exploration and exploitation. (Compare the chapters in this volume by Gamoran, Gunter, and Williams and by Frank and Zhao on this point.) That the formal incentives for exploration are few and the structural bases of local pedagogical institutionalization are strong suggests that in most schools the balance is tilted heavily toward exploitation, often the exploitation of a pedagogy not well suited to the local situation. Consequently, the probe should be directed toward discovering the conditions under which informal incentives encourage adaptation to everyday classroom problems.

One might consider, for example, the consequences of the normative grounding of informal colleague status structures. Perhaps those based on expertise, with correspondingly centralized colleague networks, provide capacity for coordinated problem-solving and the effective implementation of problem solutions. The existence of such relationships would raise the further question of the conditions for informal, expertise-based stratification in faculties, including such conditions as the criteria for faculty appointment, a distinctive school mission, and a principal's encouragement of independent faculty involvement in curricular and instructional policy.

The formal division of labor may also play a role—for example, curricula that require team teaching across subjects or grades and in effect mandate bridging. External accountability policies that allocate rewards or punishments for a school's academic performance to the faculty itself may both reward exploration and provide objective evidence that believed-in teaching methods are no longer effective. Then cumulative threshold effects, expectation states, and social control all would conspire toward teaching that is well adapted to the local situation.

IDEAS ABOUT STUDY DESIGN   In general terms, how might we design a study of students' classroom resistance? Obviously, a longitudinal design is required. The observations should occur over a sustained period of classroom life, probably an entire school year. Such sustained measurement would permit estimation of reciprocal effects of students' resistance and the teacher's instructional strategies and tactics, as well as the sequential calculation of per classroom rates of resistance episodes (the study's dependent variable). A study that spans a school year should make it possible to document shifts in the balance of teachers' engagement with colleagues and vulnerability to student demands. This design should also allow one to estimate rates of teachers' individual and collegial problem identification and problem-solving and the degree to which these efforts at organizational learning are adaptive or maladaptive in the classroom.[7]

The school sites for an initial study should be few in number, chosen on the basis of the probable exposure of their teachers to nonroutine instructional problems. My conceptualization of this research calls for fine-grained measurement of interaction among teachers and in the classroom, requiring the sacrifice of generalizability to intensive fieldwork. Should this initial study yield promising results, more economical and less fine-grained interaction measures might be derived from the initial work, allowing a later study in a larger sample of schools, selected to represent, say, the population of American public elementary or high schools. Now the sampling might be designed to take the classroom's external environment into account. If the school sites are selected to provide adequate variation in bureaucratization, centralization of decisionmaking, and administrative leadership, the study should generate findings that would connect formal organizational structure, the microsocial dynamics of the school and classroom, and socialization outcomes.

At the initial stage, the schools might be selected in two stages. At the first stage, archival or administrative data might be collected to provide some reasonable indicator of secular compositional enrollment change for a large number of schools, limited, for simplicity's sake, to public schools at either the elementary or secondary level.[8] These data might include recent trends in the school's intake achievement test scores or, as a proxy measure, the socioeconomic status of entering students' families. With these indicators in hand, it should be possible to select a small number of schools in each of these categories: schools about to experience critical, academically adverse changes in enrollment; schools experiencing incremental, but comparably adverse enrollment change; and for baseline comparison, schools with compositionally stable enrollments (at both relatively high and relatively low intake achievement levels).

The schools having been selected, the next task would be a sociometric mapping of the colleague ties within the faculty, employing some measure of interpersonal consultation about instructional matters. This map would provide a baseline measure of the social organization of the faculty, to be compared with later waves of comparable sociometric measurement. It could also provide the basis for sampling classrooms within each school—for example, one or more classes taught by teachers in subject-differentiated collegial subgroups and by isolates in the colleague network.

The Social Organization of Student Life

Let me return to the larger agenda for research on classroom events with which I began this portion of the chapter to suggest how one might move a little distance toward the incorporation of both teacher and student social organization into the same investigation. Students no less than teachers must make sense of their lives in school, and presumably they turn to other students in the attempt. In these terms, we can think of the subgroups of students that form in their networks of friendship and acquaintanceship as loci for making sense of school. The form of these networks and the content of interaction in them should be constrained by: formal procedures for allocating students to courses, course sequences, and tracks (see Friedkin and Thomas 1997); the scope and prestige structure of the athletic and extracurricular programs; the socioeconomic and racial and ethnic composition of the student body; and the number of students in the school.

Within these constraints, students presumably turn to each other to make sense of the academic part of their school lives, so that their willingness to resist teachers' demands and standards should be strongly affected by norms about levels and directions of academic effort that are induced in these subgroups. Students must make sense of many more things than academic work in their life together in school, so that their locations (for example, their centrality) and ties (for example, their involvement in relationships of obligation) should ground the identities and prestige that can become power resources in the micropolitics of the classroom.

Studying Change in the Organizational Form and Curricular Substance of Schools

The research program that I have just outlined addresses the dynamics of change in the ways teachers conduct instruction. It does not address the somewhat more macro issues of change in the formal organization of schools or in the formal curriculum. On these fronts, schools are notoriously slow to change. Dreeben (1971) has stated that many of the core attributes of school structure and physical layout observed in today's schools would also have been found in schools of the late eighteenth and early nineteenth centuries. There also is substantial evidence that contemporary schools in the United States are strongly resistant to governmental and other efforts to alter how they are organized and work (see, for example, Elmore, Abelman, and Fuhrman 1996).

However, recent findings suggest that as these efforts begin to provide incentives that matter to school districts and school principals, they are having more durable influence on school practice (Firestone, Goertz, and Natriello 1997; Muller and Schiller 2000). In this volume, Chandra Muller and Kathryn Schiller show that incentive-based state policies intended to improve the instructional effectiveness of public schools may have unanticipated consequences. How these outcomes affect the interests of powerful actors at the state or local level may affect the durability of these policies. In more general terms, my political conceptualization of institutionalization implies that institutions are likely to change when the interests of powerful actors change, when new, powerful actors appear, when the environment changes in a significant way, or when the institutionalized structure or practice loses value.

At the local level of districts and individual schools, such forces for organizational change would include substantial alteration of local political or economic structures, major changes in the composition of a school's student recruitment pool, and the disruptive consequences of either of these exogenous changes for teachers' beliefs in the effectiveness of local instructional practice. Possibly, schools characterized by efficient short-term pedagogical adaptation are less likely than others to be vulnerable to these longer-term exogenous forces. Research into the social organizational capacity of faculties for short-term problem-solving may also reveal the conditions and mechanisms that constitute latent capacity for effective adaptation to less frequent nonrandom shocks to locally institutionalized practice.

Research of this kind to date has treated nonrandom shocks to institutionalized school organization and curricula as externally generated and directed from higher levels of policy or regulation toward schools and districts. The analysis of these externally generated effects is an important line of research that should reveal consequences of environmental selection. Thus, Christopher Swanson (this volume) demonstrates the vicissitudes of initiatives in national educational policy formation in the United States created by regional environmental variation.

Research in this area also should consider the possibility that events within schools or districts themselves may constitute nonrandom shocks that alter the field of power and interests in which a school or a school district exists. If this alteration were to occur, it should set in motion a process of institutional change of organizational form or of the substance of what is taught. Presumably the effects of state-level accountability policies are themselves mediated through such local mechanisms.

To borrow a term coined by Meyer and Rowan (1977), consider also the possibility that events in schools occur as dramatic episodes that breach the logic of confidence, grounding the political or fiscal support provided by powerful local actors. Such events might include, for example, sharp declines in published test scores, local breaches of decorum like a riot at a football or basketball game, or accusations of sexual harassment of teachers by administrators or sexual abuse of students by teachers.

To reveal the action of these forces and their interaction with local district and school attributes, one might take advantage of naturally occurring events in the political or economic environments of local districts or in their recruitment pools. To do so would require something like annual waves of measurement across a large and heterogeneous sample of public school districts. This dataset might be most efficiently obtained by adding a modest number of pertinent items to the information already collected regularly by the National Center for Educational Statistics, allowing secondary analyses to address the questions that I have raised. The political practicality of this suggestion is a different matter, but it is a suggestion worth considering nonetheless.

I am grateful to the participants in the Workshop on Community and Youth Development at Stanford University, in particular Daniel McFarland and Rebecca Sandefur, and to Barbara Schneider for their helpful comments on an earlier draft.

NOTES

1. C. Wayne Gordon's *The Social System of the High School* (1957) is an exception.
2. For a comprehensive survey of the development of this body of research, see Dreeben (2000).
3. In the same vein, Marion Fourcade-Gourinchas and Sarah Babb (2002, 533) find that although market-based economies have diffused as a "nearly global policy paradigm," local institutional conditions have strong effects on the emergence of these economies in particular countries.
4. Catherine Riegle-Crumb (this volume) opens another, intriguing line of research into the national institutional context of national educational systems, namely, how cross-

national variation in social stratification (here, gender stratification) generates variation in students' experience of school and, consequently, variation in their life chances.

5. In addition to changes in the composition of student inputs to classrooms, change in the size of a school's enrollment may be pertinent. For example, growth or decline in student numbers usually results in a concomitant change in faculty numbers and, consequently, may disrupt a faculty's social structure or result in the loss or gain of younger teachers and their possibly fresh ideas about teaching.

6. Howard Becker (1952) found that Chicago public school teachers for the most part were dependent on and subordinated to the personal authority of the principal. He did not see the principal as a prime source of social support for teachers or as someone with a strong interest in the conduct of instruction. Although his study was conducted a half-century ago, his findings resonate intuitively with the conditions found in some contemporary schools.

7. A good case could be made for including students' egocentric family and neighborhood networks in the treatment of the students' microsocial environments. The school social system is indeed open to the effects of these relationships, which, so to speak, enter the school with the students. However, one must limit the causal purview of any study, so that such relationships are best treated as controls rather than as central causal elements of the study design.

8. Middle schools are an attractive possibility because they provide a modicum of curricular complexity within a relatively compact organizational setting.

Chapter 2

Ecosystems and the Structuring of Organizations

W. Richard Scott

Charles Bidwell is probably best known for his contributions to the sociology of education, and indeed, these have been considerable. However, he has also routinely been attentive to the connection between schools and the wider range of organizational forms. He frequently couches his work in more general terms, asking how organization theory informs the study of schools (Bidwell 1965) and how an understanding of school structures and educational processes informs our knowledge of organizations more generally. The latter agenda is particularly evident in his books *The Organization and Its Ecosystem: A Theory of Structuring in Organizations* (1985) and *Structuring in Organizations: Ecosystem Theory Evaluated* (1987), written in collaboration with John D. Kasarda. In these important works, Bidwell and Kasarda employ empirical research on schools to test and extend a general theory of organizational structuring. In this chapter, I seek to place this work in perspective by noting parallels to and differences from other approaches—both early and more recent—to the study of organizations.

In my reading, Bidwell and Kasarda both reflect and make independent contributions to three general trends in organization theory: the shift from closed to open system models of organization; the transition from behavioral to structural approaches to organizations; and the movement from a focus on organizational structure to a concern with organizing as a process. I structure my discussion around these three themes.

THE SHIFT FROM CLOSED TO OPEN SYSTEMS

As is clear from my own previous work on organization theory (Scott 2003), I regard the transition from closed to open-system models in the study of organizations as a watershed event that forever altered our view of organizations. The emergence of open-system models was part of a broad intellectual movement that, beginning during the mid-1950s, swept through the sciences, affected established fields such as biology, and created new fields such as cybernetics (see Bertalanffy 1956; Weiner 1954). A few scholars, in particular Kenneth Boulding (1956), quickly discerned the significance of these ideas for the study of social organization. However, it was not until the mid-1960s that open-system conceptions began to move into the mainstream in the social sciences generally (see, for example, Buckley 1967) and into organization studies more specifically (for example, Katz and Kahn 1966).

No field of study has been more influenced by open-system models than has organization studies, but those models have been accepted, and their full implications recognized, much more slowly than is commonly realized. The 1960s and 1970s witnessed a flood of new theoretical approaches, each exhibiting increased recognition of the role played by environmental conditions and forces. Among the most influential were the behavioral theory of the firm, as developed by James March and Herbert Simon (1958) and Richard Cyert and March (1963); contingency theory, pursued by Paul Lawrence and Jay Lorsch (1967), James Thompson (1967), and Charles Perrow (1967); sociotechnical theory, associated with the work of Fred Emery (1959) and Joan Woodward (1958); and transaction cost economics, as developed by Oliver Williamson (1975). While these efforts represent significant advances over previous conceptions of organizations, such as those associated with the human relations school (Barnard 1938; Mayo 1945) and scientific management (Taylor 1947), the overall tone was not "open" and welcoming. Rather, these approaches rather grudgingly recognized that organizations are susceptible to influences from the environment, but the main message conveyed was that managers must take steps to suppress and contain these forces. I concur completely with the judgment of Bidwell and Kasarda (1985, 21), who, following a careful review of work up to the early 1980s, conclude that "the widely heralded victory of open- over closed-system theory in fact is a more modest elaboration of the closed system into a control-system perspective."[1]

In developing their own ecosystem theory of organizations, Bidwell and Kasarda were important members of an emerging collection of scholars who celebrated rather than bemoaned the openness of organizations and attempted to theorize the profound ways in which organizations are dependent on and shaped and penetrated by environmental forces. In my view, two broad programs of theory and research make up this "second wave" of efforts by organization theorists to assimilate more fully the meanings of openness and pursue its ramifications: institutional theory and ecological-evolutionary theory. I briefly discuss the former and then devote more attention to the latter, since this is the strand pursued by Bidwell and Kasarda.

Institutional Theory

Although there are important earlier versions of institutional theory extending back to the turn of the nineteenth century (for a review, see Scott 2001a), institutional theory in its modern guise was first introduced into organizational studies by John Meyer and his colleagues (Meyer and Rowan 1977; Meyer and Scott 1983; Zucker 1977) and elaborated by Paul DiMaggio and Walter Powell (1983). Great emphasis is placed in this work on the environment of organizations as the source of symbolic materials—rules, norms, organizing models—out of which organizational forms are constructed. Some institutionalists (for example, North 1990) emphasize the importance of legal structures and rule systems that provide a regulative framework within which organizations can be safely created and securely operate. Others stress the importance of common values and normative systems that signify the importance of mission-setting and justification processes as a basis for organizing (for example, Parsons 1960). And still other theorists point to the importance of common cognitive frameworks that provide meaningful categories of acting and rationalized logics of organizing (for example, Meyer and Rowan 1977).

Bidwell and Kasarda acknowledge the importance of the institutional environment as a component of the "external" environment. Following Talcott Parsons (1960), they stress the "normative basis of an organization's environing social order" (Bidwell and Kasarda 1985, 40). A complex of "laws, governmental regulations, and widely shared beliefs" provides rules and guidelines that specify appropriate activity patterns and relationships for each type of organization based on its location in "the societal division of labor" (40). They conclude that, for their purposes, "the chief institutional element of the external environment is law—statutory, juridical, and administrative" (94), in particular, laws governing the formation of corporate groups, laws that structure the economy and economic exchanges, and laws regulating labor.

However, in their empirical research on schools Bidwell and Kasarda (1987) do not attempt to develop empirical measures of any of these institutional factors, no doubt because they did not differ substantially among the organizations studied—public school districts in the state of Michigan—or over the period of study—1969 to 1975. The testing of institutional arguments requires a more diverse sample of organizations or longer time periods (see Meyer 1994; Scott and Christensen 1995). Instead, Bidwell and Kasarda devote primary attention to elaborating and testing an ecological theory of organizational structuring.

Ecological Theory

Ecological theory, in its modern guise, was reconstituted under the intellectual leadership of Amos Hawley, who created a general framework for human ecology. This perspective was introduced into organizational studies through the work of a number of Hawley's students, including John Freeman, Michael Hannan, and John Kasarda, as well as more distant disciples, such as Howard Aldrich.[2] Hawley's (1950) seminal work focused on "communal" organizations (for example, communities and metropolitan systems) but also identified "associative" forms—special-purpose organizations—as an alternative basis of organizing. Hannan and John Freeman (1977, 1989), Aldrich (1979, 1999), and Kasarda, in collaboration with Bidwell (Bidwell and Kasarda 1985, 1987), employed ecological ideas to examine associative forms.

Ecologists accord primacy to the material resource environment of organizations. They view organizations as social entities competing within delimited arenas, or "niches," for the limited resources essential to their survival and growth. "Organizations, populations, and communities of organizations constitute the basic elements of an ecological analysis of organizations" (Baum 1996, 77). Organizational ecologists agree on these basic views, but disagree as to how these concepts are to be applied to organizations.

Hannan and Freeman (1989) and Aldrich (1999) focus on organizational populations—organizations exhibiting similar forms and competing for similar resources—and, to a lesser extent, on organizational communities—a set of diverse, co-evolving organizational populations linked by ties of commensalism and symbiosis (see Aldrich 1999, 298). Bidwell and Kasarda employ the same terms but develop quite different definitions and a different analytic focus. For their purposes, *organizations are themselves ecological communities, made up of diverse populations of participants*. Thus, the populations examined consist of individuals, not organizations, and the communities are not interorganizational but interpersonal systems. Whereas most organizational ecologists have primarily studied organizational populations, Bidwell and Kasarda examine the working of ecological processes at the level of the individual organization. All ecologists tend to emphasize the importance of selection over adaptation processes—differential survival rates of differing entities versus changes in the characteristics of entities (Aldrich and Pfeffer 1976). However, most organizational ecologists view selection processes as applying to organizations, whereas Bidwell and Kasarda examine selection processes at work on populations of individuals within organizations (Bidwell and Kasarda 1985, 31–36).[3]

Populations of individuals come together within organizations in order to carry out work: "an organization is an instrumental community" (36). Populations are distinguished in that each is associated with a different activity pattern in its work. "Because its activity pattern endows a population with a form, populations can be described morphologically (e.g., with respect to the specialization of its activity patterns). They can also be described demographically (e.g., with respect to their size)" (36). Bidwell and Kasarda's focus on activity patterns as a significant descriptor of organization functioning connects their work with important parallel efforts by the evolutionary economists Richard Nelson and Sidney Winter (1982, 274–75), who focus on organizational "routines"—the "repetitive patterns of activity" that underlie much of the stability of organizational behavior. Routines account for both reliable performance and organizational rigidities. Both sets of theorists embrace an evolutionary perspective of organizational change, as one set of routines or activities is displaced by a new set. Bidwell and Kasarda, however, tie such processes to the changing distribution of populations of participants in organizations.

For Bidwell and Kasarda, then, organizations consist of populations of individuals dependent on and carrying out activities intended to exchange and transform resources. They identify two environments, an *external environment* consisting of "all external phenomena that affect or could affect a community's populations," and an *internal environment* made up of the "creation, maintenance, and distribution of direct resources" resulting from the activities of an organizational population (38). The concept of internal environment "draws our attention to community structure as a locus of opportunities for and constraints upon the community's further morphological evolution" (39).

The capstone concept, the *organizational ecosystem*, embraces all of these components: "the organization's populations, resource supplies, external environmental suppliers, other external environmental actors, and relations among these components" (39). Ecologists employ this concept to bound the system under study. Otis Dudley Duncan (1964, 37) reminds us that "ecologists use the term ecosystem to refer to a community together with its habitat," or alternatively, "the ecosystem may be defined as the interacting environmental and biotic system."

The primary task undertaken by Bidwell and Kasarda is to explain the structuring of organizations by understanding the forces shaping and changing an organization's structure. What do they mean by structure? It is important to recall that this was an all-consuming topic for organizational sociologists during the 1970s. The comparative research programs of the Aston group (for example, Pugh et al. 1968; Pugh and Hickson 1976) and Peter Blau and his collaborators (Blau and Schoenherr 1971) were only the most sustained and visible instances of a concerted effort by social scientists to define, measure, and account for differences in the structure of organizations.

The conception of structure developed by Bidwell and Kasarda is too complex to permit a detailed summary, but its major dimensions will be familiar to students of organizations. They view structure as varying along two dimensions: lateral and vertical. *Lateral differentiation* (the division of labor) takes a number of forms, including the functional specialization of the organization's populations and the segmentation of subunits. *Vertical differentiation* (hierarchy) encompasses a variety of hierarchical forms and modes of coordination. The master proposition developed is that an organization's structure reflects and responds to changes in the wider environments in which it operates, its specific organizational niche, and the amount and variety of the resource flows on which it depends. Bidwell and Kasarda (1987) empirically evaluated this proposition, elaborated into multiple hypotheses, with a wealth of structural and environmental data on school districts and resource flows in Michigan for the period 1969 to 1975.

Although Bidwell and Kasarda crafted a distinctive theoretical framework, it is clear that they were working within the general tradition of ecological research, examining the effects of broader ecological processes on the evolutionary processes shaping the structure of organizations. In so doing, they were important participants in the effort to elevate the models governing organization research above the level of "clockwork," "cybernetic," and "control" systems to more fully "open" systems of organization (see Boulding 1956).

THE SHIFT FROM A BEHAVIORAL TO A STRUCTURAL FOCUS

Following their review of organizational literature as it developed during the 1960s and 1970s, Bidwell and Kasarda conclude that not only were the then-dominant approaches not truly open, but they were formulated at the behavioral rather than the structural level. They assert that "the most fully developed of the so-called open-system theories are not theories of organizational structure, but theories of individual human behavior in organizational settings, including interpersonal interaction and its microstructural concomitants" (2).

Contingency, behavioral economics, sociotechnical systems—all were based on a cybernetic model of control that differentiated between two principal components: operators and regulators. *Operators* are members of organizations who do the work; *regulators* are those who specify how and when the work is to be done. These theories all shifted attention from operators—the populations of individuals carrying on activities within organizations—to regulators: the managerial decisionmakers. In this manner, a theory of organizational change was translated into a theory of individual decisionmaking (6–19). Such a translation rests on several assumptions, all of which Bidwell and Kasarda challenge. First, it presumes that the functions of operation and regulation are performed by distinct individuals—that operators do not regulate their own behavior. Second, it assumes that organizational form is the consequence of entrepreneurial or managerial decisions. And third, it assumes that organizational form consists only of interpersonal relations, failing to recognize the import of such structural features as the size and composition of organizational membership, its stock of technological and material resources, and its distinctive institutional characteristics. For Bidwell and Kasarda, environmental forces influence organizational structuring in myriad ways that are not mediated through the boundedly rational decision processes of managers.

Many would-be open-system theorists stress the importance of the environment in shaping organizational structure. More so than other scholars working on environment-structure connections, Bidwell and Kasarda take great pains to make explicit which environmental forces are thought to be significant for schools and to examine the nested character of their effects. They develop measures of the socioeconomic and demographic characteristics of local communities as these affect the volume and composition of student inputs, and moving inside the districts to examine the organization of structural subunits, they develop measures of student and revenue inputs in order to examine their effect on the specialization and segmentation of administrative and instructional subunits. Their analyses employ both cross-sectional and longitudinal models (see Bidwell and Kasarda 1987).

In adopting this decidedly macro stance, I believe Bidwell and Kasarda were emboldened by the efforts of two of Bidwell's distinguished Chicago colleagues: Otis Dudley Duncan and Peter Blau. In their focus on the centrality of populations, environment, and technology as determinants of organizational structure, Bidwell and Kasarda embraced the central elements of Duncan's POET (population, organization, environment, technology) analytic framework, identifying basic elements of social organization (Duncan and Schnore 1959). At the same time in the same department, Peter Blau was engaged in pursuing a relentlessly macro program of comparative research on the determinants of organization structure. However, more so than Blau, Bidwell and Kasarda recognized the value of going beyond cross-sectional comparisons to conduct dynamic studies of structural change, as I discuss in the following section.

All of these macro theorists viewed organizations as collective actors with emergent properties that are more than the aggregate characteristics of their participants. Organization structures are dynamic, evolving systems influenced by the characteristics of their environments, but these environmental forces operate in many ways. In some cases, they are mediated through the decisions of managers, but in others, they enter more directly, influencing and penetrating organizations through their direct effects on participating populations, resources, and technologies. A structural analysis emphasizes these macrolevel processes.[4]

FROM STRUCTURE TO PROCESS

A third impulse represented by Bidwell and Kasarda's work is of longer duration, has greater significance, and has received less attention. I refer to a gradual shift over recent decades from a focus on organizations as "entities" to one on organizational process. My discussion of this transition is informed by the application to organizations of a general set of distinctions devised by Mustafa Emirbayer (1997), who identifies two broad approaches: substantialist and relational or process conceptions. I examine instances of each in organization studies (see also Scott 2001b).

Substantialist Conceptions

Substantialist formulations stress the priority of things or entities (substances, essences). Emirbayer (1997) identifies two subtypes: models emphasizing self-action and those emphasizing interaction. *Self-action* models assume that entities act independently, under their own power. They stress the insulation, separation, and distinctiveness of the unit under study (Emirbayer 1997, 283). In organization studies, most of the founding definitions stressed substantialist, self-action conceptions. For example, Max Weber (1921/1978, 41–50) defined organizations as closed, associative social relations oriented toward the pursuit of purposive activities directed to specified goals. And Chester Barnard (1938, 4) defined formal organization "as that kind of cooperation among men that is conscious, deliberate, purposeful." March and Simon's (1958, 4) definition is more elaborate:

> Organizations are assemblages of interacting human beings and they are the largest assemblages in our society that have anything resembling a central coordinating system. . . . The high specificity of structure and coordination within organizations—as

contrasted with the diffuse and variable relations among organizations and among unorganized individuals—marks off the individual organization as a sociological unit comparable in significance to the individual organism in biology.

Organizations were of interest precisely because they represented the "movers and shakers": collective actors capable of defining ends and mobilizing means to achieve them. Like a heroic character from an Ayn Rand novel, organizations were depicted as lonely figures struggling against the vicissitudes of a hostile environment.

As organization studies matured during the 1960s and 1970s, a different kind of substantialist model, one stressing interaction, began to appear. Stimulated by open-system theorizing, scholars began to recognize that organizations are more dependent on and affected by their social context than originally believed. *Interaction* models posit "fixed entities with variable attributes" that interact to create outcomes (Emirbayer 1997, 286). Organizational scholars developed a wide variety of interactional models of organizations that included:

- *Political models*: Organizations as coalitions of interests (Cyert and March 1963)
- *Marxist models*: Organizations as products of conflict (Collins 1975)
- *Contingency models*: Organizations as structures adapting to varying task environments (Lawrence and Lorsch 1967)
- *Resource-dependence models*: Organizations devising buffering and bridging strategies and structures as they attempt to reduce dependence and increase autonomy vis-à-vis their exchange partners (Pfeffer and Salancik 1978)
- *Transaction cost models*: Organizations as governance structures whose scope and complexity vary depending on alternatives available to reduce transaction costs (Williamson 1975)

Such interaction models take account of the effect of context on the structure and behavior of organizations but continue to privilege a view of organizations as entities that prevents recognition of the extent to which they are not simply interdependent with but creatures of their environment. Such recognition is associated with the emergence of relational models.

Relational Conceptions

Relational models recognize that, rather than being independent entities, "the very terms or units involved in a transaction derive their meaning, significance, and identity from the (changing) functional roles they play within that transaction" (Emirbayer 1997, 287). This conception remains a minority perspective in organization studies, but its acceptance is growing rapidly, fueled by a number of alternative approaches. The most general formulation is that of Anthony Giddens

(1979, 1984), who reminds us that "structures" do not exist except as processes that continually produce and reproduce rules or schema and resources, both material and human.[5] Giddens's model of "structuration" has been highly influential in shifting attention from structure to process.

Other, more specific relational or process models include:

- Karl Weick (1969, 91) insists that scholars should shift attention from organization to *organizing*, a process he defined as "the resolving of equivocality in an enacted environment by means of interlocked behaviors embedded in conditionally related processes."

- In David Silverman's (1971, 5) *action* approach, he insists, following Peter Berger and Thomas Luckmann (1967), that social reality, including organization, is "socially constructed, socially sustained and socially changed" as actors negotiate common meanings through interaction.

- In Ronald Burt's (1982) view of organizations as shifting *networks* of social relations, he asserts, along with other network theorists, that network location and the nature of the wider structure of relations in which an organization participates are more significant to its functioning than are its attributes.

- In models developed by agency theorists, such as Michael Jensen and William Meckling (1976), organizations are viewed as a *nexus of contracts* in which the conflicting objectives of individuals, some of whom represent other organizations, are brought into equilibrium.

- Many scholars in financial management hold a view of firms as a *portfolio of assets* of shifting value. Neil Fligstein (1990) details the emergence and growing acceptance of a "financial conception of the firm."

- Interpretive and postmodern models of organizations emphasize the constructive role of symbols and the building of common meanings. For example, Barbara Czarniawska (1997) has developed *narrative* models in which organizations are viewed as ongoing conversations among interactive individuals involved in formulating and reformulating intentions, interpretations, and identities.

Bidwell and Kasarda, along with other evolutionary ecologists, devised their own distinctive model stressing the importance of process over entity—structuring over structure. They describe their intention to "use a macroevolutionary approach to develop an ecosystem theory of structural dynamics in formal organizations." In particular, they propose to "specify how variation in the environment of an organization affects the organization's emerging structure under the fundamental assumption that structuring is an adaptive process" (xvi). In addition, they adopted an appropriate methodology to test their arguments. Rather than following the then-common pattern of examining cross-sectional correlation to test theories of comparative static models, they employed dynamic models to examine longitudinal data on structural change in the population of Michigan school districts.

In sum, growing evidence suggests that substantialist models of organizations are being challenged, and may ultimately be replaced, by relational models. As noted, the newer models celebrate process over structure, becoming over being. A wide range of specific models has appeared, the models differing primarily in their views concerning what is being processed. In some versions, it is symbols and discourse; in others, relations or contracts; in others, assets; and in still others, activities associated with diverse and shifting populations of participants. But throughout it all, process has begun to move to center stage (Scott 2001b).

CODA: CHANGING THEORIES OR CHANGING ORGANIZATIONS?

It may have occurred to some to ask about the source of these quite fundamental changes in our conceptions of organizations. Do they reflect merely the changing tastes and whims of organization theorists? Or do they indicate changes in the nature of organizations as social phenomena? It would be odd indeed if there were no relation between the nature of organizations as they operate in the "real" world and our theories—our ideas about organizations. I believe that, while they may be loosely coupled, there is indeed a relation between changes in organizations and changes in organization theory.

Over the past few centuries organizations have evolved from being relatively embedded and dependent components of traditional social structures, such as primitive tribes or feudal systems, to:

> more independent systems that attempt to separate and insulate themselves from the surrounding society; then to

> more interdependent systems that interact with and are affected by their social context; and more recently to

> systems that are more dependent on and more penetrated by the environment, and hence more changeable in their boundaries, populations of participants, and structures.

The shift from substantialist to relational models reflects these real-world changes. And more so than most types of organization theorists, ecologists and institutionalists have recognized these important changes in the phenomena that we are attempting to understand. Charles Bidwell and Jack Kasarda have been in the forefront of those attempting to devise and test a theoretical framework that recognizes the new realities of organizing.

NOTES

1. In a related discussion, Louis Pondy and Ian Mitroff (1979) come to the same conclusion. They argue that most discussions of organization-environment relations prior to

1980 viewed interaction with the environment as a "problem," whereas a fully developed conception of open-system models would view interaction as a "necessity" (22). They go on to argue that rather than suggesting that organizational systems should be buffered "against environmental complexity ... it is precisely the throughput of nonuniformity that preserves the differential structure of an open system" (7).

2. In the preface to his first text on organizational ecology, Howard Aldrich (1979, xiii) describes the "mind-expanding experience" of reading James Thompson and Amos Hawley "back-to-back" when he was a graduate student at the University of Michigan.

3. Throughout the remainder of this chapter, unless otherwise indicated, all references to Bidwell and Kasarda are to their 1985 book.

4. While ecologists stress the importance of material resource environments as forces that shape and constrain organizations, institutionalists focus on the role of cognitive-cultural forces. The latter remind us of the power of widely shared cultural models of schooling that provide a basis for the structuring of schooling (see Meyer 1977; Meyer et al. 1978).

5. William Sewell (1992) provides a helpful critique, clarification, and elaboration of Giddens's model.

Part II

Teaching as a Profession

Chapter 3

Teaching and the Competence of Occupations

Robert Dreeben

The idea of professionalism has been a subject of interest to sociologists at least since Talcott Parsons's (1939, 457) claim that "the professions occupy a position of importance in our society which is, in any comparable degree of development, unique in history." Many occupations have embarked on projects to transform themselves into professions, teaching conspicuously among them, and the results have been variable. The last few decades have witnessed significant advancements in treating the topic of occupational development (Abbott 1988a; Freidson 1986, 1994, 2001; Johnson 1972; Larson 1977), taking our understanding far beyond the old standby (Carr-Saunders and Wilson 1933). But professions are part of the larger division of occupational labor, and deciding which occupations to label as such is somewhat arbitrary.

It seems unlikely that any single dimension or typology will be found to classify occupations that respects their similarities and differences and defines a clear boundary between professions and nonprofessions, owing to differences in their developmental histories. With rough distinctions like professional, semiprofessional, tradesman, farmer, operative, or laborer, it is hard to know exactly what dimensions distinguish them and whether they pertain to all occupations. Parsons may have been right in stressing the importance of professions seen in the aggregate from cross-societal and historical perspectives. But in examining how particular occupations change, the idea of a course of occupational development seems to offer more analytical potential. It subsumes professionalization but also covers other kinds of occupational development.

If one had to choose a single criterion to identify a profession, it would be a practice based on a learned body of knowledge. This works well for the conventional four professions (medical, legal, clerical, and academic), but only partially for engineering and architecture. Although engineering relies heavily on physical science, the prominence of efficiency, cost, and practicality (Calhoun 1960) as standards of practice rubs some of the gloss off the academic side of the knowledge it employs. The history of civil engineering, interestingly, contains mid-nineteenth-century disputes over the balance between scholarly (including history and the humanities) and technical pursuits in training and practice (Merritt 1969). In architecture, despite the primacy of design over building construction in its self-definition (Briggs 1927; Draper 1977; Larson 1993, 4), the controversiality of aesthetic principles and the undercurrent of business interests have the same effect. Yet both engineering and architecture are commonly included among the professions despite differences in the kinds of knowledge on which they are based.

Rather than treat the professions separately, I examine an issue applicable to occupations generally: is the practice enacted with efficacy? Note that "efficacy" refers to occupations themselves, not to their members, even though members of each occupation differ in their individual competencies. The usage here is similar to Philip Selznick's (1957, 50) idea of an organization's "distinctive competence to do a *kind* of thing"; here I substitute "occupation" for "organization." Competence pertains to a collective entity. What lies behind it are the knowledge and skills available to practitioners, that is, the state of the art and its adequacy to meet the demands of the work. Here I use "state of the art" to refer to a repertoire of accepted practices appropriate to address most of the problems arising in the daily round of work, not to the familiar meaning of "cutting edge." I do not claim that competence, the capacity to perform tasks effectively (the technical component of occupations), is all there is to think about. But others have dealt with symbolic, moral, market, and other considerations. The claim is for the central importance of occupational competence; lest there be any doubt about it, witness, for example, the civil service, military, and professional reforms of nineteenth-century Britain, stimulated by the blunders of military training, recruitment, tactics, and strategy in the Crimean War (Reader 1966, 73–84; Woodham-Smith 1960), and on the comical side, Gilbert and Sullivan's spoofs of the incompetencies rampant in British institutions.

The notion of competence applies across the whole spectrum of occupations, and the level of competence of any given occupation can change over time. While there is now substantial agreement about the efficacy of medical practice—this was decidedly not the case prior to the early twentieth century (Kett 1968; Starr 1982)—there is similar agreement about the occupational competence of such trades as electrician, plumber, and machinist. Indeed, it is difficult to imagine an occupation becoming professionalized without a foundation of efficacious work, yet possessing such a foundation does not necessarily lead to professional status. Changes in the state of the art are critical in the development of occupations. They do not determine professionalism but have much to do with efficacy. From my perspective, that an occupation can deliver the goods has primacy over whether its base of knowledge is academic, it is highly remunerative, or it enjoys high prestige. Andrew Abbott (1988) argues, for example, that diagnosis, inference, and treatment are hallmarks of competence in the professions. But those elements of practice apply to all occupations.

The field of occupational studies has customarily proceeded with small to modest numbers of cases, using comparisons strategically and illustratively. Most investigations are qualitative: some are of single occupations, like Richard Ritti's (1971) on engineering and Ely Chinoy's (1955) on assembly-line manufacture; and others are comparative, like Konrad Jarausch's (1990) on teaching, law, and engineering in Germany and Daniel Calhoun's (1965) on law, the clergy, and medicine in the United States. Harold Wilensky's (1964) comparison of eighteen occupations (including six established professions) and Judith Blau's (1984) study of architecture are quantitative.

This chapter follows tradition and treats several occupations comparatively, but with a focus on teaching, in line with Charles Bidwell's contributions to understanding the work and organizational circumstances of teachers. Aside from that, teaching has been a stepchild among occupational studies, receiving little systematic attention from sociologists, Dan Lortie's (1975) *Schoolteacher* being a conspicuous exception. Teaching does not fall among the hotshot professions, even though its organizational leaders and members are preoccupied with professionalizing it, and while often scorned by public criticism, it lacks the cachet of the low-life taxi dancers, hoboes, and jack rollers whose callings have long entertained sociologists.

THE IDEA OF OCCUPATIONAL COMPETENCE

The history of work is replete with examples of the development of means to accomplish the ends in view (Adams 1996). Pre-twentieth-century medicine provides an informative example of a kind of work whose search for effective means toward ends brought contumely upon it. Respect for the occupation began to emerge late in the nineteenth century with the decline of skirmishing among allopaths, botanics, and homeopaths over patently ineffective and often lethal treatments; the growing awareness that a general theory of disease frustrated the development of sound diagnosis and treatment; the joining of surgical and medical practice; the declining animosity between practitioners and those doing laboratory research; and the replacement of the home by the hospital as a place to get well rather than to die. Most medical practice before 1900 was a showcase of incompetence; significant developments had indeed occurred, but their coalescence into competent practice would wait (Rothstein 1972; Shryock 1947; Vogel 1980).

It is easy to find evidence of competence in occupations whose practice has roots in science, medicine and engineering being the most obvious. But scientific knowledge forms the basis of practice in few occupations, and in few professions (Halliday 1987, 29–30). Among law, architecture, accounting, teaching, journalism, and many disciplines in academia, none is based primarily on science. Consider the clergy as an example. While an ability to provide evidence of salvation might be an unattainable standard for judging occupational competence, being able to attract communicants and providing enriching spiritual experiences are defensible and knowable criteria. One finds rich variation in theology, styles of sermonizing, church architecture, proselytizing, and pastoral activity directed toward keeping current members of religious congregations and attracting new ones. None of these practices, however, is based on science. Competence pertains to the *adequacy of the means* applied in occupational practice; it allows us to classify together the minister of an obscure sect with the pastor of a prestigious church, even though the former would not necessarily be considered professional based on learned knowledge.

OCCUPATIONAL COMPETENCE ILLUSTRATED

While the foregoing examples are drawn from the conventionally recognized professions, the argument applies to a wider range of occupations. Julian Orr (1996, 1), in his study of technicians who repair photocopy machines, notes the paucity of occupational studies that describe the actual practice of work—that is, "what is actually done in accomplishing a given job." In his treatment of the subjective aspects of professionalism, Abbott (1988, 40) argues that diagnosis, inference, and treatment are theoretically "the three acts of professional practice." But at a lower level of generalization, what particular activities constitute diagnosis, inference, and treatment? Orr's work addresses this question directly.

Teachers and Technicians

Copier repair is based on relations among technicians, customers, and machines (Orr 1996, 66). The knowledge of photocopy machine repair derives from technical training, repair manuals, and the pool of experience that accumulates among teams of technicians who work repeatedly on the machines. Of comparable importance are the stable informal relationships among team members who meet to discuss problems of diagnosis and repair based on their shared experience. In addition to a modicum of manual dexterity, competence depends on a storehouse of knowledge about diagnosis: ruling in and ruling out possibilities depending on machine-generated error logs, repair histories kept by technicians, current breakdown symptoms, and attempts to translate the users' lay language into information that fits the technician's mode of thinking (Orr 1996, 117). Orr states that "there is an assumption on the part of all participants in the service world that the technicians can solve any machine problem. The failure of this assumption in a problem which defies repeated attempts at solution is thus a serious *challenge to the competence of the community* and so engages their attention" (71, emphasis added).

There is also a customer relations component of the job that technicians call "fixing the customer" (Orr 1996, 82). This refers to educating customers about the proper use of the machines and getting them to understand the machines from the technician's mind-set and describe problems accordingly. This social component of the work is rife with problems because many customers do not believe there is anything to know or to report beyond saying that the machine is broken. Where the work entails changing the thinking and conduct of people (customers in this case), occupational competence is more vexed than with the mechanical side of practice. This is a vulnerability in the occupation's competence because the repair process will be impeded if the repairer cannot get appropriate diagnostic information from the user.

Several characteristics of this occupation are related to its competence. First, most of its members received their preparation for work in technical training schools and from the company that employs them, not in academic institutions. This preparation, while not academic or learned, enables them to perform both the manual and intellectual components of their work with proficiency. Second, the social organization of workers, even though jobs are located at separate sites, brings them together, usually at meals, to discuss the concrete problems of work; benefits from others' knowledge and experience are the draw. Third, the work requires detailed record-keeping in a commonly understood technical language. Fourth, aspects of the work that entail changing the beliefs and conduct of others are beset by difficulties. Finally, repair technicians want to be regarded as "professional," that is, recognized for their skill and for being businesslike (Orr 1996, 79). This view of professionalism, however, refers to specific job competence, not to the public status, power considerations, and occupational market share that motivate professionalizing projects.

Although copier repair work shows little outward resemblance to teaching, it possesses characteristics germane to occupational competence that make a comparison with teaching informative. First, although the technicians do their jobs at spatially dispersed sites, they use natural breaks in the workday to exchange experiences and knowledge over common repair problems; these problems activate the motivation to sustain a rich collegial life. Teachers in a school work at the same site, but their activities in separate classrooms restrict opportunities for collegiality. While they confront difficulties of the same general type, many of those arising in classrooms and pressing for answers tend to be particular and immediate and are seldom experienced by colleagues, directly and in common, or with reference to collectively understood documentary evidence. That is, what teachers tell each other about their work in collegial situations is mediated through their own formulation and interpretation of it, but the colleague is not a direct witness. Moreover, there is no objective record of classroom events. And unlike repair work, the day has few natural breaks that provide a spatial and temporal basis for daily collegiality.

Second, the training, technical language of manuals, error messages, and local argot arising from frequent interaction reflect the limited range of problems in copier repair compared to the wide range in teaching. The language conveys not only direct information relevant to machine and client problems but social meaning on which long-term interaction is maintained. Teaching possesses a more nebulous language with which to analyze the work and discuss it among colleagues on a technical basis; it carries information observed only by the practitioner of the activities it describes, not by colleagues or other interested parties. The language lacks standard expressions for pedagogy, significant events, practices, student conduct, conditions of classroom composition, and classroom history.

Third, teaching and copier repair both take place in organizational settings. While copier technicians are employed by a large corporation that defines their jobs, the corporation is dependent on them both to keep machines running and to protect its image. The occupation of copier repair technician, in short, holds a position of strength with both employers and customers by virtue of its competence, even though public recognition of its occupational status may not be high. Despite this, copier repair work does not seem to be an occupation that follows a path toward professionalization, presumably because it is secure based on its efficacy. Teachers, as I noted earlier, concern themselves with professional status because their efficacy has been challenged publicly and steadily. This has been the case at least since the common-school reforms of the early nineteenth century—the Massachusetts normal schools in 1837 were founded to deal with teacher incompetence (Herbst 1989a)—and later, at the end of the nineteenth century, in the large urban school systems in which teachers became vulnerable to administrative patronizing and arbitrariness (Murphy 1990). Concern with professionalism in teaching is a response to chronic assaults on its competence (for an account of a similar situation in England, see Reader 1966, 106).

Teaching and the Law

A comparison with law casts a different light on teaching. Law is customarily recognized as a profession and, along with medicine and architecture, is usually portrayed by the public as an occupation of autonomous practitioners. The reality for lawyers is actually more one of heteronomy: they work more like teachers than as the independent professional conveyed by their image. Lawyers, especially those in the most prestigious sectors of the occupation, tend to be members of large firms and to be hired as employees in the legal departments of corporations, government agencies, and other organizations (Carlin 1962, 1964; Freidson 1986; Heinz and Laumann 1994; Johnstone and Hopson 1967). Organizational employment characterizes both law and teaching. Professionalism in law, as in medicine, academia, accounting, and engineering, is by no means inconsistent with bureaucratic organization, as Parsons (1939, 466) observed more than sixty years ago, although certain differences in organizational structure are critical.

Bureaucracies vary in structure, and some variations are more consistent with professional practice than others. Bureaucracy, in other words, does not per se prevent teaching or any other occupation from engaging in professionalized work. Medical practice, for example, did not professionalize until it became attached to hospitals and universities (Vogel 1980), both being bureaucratized organizations. Electrical engineering, an occupation carried out in large bureaucratized firms, provides another apposite illustration (Ritti 1971). The projects that engineering firms pursue, as well as their internal structures and methods of operation, are governed by their business aims, not by the creative interests of research scientists. Firms hire personnel according to what their business is and whether it requires, for example, highly trained independent research scientists, more modestly trained technicians, or combinations of both. If, as Ritti (1971, 43) claims, engineers are less interested in self-generated original research than in advancement in the firm and a voice in business decisions, they still engage in work that requires imagination and initiative even if the goals are already set by the firm.

The key issue is whether an occupation can use its competence to establish its position in bureaucratized organizations so that the definition of its work is either not overwhelmed by the interests of the employing organization or is consistent with them. In law, medicine, and engineering, occupational competence exists and can flourish in bureaucratic settings. In teaching, there is reason to believe that the same reality can hold. But questions must be raised about the level of competence.

Consider law. Legal practice is highly varied: giving advice, negotiating, drafting (contracts, wills, trusts, court motions), litigating, and lobbying are but a sample of the many things lawyers do (Johnstone and Hopson 1967, 77–130). Pride of place, however, goes to research and analysis as "tasks peculiarly within the competence of lawyers. The law schools and bar exams heavily stress the development of competence at these tasks, and at least to some extent every lawyer must do legal research and analysis as part of his work" (102). The key diagnostic element of legal practice, formulating what a client's legal (and often practical or moral) problems are (Freund 1979), whether or not the client has already defined them, not done so, or done so inadequately, depends on the lawyer's capacity to do analysis, whose components Quintin Johnstone and Dan Hopson (1967, 102–3) have described as follows:

> Legal research and analysis encompass search for authoritative statements of legal doctrine, adaptation of legal doctrine to particular factual situations, prediction of how courts and other formal decision makers would decide particular cases if submitted to them, and factors that would influence these decisions. . . . [I]n part it is a creative process of seeking new relationships, developing new classifications, and originating rationales to justify them.

Erwin Smigel's (1964, 162) respondents in his study of Wall Street firms referred "to the fact that they were working in grey areas of the law—those portions of it which no one really knows and where what is done may help define the law." This is a kind of work that requires substantial intellectual independence in the exercise of judgment (344).

Central to legal practice, as well as to preparation to enter the occupation, are the written records of legal proceedings (briefs, trial transcripts, legal forms and instruments, contracts, statutes, codes, court decisions) and commentaries on them and on legal practice itself (law review articles, reports by bar associations, and the like). As do medicine, accounting, and engineering, law voluminously records its own practice, not just as statements of precedent but as records of the practice itself, expressed in a language common among lawyers, from which new problems can be defined and approached. The contrast with teaching, whose day-to-day activities leave little trace, is striking. Teaching activities, which consist of oral expressions and unrecorded and rarely observed actions, remain largely out of analytical reach and unavailable for the preparation of new recruits. Academics study teaching, but from numerous perspectives and without common categories or language; their findings are then written for an audience primarily of other academics, not of teachers. Moreover, teaching's organizations, both national and local, have not undertaken the task of observing, conceptualizing, analyzing, and publishing the activities entailed in the occupation. This undermines the generation, accumulation, and codification of knowledge about teaching as work and stands in contrast to the case of law, for which the written record of legal activity and commentary forms the raw material for training.

The comparison between law and teaching highlights another consideration related to occupational competence: the presence of a clientele faced privately, one at a time, and for the duration of the case, distinguished from a clientele faced collectively, publicly, and continuously. Lawyers and other individual practitioners apply their knowledge and procedures to the particulars of separate cases. The cases themselves are not intermingled, and lawyers need not pay much attention to how their actions in one case reverberate among the other cases they are handling. A legal case has an end to it, and the result can be assessed in light of what was done. Teaching, by contrast, poses a different set of contingencies because teachers have responsibility not just for the instruction of a diverse aggregate of individual students but for the long-term conduct of a class as a collectivity. The work ends not with a result tied to preceding efforts, but with an arbitrary date on the calendar—the end of the school year. The connection between efforts and results is hard to establish.

The knowledge for carrying out this sort of activity, with due regard for how decisions made at a given moment will play out hours, days, weeks, and months down the road, is simply not available in well-established form, though teachers act in such circumstances and, by necessity, devise their own solutions, some of them highly effective, others inept. As noted earlier, the evidence about teaching that could form the basis of such knowledge largely evaporates, unobserved, unrecorded, uncodified, and unconceptualized. The situation of teachers in working with collectivities in public over time is duplicated in a small number of other occupations that share the same predicament of lacking effective procedures: corrections is the most obvious case (Conover 2000; Jacobs 1977; Sykes 1958), and group social work is another. In all these cases, occupational competence itself is problematic because the connections between activities and outcomes—consisting of diagnoses, inferences, and treatments—are difficult to specify. Indeed, all occupations that entail the management of people to achieve individual and organizational goals—for example, in business, in the military, in athletics—experience uncertainties in attaching the selection of means to the achievement of goals.

TEACHING PRACTICE

Teaching activities that challenge occupational competence arise through the tasks of organizing classrooms, establishing routines, imparting information and skills, explaining new material, changing activities, and coping with the patterns of sociability among students, especially when they upset the flow of events (McFarland 1999, 2004, this volume). Their nature and difficulty depend on school level and the composition of the student population. In some elementary schools whose students come from troubled families, lack adequate language facility, or attend sporadically, difficult teaching conditions arise. The same is true with similarly composed secondary schools. Academic high schools pose less difficulty because the conduct of classes is based on the assumption that students not only possess reading skills that allow them to apply knowledge in all subjects but also recognize how academic subjects connect to college attendance and subsequent career advantages. Such schools aim to hire teachers with specialized command of academic subject matter that is integrated with that of the university system (Clark 1983).

No one claims that academic high schools are problem-free. But there are conventional ways to teach an academic curriculum in high schools premised on students' motivation and ability to read well and on teachers' ability to elicit and test students' knowledge and prepare them for college entrance exams—perhaps even for college. If teachers in academic high schools have mastered their subjects and can control their classrooms, they can still prepare students for college using traditional, unimaginative, or dull methods of instruction. The occupational challenge is manageable because viable means are at hand. Lortie (1975) has famously commented that teachers teach the way they were taught; in academic high schools, it may be how they were taught in college.

In high schools with students who enter two or more years behind in reading and mathematics, whose elementary and middle school experiences have been negative, whose attendance has been uneven, whose social and family circumstances have been unsupportive, or who have found little positive in their past schooling, carrying out instruction and keeping order are notoriously difficult, even for experienced teachers (McFarland 2004). The largely unacknowledged reason for this difficulty is that the knowledge and skills for dealing with hard cases are not broadly available in technically viable ways when the assumptions of academic schooling do not hold. This is not to deny that some teachers do very well under difficult circumstances, but they are effective because they have figured out how to deal with particular problems, not because the principles and techniques underlying their practice have been formulated or built into the preparation of teachers or become part of teaching's state of the art. Occupational competence for tough circumstances is limited. This situation, of course, is not peculiar to teaching, as Charles Bosk (1979, 1992) and Renée Fox (1959) have shown for the medical treatment of extreme cases. But it is particularly acute in occupations that deal with hard cases on a continuous basis—prison guards maintaining order on a cell block, for instance, or police reducing gang violence.

Teaching, with virtually no occupational tradition of practitioners collectively designing practices to deal with hard problems, has remained remarkably unchanged in its technological repertoire, despite variations associated with a dizzying array of fads and reforms. *Indigenous* research and development addressing the work of teaching has not been part of the occupational culture (though an exception to this generalization may be found in the practice of "lesson teaching" in some Japanese school districts [Yoshida 1999]). The discourse on teaching practice tends to be abstract, ignoring the day-to-day realities of classroom life. It fastens mostly on the "treatment" side of things to the exclusion of the "diagnostic" and "inferential." For example, there is little in teaching that speaks directly to the diagnosis of problematic *classroom* situations and is comparable, say, to physical diagnosis in medicine, the repair technician's questioning of copy machine users to identify what went wrong, or the lawyer's initial interview with a prospective client. When diagnosis is primitive, unsystematic, or not expressible in known categories or within agreed-upon parameters, there is not much need for inference to link it to treatment.

The tasks entailed in the running of classrooms—the foundation for identifying the dimensions of the work and its competent performance—have scarcely been categorized. For at least a half-century, teaching has proceeded on the assumption that poor student achievement is the central problem facing the occupation. Although it is certainly the case that many students do not perform well, it is not entirely clear whether poor achievement represents a proper diagnosis or a cluster of symptoms of more underlying difficulties. This is an open question that is chronically viewed as closed, or at least not worthy of much examination. Teaching is a prime example of Orr's (1996, 1) observation about the limits of our knowledge of "what is actually done in accomplishing a given job."

Like other lines of work, teaching requires command over a technology that includes, for example, starting and ending a class, carrying out lessons in classrooms diverse in student talents, coping with disruptions, deciding when and how to proceed to the next activity, assisting students with problems while minding the rest of the class, deciding what classroom formats to use for different curricular purposes, managing the ebb and flow of students' social activities in classrooms as well as the academic ones—all elements of the daily round. Identifying activities of this nature suggests areas for diagnostic attention. Treating correctly diagnosed situations may then lead to remedies for poor achievement, especially since poor achievement may be the product of prior causes that are more appropriate targets of direct treatment than poor achievement itself.

The absence of serious attention devoted to the problems of classroom diagnosis has left the door open to an endless array of educational "treatments" (or "reforms") rooted more in doctrine, "theory," and "philosophy" than in analysis of classroom events. (But as I noted earlier, teaching, unlike other occupations, pays little attention to the systematic observation, conceptualization, and codification of those events.) The discourse of teaching has vacillated over time between the abstractions of "traditionalism" and "progressivism," whose relevance to the activities of teaching is minimal. But knowing how to engage in appropriate instruction and classroom management does not derive directly from general precepts and ideological postures because they do not connect to the contingencies that arise from the particularities of classroom events.

The brevity of initial training—and accordingly the brevity of practice teaching—the difficulty of carrying out both student instruction and the training of new teachers in the same place at the same time, the difficulty of identifying the mid- and long-term classroom consequences of actions taken in a moment of time, the lack of records documenting work, and the lack of a standard language to report it are all conditions that have taxed the occupation in defining the nature of its work and its competence. Compared to other occupations, teaching is also less embedded in collegial life. Workshops and in-service activities to improve practice (generally referred to in question-begging fashion as "professional development") are common, although they tend to be short and sporadic and are often faddish. Knowledge about work circulates among teachers in local networks organized around secondary school departments and those formed around friendship and grade taught (Bidwell and Yasumoto 1999; Siskin 1994). Teachers, however, are characteristically left to assess their own situations and develop individual solutions to classroom quandaries, with the alternatives constrained by the conventional constants of classroom existence: an enclosed space, a textbook, a class period, the school year, and the variability of classroom composition. In fact, the implications of these combined conditions for the definition of teachers' work have yet to receive serious analysis. The occupational state of the art gives teachers less to go on than workers in many other occupations.

HISTORICAL CONTRASTS OF TEACHING AND ENGINEERING

All occupations experience some course of development that influences their competence, shaped by changes in knowledge, technology, societal opportunities and constraints, and programmatic efforts. The historical development of occupational competence, like professionalization, can be examined comparatively. Two markedly different occupations, teaching and engineering, possess certain similarities that highlight their differences. They began to develop as occupations at about the same time—in the decades surrounding the turn of the nineteenth century—and they have in common the fact that they both originated in organizational settings. However, this contrast, as I have just presented it, is too simple. Engineering is not a single occupation; it is a collection of them, four of which—civil, mechanical, mining, and electrical—out of a large number, gained prominence through their organizations. It is civil engineering that originated in organizational settings, not mechanical, but both serve as informative contrasts to teaching.

The Development of Occupational Competence in Engineering

Mechanical engineering developed out of small, independent machine shops devoted to innovative methods of working metals to build machines, tools, and machine parts. The shops did not produce primarily for retail commerce but rather to supply factories (for example, in the railroad and textile industries) and the military. There was an important intellectual component to this work, and its advocates were intent on developing it as well as distinguishing it from occupations that depended largely on physical strength and practical knowledge, the main talents required, say, for stationary engineers and locomotive drivers, who were considered machine tenders rather than engineers. The interests of mechanical engineers, according to Monte Calvert (1967, 8), were supported by an upper-class social elite who held an interest in "creating and preserving engineering as a gentlemanly profession" through the agency of small machine shops. The operation of these shops was stimulated by the profit motive, yet "transcended the non-professional, competitive business world" (13) and provided both intellectual challenge and respectability.

As with other occupations, controversy brewed over the appropriate way to train engineers. Early in the history of the occupation, the importance of fundamental knowledge underlying practice was accepted (a key difference from the case of teaching). Contributions from European research into thermodynamics and metal fatigue were known, and the importance of calculus was well recognized. Contention, however, developed between those who believed that engineering education was best carried out in university laboratories, where scientific principles could be applied to practice, and those who believed that practical shop experience was the preferable route to gaining fundamental knowledge. By the end of the nineteenth century, the "educators" had largely won out over the shop advocates. This victory came with the emergence of the large electrical equipment companies, General Electric and Westinghouse, which provided the graduates of engineering schools with shop experience in their laboratories (Calvert 1967, 74–76, 216). The victory took various forms in which academic, scientific engineering education was combined with practical shop experience.[1]

Civil engineering differs from mechanical engineering in that it did not arise out of small-shop entrepreneurship. The occupation grew out of the employment of men who gained construction "experience and practical skill" (Calhoun 1960, 35) on public works projects, like dams, canals, roads, and drainage projects. As a base of knowledge underlying these efforts developed experientially, and the similarity between the projects undertaken in the civil and military sectors of society became recognized, the U.S. Military Academy at West Point became the site for training in engineering skills. In the mid-1830s, training also became available at such engineering schools as Rensselaer, Partridge's School, and Stevens Institute (Calhoun 1960, 47–52). The dominant pattern, however, was that "engineering projects . . . served as schools of engineering. . . . Th[e] civil engineer was the creature of the organizations in which he worked" (51, 53). That much could be said of teaching. In teaching, however, the school was scarcely the training ground for new teachers.

At the heart of engineering activities is judging the practicability of a project, a task that requires advance planning, bringing relevant evidence to bear, and assessing cost (Calhoun 1960, 55–57). Determining elevations, slopes, and soil composition and planning the routes of canals, roads, and railroad track (58–60) were the kinds of activities whose performance benefited from both practical experience and mastery of scientific principles and whose performance and results could be assessed with considerable reliability. The increasing size of projects led to the hiring of full-time specialized experts by large engineering firms. This development opened up paths of career mobility in which the mastery and accumulation of skills allowed for advancement toward the grade of chief engineer (Merritt 1969,

10). These characteristics of civil engineering as an occupation—cumulative skill acquisition, objective assessment of work activity, and the mobility provided by a hierarchical organization—have been notably absent from teaching.

As projects and organizations that employed engineers increased in size, they also expanded in their implications for economic, political, and social policy beyond the scope of the practical goals tied immediately to the projects themselves (Calhoun 1960, 162–63). In effect, civil engineering became an occupation that attempted to define its place in and contribution to society through what it considered to be valuable public projects. By the late nineteenth century, engineering tended to gravitate toward large organizational forms, with the result that the technical and managerial components of engineering became closely interwoven. It moved beyond a narrow preoccupation with technical mechanics to include the institutional concerns that large corporate enterprises confront in tying their activities not just to corporate management but to matters pertaining to the public welfare as well (Merritt 1969, 87).[2]

Despite a long history of jurisdictional disputes among different branches of engineering and disagreements about the appropriate forms of training and the relative importance of scientific, practical, business, and managerial knowledge, engineering, in most of its manifestations, has consistently concerned itself with the efficient performance of goal-directed practical activity. Although the chronic disputes may have frustrated the attempts by some engineers to succeed in a professionalizing project on the model of medicine—the close connection with business activity being one of the main obstacles—professional values related to science, mathematics, and a larger world of ideas have nevertheless remained present, if insufficient to guarantee professional recognition of the occupation as a whole.[3] Teaching, by contrast, has never succeeded in rooting its practice in some larger intellectual scheme of thought, scientific or otherwise, nor has it succeeded as an occupation with strong claims to efficiently performed, goal-directed practices.

Challenges to the Occupational Competence of Teaching

The case of teaching reveals significant historical similarities to as well as differences from engineering. Private venture schooling existed in the American colonies, first as household-centered dame schools and later as entrepreneurial efforts to offer instruction, often in evening schools, in a variety of skills and areas of knowledge: arithmetic, surveying, embroidery, navigation, playing musical instruments (Cremin 1970; Seybolt 1925, 1935). But in the early nineteenth century, with the increasingly successful efforts to establish local and state systems of common public schooling, these independent efforts dried up. Unlike the case of mechanical engineering, where the shop was a unit of production and the "shop culture" that accompanied it remained a significant influence in defining the occupation, teaching as a pursuit undertaken in small entrepreneurial settings gave way to one whose existence and character were defined by an organizational entity: a local school, and eventually a school system. But even when schools were based in households or organized as small entrepreneurial units, the tasks of teaching were those of conveying existing knowledge and skills. They did not entail heavy societal responsibilities beyond the fulfillment of basic community expectations (like literacy and morality) and the provision of the specialized skills students wanted to acquire. Although early school settings were far from bureaucratic, teaching nevertheless arose as an occupation dedicated to meeting obligations set by external agencies: families, local communities, interest groups, counties and municipalities, states, and the federal government. And while school systems are more bureaucratized now than at the beginning, the conditions and daily tasks of teaching predate bureaucracy.

In the seventeenth and eighteenth centuries, the qualification to teach appeared to depend on the level of education attained by the teacher. Initially, women did not teach Latin or advanced English, because preparation in Latin and writing was closed to them. They were relegated to teaching young children until educational opportunities opened up for them, a transition that occurred from the late eighteenth to the early nineteenth century (Perlmann and Margo 2001). The source materials on the history of teaching, however, do not describe the particulars of what teaching at any level entailed, at least as far as instruction is concerned.[4]

The situation is different from what prevailed in engineering at about the same time. It has been possible to identify the activities entailed in that line of work and whether they were effective. In teaching, however, a teacher's qualification was signaled by being able to control a class and having been exposed to the curriculum in question as a student—or at least having learned to read. "It should be recalled that teaching the New England summer sessions of 1820 did not require educational adornments much loftier than literacy" (Perlmann and Margo 2001, 66). As educational opportunities for girls increased in the early nineteenth century, the ideology of domesticity turned nurturance into a justification for women to teach—even to teach older boys—thus transforming adherence to values about family life into a standard of teaching competence (30–31).[5]

Horace Mann was acquainted with Victor Cousin's report and envisioned a scheme in this country that would offer full-time teacher training, similar to the practice in Prussia. But Massachusetts normal schools, beginning in 1837, were established for a different purpose: a remedial one designed for temporary, mostly female teachers of modest talents who by the 1830s were teaching both summer and winter, while males taught in the winter. Normal school enrollments were lower than expected, and many of the women who attended never entered teaching (a pattern that continues to occur to the present day [National Center for Educational Statistics 1983]), because a normal school education opened up other pursuits besides teaching (Herbst 1989a, 219–20, 1989b; Theobald 1995). Nothing in the American experience would support a training system like the Prussian one, which was favored by Whigs like Mann and aimed at solid preparation for men who expected to follow lifetime careers in teaching. A prevailing view in Massachusetts at the time was that anyone could teach, would do so for little pay, and would leave teaching when better opportunities arose (Messerli 1971, 253–54). Indeed, many of the men who taught did so part-time to support themselves while preparing for other pursuits. A common notion was the idea of the citizen teacher: anyone who acquired some education could teach, at least for some time in a life of work (Herbst 1989b, 83). Even as late as the 1910s in Iowa, country school teachers, the largest component of the occupation, went unrecognized by the Iowa State Teachers Association and were otherwise treated with disrespect. "Part of the reason for this was that teaching in the country schools did not require any formal training" (Reynolds 1999, 63), and the state provided no incentives for country teachers to acquire normal school training when it became available in 1911.

The occupational competence of teaching resolved itself into an issue of training. Training took different forms related to region of the country, state, sex of the teacher, and the power of different groups dedicated variously to the presumed interests of rural elementary teachers, high school teachers, school administrators, academics in the business of teacher training, and institutions such as colleges, academies, normal schools, and universities vying to establish their own positions of dominance and reap the benefits of tuition monies (Herbst 1989a, 222–29). The battles were over whether the state or localities (towns, counties) should take responsibility for training young rural women to teach in grade schools, men to teach in high schools, instructors in normal schools, town and county administrators, and so on; there was also conflict over which training institutions should be responsible or not responsible for which kind of teachers. For example, was it appropriate for a university to train grade school teachers? If so, did it matter whether the teacher would be working in the city or in the countryside? And while the competence question emerged as a matter of training, training turned into a problem of politics, of who should control what. The situation with teaching was far different from the case of engineering, in which a consensus prevailed over the fundamental significance of the knowledge informing the work; the only area of disagreement was over how best to transmit that knowledge.

Competence is not simply a matter of training. Identifying it requires a description of the activities entailed in the work. Visible activities, such as those found in architecture, engineering, medicine, copier repair, and the skilled trades, can be identified and also conceptualized in light of the thought processes associated with them (for example, Abbott's idea of "inference"). The identification of the activities associated with teaching, however, has remained notoriously difficult. It is no mean task to describe what teachers do in the course of their work, let alone to conceptualize it. A partial exception to this claim can be found in James Leloudis's (1996, 16) portrait of schooling in North Carolina in the late nineteenth to early twentieth centuries. He notes that:

> memory drills dominated reading lessons just as they did ciphering lessons. Common school students learned to read by learning to spell. "Over and over again" was the rule of the day in most classrooms, as children labored to conquer lists of words without definitions. Textbook authors assumed that their young audiences would communicate through speech more than writing and that patterns of local usage would supply meaning. In most communities, reading was an oral, often collective activity, not the private and silent one it is today.

This description indicates what students did; from it one can only infer the classroom conduct of teachers—and then only for those fragments of the school day devoted to reading and spelling. Leloudis (1996, 11–13) also identifies the conditions of teaching: teachers' subservience to the preferences of parents and local school officials; the school calendar that kept schools open seasonally and for long hours during the day so that students could come and go according to their household obligations; and the curriculum that permitted the use of family-owned books combined sometimes with more standard textbook fare.

In contrast, the work of engineers from the beginning was defined by a project, whether a sizable public works undertaking or the design and fabrication of a machine in a small shop. There were palpable ways to determine whether the production succeeded and whether it could be done more quickly, less expensively, or in an alternative manner that would reduce effort and waste and perhaps lay the groundwork for a better design. Public works projects and machine shops were hierarchical, the former more so than the latter, and both provided experiences for the supervision and training of new recruits simultaneously with the activities of production—in fact, as part of them. Teaching is starkly different, even though in both engineering and teaching what is to be done is defined by others, specifically so in the case of engineering, generally so in the case of teaching. No one expressed precisely what teachers were supposed to do, but whatever it was, they were expected to be better at it if they had had more rather than less education. The training element present in engineering was absent in teaching. It still is. Rather than being built on projects (as in engineering and architecture) or cases (as in medicine or law) or discrete problems (as in repair occupations), teaching is premised on the performance of work for a period of time (months, terms, years) and without a clear-cut indication of task completion. Teachers are also subject not to the direct authority of more experienced workers, as is true among engineers, but indirectly to public officials and others in the community who know as little if not less about the work than the teachers themselves.

From the outset, the working situation of teachers has not been one that stimulates the analysis of work. Rather, its circumstances have been those of subordination and exposure to the sometimes arbitrary expectations of community members, official and otherwise, unaided by a work technology that would allow teachers to demonstrate their effectiveness. Despite the professionalizing campaigns of the National Education Association (NEA)—expressed through a rhetoric of professionalism that dates from the time of Mann—and the migration of teacher training from the high schools and academies to the normal schools, and then to the universities, the basic working situation has remained much the same for a century, as Willard Waller's (1932) portrayal of rural teachers testifies—and even to the present day.

Notwithstanding these changes in the location of and responsibility for teacher training, the comparison of teaching to mechanical engineering reveals a significant reality for the occupational development of teaching. In both cases, the occupation began in the early nineteenth century with the practice taking place in small, independent work units: machine shops and local schools. Despite this similarity, the major difference was that in machine shops, work transpired in open, collective settings in which neophytes participated as apprentices, visible to their more highly skilled colleagues. They learned their trade through this experience. Teachers, however, taught alone and unobserved and learned their trade through that experience. Even though formal pre-service training has become a larger component in the worklife of teachers, the inability of the classroom to integrate both work and training activities simultaneously has remained a stable occupational property of teaching to the present time, no technical solution to the problem having emerged. One is reminded here of Arthur Stinchcombe's (1965, 143) proposition about the founding of organizations, namely, there is a "correlation between the time in history that a particular type of organization was invented and the social structure of organizations of that type which exist at the present time." Absent technological innovations that alter the nature of the work and perforce the relation between training and work performance, organizational structure endures, and this proposition, I suggest, may hold for occupations and their work activities in the same way it does for structure.

PROFESSIONALISM AND COMPETENCE

The history of occupations over a span of centuries shows the multiplicity of courses they have followed. A small but disputed number of them, through their efforts to change the nature of their work—to distinguish themselves from other occupations, to claim work jurisdiction, or to mobilize themselves socially, politically, and economically—have sought and gained status as professions. The symbolism of professionalism is potent, and occupations have been drawn to the illusion that there is a conventional main road to becoming a profession. A small number of occupations have gained uncontroversial recognition as professions, but why this list of cases has received so much scholarly attention is not entirely clear. In addition, there have been numerous—and sterile—attempts to identify criteria that distinguish professions from nonprofessions. The developmental histories of other occupations, however, raise questions equally as interesting.

As I noted earlier, teachers and their organizations have long used the rhetoric of professionalism to characterize their work and its status. Since the 1830s and the advent of normal schools, the public status of the occupation has been a source of concern to its members. The professional rhetoric has referred to public prestige, autonomy, and high remuneration, characteristics that spokespeople for teachers conventionally attribute to medicine and law, based on a presumption that professional status will be achieved by seeking these indications of professionalism through collective action. It is noteworthy that historically the NEA has been adamantly opposed to unionism, regarding it as a threat to professionalism, which it defined in status terms, but over the last thirty or so years it has emulated the bread and butter unionism of the American Federation of Teachers (AFT). Both consider themselves to be following a professionalizing agenda through political lobbying and collective bargaining; neither, however, attends much to the components of teaching practice and the activities it comprises. They assert the professionalism of teaching yet bemoan the fact that the occupation does not command the prestige and emoluments of other professions, nor the power to define what education means for society in the same way that medicine defines health, law defines justice, the clergy defines faith, journalism defines news—in Everett Hughes's (1958, 79) words, by claiming a mandate "to tell society what is good and right for the individual and for society at large in some aspect of life."

The central occupational problem of teaching, I argue, is not professionalism or the lack of it: it is the issue of competence in dealing with hard situations. Teachers, collectively organized, or in school systems or schools, have not addressed this question. Educational reforms of one sort or another have been proposed to improve the efficacy of teaching—new curricula, new forms of school organization, new methods of management, new pedagogy, new testing programs, new standards—but these almost invariably originate outside the occupation, from academia mostly, but also from the programs, nostrums, and ideologies of interest groups. They have no hold on teachers; they represent the advocacy positions of others intended to make teachers change the nature of their "treatment." As efforts to raise the level of competence on an occupational basis, they go nowhere.

What would be entailed if teaching were to raise its level of occupational competence? What changes in work activities and school organization would contribute to this goal? These are not easy questions to answer. The conventional approach to them—to the extent they have even been asked—has been to search for solutions in the realms of public policy and research. Efforts to address the competence problems of teaching—leave the matter of the effectiveness of such efforts aside—tend to originate outside the occupation. They tend to define what is problematic in terms of failures in student achievement—the overwhelming focus of public policy and academic research attention—as if remedies addressed to that end would simultaneously improve the state of the art in teaching.

Over the past half-century at least, the educational terrain has become littered with the debris of attempts to change curricula, pedagogy, classroom design, management principles and techniques, testing, and other aspects of educational practice. Some of this debris has been dusted off, renamed, and tried again, as if the first failure was not sufficient to demonstrate lack of viability. In some cases, like the post-Sputnik science curriculum reforms, academia was the breeding ground. In other cases, reforms originated with prominent individuals (Conant, Rickover, Bestor, Comer, Sizer, and others), some of whose designs for schooling became briefly eponymous before fading away. And in still other cases, agencies of federal and state government have been the prime movers. What is so conspicuous about these efforts is their remoteness from the day-to-day work of school administration and teaching. In effect, they do not identify or provide the conditions for teachers to define the major categories of their work, document the flow of it, develop diagnostic procedures for classroom events, consider the alternative treatments for those diagnoses, and develop a collegial life that supports both the analysis of work and its practice. In other (but certainly not all) lines of work located at most levels of the socioeconomic hierarchy, such conditions do exist to support occupational competence.

Although much of the impetus to raise the competence level of teaching originates in the realm of public policy, another source of such efforts is academia. This is hardly surprising since the training of teachers represents a huge enterprise in the world of higher education, and especially in the state-controlled schools and colleges of education. Indeed, as part of their own status-raising efforts, schools and colleges of education have invested heavily in programs of research and in their attachments to the American Educational Research Association. This commitment to research, however, is not simply part of a prestige-generating enterprise; it is also premised on the notion that educational practice will benefit from research efforts located in schools and colleges of education. The research in question is scientific, and those performing it assume that the intellectual base of knowledge that supports teaching is scientific and accordingly is most appropriately carried out by members of the academy. This is the model of medicine—the lodestar profession—and to a lesser extent engineering. It would be erroneous to believe, however, that medicine achieved its status strictly through scientific advances. It is also strange that teaching, like some other occupations, compares itself to medicine in the scramble for status since their respective histories have been so conspicuously different. Indeed, medicine may not be the lodestar but a grand exception, a distinctive case.

Teachers pay little attention to the research findings of academic scholars using scientific methods. There is not much evidence that teachers read it or that the research, if they did read it, would contribute much to their practice. To put it mildly, skepticism about the value of scientific research for their work runs high among teachers—and reasonably so. As I indicated earlier, many if not most occupations—including the professions defined broadly—are not based on scientific evidence and do not depend in their practice on advancements in science. The law—despite a (failed) late-nineteenth-century movement to establish a science of law—and the clergy are obvious cases. Certain academic fields, especially the humanities, are devoted to systematic inquiry but are hardly tied to science. And fields in which occupational competence is high, like copier repair, journalism, architecture, and the skilled trades, do not look to science, although they may benefit indirectly from scientific developments.

It seems that the most serious obstacles to establishing a satisfactory level of competence as an occupational property of teaching lie in shortcomings related to an underdeveloped technical language for expressing the characteristics of the work; the evanescent nature of the work activities of teaching and the failure to capture, document, and classify them; the invisibility of teaching to collegial observation and scrutiny; and, given the highly decentralized nature of the American educational system with regard to teacher training, curriculum, and the local political control of schools, the difficulty of diffusing knowledge about practice. How to overcome these obstacles is no simple matter. In the Japanese scheme of lesson teaching (Yoshida 1999), which is far from universal in Japan, teachers at given grade levels in local schools design curriculum and lessons, try them out while being observed, document them, revise them over several iterations, enact them, and publish the results. Although lesson teaching is an exceedingly time-consuming and labor-intensive process, it is also tied directly and visibly to the experience of teachers at work. It is systematic, analytical, and synthetic. Teachers' unions in the United States, ever protective of the hours and conditions of work, would scarcely warm to such a process. Even though occupational competence requires substantial investments of time and effort, first-level teacher training in the United States requires only a minimal investment—a fact that no doubt works to the economic advantage of teacher training institutions by virtue of the tuition monies generated.

It is difficult to see where an incentive for teachers, not outside parties, to engage in indigenous efforts at systematic inquiry into the nature of their work will originate, flourish, and become institutionalized. To understand why this systematic inquiry is not found in teaching but does occur in occupations that are more secure in their competence, we might turn to one of Abbott's (1988) arguments about professionalizing as a historical process of jurisdictional conflict over domains of work. Teaching has been free of jurisdictional conflict because no other occupational group has sought to take over its line of work. The value of jurisdictional conflict is that it forces the practitioners of an occupation to define the basic work activities over which it claims control and defend the claim from invaders and schismatics. Teaching has not had to do that; it has had critics, but it has not faced occupational enemies or aggrandizers. Schools are a public utility. They must provide their service, their "treatment," every day, whatever the quality. The absence of jurisdictional conflict in teaching has taken its toll in the lack of attention paid to the diagnostic and inferential components of the work, which are closely tied to treatment in both professional and other occupations whose efficacy is their competence.

Finally, for reasons difficult to explain, teaching has never found a body of ideas—pedagogical principles, in effect—under which to subsume its practices. There has been nothing comparable to the aesthetics of design in architecture, the principles of jurisprudence and precedent in law, or science in medicine and engineering to provide an intellectual basis for practice. This circumstance, combined with the reluctance of *teachers themselves* to pursue an ideational agenda derived from their own work experience, undercuts the development of a distinctive competence, in the first instance, and derivatively, to undertake a professionalizing project, in the second. The agenda for identifying a distinctive competence, especially for dealing with hard cases, must overcome this historical impediment— which still exists—as well as the prevailing conditions, enumerated here, that stand in the way.

NOTES

1. What also underlay the conflict between the academic and shop cultures was the difference in the claims for status invoked by the advocates for each side: in one case, sta-

tus was gained through the educational mastery of the scientific and mathematical knowledge available through universities; in the other, status was based on elite family origins and social networks, sometimes a classical education, and wealth gained from successful entrepreneurship (Calvert 1967, 153–54). From the outset, mechanical engineering was imbued with a sense of high social status conventionally construed: through mastery of university-based knowledge and elite family lineage. In contrast, teaching in small entrepreneurial schools could bring no such status resources to its occupational position.

2. As a historical note, this development found expression in Frederick W. Taylor's scientific management movement and in the technocracy movement of the early twentieth century (Layton 1971, 134–78; Smith 1984).

3. "Engineers," according to Robert Zussman (1985, 222), "have never succeeded in a 'collective mobility project' equivalent to that of doctors and lawyers. With occasional exceptions in civil engineering and among some executive officers of industrial corporations, practice is not restricted to certified engineers, and there is no restriction on the use of 'engineer' as an occupational title."

4. In 1831, Victor Cousin, a French professor of philosophy, made detailed observations of Prussian schools and teacher training institutions for the French minister of public instruction. About this venture, Jurgen Herbst (1989a, 216) comments: "It seems strange ... that in reviewing plans and curricula of the seminars [to train teachers], Cousin found relatively little to report on instruction in pedagogy proper. ... The first requirement for a candidate for a teaching position was a pure heart and an upright character."

5. The North-South regional differences that Perlmann and Margo (2001) discuss are beyond the scope of this chapter.

Chapter 4

The Prospects for Teaching as a Profession

Susan Moore Johnson

In the eyes of the public, teachers have long been regarded as second-rate professionals. Twenty years ago Gary Sykes (1983, 98) observed that although teaching "has enjoyed a measure of public esteem and gratitude through the years . . . there is a long-standing taint associated with teaching and corresponding doubts about those who chose this occupation." Unlike medicine and law, the field of education has struggled unsuccessfully to achieve a level of respect and recompense for teachers that reflects the importance and demands of their work. Dan Lortie (1969, 29), who examined the work of elementary school teachers, similarly concluded that "the general status of teaching, the teacher's role, and the condition and transmission arrangement of its subculture point to truncated rather than fully realized professionalization." Walter Metzger (1987, 10) observed that when sociologists drew up a list of attributes that defined a profession, they intended to "distinguish the genuine article from the unworthy pretentious rest." Those lines of work that did not measure up had been designated "the semi-professions, the quasi-professions—where they could receive a silver medal until such time as they earned the gold" (11). One of these was teaching.

There are various plausible explanations for why teaching had achieved little more than a toehold of professional standing by the mid-1980s. Until the 1950s, teaching was short-term, itinerant work taken up by men on their way to a "real" profession—or at least a better-paying job—and by women who taught for a short time before marrying or having children (Rury 1989; Tyack 1974). Teacher education programs, where they existed, were brief and seldom regarded as substantive or challenging (Lortie 1975). The ongoing need for over two million teachers to staff classrooms across the country made it difficult to be selective in hiring and thus elevate the public status of the work. This problem of status was further exacerbated by the fact that, because teaching is akin to child care, it has long been seen as women's work (Hoffman 1981) and therefore not deserving of the status of medicine or law. Also, because teaching was locally funded, teachers' salaries, like those of firefighters and police, remained subject to public scrutiny and control, a factor that routinely limited pay (Johnson 1990). Further, because teachers were publicly paid and thus publicly accountable, they were never granted the formal autonomy in their work that is often said to be essential for true professionals (Lortie 1975). Finally, while professionals are expected to possess "a body of complex knowledge" (Metzger 1987, 10), pedagogy had by the 1980s only a weak and contested knowledge base (Good 1983). The only firm purchase on professionalism that educators had by the 1980s was a claim to the "service ethic" (Metzger 1987, 10), and even that was subject to skepticism.

Following publication of *A Nation at Risk* (National Commission on Excellence in Education 1983) and the failure of initial efforts to improve teaching with greater top-down control, education reformers developed a plan to improve schools by professionalizing teaching. Policy analysts, practitioners, politicians, education school deans, and scholars combined their efforts to develop and promulgate a strategy linking the professionalization of teaching with school improvement. Richard Ingersoll (1997, 1) elaborates on their rationale:

> Proponents of this view hold, for example, that teachers are underpaid, have too little say in the operation of schools, are afforded too few opportunities to improve their teaching skills, suffer from a lack of support or assistance, and are not adequately rewarded or recognized for their efforts. The key to improving the quality of schools, these critics claim, lies in upgrading the status, training, and working conditions of teaching, that is, in furthering the *professionalization* of teachers and teaching. The rationale underlying this view is that upgrading the teaching occupation will lead to improvements in the motivation and commitment of teachers, which in turn will lead to student learning.

Now, over twenty years after this concerted effort to professionalize teaching began, it is time to take stock of this initiative and consider what the prospects are for the future of teaching as a profession. It is particularly appropriate to assess the standing of teaching as a profession at this time when public schools face a wholesale replacement of their teachers within the next decade. How close are teachers to "earn[ing] the gold" medal of professionalism (Metzger 1987, 10)? Will the next generation of teachers be the first to know teaching as a full-fledged profession?

In the following discussion, I first consider the characteristics of professions and review the elements of professionalism that have proven to be problematic for teachers over time, identifying for each how changing times and circumstances might provide new opportunities for teaching to advance its standing as a profession. Next, I consider the reforms introduced since the mid-1980s to address these shortcomings. Finally, I assess the prospects for education as a profession in light of new evidence about the next generation of teachers and the current context of public education.

THE PROFESSIONAL STANDING OF TEACHING

Sociologists have written extensively about the essential features of professions. Although there is general agreement about some, there is no single list of characteristics to which all subscribe. Eliot Freidson (1994, 128) observes that "professionals have been singled out as occupations that perform tasks of great social value because professionals possess both knowledge and skills that in some way set them apart from other kinds of workers." Scholars of education have also identified the primary conditions that "distinguish a profession from other occupations," including: "a specialized knowledge base and shared standards of practice"; "a strong service ethic, or commitment to meeting clients' needs"; "a strong personal identity with, and commitment to, the occupation"; and "collegial versus bureaucratic control over entry, performance evaluations, and retention in the profession" (128).

Andy Hargreaves and Ivor Goodson (1996, 1) observe that "teacher professionalization has been a historically precarious project: resisted by governments, bureaucracies and business interests without, and undermined by ambiguities of loyalty, strategy and identity within." Over time, a variety of factors have contributed to teaching's standing as a semiprofession. Some endure today, such as the perception of teaching as women's work, and therefore as an occupation that does not warrant professional status. Other factors, such as teachers' historically brief tenure in the occupation, their lack of access to specialized knowledge, the absence of an established credentialing process, and the absence of a staged career, have undergone change.

Teaching as Itinerant Work

The sociologists who study professions do not include on their list of criteria the expectation that professionals will make a long-term commitment to their occupation; that goes without saying. In teaching, however, such commitment has never been a certainty. Although the cohort of teachers now approaching retirement has made teaching a lifetime career, they are the first to do so (Evans 1996). To the extent that history shapes current beliefs, it is important to acknowledge that teaching was itinerant work for close to a century. As Lortie (1969, 17) observes, during the colonial period "those who taught did so for limited periods of time, for most of them were on the way to something else—ministerial students preparing for a pulpit, indentured servants accumulating the price of their bond. Incomes and prestige were low." With "urbanization, secularization, and school expansion" in the late nineteenth century, "teaching became work performed by young women" (12). Lortie explains that, "given the relative position of the young and the female in the nineteenth century . . . [that fact] probably reduced rather than augmented its social rank" (12). Those women, however, were not permitted to continue as teachers once they married or became pregnant; the result was steady and inevitable teacher turnover.

In the 1950s school districts dealt with the teaching shortage following World War II by eliminating restrictions on married and pregnant women so that they could continue to teach (Spencer 2001). By the late 1960s, when access to other professions was still restricted for women and people of color, teaching attracted many able recruits seeking to do meaningful public service. Unlike those who preceded them, this cohort of new teachers has remained in teaching over time, gradually changing the public's perception of teaching as temporary employment and increasing the chance that teaching will be regarded as professional work.

Lack of Specialized Knowledge

Ingersoll (1997, 5) explains that professions are often said to be the "knowledge-based" occupations: "The assumption is that professional work involves highly complex sets of skills, intellectual functioning, and knowledge that are not easily acquired and not widely held." This standard presents several challenges for those who would professionalize teaching. First, the public does not widely believe that specialized knowledge is needed to succeed in teaching. Lortie (1969, 24) emphasizes that professional status requires that the "relevant publics (clients, political agencies, and the like) *believe* that knowledge to be both essential and restricted to members of the professional group. The possession of esoteric knowledge over a period of time strengthens those within the profession vis-à-vis the public in *general* terms." However, as Linda Darling Hammond (2001, 761) observes, "The view of teaching as relatively simple, straightforward work, easily controlled by prescriptions for practice, is reinforced by the 'apprenticeship of experience' adults have lived through during their years as students in schools."

Second, as Lortie noted in 1969, it is pedagogy—not the subject matter taught—that is the unique province of teachers. Scientists, not teachers of science, lay claim to scientific knowledge. For elementary teachers, "the subjects teachers themselves believe useful in teaching (e.g., child psychology) are primarily the property of others" (Lortie 1969, 24). Only recently has pedagogy begun to gain recognition as a challenging and complex topic worthy of inquiry and mastery.

Third, systematic research on teaching was, until the 1980s, very scarce. Thomas L. Good (1983, 42), reviewing research on classroom teaching in 1983, notes that "we know considerably more about classroom teaching than we did a decade ago. In 1970 the accumulated knowledge about the effects of classroom processes on student achievement was weak and contradictory." Yet, even as Good surveyed the field in 1983, there were relatively few carefully conducted, well-regarded studies of teaching practice, and many important questions, such as how best to teach reading or mathematics, remained largely unexplored. Therefore, by the mid-1980s the teaching occupation did not have a substantial and specialized knowledge base on which to rest its case for professional standing.

Uncredentialed Work

Colonial teachers had no special training: "No special arrangements existed to regulate entry, and the necessary credentials were limited to sufficient literacy to teach reading, writing, and elementary arithmetic" (Lortie 1969, 16–17). There was an understanding that a teacher "should have completed the level immediately above that which she aspired to teach" (18). Between 1900 and 1950, states gradually increased requirements for teaching licenses, although the required courses were few, and the content standards loosely defined. In marked contrast with the formal preparation, apprenticeships, and licensing required in law or medicine, there were no formal examinations to ensure that aspiring teachers had mastered the material. As Ingersoll (1997, 5) explains, "Nearly all professions require completion of an officially sanctioned or accredited training program and passage of examinations in order to obtain certification or licensure to practice. Indeed, it is illegal to practice most professions without a license. These credentials serve as screening devices." However, throughout much of the twentieth century states had inconsistent requirements for new teachers, there were no examinations to screen or certify candidates, and many unlicensed teachers hired to meet a shortage practiced under emergency certificates (Darling-Hammond 2001).

A Flat Career Structure

Since the mid-1900s, the professions of law and medicine have instituted mechanisms for induction and advancement to ensure that new entrants are supervised early in their practice and progressively assume more responsibility. However, well into the 1980s teachers' roles remained largely undifferentiated; the first day of classroom teaching looked much like the last.

In part, this uniformity of role is driven by the "cellular" organization of schools (Lortie 1975, 14), which isolates teachers in their classrooms and discourages colleagues from working in interdependent ways. Also, there is an assumption of "rationalized activities" and demand for a "uniform product" (Bidwell 1965, 974). Thus, throughout the last century most schools treated teachers as replaceable workers with generic but minimal skills rather than as specialists with advanced training.

The problem of undifferentiated roles and unstaged careers, however, is arguably self-imposed by teachers themselves. They are wary about administrative favoritism and consequently prefer a kind of uniform treatment that discourages superiors and the public from making distinctions among them (Johnson 1990). As a result, teaching assignments and pay have long been regulated by standardized rules and seniority-based criteria. This lockstep treatment, coupled with the lack of systematic induction for novice teachers, has reinforced the view of teaching as nonprofessional work.

Public Funding and Public Accountability

The fact that teachers' pay depends on public funds also has implications for education's status as a profession. It is clear that the process of collective bargaining has standardized pay for teachers (Odden and Kelley 1997). However, the fact that local budgets restrict negotiated salary settlements and often require achieving equity across other groups of public service employees makes it virtually impossible for teachers to achieve financial standing and status comparable to that of independent doctors and lawyers.

There is also considerable evidence that teachers are primarily focused on the intrinsic, rather than extrinsic, rewards of their work (Lortie 1975). They do not enter teaching expecting to earn high salaries, although they do expect pay that will allow them to live comfortably (Johnson 1990). Although teachers have not expected or aggressively pursued pay levels comparable to those of law or medicine, achieving sufficient pay to make teaching affordable work has been a perennial concern. The process of collective bargaining, which puts decisions about salary in the hands of a few, tends to make this an institutional issue rather than an individual one. As Lortie (1969, 23) has observed, "The established practitioner in a well-established profession occupies a favored position in the market. He can assert himself vis-à-vis a single client without serious economic risk. . . . Elementary teachers receive their income from 'one big client.'" In 1984 the average teacher's salary was $21,974, substantially less than that of accountants ($28,721), attorneys ($44,743), and engineers ($34,443) (American Federation of Teachers 2000, 27).

Because public schools depend on public funds, local communities and states are entitled to hold teachers accountable for their performance. They typically do so through senior school administrators who serve as the agents of publicly elected school boards. It is often noted that teachers have considerable autonomy behind the closed doors of their classrooms. However, this independence is inadvertent rather than deliberate, and teachers' autonomy ultimately remains constrained by policies that limit such things as textbook selection and equipment purchases. In 1969, Lortie observed, "the current situation reflects the centuries during which teachers were defined solely as employees. It is interesting that teachers have not challenged their formal subordination; unlike most who claim professional status, teachers have not contested the right of persons outside the occupation to govern their technical affairs" (19). By the mid-1980s, teachers had begun to challenge "their formal subordination" through their unions, but they were not actively asserting their right to be accountable to their colleagues and a set of professional standards rather than to higher-ups in the school department.

Therefore, prior to 1985, many features of teaching and schools combined and interacted to make it unlikely that education would approach, let alone meet, the sociologists' standards for a profession. The fact that, until the mid-1960s, most teachers made only a short-term commitment to their work is consistent with a scanty credentialing process, the absence of systematic induction, and the lack of opportunities for advancement in teaching. The field's failure to document teachers' skills and specialized knowledge about instruction further reinforced the uniformity of teachers' roles. Finally, teachers' dependence on the public dollar made it unlikely that they could earn substantially more money or seize control of their work and elevate it to that of a profession.

EFFORTS TO PROFESSIONALIZE TEACHING, 1985 TO 2000

When *A Nation at Risk* was published in 1983, the basic outlines of teaching had remained unchanged and largely unchallenged for decades. Teachers continued to be isolated and autonomous within their classrooms, yet they lacked the authority to control their work or workplace. When the alarm sounded in 1983 about schooling's failures and "a rising tide of mediocrity," states and districts instituted policies to control and closely inspect teachers' work. However, within several years it became apparent that external efforts to regulate teaching had done little to improve students' performance. Therefore, reformers abruptly turned to teachers as the agents of school improvement.

Reformers who promoted teachers' increased control of their work in the mid-1980s held that teachers' lack of autonomy was a major deterrent to improved practice, and thus they devised an explicit exchange of autonomy for obligation. At the time, Sykes (1983, 19) explained:

> A profession agrees to develop and enforce standards of good practice in exchange for the right to practice free of bureaucratic supervision and external regulation. At the policy level, this contract applies to standards for licensure, certification, and program accreditation. . . . At the practice level, this contract applies to the organization and management of work. Collegial norms and peer evaluation direct work that is amenable neither to administrative oversight nor to routinization.

In laying out the possibilities of professionalizing teaching, Sykes further explained that the work of professionals must be organized to "encourage collegiality and norm enforcement together with continued growth in professional knowledge and skill" (19). Given the history of teaching as subordinated, regulated work, the proposed trade of autonomy for obligation was unprecedented and promising.

In the broad coalition of those who were intent on elevating teaching to professional status, teacher educators and education scholars were joined—some would say led—by prominent businesspeople, politicians, and union leaders. This alliance was most apparent in the membership of the Task Force on Teaching as a Profession, sponsored in 1985 by the Carnegie Forum on Education and the Economy. Chaired by Lewis Branscomb of IBM, the task force included, among others, former North Carolina governor James B. Hunt and New Jersey governor Thomas H. Kean; the writer and consultant John W. Gardner; Fred M. Hechinger of the *New York Times*; and Albert Shanker and Mary Futrell, presidents of the two major teacher unions.

The influential report of this group, *A Nation Prepared: Teachers for the Twenty-first Century* (Carnegie Forum on Education and the Economy 1986, 3), called for teachers to hold "a bachelor's degree in the arts and sciences as a prerequisite for the professional study of teaching" and the development of "a new professional curriculum in graduate schools of education leading to a Master in Teaching degree, based on systematic knowledge of teaching and including internships and residencies in the schools." The report emphasized the importance of professional autonomy for teachers, citing it as "the first requirement. If the schools are to compete successfully with medicine, architecture, and accounting for staff, then teachers will have to have comparable authority in making the key decisions about the services they render" (58). Calling for teachers to assume greater leadership in their schools, the report noted that "in most professional organizations those who are most experienced and highly skilled play the lead role in guiding the activity of others" (58).

Within the next decade, an unprecedented coalition of reformers allied to advance a set of initiatives: shoring up the knowledge base of teaching, strengthening teacher preparation programs, increasing licensing requirements, creating an advanced level of teacher certification, introducing local peer review and career ladders, and decentralizing school governance to provide teachers with greater influence in matters of school policy and practice.

Strengthening the Knowledge Base of Teaching

Since 1985, education researchers have studied classroom teaching closely in an effort to demonstrate that effective instruction depends on specialized knowledge and skills rather than on idiosyncratic characteristics such as being a "born teacher." In his landmark 1987 article "Knowledge and Teaching: Foundations of the New Reform," Lee Shulman observes that the reformers' "rhetoric regarding the knowledge base . . . rarely specifies the character of such knowledge. It does not say what teachers should know, do, understand, or profess that will render teaching more than a form of individual labor, let alone be considered among the learned professions" (4).

Shulman (1987, 8) then identifies the components of a proposed knowledge base of teaching, including "content knowledge, general pedagogical knowledge, curriculum knowledge, pedagogical content knowledge, knowledge of learners, knowledge of educational contexts, and knowledge of educational ends, purposes and values." He highlights the importance of pedagogical content knowledge, "that special amalgam of content and pedagogy that is uniquely the province of teachers, their own special form of professional understanding" (8). This definition of, and attention to, pedagogical content knowledge subsequently spawned intensive studies of teaching in a wide range of subjects, including writing (Sperling and Freedman 2001), reading (Barr 2001), literature (Grossman 2001), mathematics (Ball 2001), science (White 2001), history (Wilson 2001), and social studies (Sexias 2001). As a result of such research, it has gradually become apparent that good teaching is not simply the product of good intuition. A teacher of reading, for example, must be equipped with a range of diagnostic and pedagogical strategies to meet the needs of different students, while a mathematician seeking to instill mathematical competence must understand not only mathematical concepts but also students' various strategies and approaches to mathematical reasoning. While the knowledge base of teaching is far from complete, this ambitious scholarship has established respectable groundwork for the long-term effort.

Improving Teacher Education

While researchers were building the knowledge base, reformers began to redesign teacher preparation programs to ensure that such knowledge would be transmitted and effectively enacted by aspiring teachers. The Holmes Group, a consortium of deans of schools of education, was formed in 1986 "to *enhance the quality of schooling* through research and development and the preparation of career professionals in teaching" (Holmes Group 1986, as quoted in Holmes Group 1990, vii, emphasis added). The Holmes Group "wished to see nothing less than the transformation of teaching from an occupation into a genuine profession that would serve the educational needs of children. To this end, the deans sought to align themselves with other organizations, agencies, and institutions that supported their goals and general directions" (Holmes Group 1995, i).

In their publications *Tomorrow's Teachers* (1986), *Tomorrow's Schools* (1990), and *Tomorrow's Schools of Education* (1995), the Holmes Group built a case for a new approach to teacher preparation that would require aspiring teachers to hold undergraduate majors in substantive fields and graduate preparation in teaching. Key to their strategy was the creation of professional development schools run by partnerships of university faculty, experienced teachers, and school administrators. Modeled on teaching hospitals, these preparation sites for new teachers were meant to provide clinical training. The most ambitious of these programs established full-time, fifth-year internships for prospective teachers, engaging them in all aspects of teachers' work. "These schools will serve as settings for teaching professionals to test different instructional arrangements, for novice teachers and researchers to work under the guidance of gifted practitioners, for the exchange of professional knowledge between university faculty and practitioners, and for the development of new structures designed around the demand of a new profession" (Holmes Group 1995, vi). Subsequently, universities and schools established several hundred professional development schools across the nation (Darling-Hammond 2001).

Central to the reformers' goals for teacher education was the replacement of a list of required teacher education courses with a set of competencies. Rather than relying on academic evidence (attendance, course credit, grades, or test scores), reformers sought to assess teachers' knowledge and skill by observing their practice or directly inspecting—in documents or via videotape—the process and products of their practice. The National Commission on Teaching for America's Future (1996, 67) called such standards "the linchpin for transforming current systems of preparation, licensing, certification, and ongoing development so that they better support student learning." They concluded: "Of greatest priority is reaching agreement on what teachers should know and be able to do to teach to high standards" (67).

Darling-Hammond (2001, 763) reports that the new standards

> incorporate knowledge about teaching and learning that supports a view of teaching as complex, contingent on students' needs and instructional goals, and reciprocal, that is, continually shaped and reshaped by students' responses to learning events. The new standards and assessments take into explicit account the teaching challenges posed by a student body that is multicultural and multilingual, that possesses multiple intelligences, and that includes diverse approaches to learning.

The shift toward performance-based rather than course-based standards, Darling-Hammond notes,

> could enable states to permit greater innovation and diversity in how teacher education programs operate by assessing their outcomes rather than merely regulating their inputs or procedures. Well-developed assessments of candidates, if they actually measured the important attributes of teaching knowledge and skill, could open up a variety of pathways and types of preparation for entering teaching without lowering standards.

Knowledge-based standards were to be at the core of a new initiative by the National Council for Accreditation of Teacher Education (NCATE) in 1987 to "ensure that teacher education programs were grounded in knowledge about teaching and learning" (Darling-Hammond 2001, 763). In 1994 NCATE revised its standards to focus more on competencies. By 2000, fifteen states were using NCATE standards as the basis for approving all of their teacher preparation programs, a "five-fold increase over the previous three years" (768). Although it is by no means certain that the number of states embracing the NCATE standards and review process will increase steadily, it is clear that states and colleges have begun to systematically review the quality of their teacher education programs.

Increasing Licensing Standards

Efforts to define education's knowledge base and to create new structures for teacher preparation were closely linked to various states' initiatives to raise the bar for entry into teaching. Wide variation existed in the breadth and depth of the states' requirements. Darling-Hammond, Arthur Wise, and Stephen Klein (1999, 90, 189) describe Minnesota's professional standards board, which "has assumed full responsibility for conceiving and creating its own assessment system," a system that includes subject-specific knowledge and skills. A similar approach was adopted by INTASC, an interstate teacher licensing consortium of thirty-four states, twenty-four of which had "formally adopted or adapted the INTASC standards for beginning teacher licensing" by 1997 (Darling-Hammond 2001, 768). Many states that had not joined INTASC also increased licensing requirements after 1985, specifying more explicitly the topics that teachers had to study or extending the duration of required student teaching.

States also began to adopt licensure tests and to require minimum GPAs for teaching candidates. Darling-Hammond (2001, 762) reports that

> between 1980 and 1990, at least twenty-two states enacted some form of testing for entry into teacher education and fifteen states set minimum GPAs for entry. Fifteen states required both testing and minimum GPAs. On their own initiative or as a result of state mandates, at least 70 percent of teacher education programs established minimum grade requirements that must be met before a student is admitted. More than half also required that students pass a proficiency test before completing the program. During this decade, more than forty states introduced tests for initial licensure.

Creating a System of Advanced Certification

A Nation Prepared called for the creation of a National Board for Professional Teaching Standards, which would "establish high standards for what teachers need to know and be able to do, and . . . certify teachers who meet that standard." The task force envisioned that teachers who achieved such advanced certification would then serve as lead teachers in their schools, "guid[ing] and influenc[ing] the activity of others, ensuring that the skill and energy of their colleagues is drawn on as the organization improves its performance" (Carnegie Forum on Education and the Economy 1986, 58). Advanced certification for teachers was to be modeled on medicine's practice of board certification for doctors.

The successful establishment and funding of the board and its subsequent development of performance-based assessments of teachers' work in twenty-five instructional fields by 2002 is one of the most remarkable accomplishments of the post-1985 professional reforms. A majority of the board's members are classroom teachers, in keeping with plans to create a self-regulated occupation. By 2002 the board had certified over 16,000 "accomplished" teachers, with the goal of reaching 100,000 by 2006 (National Board for Professional Teaching Standards 2002, 1).

Although the board's funding and assessments remain controversial (Wilcox 1999), there is considerable public recognition and reward for teachers who achieve board certification. By March 2002, 48 states and approximately 411 local districts had established financial incentives and recognition; 32 states supported individuals' assessment fees, and 33 provided salary supplements for those who succeeded. For example, North Carolina increased by 12 percent the portion of board-certified teachers' salaries paid by the state. California paid a onetime bonus of $10,000 and an additional $20,000 for board-certified teachers who stayed in low-performing schools for four years. In one of the most generous offers, Mississippi paid board-certified teachers $6,000 per year for the ten-year life of the certificate (National Board for Professional Teaching Standards 2002).

Central to the vision of creating a board that would certify accomplished teachers was the expectation that these teachers would then assume roles as lead teachers in their districts. Although the potential for such roles exists, the relative number of certified teachers remains small. If the board achieves its goal of certifying 100,000 teachers by 2006, that would still be only 3 percent of the teaching force (Johnson 2001, 394). As yet, few local districts have developed roles for board-certified teachers that would institutionalize the ideal of collegial control of teaching.

Introducing Peer Review and Career Ladders

While national consortia and task forces were planning to improve schooling by professionalizing teaching, local union leaders and school administrators were experimenting with ways to advance the premise that if teachers are to become true professionals, they must be responsible for monitoring the performance of their colleagues. Beginning in the mid-1980s, a small number of unionized districts began to collaboratively create and negotiate policies and programs to increase teachers' roles in the induction and assessment of their peers (Kerchner and Koppich 1993).

Toledo, Ohio, was the site of the first and longest-running peer review plan (Gallagher, Lanier, and Kerchner 1993). Created jointly by labor and management, this program selected and trained a group of experienced teachers who would leave their classrooms for two years to mentor and evaluate novice teachers. After one year of closely supervising new teachers' work and modeling expert practice, the peer reviewers recommended to a joint labor-management committee whether these new teachers should be reemployed or terminated. The program proved to be so successful that it soon became the model for comparable efforts in Cincinnati (Johnson 1989; King 1993), Rochester, New York (Grant and Murray 1999; Koppich 1993), and Columbus, Ohio. Over time, peer reviewers assumed responsibility for assessing not only new teachers but also experienced teachers judged by peers or administrators to be in need of assistance.

Such programs won recognition because of both their effectiveness in providing the support needed to retain effective teachers and the difficult judgments required to dismiss weak ones. Moreover, these efforts represented the first time that teachers, led by their unions, had assumed responsibility for such decisions. Teachers' deeply rooted and enduring concerns about equity had long played out in collective bargaining provisions that treated all teachers as a group and proscribed efforts to distinguish among them on the basis of quality. Given that history, the institution of peer review was indeed noteworthy.

In establishing its peer review program, Rochester's union president, Adam Urbanski, and superintendent, Peter McWalters, also created a career ladder, which included different steps for teachers with varying levels of experience and expertise (Grant and Murray 1999). In doing so, they established the position of lead teacher called for by the Task Force on Teaching as a Profession. Rochester's lead teachers were to serve as peer reviewers in a Peer Assistance and Review Program, modeled on Toledo's program. With the approval in 1987 of a pay scale that increased teachers' salaries by 40 percent and allowed lead teachers to make as much as $70,000 a year (Koppich 1993), Rochester made real the proposition that differentiating teachers' roles and responsibilities could lead to higher pay for teachers.

Notably, while a small number of "lighthouse" districts were adopting collaborative approaches to collective bargaining and creating professional kinds of reforms, other districts relied on conventional, adversarial bargaining to settle contract disputes. As a result, collective bargaining agreements that narrowly define teachers' responsibilities and carefully specify their rights and protections perpetuate the image of teachers as laborers rather than professionals (Johnson and Kardos 2000).

Decentralizing School Governance

Meanwhile, local school reformers in Miami-Dade, Florida, were creating the prototypes of school-based governance boards, composed of teachers, administrators, and parents (Phillips 1993). Such shared-decision-making councils, or school-site councils, were designed to decentralize decisionmaking about policy and practice, which in some districts meant control of hiring and spending. Where such councils were established through collective bargaining, teachers typically held the majority of seats, although this did not necessarily mean that they had the final say. In Boston, for example, principals continued to hold veto power in school-site council decisions.

The idea of school-based management (SBM) was adopted by many districts in the early 1990s. Notably, however, district offices seldom granted these councils the authority and control over resources specified by such arrangements. Also, councils often became embroiled in details of administration and school maintenance, while finding it hard to address instructional issues. In the mid-1990s, Rodney T. Ogawa and Paula A. White (1994, 54) concluded that there was "little evidence that SBM has significantly enhanced conditions in schools and districts or improved students' academic performance."

There is little to suggest that this changed over the next decade. Moreover, it is not clear that decentralized governance resulted in greater empowerment for teachers. Ingersoll (1997, 7) explained that "reformers have argued that teachers cannot be expected to be highly committed to school decisions over which they have had no say." However, when he analyzed data from the 1990–91 Schools and Staffing Survey, in which principals reported on the extent of teachers' authority in "decisions concerning curriculum, discipline, and hiring in schools," he found that "in comparison to principals, teachers appear to have had limited professional authority over these school educational decisions" (21). Thus, there is no evidence yet that teachers have widely attained significant influence in school governance.

Taking Stock

Some fifteen years after the institution of these reforms to professionalize teaching, each endures, although some are far stronger than others. The National Board for

Professional Teaching Standards, for example, has grown steadily and become well established, while the prominence of school-based management has faded. Most reforms vary tremendously in how they have been enacted in practice and, therefore, what their implications are for the professional standing of teachers. For example, there are vibrant professional development schools serving as exemplary sites for the clinical training of intern teachers, and there are so-called professional development schools where little more than the name indicates a change from business as usual. Similarly, there are sites, such as Toledo and Columbus, where peer review is an established and respected process for teachers' induction and assessment, and others, such as the state of California, where peer review is more a paper requirement than a day-to-day reality. There are districts where labor-management relations are collaborative and professional, and others where they are contentious and industrial in character.

Overall, the components of this comprehensive strategy to professionalize teaching have not yet merged to create a system of preparation and practice for teaching that will advance its standing as a profession. Teachers certified as "accomplished" by the National Board for Professional Teaching Standards have not assumed new roles as lead teachers in many schools. Competency-based standards for teachers' work have been incorporated effectively into the board's assessments of experienced teachers, but far less so into pre-service preparation or the states' and districts' evaluations of other teachers. To be effective levers in professionalizing teaching, these components must be established both broadly and truly, embodying the original purposes and principles of design and interacting to support and enhance each other.

Elements Beyond the Control of Reformers

These concerted and comprehensive efforts to professionalize teaching differ markedly both in scope and sponsorship from the piecemeal efforts that preceded them. However, even if they are fully and robustly implemented, they cannot guarantee that teaching will achieve professional status. Public education is not a closed system, and thus the outcome will be influenced by other factors, including pay limited by public budgets, demographic changes in the teaching force, and other education policies.

Throughout this reform effort, the goal of achieving higher pay for teachers has remained in the background. It was to be an important, but not explicit, consequence of successfully enacting other elements, such as roles for lead teachers or certification by the national board. Although this strategy has achieved some success, particularly in the legislated bonuses to board-certified teachers, overall salaries have risen little, despite early progress.

The National Center for Education Statistics (2001, 26) reports that teachers' salaries rose 20 percent between 1980–81 and 2000–2001, although "virtually all of this increase occurred during the mid-1980s. Since 1990–91, the average salary for teachers fell slightly, after adjusting for inflation." Average salary levels can be

somewhat misleading, however, since they are influenced at any time by the demographic profile of the teaching force. The fact that the age of the average teacher
increased during this period suggests that salary levels were even lower than these
figures suggest. The American Federation of Teachers' *Survey and Analysis of
Teacher Salary Trends, 2000* (2000, 15) reports that the average beginning salary for
a teacher with a bachelor's degree in 1999–2000 was $27,989, while the average
salary of all teachers was $41,820. "After adjusting for inflation, the 1999–2000 av-
erage teacher salary of $41,820 is only $46 above what it was in 1993. It is just
$2,087 more than the average salary recorded in 1972—a real increase of only
about $75 per year." Similarly, *Education Week* (2000) reports in *Quality Counts 2000*
that the earnings gap between teachers and nonteachers with bachelor's degrees
increased between 1994 and 1998 from $12,068 to $18,006, while the gap between
teachers and nonteachers with master's degrees increased from $12,918 to $30,229
(Boser 2000). Ingersoll (1997, 8) argues that "the gap between starting salaries and
end-of-career salaries provides some indication of the extent of opportunity for
promotion, and the range of monetary rewards available to employees as they advance through their careers. From this viewpoint, a professionalized teaching job
would offer salaries and benefits competitive with those in the established professions." Analyzing data from the Schools and Staffing Survey, he found that the
mean starting salary in all public school districts in 1990–91 was $20,918, while the
mean maximum salary was only $39,348 (14). To the extent that opportunities to
earn high pay over the course of a career reflect professional standing, teaching
has made little progress in the last two decades.

CHANGES IN THE TEACHING FORCE

With the impending retirement of a large portion of the teachers who have staffed
the nation's schools since the move to professionalize teaching began, we must ask
what the future holds. Will the goals and expectations of the next generation of
teachers be compatible with this strategy for professionalizing teaching? And how
might changes in the economy and job market for teachers affect their standing
and leverage as professionals?

Who Enters Teaching?

The cohort of teachers who are now approaching retirement were hired between
the mid-1960s and mid-1970s, when women entered the workforce in large numbers and were permitted to continue teaching after marriage and childbearing.
The full array of professional opportunities had not yet opened for women and
persons of color, and thus large numbers of well-schooled individuals entered
teaching and remained over the course of their careers. This phenomenon, sometimes called the "hidden subsidy" of teaching, began to evaporate in the 1980s as
other fields, such as engineering, law, and business, not only opened but also ac-

tively recruited entrants. However, the effects of this change were not immediately felt since enrollments stabilized in the 1980s and districts hired few teachers.

While reformers were designing more challenging standards for assessing teachers' work and creating structures that would make greater demands on their knowledge and skills, the quality of entering teachers was in decline, a fact that became apparent in the early 1990s. Using the U.S. Department of Education's study "Baccalaureate and Beyond," *Education Week* tracked the top-scoring 1992–93 college graduates, "defined as those who had scored in the top 25 percent of everyone who took the SAT or ACT college-entrance exam," and found that "college graduates who actually taught in public schools by 1996–97 were much less likely to have scored in the top quarter on the tests (14 percent) than those who chose other professions (24 percent)" (Boser 2000, 16–17).

Implicit in the logic of the professional reforms of the 1980s was the expectation that teachers would continue to make a long-term commitment to the classroom. Also, reformers' efforts to extend and enhance teacher preparation programs assumed that aspiring teachers would continue to prepare to teach in traditional, pre-service programs. However, early evidence about the next generation of teachers indicates that only some may approach teaching as a long-term commitment and that many will seek to enter the classroom with minimal prior preparation.

Those who enter teaching today live in a time when serial careers are the norm and short-term employment is evidence of versatility and vitality rather than irresponsibility or failure. Interviews conducted with a purposive sample of new teachers (Peske et al. 2001) suggest that a long-term commitment to classroom teaching may soon become the exception rather than the norm. Out of fifty teachers interviewed in 1999 by researchers at the Project on the Next Generation of Teachers, only three said they plan to remain classroom teachers for their entire careers. Some had entered teaching to explore the possibility of staying longer, while others were planning to make a contribution to public education before moving on to other work. There were midcareer entrants who had significant experience in other fields as well as "capstoners" (Peske et al. 2001, 308) who entered teaching for a stint before retirement. Most respondents who said that they planned to remain in education for the rest of their careers but not in the classroom anticipated taking on differentiated roles in curriculum development, mentoring, or professional development. In their plans and their tentative commitment to the classroom, this entering cohort differs significantly from their retiring colleagues (Johnson and the Project on the Next Generation of Teachers 2004).

A surprising proportion of new teachers today are midcareer entrants. Emily Feistritzer (1999) reports that more than half of the people admitted to teacher preparation programs in 1998 came from occupations outside of education. A 2001 random sample survey of 110 first- and second-year teachers in New Jersey (Liu and Kardos 2002) found that 46 percent of respondents were midcareer entrants. Interviews by the Project on the Next Generation of Teachers with twenty-four midcareer entrants revealed that they entered teaching seeking meaningful work but were quick to move to a new school or to leave teaching altogether if they found that working conditions made good teaching impossible (Johnson and Birkeland 2003).

Notably, an increasing proportion of new teachers—particularly those who enter from another career—participate in alternative route programs, which may reduce or even dispense with the state's licensing requirements. Teach for America, which is designed to attract and accommodate young graduates who want to make a two-year contribution to public education, provides new teachers with seven weeks of summer training before they receive an emergency license and full-time responsibility for a class in a low-income school. An increasing number of alternative certification programs, such as the Massachusetts Institute for New Teachers (MINT), recruit midcareer entrants and then rely on short-term summer training before granting the recruits full-time employment and accelerated licenses. There is wide variety among alternative route programs: some are carefully conceived to provide job-embedded learning and ongoing support in the classroom, while others adopt a sink-or-swim approach to entry. These programs are driven in part by the teacher shortage and in part by opposition to traditional teacher education. Their overall effect, however, is to challenge the merits of pedagogical training and the need for intensive pre-service education, such as that developed by reformers seeking to professionalize teaching.

Effects of the Economy and Job Market

During the first years of the teacher shortage (1999 to 2001), it appeared that the move to professionalize teaching might get an extra boost from a projected teacher shortage in which the demand for certified teachers would far exceed the supply. Teachers reasonably expected to command higher salaries and demand better working conditions, and in fact districts began to recruit teachers—sometimes poaching them from nearby districts or states—and offer them signing bonuses or forgiveness of their education loans. However, when it became clear that districts could not staff their classrooms with certified teachers, states began to reduce or waive the requirements for entry, many of which had been carefully developed over the past fifteen years of reform.

Sudden and dramatic budget cuts incurred by districts and states following the attacks of September 11 and subsequent economic failures revealed just how fragile teachers' newly elevated standing actually was. Urban districts, such as Detroit and Buffalo, which had recruited teachers only six months before, began to issue layoff notices. Teachers' ultimate reliance on public funds made it impossible for them to take full advantage of their scarcity, which otherwise might have helped them command the pay and respectful treatment generally afforded professionals.

The Standards and Accountability Movement

Probably the single most important education policy initiative in the last decade is the movement for high standards and accountability, geared to advance systemic, demonstrable improvement in student learning, especially in low-performing, urban districts (Elmore 2000). This concerted effort is in part a response to the slow pace and inadequate gains in students' performance achieved by the movement to professionalize teaching, particularly in low-income communities. Predictably, however, there is great variety in what the states' versions of standards and accountability mean for teaching and student learning, ranging from repeated and numbing test preparation to focused and challenging instruction.

The standards and accountability movement initially was fully consistent with the model of a professionalized teaching force, with expert teachers assuming roles as professional developers (Elmore and Consortium for Policy Research in Education 1996). However, in many districts accountability has introduced a decidedly top-down tenor, and standardized test scores are increasingly emphasized as the single measure of student learning. Superintendents' pay is frequently pegged to students' test scores, and local real estate agents tout communities where students score well. In many urban districts the pressure to perform well on standardized tests drives like a piston down into the schools; an organization that was once loosely coupled (Meyer and Rowan 1978) now tightly regulates time and task, with principals insisting that teachers exact higher performance from their students. Teachers, whose lesson plans now are regularly monitored, often find that they have less autonomy than they once did to devise curriculum, choose texts, and create interdisciplinary projects. Notably, teachers hold differing views of this movement: some welcome the focus and resources that accountability has delivered, and others feel oppressed by hierarchical control. Whether this situation is ultimately good or bad for teachers and students, it is certainly very different from the teacher-run schools envisioned by the Task Force on Teaching as a Profession.

THE PROSPECTS FOR TEACHING AS A PROFESSION

There are many ways in which teaching has made real progress toward professional standards since 1985. Research into teaching practice and its effects on student learning has advanced steadily, as have understandings of pedagogical content knowledge. Arguably, the knowledge base of teaching is increasingly solid. The National Board for Professional Teaching Standards' success in developing performance assessments grounded in that knowledge base augurs well for establishing a broadly recognized system of competency-based standards for teachers. Although it is challenging to implement such standards in a state licensing system, there is evidence that this can be done. Districts could also use these standards in selecting lead teachers and developing differentiated staffing patterns and career ladders that encourage individuals to learn new skills and assume greater responsibility over time. Further, districts that have established effective peer review programs demonstrate the readiness and capacity of expert teachers to induct and supervise their new colleagues. Overall, the movement to professionalize teaching has been purposeful, continuous, and consequential.

Other factors, however, are beyond the reach and control of these reformers.

Teacher pay levels continue to be subject to public scrutiny and budget constraints, thus remaining far below those of doctors, lawyers, and engineers. Other careers, many of which offer higher pay and better working conditions, now successfully recruit and attract women and persons of color who once would have become teachers by default. As a result, the quality of the teaching force, as defined by test scores or GPAs, has diminished, and with it the likelihood that teachers will garner public respect as professionals. Increasing student enrollments, coupled with greater numbers of teacher retirements, may have made well-prepared teachers a scarce and valued commodity. Early evidence suggests that states and districts have responded to the teacher shortage by granting emergency credentials and reducing licensing requirements, thus increasing the supply of teachers and giving credence to the belief that "anyone can teach." Also, if the federal government's demand for standardized tests causes teachers to rely primarily on scripted curricula and to concentrate instruction on test preparation, the image of teaching as mechanical, nonprofessional work will displace any picture of professional practice that reformers have been carefully framing. As Hargreaves and Goodson (1996, 3) have observed, "Teacher professionalization appears to be advancing in some respects; retreating in others."

It seems unlikely that education will achieve the kind of professional character, status, or pay that medicine and law have today. Considerable progress has been made in professionalizing certain important aspects of teaching—establishing a knowledge base, developing competency-based assessments, and creating the beginnings of a differentiated career structure. However, because education is publicly funded, teachers' salaries will always fall behind those of the "real" professions. Because schools are publicly accountable, teachers' autonomy will always be constrained. Because the nation's many classrooms must always be staffed, standards for entry to teaching will fluctuate. Despite advances that improve the prospects for students, teaching likely will remain a "silver medal" profession.

Chapter 5

The Anomaly of Educational Organizations and the Study of Organizational Control

Richard M. Ingersoll

Those who study organizations have long considered elementary and secondary schools to be an interesting anomaly—an odd case. In the interdisciplinary field of organization theory and among social scientists who study organizations, occupations, and work, schools have seemed unusual because, while they appear to look like other large complex organizations, such as banks, agencies, offices, and plants, they do not seem to act like them. In particular, schools do not seem to have the degree of control and coordination that rationalized, centralized organizations are supposed to have. Schools have all the outward characteristics of such organizations, including a formal hierarchy, a specialized division of labor, and a formal structure of rules and regulations. However, according to many organizational analysts, schools exert very little control over their employees and work processes. Because of this seemingly contradictory behavior, organization theorists have adopted a colorful vocabulary to identify such settings. Educational organizations, they hold, are extreme examples of "loosely coupled systems" and "organized anarchies." In this view, schools are oddly debureaucratized bureaucracies and, paradoxically, disorganized organizations. For four decades this image of schools has been the conventional wisdom in the field of organization theory and a dominant perspective in theory and research on school organization. It has also had a large impact in the realm of school reform and educational policy.

This chapter evaluates this view of schools, which I refer to as the loose-coupling perspective on schools. Although this perspective on schools has long been widely accepted, there are good reasons to reexamine its arguments and claims about the structure of school organizations. Loose-coupling is not the only perspective on the organization of schools and on their degree of control and coordination. Indeed, much evidence supports an antithetical view of schools that is also popular, though held by a different group of education researchers, reformers, and policymakers. Schools are not too loose, this opposing view holds, but are exactly the opposite—the epitome of top-down, overly controlled, centralized bureaucracies.

The loose-coupling perspective has insightfully illuminated the extent to which schools are indeed an unusual kind of organization, with characteristics that have posed challenges for both research and reform. Schools do not fit into tidy rational and efficiency models of organization and are not well explained by economic-production models of industry, and these characteristics have large implications for their coordination and control. My argument, however, is that theory and research influenced by the loose-coupling perspective have not gone far enough and have not fully brought out the implications of these insights for understanding the organization of schools. Distinguishing the degree and character of control in schools depends on where and how one looks. My contention is that the loose-coupling perspective has underemphasized some of the institutional functions of schools, neglected to look closely at the social organization of teachers' work, and, as a result, overlooked and underestimated organizational control in schools.

In this chapter, I lay out the intellectual roots of the loose-coupling perspective. I explain how the study of educational organizations has come to be an important problem—an anomaly—in the interdisciplinary field of organization theory. I try to build on this perspective by further elaborating the teaching occupation's unusual combination of characteristics and the limits these place on the bureaucratization and rationalization of schools. I also turn to what I believe are several key limitations underlying the loose-coupling perspective.

THE ANOMALY OF EDUCATIONAL ORGANIZATIONS

One of the first and most insightful accounts of the anomalous character of schools came from educational sociologists based primarily at the University of Chicago, particularly Charles Bidwell.[1] Bidwell's seminal contribution was to use the perspective of organization theory to bring to light a fundamental tension in organizations charged with the task of educating the young: the inherent incompatibility between the nature of formal organizations and the nature of the work of teaching.

The objective of the public school system is to provide a mandatory, publicly funded service for a mass clientele. Hence, the job of those charged with administering this system lies in seeing that large numbers of students are similarly educated as efficiently as possible. From a managerial and organizational perspective, the obvious mechanism by which to undertake this kind of task was and is rationalized bureaucracy. The bureaucratic model of organizational administration emphasizes impersonal systems of selection and assignment, standardized operating procedures, formalized routines, and written records and rules. Contrary to the conventional stereotype, from a managerial and organizational perspective, bureaucracy is among the most efficient and functional methods for those concerned with the problem of coordinating and controlling large numbers of individuals collected to accomplish complex, large-scale tasks.

Although the mass character of education suggests the use of the bureaucratic mode of organization, other aspects of education do not. The bureaucratic model is preferable from an administrative viewpoint, but it is not, Bidwell argues, from a teaching viewpoint. Like many other human services occupations, teaching involves tasks, knowledge, and skills that are less tangible and more indeterminate than those of traditional production-oriented occupations. Teaching is inherently fluid work; it requires flexibility, give-and-take, and the freedom to make exceptions.

From this viewpoint, the unusual characteristics of teaching limit the bureaucratization and rationalization of teachers' work. The task of teaching, which requires a personal orientation and professional autonomy, clashes with bureaucratic rationalization, which requires an impersonal and hierarchical orientation. In short, while the large-scale and mass character of schooling dictate bureaucracy, the character of the work of teaching itself dictates the opposite. The result, Bidwell concludes, is that schools have developed an unusual degree of "structural looseness," and the work of teachers, compared to other kinds of jobs, is subject to few rules and regulations and little administrative surveillance; this structural looseness gives teachers a lot of room to exercise personal discretion and make decisions, particularly within the confines of the classroom. Bidwell argues that structural looseness in schools, while perhaps dysfunctional in some ways, is an inevitable and functional condition of these organizations. By granting an unusual degree of discretion over classroom instructional matters to faculty, administrators are able to harness the skills and expertise of teachers and generate their consent to organizational arrangements. Schools, he concludes, while necessarily bureaucratized, are also necessarily debureaucratized.

Dan Lortie's (1969, 1973, 1975, 1977) seminal research on teaching has provided the most prominent empirical support for this view of schools. Teaching, he holds, is "least controlled by specific and literally enforced rules and regulations" (1969, 14). Moreover, "compared to other systems of work, schools still provide considerable occasion for the exercise of personal discretion by classroom teachers" (1977, 30). As a result, Lortie concludes, "self-contained classrooms are small universes of control with the teacher in command; administrators refer, ambivalently, to the 'closed door,' which the teacher can put between herself and administrative surveillance" (1969, 9).

These characteristics, Bidwell, Lortie, and others in this tradition have persuasively argued, make schools a theoretically significant case of modern bureaucratic organization. The apparent looseness of schools offers one of the clearest illustrations of the limits to organizational rationalization. The tension between these contrary tendencies, in the loose-coupling perspective, is both inevitable and a source of never-ending challenges to those entrusted with the management of schools. The insights embedded in this theoretical framework have shaped thinking on school organization for the past four decades. Indeed, it is precisely because of this tension and these characteristics that educational organizations have assumed an interesting and important place in the larger study of organizations, occupations, and work.

The Loose-Coupling Perspective

Since the translation of Max Weber's (1946, 196–244; 1947, 324–41) famous studies of bureaucracy, research traditions both celebrating and debunking the theoretical and practical usefulness of bureaucratic rationality have dominated thought on organizations. The study of complex organizations has been characterized since its inception by debate over both the explanatory power and the practical applicability of the classic Weberian "machine" model of organizational administration. Numerous empirical studies have sought to apply Weber's narrow model of organizational administration to a wide range of aspects of a wide variety of organizations. Much of the theory and empirical research in the field has been an extended argument over to what extent, and with what consequences, different kinds of organizations are bureaucratic. Likewise, work in this field has been marked by the development of numerous parallel analytic dichotomies and tensions—organic-mechanical, open-closed, informal-formal, natural-bureaucratic, institutional-organizational, bureaucratic-professional—all of which seek to capture, in one way or another, variations of this tension within and between organizations. At the heart of the debate are two questions: To what extent are modern complex organizations the controlled and coordinated entities described by the bureaucratic model? And to what extent should they be so? (see, for example, Pfeffer 1982; Zey-Ferrell and Aiken 1981).[2]

From the standpoint of understanding research on the organization of schooling, the most significant event in this long tradition was the ascendancy of a group of organization theories beginning in the 1970s. These theories offered a new and colorful vocabulary to describe work and organizations that are difficult to rationalize because of this tension: "loosely coupled systems," "organized anarchies," and "decoupled organizations." The theme common to this group of theories was the insightful emphasis on the degree to which organizations that appear to be rational—that is, the coordinated, controlled entities described by the bureaucratic model—are not so, and in fact cannot be so.[3] This tradition focused on illuminating types of organizations that are necessarily far more complex, less stable, less coherent, and, especially, less controlled than what is described by the bureaucratic model.

The ideas of this perspective have generated a great deal of interest in the sources, forms, and variations of organizational looseness and tightness. The result is a body of writing and research that is highly varied, depending on the units and levels of analysis chosen and the definition of loose coupling utilized. Some analysts, for example, focus on the connections between individuals within organizations; others focus on the degree of coupling between organizations; still others focus on linkages between sectors or populations of organizations. Moreover, a great deal of ambiguity holds in this theory and research when it comes to the question of whether organizational tightness or looseness is necessary or unnecessary, functional or dysfunctional, efficient or inefficient, effective or ineffective.

Despite the wide range of uses to which the ideas of loose coupling have been put, there is nevertheless common ground. Specifically, loosely coupled organizations are those that have undefined, unclear, diverse, or ambiguous organizational means and goals and as a result have low levels of organizational control and coordination of employees' productive activities. At the root of looseness is the balance of power in the organization. As Howard Aldrich (1978, 52) notes, "The major determinant of coupling [is] the degree of hierarchical control by a central authority."

The tension—between bureaucratic and nonbureaucratic modes of organization—is more acute in some kinds of work and occupations and less acute in others. Most agree that such tensions are especially exacerbated in human-service, client-serving, and people-intensive jobs, particularly in white-collar occupations in complex organizations. Work in such settings often requires increasing amounts of both employee autonomy and cooperation and is less amenable to formal definition, assessment, and evaluation. In short, these kinds of jobs seem to intensify these fundamental tensions and, as a result, are primary sites of loose coupling. In particular, elementary and secondary schools assume a central place in this perspective. Schools, these analysts have concluded, are the archetypal loosely coupled systems.

Schools have long been unexplained Kuhnian anomalies for the rational paradigm. William Ouchi (Ouchi and Wilkins 1985, 467), in his review of organizational culture analysis, goes so far as to claim that "it was the resistance of school systems to bureaucratic interpretation that brought to an end the study of formal organization structure." Drawing from the research of individuals like Bidwell and Lortie, organization theorists over the past few decades have ascribed to the conventional wisdom that schools are an example of an extreme case of decoupling and debureaucratization (Tyler 1985, 1988). Karl Weick (1976, 11) concludes, for instance, "that in the case of educational organizations there is loose control of the work—the work is intrinsically uninspected and unevaluated or if it is evaluated it is done infrequently and in a perfunctory manner." As John Meyer and W. Richard Scott (1983, 48) put it: "The standard social science portrait of schools depicts weak and ineffective organizations with little internal rationalization of work, and little capacity to produce useful effects as measured by student performance."

Notably, researchers have not been the only group to give credence to the view of schools as loosely structured, relatively undercoordinated, and undercontrolled. This has also been a recurrent and popular theme in the realm of school reform and educational policy. Although organizational researchers generally have come to mixed conclusions concerning the positive and negative consequences of loose structuring and whether change is necessary, beneficial, or even possible, those involved with educational reform have been less ambivalent. Indeed, if schools lack control and coordination, then one obvious conclusion is to "tighten the ship." This desire to increase the control of what goes on in schools and what teachers do in their classrooms regularly resurfaces as a central tenet underlying education reform (see, for example, Hannaway and Carnoy 1993; Elmore 2000). Both loosely controlled and poorly performing schools in general and loosely controlled and poorly performing teachers in particular have been blamed for the decline of American economic competitiveness and productivity, the decline in student academic achievement, increases in teenage pregnancy and juvenile delinquency and crime, the coarsening of our everyday discourse and culture, a decline in morals, gender and racial discrimination, and on and on.

In sum, the loose-coupling perspective has insightfully brought to light some of the unusual characteristics of schools and their implications for the organization of schooling. My argument, however, is that this perspective has not gone far enough and has not fully brought out the implications of these insights for understanding the kinds of coordination and control that exist in schools. In the next section, I elaborate on the implications of these insights.

The Unusual Characteristics of Schools as Organizations and of Teaching as an Occupation

Who are the "clients" and what are the "products" and "technologies" of schools and teaching? And what are the implications of these for the organization and control of this work? The clients of teachers are an odd mix—they are at once obligatory, mandatory, multiple, diverse, and many. Schooling is a mass public-service "industry." All school-age members of the public have the right to a publicly funded education. Schools and teachers are obligated to educate all youngsters, regardless of how cooperative, motivated, prepared, or deserving they are. Those of legal school age, however, are not only entitled to a tax-paid education but obligated to receive it. Elementary and secondary schooling are mandatory, whether the student wishes to be in school or not. In short, the relationship between teacher and student is what Lortie (1977) calls "dual captivity"—teachers are public servants who are obligated to serve their clients, and their clients are recipients of a public service who are obligated to be served.

Parents and their children are not the only clients of teachers and schools. In a broad sense, the entire society is the client of the public servants who have been delegated the task of preparing future citizens. Regardless of whether they have school-age children or not, every member of the public is financially responsible, through taxes, for the moral, civic, and academic training of the young. The fiduciary responsibility of the general public even extends to some extent to students enrolled in private schools. Certain private school expenses, such as textbooks, transportation, and special education, are funded through state and federal taxes. As a result, a wide variety of groups, representing a wide diversity of interests, see themselves as the fee-paying clients of the services provided by schools. This unusual mix of client characteristics in turn has implications for the services provided and the expected "products" of schooling.

Perhaps the most obvious and straightforward goal of schooling is teaching the young essential academic skills and knowledge, and the most obvious and straightforward product is student academic achievement as measured by test scores. But teachers do not simply teach academic subjects. Schools and teachers are also responsible for socializing children and teaching societal values, behavior, attitudes, mores, and norms—that is, for teaching proper behavior. Both implicit and explicit socialization is, of course, an important part of all jobs, occupations, and organizations. All employees and clients are shaped by their organizations, but in schools socialization is not simply a by-product or even a means to an end—it is one of the major "products."

Such outcomes, analysts such as Bidwell and Lortie have noted, are indeterminate and intangible. This is true not only for teaching, they point out, but for most human services work. For example, a central tension in hospital administration is the difficulty in assessing the quality of nursing, where the major "product" that nurses "make" is patient care. The job and major outcomes of teaching are not simply indeterminate and intangible but also a source of conflict. Teaching involves a value-laden social task—the "production" of socialized adults from unsocialized children—and there is much disagreement over exactly what the end product ought to be.

This unusual combination of clients and products sets schools apart from many other organizations, and teaching apart from many other occupations. But there is an additional and related aspect that makes teaching an unusual occupation. Not only are the tasks of schooling important, multiple, contradictory, ambiguous, and contentious, but the process of undertaking and achieving them—the "technology" of teaching—is both complex and uncertain. In the auto industry, a well-developed technology results in the production of automobiles. In teaching, however, there is very little consensus as to what the end products ought to be, very little consensus as to the best process, method, or means of reaching these ends, and very little consensus as to how to go about measuring whether these ends have been achieved.

Teaching is an interactional type of work: in the production process employees work not with raw materials or objects but with other individuals. In such settings cooperative relations are not only conducive to productivity but in many cases *are* productivity. Moreover, the individuals with whom teachers work are neither mature, socialized adults nor voluntary participants; indeed, as Willard Waller (1932, 10) aptly puts it in his classic book on the sociology of teachers, they are "at once the most tractable and the most unstable members of the community." For all these reasons, teaching is an inherently ambiguous, unpredictable, and fluid craft. Teaching requires flexibility, give-and-take, and an ability to make exceptions, and it can present formidable and unusual challenges.

Finally, teachers themselves are an unusual group. Their motives, values, and aspirations upon entering teaching differ dramatically from those of entrants to many other occupations. Research on occupational choice and values has shown that an unusually large proportion of those entering teaching are motivated by what is called an altruistic or public-service ethic. Such individuals place less importance on extrinsic rewards (such as income and prestige), less emphasis on intrinsic rewards (such as intellectual challenge or self-expression), and more importance on the opportunity to contribute to the betterment of society, to work with people, to serve their community, to help others—in short, to "do good." Those with a public-service orientation prefer careers and jobs with a high "social" content, such as medicine, social work, and especially teaching. Numerous studies over the past four decades have shown that those entering teaching are more likely to value service and less likely to value pecuniary rewards than those entering most other occupations, including law, engineering, natural or social science, sales, advertising, business, architecture, journalism, or art (see, for example, Davis 1965; Miech and Elder 1996; National Education Association 1972, 1982, 1987, 1992, 1996; Rosenberg 1957). This trend continues to hold. For instance, a poll conducted in 2000 asked a national sample of recent college graduates their feelings about the importance of particular job characteristics, including "that a job contributes to society and helps others." Only 39 percent of nonteachers felt that this characteristic was "absolutely essential" in their job, while 72 percent of teachers felt this way.[4]

Teaching's unusual combination of qualities—important tasks, multiple and often contradictory demands, mandatory, obligatory and non-adult clients, altruistic practitioners, ambiguous processes, and, finally, uncertain outcomes—poses unusual difficulties for those who manage and work within schools. The work of teachers brings the basic organizational tension surrounding the competing needs for both control and autonomy to a peak. Because of the unusual characteristics of schooling, organizational control is especially important and necessary, but for the very same reasons teacher autonomy is especially important and necessary.

Owing to its democratic character and its public funding, the school system is charged with providing a relatively standard and equal service to large numbers of clients in as efficient a manner as possible and at as low a cost as possible. Moreover, because of teaching's inherent importance and inherent uncertainties, the public—and in turn, school administrators—have an understandable need to take great pains to ensure substantial control and accountability over those doing the work, teachers. Parents, for instance, typically want—and deserve—to know that the quantity and quality of what their child is taught in one classroom or school is no less than what their neighbors' children are taught in other classrooms and schools. As Bidwell points out, all these needs dictate the use of a formalized, standardized, and hierarchical—that is, bureaucratic—mode of organization for the provision of these services. And indeed, beginning in the early twentieth century the American school system quite consciously adopted the bureaucratic mode of organization (Tyack 1974). The advantages of these kinds of mechanisms should not be underestimated. They foster consistency and predictability and curb arbitrariness, favoritism, and inconsistency. All of these conditions are important and necessary given the particular character of the clients, objectives, processes, and products of schooling. However, bureaucratic mechanisms also have distinct disadvantages for this kind of work and for the very same reasons—because of the particular character of the clients, objectives, processes, and products of schooling.

As both Lortie and Bidwell have noted, regulations often do not work well for irregular work. Unlike automobile production, for example, much of what teachers do is not routine—that is, it can be difficult to codify and "freeze" the work of teachers into set routines, standard operating procedures, and measurable products (for a discussion of measurement issues in work, see Sørenson and Kalleberg 1981). Rules can never cover all the issues and contingencies that arise in work like teaching, where there is little consensus and much ambiguity surrounding means and ends. For each issue governed by rules, there are equal numbers of issues for which no rules exist. It is difficult to significantly reduce uncertainty and ambiguity—the very point of bureaucracy—in work that is inherently uncertain and ambiguous. As a result, rules and standardized procedures are rarely sufficient to establish adequate control in settings such as schools. In short, opportunities and allowances for discretion inevitably arise in teaching, despite the breadth and depth of rules and procedures.

Moreover, rules can be a relatively costly and time-consuming method of employee control. Rules are vulnerable to circumvention, and they require continual oversight and enforcement. Even if it were feasible and possible to achieve adequate control through the use of rules, such a mode of organizational control can be self-defeating. The advantage of rules—their consistency—can be a decided disadvantage with work that requires give-and-take. Discretion is not simply inevitable but necessary in the work of teaching. The one-size-fits-all approach of rules can deny teachers the flexibility necessary to do the job effectively. For just these reasons, rules can generate resistance. Like all organizations, schools need control, but they also need the consent, goodwill, commitment, and cooperation of their employees. This is perhaps even more true in teaching because the work involves unusual clients—children—and unusual practitioners—altruists. Precisely because of teaching's unusual combination of clients, products, and technologies, schools are unusually dependent on the cooperation, motivation, and commitment of those actually *entrusted* with the work of teaching. If the enforcement of rules and other direct modes of control become coercive, teachers may become resentful. "Sticks and carrots" may motivate low-performing employees, but that approach may also demotivate high-performing employees, with detrimental effects for the organization.

For these kinds of reasons, analysts of organizations, occupations, and work have long argued that bureaucratic and direct mechanisms, such as rules and sanctions, are often not the most effective mechanisms for ensuring organizational control and accountability in settings such as schools (see, for example, Bidwell and Quiroz 1991; Gaventa 1980; Ouchi 1977; Perrow 1986, 128–31). But in contrast to the conclusions of those subscribing to the loose-coupling view, this does not mean that schools are without control and coordination.

THE LIMITATIONS OF THE LOOSE-COUPLING PERSPECTIVE OF SCHOOLS

In this final section I turn to what I believe are several key limitations underlying this perspective. Distinguishing the degree and character of control in organizations depends upon where and how one looks. Given the unusual characteristics of schools as organizations and of teaching as an occupation, defining what teachers do in their jobs and assessing the extent to which their work is subject to organizational control are not straightforward issues.

Defining the Work of Teachers

Analysts of power and control in organizations have long stressed that it is important to distinguish which issues and activities are central to the roles and work of particular groups and which are not. The power held by particular groups or individuals in an organization is a function of the extent to which they influence decisions surrounding the goals and activities that are most central to their jobs. Perhaps most importantly, control of these issues is the most consequential for those groups.[5] Real power does not reside in responsibility for, and control over, less important or less central issues and decisions; indeed, the delegation of control over marginal and non-essential issues is often used as a form of co-optation and a subtle means of centralizing power. In such cases, employees can be led to falsely believe they have a voice in the management of their jobs and organization when in fact they do not (Selznick 1949).

What are the key decisions, issues, and activities involved in the work of teachers in schools? Most empirical research on the organization of schools assumes, reasonably enough, that the core of what teachers do is academic instruction in classrooms. But that is not the entire story.

As mentioned earlier, instructing youngsters in the "three Rs" and passing on academic skills and knowledge are not the only goals of schooling or the sole substance of teachers' work. Schools and teachers are also responsible for passing on society's way of life and culture. This social dimension of schooling has been a central theme of educational thought since the beginning of the twentieth century. Starting with the classic studies of education by John Dewey and Émile Durkheim and continuing through midcentury mainstream educational theory and up to the revisionist and critical educational analyses that dominated the last quarter of the twentieth century, social science has held that a major purpose of educational organizations lies in their social functions (see Bowles and Gintis 1976; Bourdieu and Passeron 1977; Dewey 1902/1974, 1934; Dreeben 1968; Durkheim 1925/1961; Grant 1988; Henry 1965; Kirst 1985; Parsons 1959; Schneider and Stevenson 1999; Waller 1932). Both Dewey and Durkheim, for example, argued that schools have, in essence, the same purpose as religion—to pass on moral order. Moreover, more recent researchers, such as James Coleman and Thomas Hoffer (1987), have argued that this social role is expanding as schools are being increasingly called upon to accept responsibility for additional tasks once solely reserved for parents, churches, and communities. In short, educational theory has long held that one of the central goals of schooling is helping to rear the next generation.

This line of education theory draws attention to the fact that what students learn in schools has as much to do with social relations as it does with the content of the academic curriculum. Much of this social activity is implicit, informal, and unstated, prompting observers to use the term "hidden curriculum" to refer to the norms, behaviors, and roles transmitted to students. Although often integrated with the "official curriculum," this social learning is distinct from academic learning.

Perhaps one of the clearest attempts to capture this academic and social distinction is in the contrast between the concepts of "human capital" and "social capital," popularized by Coleman and Hoffer (1987) in their research on schools. In the context of education, the former refers to the skills and knowledge passed on to students by schools, and the latter refers to the social relations that establish and communicate norms and sanctions. Just as financial capital and human capital are valuable assets to be acquired, social capital, while less tangible, is no less valuable a resource and asset to be acquired.

Sociologists in particular have distinguished two overlapping types of activities within this social dimension of schooling—socialization and stratification. The first involves the inculcation of societal norms and rules, in short, the parenting of children. The second involves the assessment, sorting, and channeling of students into ranks, roles, and statuses according to their abilities and behavior, often referred to as the tracking of students.

Despite the widespread recognition of the theoretical importance of the broader social goals and dimensions of schooling, these are often deemphasized in empirical research on school organization. Many analysts begin with the assumption that what teachers do in the educational and productive core of schools is primarily classroom academic instruction. In turn, researchers often assume that the ultimate and most important outcome of schooling is student academic performance. Finally, many end up assuming that student scores on pencil-and-paper, mass-produced, standardized tests are "the bottom line" and the be-all-and-end-all of education.

Underlying this view is an economic production-oriented model that is drawn from organization theory and research in industrial settings. In this framework, the objective of schools, as with industrial and business organizations, is to produce outputs from inputs. The latter usually include teacher, school, and student characteristics and resources; the former usually is student academic learning. Even those who stress the importance of the social aspects of schooling, such as a school's "community," "climate," or "ethos," often end up treating these as subsidiary preconditions and as inputs necessary for academic learning to take place.

Again, Coleman and Hoffer's (1987) research provides a prime example of this tendency. The force of much of Coleman's later work derived from his insightful illustrations of the importance of "functional community" and social capital in schooling, especially in his analysis of the differences between public and private schools. But in his analyses, these concepts are largely treated as inputs into the process of schooling, and he ultimately justifies them as important because of their positive effects on the "real" output of schooling—student test scores.[6] Others have gone even further in this tendency to blur the distinction between academic and social learning by assuming that student scores on academic achievement tests are *themselves* accurate measures of behavioral maturity, character, moral growth, and other key aspects of social learning (see, for example, Murray and Herrnstein 1996).

My point is not that academic instruction and achievement or student scores are unimportant. Nor am I arguing that they are not integrally related to the socialization and sorting processes in schools. Indeed, instructional and social objectives and processes are often inextricably mixed and merged within classrooms. My point is that the academic goals and activities of schools are not the same things as the social goals and activities of schools. The behavioral growth and learning of students, the transmission of norms and roles, and the character of social relations are all equally important aspects of the job of teachers and equally important outputs of schooling. Schools are formal organizations—in the sense that they are tools engineered to do a job—and hence they are in some ways similar to economic production-oriented industrial operations. But schools are also social institutions—in the sense of being small societies infused with normative values and purposes. In this latter sense, the purposes of schools overlap with those of another socialization institution—the family.[7]

Emphasis on the academic and instructional aspects of the job of teachers has led to a deemphasis on the social dimension of teaching in empirical research on school organization. When it comes to examining the organization and control of the core educational activities in schools, researchers usually focus on the control of decisions commonly associated with formal academic instruction, such as the selection of instructional texts and the choice of teaching methods. In contrast, researchers less often examine who controls decisions surrounding behavioral, social, and normative activities in schools.

For instance, tracking is one of the most important topics in sociological research on education and the subject of voluminous research, much of it focused on the extent to which the sorting of students in schools is based on background factors, such as their socioeconomic status, rather than their actual ability and achievement (Bidwell and Friedkin 1988). In essence, tracking is concerned with how students are to be stratified into low, middle, and high ranks—one of the most crucial teaching and educational activities transpiring within classrooms and schools. But in research on school centralization and decentralization, there has been little examination of who controls these activities. There has been, for example, almost no investigation of the extent to which teachers influence or control decisions surrounding these gatekeeping processes and with what implications for the schools and students.

Likewise, student discipline is one of the most important aspects of the social side of schooling. In the first place, classroom order is fundamental—without the maintenance of some degree of classroom order and student discipline, education processes cannot proceed at all. Student discipline, however, is not simply a prerequisite for the successful transmission of instruction. Teaching discipline to children—the ability to behave according to the social norm—is at the heart of school socialization and ultimately societal survival. Durkheim makes a compelling case that a necessary adherence on the part of students to social norms—what he refers to as the "spirit of discipline"—is *the* basic element of the moral and social order transmitted in schools (see, for example, Durkheim 1925/1961, chs. 2 and 3). Moreover, discipline is concerned with which and whose set of values are to dominate school life—one of the most crucial educational decisions and activities transpiring within classrooms and schools.

However, researchers often do not place great importance on student discipline in schools. For example, a national poll of professors of education, who represent a large portion of those doing research on schools and also of those who teach future teachers, found that most place student discipline, along with neatness, punctuality, and manners, at the bottom of their list of priorities for schools. For example, only about one-third of the education professors felt it was "absolutely essential" to prepare or train teachers in maintaining classroom discipline. In contrast, an overwhelming majority placed academic learning and achievement at the top of their list of priorities for schools (Farkas, Johnson, and Duffett 1997). A similar deemphasis holds in empirical research on school organization. There has been little interest in examining the extent to which teachers control or influence key decisions surrounding behavioral codes and discipline policy and the implications for schools.

In contrast, teachers, administrators, and the public place great importance on these issues. Numerous surveys have found that both teachers and principals feel that promoting good work habits and self-discipline in students is as important a part of schooling as building basic literacy and encouraging academic excellence. Likewise, the well-known poll of the "Public's Attitudes Toward the Public Schools," conducted annually by Phi Delta Kappa and Gallup, has shown that moral and social issues—such as student discipline, lack of respect for teachers, and improper behavior in classrooms—have consistently been among the most important educational concerns of the public for decades (Elam 1995). The public overwhelmingly feels that an important goal of elementary and secondary schools is and should be to shape conduct, develop character, and impart values, and an important output is, in plain terms, well-behaved children and youth. Teaching "good behavior" is a large part of the job of elementary and secondary teachers, something new teachers quickly learn once employed at schools. The centrality of these issues to their job is also probably something that sets elementary and secondary teaching apart from college-level teaching.

Given its central importance to the public, the dimension of social learning in schools is also, not surprisingly, a major source of conflict among competing school reform movements. Conservative Christian groups, for instance, have attacked the school system for a number of years, complaining that public schools teach values and a "religion"—"secular humanism"—contrary to their own beliefs (Crawford 1980; Kellman 1982). Conservative Christians, in insisting that the inculcation of values is fundamental to schooling, are ironically in agreement with liberal-left reformers. The latter also criticize the values transmitted in schools, although in their view the problem lies in the prevalence of class, gender, and racial bias in the social dimension of schooling (see, for example, Giroux 1981).

In sum, organization theory suggests that assessments of the distribution of control in schools must focus on who controls the key decisions that affect the content and terms of the work of teachers. In turn, educational theory tells us that the educational work of teachers in schools includes two distinct dimensions—the academic and the social. Research on school organization has shed much light on who controls the former, but it has shed much less light on who controls the latter. This is an important limitation. The social side of the teaching job includes some of the most consequential activities going on in schools. A key but overlooked question is, who controls these issues, and what effect do they have on life in schools?

In fact, a close look reveals that socializing and sorting work is one of the most crucial and highly controlled aspects of schools. I have found both in analyses of large-scale national survey data and in fieldwork in schools that teachers have far less influence over—and autonomy in regard to—social and behavioral decisions and issues in schools than they do in regard to academic instructional issues. In a series of multivariate analyses, I have also found that just as the amount of autonomy and control held by teachers varies by the type of decision or issue involved, so the effects of teacher autonomy and control of teachers and schools vary by the type of issue involved. Although teachers have more control over instructional issues (such as the selection of course textbooks, topics, materials, and teaching techniques), this appears to count for little if they do not also hold substantial decisionmaking control over social issues, such as school and classroom student discipline policies. For those activities that are most fundamentally social—where the educational process involves the socialization and sorting of students—a lack of teacher control shows the strongest impact on how well schools function. Schools that allow more teacher control over social issues have fewer problems with student misbehavior, more collegiality and cooperation among teachers and administrators, a more committed teaching staff, and lower teacher turnover (Ingersoll 1994, 1996, 2003).

Measuring Organizational Control in Schools

In addition to where one looks and how one defines the issues and activities central to the work of particular organizational groups, assessments of organizational power and control also depend on how one examines and measures these phenomena. Research on school organization has often focused on direct, visible, and hence more obvious mechanisms and aspects of employee control, accountability, and influence. Typical of this approach is the influential work of John Meyer and Richard Scott. Using quantitative survey data primarily from elementary schools in one state, they focus on three means by which school organizations control the work of teachers: detailed school policies; administrative inspection of teachers at work; and administrative use of students' examination scores to evaluate teacher performance. They find that "schools develop few policies in the areas of greatest significance for their central goals and purposes" (Meyer and Scott 1983, 75). Moreover, they find little follow-up for those policies that do exist: "Neither teaching nor its output in student socialization is subject to serious organizational evaluation and inspection" (74). Finally, even if there are rules and even if they are monitored for compliance, such control would not be possible, they conclude, because school administrators' "authority to carry out these activities is in fact evanescent" (75).

Policies, inspections, and performance evaluations are all among the most important and most widely used mechanisms of employee control and accountability. Moreover, quantitative survey data on school rules or other aspects of organizational accountability can provide a valuable and necessary overview of the forms, distribution, and variations of control in educational organizations. Indeed, one of the strengths of survey data is their ability to provide an accurate picture of variations in organizational structure across many types of schools.

But policies, inspections, and performance evaluations are not the only mechanisms and forms by which control may operate in workplaces. In recent decades a variety of research on organizations and occupations has insightfully mapped out a whole range of alternative forms by which organizations control their employees (see, for example, Braverman 1974; Burawoy 1979; Edwards 1979; Gaventa 1980; Simpson 1985). Moreover, some of the most effective of these forms of organizational constraint, accountability, and control are difficult to capture through survey questionnaires; they require close examination of the day-to-day organization of employees' work.

Charles Perrow (1986), for instance, has persuasively argued that far more effective than direct controls, such as rules, regulations, and sanctions in organizations, are other types of structural controls that restrict the range of behavior and responsibility through the way production is organized and the way jobs and tasks are subdivided. The hierarchical structure of organizations, by definition, delimits the areas in which members have both responsibility and power and hence functions as a less visible means of both organizational coordination and control.

Besides these structural kinds of controls, Perrow also suggests the crucial importance of the even less visible organizational controls that are built into the culture of workplaces and organizations. In this case, behavior is circumscribed by taken-for-granted norms, expectations, and precedents. In both of these less direct forms of control, employees may seem to have autonomy and independence precisely *because* of the centralization of the power of employers. As a result, the absence of obvious controls may be an indicator not of looseness but of the efficacy of these other mechanisms.

Further contributing to a limited understanding of power and control in organizations are a series of misconceptions surrounding the concept of bureaucracy itself. A common mistake is to confuse bureaucracy with organizational control and to assume that "bureaucracy" is synonymous with "centralization" and in turn that a lack of bureaucracy is synonymous with decentralization. Bureaucracy, however, is only one mode of many by which individuals may be hierarchically organized in the pursuit of larger goals and tasks. Bureaucratic mechanisms are a method of achieving centralized control in organizations, but they are not the only mechanism for doing so. Weber (1946, 1947), for instance, described two other modes of organizational authority: that based on personal loyalty to a leader, and that based on taken-for-granted norms and traditions. An organization that does not exhibit the characteristics of the bureaucratic model is not necessarily one that lacks control and coordination. What distinguishes the bureaucratic mode of control is rationalization. Rather than control and coordinate individual members through, for example, personal allegiance or obedience to individuals, bureaucracies emphasize control through formalization, standardization, and routines.

Moreover, bureaucratization is variable: there is great variation both within and between organizations in their degree of bureaucratization. Most organizations are a mixture of both bureaucratization and debureaucratization and of both rationalization and nonrationalization.

Another related misconception is the assumption that bureaucratic modes of control are applicable solely to subordinates and lower-level employees. For instance, some of those subscribing to the loose-coupling perspective have argued that the formal regulation of administrative prerogative in schools is an impediment to organizational control—almost as if constraints on managers were a wrongful use of bureaucratic rationality. It is certainly true that superordinates are often subject to fewer bureaucratic controls than subordinates. Organizational analysts have long observed that the further one goes up the hierarchy in most organizations, the less rationalized controls there are (see, for example, Caplow 1954, 66; Kanter 1977, 73, 118; Kohn and Schooler 1983, ch. 2). While they are often the first to prescribe routine for the rest of the organization, those at the top of organizations often staunchly resist rules and regulations for themselves. But the point of standardized regulations is to minimize such exceptions, that is, to try to ensure that no one is above the law, not even the boss or the president. Standardization, by definition, strives to be universalistic and to constrain everyone alike, both subordinates and superordinates.

Similarly, some assume that increased regulation of higher-level managers necessarily results in decreased regulation of lower-level employees. For example, Lortie (1969) has argued that the standardization of teachers' salaries and promotions lessens teachers' dependency and thus undermines their loyalty and obedience to particular school administrators. This is certainly the case, but Lortie misses what this kind of rationalization, so fundamental to bureaucracy in general, does provide—the loyalty and obedience of employees to the organization.

As Weber pointed out, the point of formalized organizational regulations is not simply to control employees but to foster their commitment and allegiance to the organization. Regulations and procedures, for instance, that are designed to protect against the arbitrary dismissal of employees, foster fairness, and undermine favoritism and cronyism promote the security of employees as well as organizational efficiency (see Kohn and Schooler 1983; Weber 1946, 202). In this sense, limitations on superordinate prerogatives are not necessarily a form of decentralization but can be a different—and in Weber's view, innovative—form of centralized control and coordination. In short, organizational control of school administrators does not result in a lack of organizational control of teachers.

A final and related misconception is the assumption that the absence of bureaucracy in organizations is synonymous with organizational decentralization and employee autonomy. For instance, some of those who subscribe to the loose-coupling perspective associate debureaucratization solely with a paucity of rules and regulations for teachers or teachers' ability to bypass rules and regulations. But pockets of nonrationalization and debureaucratization are not limited to subordinates in organizations. Administrators and superordinates may also be subject to too few rules, be inadequately accountable, or enjoy wide autonomy. Or they may also be able to evade, ignore, or resist the rules that do exist—with important consequences for employee control. Indeed, a lack of standardized, authorized regulations, or a disregard for them, can be a source of administrative power and organizational centralization rather than the opposite.

The lesson for research on schools is that to more completely understand the distribution and forms of control in schools we must examine more than only the visible, direct, and obvious means of influence and employee control and move beyond stereotypes of bureaucracy. The key question is, what can we discover about control in schools if we use a wide range of data to examine possible mechanisms, direct and indirect, bureaucratic and nonbureaucratic, formal and informal?

In my own research, I have found that school administrators, like managers in other organizations, do indeed have access to a host of alternative means by which to supervise and sanction the behavior of teachers (Ingersoll 2003, chs. 4 and 5). The data reveal that teachers in most schools are subject to a great deal of constraint through a variety of modes of workplace control. I found that in schools, as in all bureaucratic organizations, there are many rules, policies, regulations, employee job descriptions, and standard operating procedures designed to direct and control the work of teachers. I also found that school administrators have a great number of means, both formal and informal, by which they can supervise, discern, and evaluate whether teachers are complying with the rules and policies. In addition, I found that school administrators have numerous mechanisms to discipline or sanction those teachers who have not complied with the rules or have not performed adequately. A close look at schools reveals that administrators have a great deal of control over key resources and decisions crucial to the work of teachers, and these provide a range of direct and indirect levers—sticks and carrots—to exert accountability.

I also found that rules, regulations, supervision, and sanctions are not the only, nor perhaps the most effective, means of controlling the work of teachers. Teachers are also controlled in less visible and less direct ways. Schools are an odd mix of bureaucratic and nonbureaucratic characteristics. Some of these other methods of control are built into the formal structure of schools and the way the work of teachers is organized. Others are embedded in the workplace culture—the informal or social organization of schools. Although these mechanisms are less direct and obvious than formal rules and regulations, they are no less real in their impact on what employees actually do. Indeed, in some ways the pervasiveness of these other kinds of controls makes it less necessary for school administrators to implement and require formal regulations and elaborate mechanisms of accountability. In some cases, higher-order decisions, over which teachers have little influence, set the parameters for the lower-order decisions delegated to teachers in their classrooms. In these cases, the use of relatively crude and direct levers is not necessary because, by definition, little of consequence is actually delegated to teachers.

These less obvious controls are reflected in the role of teachers in schools. Teachers are a good example of men or women in the middle. The inherent character and tensions of "in between" roles were originally captured in the classic research on "men in the middle" by William Foote Whyte and Burleigh Gardner (1945). Most work roles and occupations—except of course those at the very top and very bottom—involve being in between two or more groups: most employees receive as well as give orders and must deal with demands from both above and below. Problems arise when those in the middle are subject to unreasonable or competing or contradictory demands or are not provided with the necessary power and resources to get the job done adequately. In the extreme case, those caught between impossible demands and limited resources illustrate one of the classic problems of management: holding employees accountable for things they do not control.

Teachers are not actually the "workers" themselves and do not do the "work" of learning. Teachers supervise and direct those who do the work—the students. Nor are teachers part of the management of schools; the role of teachers lies in between that of "management" and "workers." Teachers are delegated only limited input into the management of schools and crucial decisions regarding their work, but they are delegated a great deal of responsibility for the implementation of these decisions. Like other middle men and women, teachers usually work alone and may have much latitude in seeing that their students carry out assigned tasks. This responsibility and latitude can easily be mistaken for discretion and control, especially in regard to tasks within classrooms. A close look at the organization of the teaching job shows, however, that it involves little real power. Indeed, contrary to some critics, a close look at the job of teaching reveals that teachers are pushed to accept a remarkable degree of personal accountability in the face of remarkable lack of collective accountability on the part of the schools that employ them. In turn, while teachers have little input into the way schools are run, they are routinely held accountable and often blamed for the apparent failure of schools.

CONCLUSION

What can we conclude from this discussion of the loose-coupling perspective of schools? Our understanding of the character of schools as organizations and of the character of teaching as an occupation is indebted to the work of Bidwell, Lortie, and others in this tradition. Teaching is indeed an unusual kind of occupation, schools are an unusual kind of workplace, and education is an unusual kind of industry. Schools are not well explained by a rational economic-production model of organization. School settings must cope with fundamental tensions that pose critical problems for their management and design, have large implications for control, and pose challenges for reform.

My argument, however, is that much of the theory and research influenced by the loose-coupling perspective has not gone far enough and has not fully brought out the implications of these insights for understanding the organization of schools. Schools are indeed loose in important ways. Teachers do report high levels of autonomy for some issues, and schools do have problems of cohesion, cooperation, communication, and coherence. But many of these problems appear to be largely due not to a lack of organizational control but to precisely the opposite.

When we look closely at the less technical and more institutional functions of schools and at the social organization of teachers' work, it appears that the classroom is not a separate, inviolate zone of teacher autonomy. Rather, the work of teachers is subject to a great deal of control and constraint.

This chapter draws material from *Who Controls Teachers' Work? Power and Accountability in America's Schools* (Ingersoll 2003).

NOTES

1. My summary here draws from two classic pieces by Bidwell: his 1965 interpretive review of the formal organization of schools, and his 1970 article on the unusual characteristics of the work of teachers. The more recent work of Bidwell (see Bidwell, Frank, and Quiroz 1997; Bidwell and Quiroz 1991) has further elaborated the sources and variations of looseness in schools. He and his associates developed a typology of different mechanisms by which the work of teachers is organizationally controlled across different kinds of schools. In their model, organizational control systems in schools vary from top-down, highly bureaucratized, and highly centralized to loosely coupled, highly debureaucratized, and highly decentralized, depending on the size of the schools and the socioeconomic status of the school community. Their focus was on the different forms of workplace control in schools and how these are embedded in the social organization of school workplaces and affect a range of student outcomes.

2. My brief sketch of organization theory, the study of bureaucracy, and Weber's concept of rationality draws from Richard Scott's (1987) standard text. It is important to recognize that in the context of bureaucratic organizations, the term "rationality" is used here in the narrow sense of formal or technical rationality. The latter refers to the rationality not of the goals but of the means by which they are achieved. In contrast to formal rationality, substantive rationality is concerned with how sensible and valuable the goals of the entity are. It is of course possible to use rational means to obtain nonrational ends. Weber (1947, 185, 215), for instance, pointed out that regardless of the degree of formal rationality, whether observers find organizations to be characterized by substantive rationality depends on the values and standards held by the observers themselves.

3. This body of work comprises several different streams of thought and research: "garbage can" theory (see, for example, Cohen, March, and Olsen 1972; March and Olsen 1976), the organizational social psychology of Karl Weick (1976, 1979, 1984), and institutional theory (for example, Meyer and Rowan 1977, 1978; Meyer and Scott 1983).

    Although it shares an emphasis on loose-coupling, institutional theory is a distinctly different approach to organizational analysis from that of Weick and March. Moreover, institutional theory is not one theory but rather several theories and approaches that are not entirely consistent or cohesive. For reviews of this genre, see Zucker (1987) and Scott (1988). My discussion of the loosely coupled organizations view refers to that branch of institutional theory associated with the work of Richard Scott, John Meyer, and their associates. Its contribution has been to transcend traditional task-oriented explanations of organizations and resurrect and reconstruct Philip Selznick's (1949) notion of institutionalization as the driving force shaping organizational order and disorder. Indeed, this variant of institutional theory is often credited (for example, Dreeben 1994) with providing an intriguing explanation of the anomaly of loosely coupled organizations: tight coupling at the interorganizational level leads to loose coupling at the intraorganizational level. For a more detailed summary and critique of these streams of theory and research on loosely coupled systems, see Ingersoll (1993).

4. These data are from a 2000 survey conducted by Public Agenda, an education-oriented public opinion research group. The sample size was 664 K–12 public school teachers and 802 nonteachers. For details on the data and survey, see Farkas, Johnson, and Foleno (2000).

5. Eliot Freidson (1973), for example, distinguishes between control over the content of work (the what and how of tasks) and control over the larger terms of work (the organizational and social context that defines and regulates the work). Groups that control important parts of the larger terms of their work are in turn likely to have substantial control over the content of their work. For a useful review of the sources of workplace control, see Simpson (1985). For other work on organizational control, see, for example, Crozier (1964), Perrow (1986), Kanter (1977), Selznick (1949), and Hinings and others (1974).

6. It is necessary to recognize that although Coleman and others emphasize academic scores, they do not totally ignore non-academic outcomes. Some, of course, do examine student dropout, delinquency, alienation, and so forth, as valid outcomes of schooling.

7. Like the concept of "bureaucracy," the concept of "institution" is also defined and used in numerous ways. Some, for instance, use the term to refer to organizations, while others are referring to a normative principle behind organized behavior. In organization theory there is a long tradition of concern with the distinction between organizations and institutions. Following Selznick (1957) and Scott (1987), by "institution" I mean an entity that is infused with meaning and value beyond the technical requirements at hand. A "formal organization" refers to a rational tool geared to specified goals, and an "institution" is a more natural, more normative, less technically oriented collectivity.

Chapter 6

Professional Community by Design: Building Social Capital Through Teacher Professional Development

Adam Gamoran, Ramona Gunter, and Tona Williams

The social organization of teachers in a school has long been of interest to scholars (Bidwell 1965; Waller 1932). Many have noted that teachers work in isolation from one another owing to the physical layout of schools and the ways in which the tasks of teaching are organized (Bidwell 1965; Jackson 1968; Johnson 1990; Lortie 1975). Consequently, most schools offer few opportunities for teachers to collaborate on instructional matters. Cases of high levels of collaboration are rare and until recently have not received much attention. As Charles Bidwell (1965, 1008) has explained, "Within school systems the formation of strong colleague ties depends chiefly on situational factors." For most of the period since Bidwell's classic 1965 essay, the situational factors that promote strong colleague ties have not been explored.

In the past decade, researchers have turned greater attention to understanding the conditions that promote collegiality and collaboration among teachers in a school system (see, for example, Bidwell, Frank, and Quiroz 1997; Johnson 1990). A major impetus for this line of work has been recognition of the crucial role played by the teacher colleague group, often referred to as a "professional community," in the success or failure of reform efforts. Studies of school reform claim that establishing a professional community is crucial for supporting change in teachers' work because it provides a context in which reforms can be disseminated and norms supporting the reform can emerge (see, for example, Newmann and Associates 1996). How do professional communities of teachers form and develop? This chapter examines a case of professional community by design in which professional development was used in an explicit attempt to create "strong colleague ties" focused on teaching and learning. Analysis of workshop observations, teacher interviews, and survey data show how teachers drew on their social relationships within the community to support new teaching practices.

PROFESSIONAL COMMUNITY AND TEACHER CHANGE

What do we mean by "professional community"? A useful definition comes from Fred Newmann and Associates (1996), who view professional community as a group of educators who:

- exhibit shared values;
- focus collectively on student learning; collaborate;
- engage in reflective conversations about student learning; and
- share their practices with one another.

The claim that a professional community is necessary to support teacher change carries an implicit critique of several earlier notions. First, it challenges the view that "resource allocation" is the primary mechanism of organizational control over teaching (Gamoran and Dreeben 1986). The idea that administrators can use resources to leverage teacher action falls short because teachers have so much autonomy after the classroom door is closed that they can use many of their resources as they wish. A professional community, however, provides both technical expertise and normative pressure so that resources allocated by districts and schools may be used in ways that are consistent with the goals of the community, thus supporting the process of change (Gamoran et al. 2003).

Second, the emphasis on professional communities of educators addresses shortcomings in common approaches to "restructuring" schools. In the restructuring notion, school systems can induce changes in teaching and learning by pressing on the right "levers" of change—detracking, shared governance, site-based management, and so on (Lewis 1989). Yet structural changes typically have weak effects, and studies of school restructuring have concluded that teacher change is primarily a response to teacher learning rather than to structural shifts (Elmore, Peterson, and McCarthey 1996; Newmann and Associates 1996). Teacher learning in turn may be enhanced and supported by the presence of like-minded colleagues engaged in a common enterprise (Gamoran et al. 2003).

Third, the idea that communities of educators are necessary to support change raises questions for today's prevailing trends in educational reform, which emphasize accountability measures tied to district or state testing systems as the means to change what teachers do in classrooms. According to the critique, teachers need enhanced professional knowledge to respond to accountability demands, and this knowledge will be supported by treating teachers as professionals and by creating contexts in which communities can emerge (McNeil 2000).

Professional Community and Teaching for Understanding

While Bidwell (1965) notes that colleague ties are situational, the salience of col-league ties in supporting change is also a matter of context. That is, the importance of collegial relations for teacher change may depend on the content of the change that is being attempted. If the desired outcome is maximizing student perfor-mance on a narrow range of skills, then providing strict instructional guidelines may be the best lever for change, and a community of teachers may not help and could even impair the change process (for instance, if teachers banded together to resist).

By contrast, an effort to promote instruction that emphasizes deep understand-ing of powerful ideas may be especially sensitive to the presence or absence of a community of teachers. This approach is sometimes called "teaching for under-standing," and it emphasizes three principles (for a review, see Gamoran et al. 2003): a focus on student thinking, powerful content, and an equitable classroom community.[1] The emphasis on student thinking forces teachers to confront uncer-tainties that they might otherwise avoid. While teaching is always an uncertain technology, teachers can typically circumvent uncertainty by following pre-dictable patterns of practice.[2] In teaching for understanding, however, teachers cannot follow routine scripts because they attend to students' ideas and may need to modify their approach in response to student thinking. A professional commu-nity of educators offers a different sort of resource to draw upon for resolving un-certainties. It provides teachers with colleagues who have similar commitments and can provide feedback, collaborate on solutions, and reinforce norms about teaching for understanding. For these reasons, teachers working toward teaching for understanding may be especially likely to benefit from a strong professional community.

Professional Community, Professional Development, and Social Capital

A professional community, as we have defined it, is vibrant with social capital. It embodies four hallmarks of social capital in a community: trust, reciprocity, infor-mation flows, and emerging norms. Conceiving of a professional community of educators in terms of social capital emphasizes that the community has value as a *resource* that teachers can draw upon to improve their teaching. Social relation-ships embodied in a community serve as a resource by providing new ideas and feedback on the technical tasks of teaching and by generating and supporting norms consistent with the new practices.

According to Adam Gamoran and his colleagues (2003), professional develop-ment that is coherent, sustained, and focused on collaboration and inquiry can generate social capital within a professional community. In this context, social capital emerges as teachers work together to focus on student learning. Social capital in this conception is part of a larger framework that examines resources of three types: material resources, such as equipment, curricular materials, and time for meetings; human resources, that is, the knowledge, skills, and commitments of teaching; and social resources (which are forms of social capital), the relations of trust and expectations that teachers draw upon to ask questions and try out new ideas. Following Gamoran, Walter Secada, and Cora Marrett (2000), we view material, human, and social resources as both affecting and affected by teacher professional development. Thus, we may expect professional development to strengthen social ties, just as strong social ties among teachers may encourage further collaboration and professional development.

Critics of research on social capital point out that the concept has often been defined by its functions and that this makes it difficult to assess its effects (Durlauf 2002; Portes 1998). For example, if the presence of a norm is evidence of social capital, how can we say that social capital helped bring about the norm? We aim to move beyond this quandary by asking whether collaborative professional development is associated with collegial ties, and whether collegial ties that reflect social capital can serve as resources to support teaching for understanding. We do not envision this as a one-way process from social connections to teaching for understanding, but rather conceive of a dynamic process in which teachers' professional relations with one another and their classroom experiences of teaching for understanding have continuous mutual effects (Gamoran et al. 2000). Do teachers' beliefs and practices in teaching for understanding reflect their relationships as colleagues? When do teachers draw on collegial ties for help with their concerns about teaching? To address these questions, we turn to a study of teacher development in one school district.

A CASE OF PROFESSIONAL COMMUNITY BY DESIGN

Science and Mathematics Modeling (SAMM) is a professional development program for elementary teachers in Europa, Wisconsin, a small district that draws students from both a midsized city and a nearby suburb.[3] The district serves about four thousand students, a number that represents substantial growth over the past decade. The population growth has been accompanied by increasing diversity. For example, the portion of the district's students who receive free or reduced-price lunch grew from about 4 percent of students in 1990 to over 10 percent in 2000. The district averages mask important differences between schools: two of the four elementary schools contain almost no children living in poverty, while the other two schools average almost 25 percent of students receiving free or reduced-price lunch.

The professional development program began in 1992 with a pilot project that involved a group of university researchers and ten teachers who collaborated in seventy-five hours of workshops during that school year and a weeklong summer seminar. In 1995 a new version of the project emerged through additional support from the district and outside grants. At this point, the participants named the group "SAMM." During this phase of formal teacher-researcher collaboration, teacher participation grew from twenty-five (in 1995 to 1996) to thirty-four (in 1997 to 1998). At the end of this three-year collaboration, the team of researchers ended their active participation in the group, while over twenty teachers continued to organize monthly full-day workshops, with the district's financial support. These teacher-led activities continued beyond the researchers' involvement for at least two years.

Data Sources

As part of a larger study of the organizational context of teaching reforms, we collected data about SAMM during the last two years of the teacher-researcher collaboration (1996 to 1997 and 1997 to 1998) and during one additional year (1998 to 1999) when the program was led solely by teachers. Our evidence comes from four sources: observations of twenty-six professional development workshops; interviews with teachers who participated in SAMM (twenty-two teachers in 1997, twenty-one in 1998, and eighteen in 1999); interviews with four or five district and school administrators each year; and surveys of all classroom teachers of mathematics and science in the four elementary schools in 1997, 1998, and 1999. Surveys were obtained from seventy-three, seventy-five, and sixty-nine teachers, respectively, reflecting response rates of about 80 percent in each year.

Professional Development Activities

The SAMM group developed a dual focus: collaborative planning among the teachers and examination of student work. This encouraged the emergence of group norms, reciprocity in their relationships, trust, and information-sharing among the teachers—all elements of social capital. The group's primary professional development activity was examining student work in order to understand student thinking. Nearly all of the monthly professional development seminars featured student work in some way, often as a session's core focus. Generally the work examined came from students in different classes, and often different grade levels. By examining student work collaboratively, the teachers gained insight into what students were thinking and how student thinking changed over time and in response to classroom activities. A typical instance is related in field notes from a three-hour whole-group professional development meeting that took place after school in the library of one of the elementary schools:

> In this section of the meeting, the teachers broke into small groups to examine samples of children's work. The discussion in one group focused on whether and how children came up with a format for classifying. The group I was with looked at two types of classification systems. One was a system for classifying self-portraits of

young children and another was a system for classifying drawings of houses made by young children. . . . The teachers in the small group I observed were very enthusiastic and engaged. . . . All of them were trying to figure out what the kids' classification systems were. . . . Their comments suggested that they were trying to understand children's thinking that was underlying their classification systems. . . . After this discussion, participants got up to look at the actual pictures that had been used by the children in their classification systems to see if they could match the actual pictures to the classification systems. . . . Next the whole group came together for a discussion and a report on the small groups. The main question was: How did progression in the classification system occur?

This example, one of many that could have been selected, illustrates several points about the work of the SAMM group. First is members' unwavering attention to what students were learning. What did students know? How did they represent their knowledge? Addressing these questions constituted the central subject matter of SAMM meetings. Second is the collaborative nature of the teachers' work. Teachers collaborated to implement classroom activities whose results furnished the subject matter of the workshop, and they also collaborated to analyze and discuss the evidence of student thinking. The collaborative nature of this discussion is essential; it was through ongoing dialogue that teachers reflected on what they were learning, tried out their ideas with colleagues and university researchers, received feedback, and considered how to incorporate what they had learned into subsequent teaching. Moreover, working new ideas into instruction typically occurred in collaboration with colleagues, university researchers, or both.

Third, one can observe the teachers' reliance on a shared technical vocabulary. In this case, the teachers used the term "classification system" to refer to a systematic way of organizing data. Teachers in this group employed a wide range of shared terms, such as "coordinate system," "skip counting," "clustering," "scaffolding," "jigsaw," and "division notation." A shared vocabulary is an indicator of professional knowledge that is often lacking among groups of teachers. Typically, teacher talk relies on lay terminology and does not focus on student learning (Jackson 1968). In the SAMM group, much of the teacher talk focused on student learning, and a technical vocabulary had been adopted to enable the conversation. Many of the terms are common within the field of mathematics education, and their use among elementary teachers suggests a point of contact with a larger professional field, presumably a result of contacts with university-based mathematics educators through the SAMM project.

Fourth, this example illustrates how the seminars provided a forum for teachers to make their work public. Conventionally, teachers work in isolation from their colleagues. They shut their classroom doors and their teaching is shielded from inspection from any outsiders, including their peers (Lortie 1975). By contrast, SAMM teachers frequently displayed their work for examination by colleagues. Occasionally this occurred through peer visits or videotaped class sessions, but more often, as in this example, teachers described an activity they had carried out in class and presented the materials they used for the activity and the student products of the activity for deliberation by the group. The public display of teaching was necessary for providing evidence of student thinking. It was also important because it gave teachers a rare opportunity to explore questions and concerns about their own teaching with colleagues and others they perceived as experts.

In addition to examining students' work, SAMM meetings and workshops included substantial time for teacher collaborative planning. On these occasions teachers worked together to plan classroom activities. Planning teams often involved teachers from different schools or different grade levels. During the three years of teacher-researcher collaboration, planning teams also involved teachers and researchers working together. The meetings and workshops provided an opportunity for these joint ventures. Activities such as the classification exercise described here were the result of such collaborative planning.

Analysis of Social Relationships and Support for Teaching for Understanding

Did the SAMM project contribute to "strong colleague ties" that constitute a resource in the form of social capital that supports teaching for understanding? To address this question, we drew on data from teacher interviews and surveys. In the interviews, we asked teachers, "If you were to have any questions, concerns, or ideas about teaching mathematics and science, to whom would you go to discuss those issues?" We used teachers' responses to this question to identify collegial ties. From questionnaires, we drew information on teachers' beliefs about teaching for understanding and the extent to which their self-reported teaching practices reflected teaching for understanding. We constructed scales for teaching-for-understanding beliefs and practices; scale items and reliabilities are reported in the appendix, as are means and standard deviations for these and other variables used in the analyses.

If collegial ties support teaching for understanding, we might expect to find that teachers who name one another as colleagues tend to express more similar teaching beliefs and practices. To test this notion, we conducted a network analysis (Frank 1996) in which the network tie ("other" is named as a colleague) is a function of characteristics of the interviewee, or "ego," as well as characteristics of the other and characteristics of the dyad, including the similarity of their teaching beliefs and practices. The surveys furnished additional data on teacher experience, and we used district and professional development group records to indicate school, grade level, and professional development group membership. We also included two important network controls in the analysis: ego's "gregariousness," or the number of others whom ego named in total, and other's "popularity," or the total number of times other was named as a colleague.

This analysis has one important limitation: whereas all elementary teachers of mathematics and science in the district were targeted as others, and the large majority are included in the analysis, only teachers who were members of SAMM were potential egos because only they were interviewed. Thus, the analysis does not incorporate the full range of teachers in the district. This suggests a possible modification to our main hypothesis about the association between approaches to teaching and collegial ties. Although teachers deeply committed to teaching for understanding may tend to seek out others with similar views, what about teachers who are in the professional development program but have not grasped the approach in full? These teachers may be more likely to speak with others whose approach differs from their own, as a way of learning more about teaching for understanding. Thus, the strength and direction of the association between approaches to teaching and collegial ties may depend on the nature of ego's approach to teaching.

Another limitation of the analysis is that it cannot distinguish between *influence* in the teacher network and *selection*. If teachers with similar approaches to teaching are likely to speak with one another, is that because similar teachers seek out one another, or because teachers who speak with one another become more alike over time in their views of teaching? Although the network analysis does not address this question, our three years of survey data and rich base of interview material helped us gain some purchase on this issue.

SURVEY RESULTS   Table 6.1 displays results of the logistic regression analyses. The table displays three columns of results, one representing each year of the study. The main finding in this analysis is the strong role of formal structure in organizing collegial relations. Teachers are much more likely to name others as colleagues they would go to with a question about their mathematics or science teaching when they are: in the same school; in the same grade level; and members of the same professional development group (that is, SAMM). These effects are generally stable across the three years of data collection. The finding regarding same-grade contacts is particularly interesting, because it suggests that the grade level serves as an axis of organizational differentiation in elementary schools, much as the department does in high schools.

In 1997 and 1998, neither beliefs nor practices related to teaching for understanding were associated with the likelihood of choosing a colleague for help. In 1999, however, the results are different. First, the absolute value of the difference between ego's and other's teaching practices is *positively* associated with naming a colleague, contrary to our prediction. At first glance, this result seems to indicate that teachers were more likely to name colleagues whose teaching practices were different from their own than they were to name colleagues whose practices were similar. But this coefficient must be interpreted in light of the interaction term, which is *negative*. The positive main effect coupled with the negative interaction term indicates that teachers who were low on the scale of teaching for understanding practices were likely to name colleagues who differed in their teaching practices, but teachers who were high on the scale tended to name colleagues whose practices were similar. For example, a teacher who is one standard deviation above the mean on the practices scale $(11.3 + 3.1 = 14.4)$ would increase her likelihood of choosing a colleague with the same score by 2.46 in the logit metric $((11.3 + 3.1)(.1708) + 0(.5795) + 0(-.043) = 2.46)$. By contrast, a teacher who scored

TABLE 6.1 / Association Between Teaching for Understanding and Colleague Ties

Predictor	1997		1998		1999	
Ego's background						
Experience in this school	−.04	(.04)	−.02	(.02)	−.14	(.08)
Grade level	.06	(.12)	.26*	(.12)	.09	(.15)
Year in SAMM[a]			−.99	(.55)	.29	(.43)
Other's background						
Experience in this school	−.00	(.03)	−.04	(.03)	−.14*	(.07)
Member of SAMM	5.65*	(.83)	3.82*	(.82)	2.44*	(.65)
Year in SAMM[a]			.38	(.42)	.45	(.29)
Dyad context						
Same grade	1.75*	(.36)	2.49*	(.37)	1.20*	(.39)
Same school	2.30*	(.37)	3.03*	(.36)	2.18*	(.39)
Teaching for understanding						
Ego's beliefs	.68	(1.30)	1.25	(1.41)	−1.16	(1.55)
|Ego—other's beliefs|[b]	−6.86	(8.06)	6.93	(11.05)	−2.71	(11.51)
Interaction (beliefs)[c]	2.06	(2.35)	−2.30	(3.33)	.77	(3.49)
Ego's practices	.12	(.11)	.03	(.11)	.17	(.10)
|Ego—other's practices|[d]	.12	(.23)	.16	(.20)	.58*	(.23)
Interaction (practices)[e]	−.02	(.02)	−.01	(.02)	−.04*	(.02)
Network controls						
Gregariousness	.21*	(.02)	.19*	(.02)	.27*	(.03)
Popularity	.43*	(.07)	.35*	(.09)	.65*	(.11)
Constant	−11.76		−15.16		−9.52	
Number of dyads	1,584		1,638		1,292	
Model fit (cases predicted correctly)	96.8%		97.0%		96.5%	

Source: Authors' calculations.
Note: Parameters are logistic regression coefficients, with standard errors in parentheses. Dependent variable: Other is named as colleague.
[a]All egos were members of SAMM, but some joined after 1997. About one-third of others were members of SAMM.
[b]Absolute value of difference between ego's and other's beliefs.
[c]Interaction between ego's beliefs and absolute value of difference between ego's and other's beliefs.
[d]Absolute value of difference between ego's and other's practices.
[e]Interaction between ego's practices and absolute value of difference between ego's and other's practices.
*p < .05

one standard deviation below the mean (11.3 − 3.1 = 8.2) would increase her likelihood of choosing a colleague with an identical score by only 1.4 ((11.3 − 3.1)(.1708) + 0(.5795) + 0(−.043) = 1.40). Figure 6.1 uses these and similar computations to compare effects on the likelihood of naming a colleague for teachers who are high and low on the practices scale and for others who are high and low on the same scale. Each bar in figure 6.1 represents the change in the likelihood of one teacher nam-

FIGURE 6.1 / Logit Estimates for Change in Likelihood of Seeking Help from a Colleague at Different Levels of Teaching for Understanding

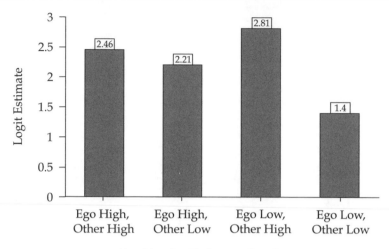

Source: Authors' calculations.

ing another depending on each teacher's level of teaching-for-understanding practices. The figure reveals that teachers who are low on teaching-for-understanding practices are much more likely to name a teacher who is high on the scale than one who is equally low. By contrast, teachers who are high on teaching-for-understanding practices are only slightly more likely to name a colleague who is similar than they are to name one who is different.

The logit coefficients in figure 6.1 can be expressed as probabilities. Because the logit function is nonlinear, a change in probability related to one variable depends on what values are set for the other variables. For teachers in different schools and grade levels, the overall probability of naming one another as colleagues is very low (around 1 percent), so variation in teaching-for-understanding practices matters very little. Among teachers in the same school and grade, and where both participated in SAMM, differences in self-reported teaching-for-understanding practices are much more consequential. Teachers who are high in teaching-for-understanding practices are a little more likely to name a colleague who is high on the scale than one who is low (12 percent versus 10 percent, respectively). However, teachers whose own reported practices are low on the scale are especially likely to name a colleague who is high on the scale (17 percent) and especially unlikely to name a colleague who is low (5 percent).[4]

Interpretation of figure 6.1 along with the associated probabilities suggests that teachers who are high on teaching for understanding are likely to identify colleagues they would talk to regardless of their location on the scale, while teachers who are low on teaching for understanding tend to select only those who are on the opposite end of the scale. This pattern may reflect two separate phenomena. First, it is consistent with our earlier claim that teachers engaged in teaching for understanding tend to use their relationships with colleagues as a social *resource*, or social capital, that they draw upon to work out the challenges of their practice. Second, teachers who do not exhibit these practices but are involved in professional development aimed at teaching for understanding may seek out the leading practitioners for advice. If all teachers in the district were available to serve as egos in the analysis instead of only those in the SAMM program (that is, if a control group were available), we might have found teachers who are low in teaching-for-understanding practices and who have no interest in seeking out fellow teachers with differing approaches to teaching. This question awaits further research with a more inclusive sample.

Because the effects for teaching practices occur in only one of the three years of data, it is hard to be confident in their validity. Note, however, that as the teachers' practices became more visible within the professional development group over time, their likelihood of seeking out colleagues based on those teachers' membership in the SAMM group diminished. This may mean that formal structure becomes less important, and what teachers are actually doing in their classrooms becomes more salient, as the collaboration progresses. Support for this notion comes from the fact that teachers continually present their work and that of their students in the SAMM workshops. By the third year of the study, it may be very clear which teachers are the experts and are truly engaged in teaching for understanding.

Do these patterns reflect selection or influence? That is, do teachers high in teaching-for-understanding practices name others who are similar, or do teachers become more similar by talking to the colleagues they have named? The negative association between similarity of teaching practices and seeking help from a colleague for those low in teaching-for-understanding practices seems most interpretable as a matter of selection. We can use the interview data to help sort out these issues and to address the broader question of what teachers talked about when they exercised their collegial ties.

INTERVIEW FINDINGS   Do teachers seem to be influenced by those they name, or do they select others who are similar (for those high on teaching-for-understanding practices) or different (for those low on the scale)? To address this question, we examined interview responses for teachers at different levels on the teaching-for-understanding practices scale. We focused on the interview question noted earlier and on a follow-up question: "Think back to an event where you discussed something with one of the people you just named. Describe the incident, what you talked about, how you tried to resolve the issue, and what the outcome was."

The interview analysis shows that processes of influence and selection in the teacher networks are deeply intertwined. Generally, it is impossible to disentangle the two, because both are reflected in the same interactions. Teachers who reported low levels of teaching-for-understanding practices clearly sought out colleagues they perceived as experts. Peter, a fourth-grade teacher, pointed to a colleague who served in both formal and informal leadership roles in the group:

> My first step would probably be to [go to] Lisa. She's just been so involved. And she really understands and she's very enthusiastic about, basically, just helping out. But she knows so much. She's a great resource. Even though we're in such different grade levels. She has some really wonderful ideas. Has a great approach to how kids think. And interpreting that. So when I have had questions, that's who I've gone to first.

The same teacher's interview also illustrates how teachers low in teaching-for-understanding practices are reluctant to turn to others who are similarly low: "Unfortunately, there . . . [are] not a lot of people that are really involved right now in this project. So it's hard to go to them. The people who aren't involved, it's hard to go to them because they don't know. They're taking a totally different approach." In conversation with teaching-for-understanding experts, Peter is clearly influenced by what he learns:

> Lisa and I spent a lot of time just talking about, "Well, you know, what tools can they use within this activity," and I think it was interesting because I thought, "Kids should be able to use rulers if they understand," and her ideas were, "No, they should use nonstandard units and things like that to measure with." So we had . . . a difference of opinion there. And we also . . . got into talking about what is height in a rectangle and what is width and what is wideness and how do you know what is bigger, comparing height and things like that. And she knocked my socks off because she gets so particular and she pays such attention to details where . . . I don't always see those details and those things like that. So those are a big help.

It seems likely that as a result of these encounters, Peter's practices would become more reflective of teaching for understanding. Indeed, his score on the self-reported scale of teaching-for-understanding practices rose from 1997 to 1999.

A similar example of both influence and selection comes from another teacher who reported low levels of teaching-for-understanding practices and who sought out a colleague with greater expertise:

> Phil Cannon and I both did a unit about seeing silhouette solids, and we both did the task at the end, the problem at the end, which was constructing a three-dimensional toy representing it in two-dimensional space. And we talked with each other about what kinds of materials you could provide with kids to help them do that because it was a really difficult thing. And I know I gave him some stuff. And he showed me something else. And we kind of shared materials about it. . . . The outcome was, we both got some better stuff than we had before.

This teacher's practices also became more reflective of teaching for understanding over time, although the change was less extensive than with Peter.

Consistent with the survey results, we found that teachers who were high in teaching-for-understanding practices often spoke with colleagues who scored very differently in teaching-for-understanding practices (though their predilection was to speak with those whose scores were slightly greater). For example, Lisa, the expert mentioned by Peter, referred to Peter as someone to whom she herself would go with a question. Her examples of such interaction, however, referred to teachers who were SAMM veterans like herself and close to her level or higher in teaching-for-understanding practices. In these encounters, teachers were clearly influencing one another by exploring student thinking and its relation to their teaching. For example, here is the description provided in 1997 by Carol, the most prominent teacher-leader in SAMM:

> Lisa and I talk[ed] about way-finding [a mapping activity] with kids and tr[ied] to make more sense of that. I did go to plan with her, and I watched video and saw some of the work her kids did and looked . . . to see where her kids had been working . . . and that was more to figure out how we were gonna share those ideas with teachers. . . . So we weren't co-planning for similar groups of kids at that time, but we were sharing ideas and modifying things either way, things her kids had done that could work with my third-graders and things my past second-graders had done that would help her first- and second-graders now.

These analyses clarify questions that were raised by the survey analyses. They demonstrate that network ties reflect both influence and selection. Moreover, they show how teachers learn from their colleagues. Consistent with our conceptualization, teachers who are highly engaged in teaching-for-understanding practices tend to learn from a wide range of colleagues, while teachers whose practices reflect teaching for understanding to a lesser degree learn mainly from those more involved in teaching for understanding than they are.

CONCLUSION

This chapter offers a case study of professional development as an engine of change. The analyses show how sustained, coherent, collaborative professional development can be used to create strong colleague ties in a professional community. These ties constitute social capital—a resource teachers draw upon to address issues and concerns in their teaching.

The network analysis shows the importance of formal structure in establishing colleague ties: working at the same school, teaching the same grade level, and participating in the same professional development program were the most salient predictors of network relations. The network analysis also suggests that similarities and differences in teaching practices may affect colleague ties, although the impact may be different for teachers who take different approaches to teaching. By analyzing interview responses, we confirmed that causality in the network models runs in both directions: fellow teachers are chosen as colleagues in part owing to their practices, but teaching practices are also affected by network connections. Selection and influence patterns both demonstrate the mechanisms through which social relations among educators support teaching for understanding.

How much should we make of one case study? The case of Europa Elementary is part of a larger set of six cases that reveal not only varying levels of professional development's influence on teachers' reflections about their practice but also the creation of professional communities that are rich in social capital (Gamoran et al. 2003). Europa is a case in which the capacity for professional community was especially high owing to long-standing relationships with outside researchers, a supportive administration, and committed teachers. Thus, while Europa suggests one route to professional community, it may not be the only one, and it may not be replicable in all contexts. The case of Europa does confirm, however, that colleague ties are indeed "situational" and that, as a form of social capital, they constitute a valuable resource when activated.

APPENDIX: SCALE ITEMS AND RELIABILITIES

To rate teachers' teaching-for-understanding beliefs, we asked them whether they strongly disagreed, disagreed, agreed, or strongly agreed with the following statements:

1. Teachers should plan instruction based upon their knowledge of their students' understanding.

2. Teachers should encourage children to find their own strategies to solve problems even if the strategies are inefficient.

3. Teachers should always know the answers to questions posed by their students. (*scoring is reversed*)

4. Teachers should structure their instruction to follow the progression in the textbook. (*scoring is reversed*)

5. Students must learn basic skills before they can be expected to analyze, compare, or generalize. (*scoring is reversed*)

6. Instruction should include many open-ended tasks.

7. Instruction should provide step-by-step directions. (*scoring is reversed*)

8. Students should understand what they are learning before they attempt to discuss their thinking. (*scoring is reversed*)

9. Students should learn mathematics and science through regularly debating their ideas with other students.

To rate teachers' teaching-for-understanding practices, we asked them how often they engaged in the following practices: rarely or never (0), one to three times a month (2), one to two times a week (6), three to four times a week (14), or every day (20).

TABLE 6A.1 / Means and Standard Deviations of Independent Variables

Predictor	1997 Mean (Standard Deviation)		1998 Mean (Standard Deviation)		1999 Mean (Standard Deviation)	
Ego's background						
Experience in this school	5.48	(5.38)	6.26	(5.30)	5.53	(3.05)
Grade level	2.86	(1.32)	2.86	(1.36)	2.37	(1.72)
Year in SAMM[a]	1	(0)	1.90	(.29)	2.58	(.75)
Other's background						
Experience in this school	5.87	(5.40)	5.97	(5.75)	6.47	(5.40)
Member of SAMM	.39	(.49)	.36	(.48)	.31	(.46)
Year in SAMM[a]	.39	(.49)	.67	(.86)	.96	(1.20)
Dyad context						
Same grade	.27	(.44)	.25	(.43)	.20	(.40)
Same school	.23	(.42)	.23	(.42)	.21	(.41)
Teaching for understanding						
Ego's beliefs	3.40	(.27)	3.32	(.23)	3.34	(.25)
| Ego—other's beliefs |[b]	.41	(.31)	.33	(.25)	.38	(.28)
Ego's practices	11.48	(3.13)	11.06	(3.08)	11.33	(3.11)
| Ego—other's practices |[c]	4.12	(3.00)	4.04	(2.80)	4.38	(3.18)
Network controls						
Gregariousness	8.27	(11.60)	9.33	(12.48)	8.58	(9.11)
Popularity	2.08	(3.12)	2.21	(2.86)	1.67	(2.63)
Number of dyads	1,584		1,638		1,292	

Source: Authors' calculations.
[a]All egos were members of SAMM, but some joined after 1997. About one-third of others were members of SAMM.
[b]Absolute value of difference between ego's and other's beliefs.
[c]Absolute value of difference between ego's and other's practices.

1. Provide step-by-step directions for students to follow in solving problems (*scoring is reversed*)
2. Allow students to devise their own strategies to solve problems
3. Have students explain their approach to solving problems
4. Engage students in drill and practice in basic facts, definitions, computations, skills, or procedures (*scoring is reversed*)
5. Engage students in problem-solving or research that requires organizing and integrating knowledge
6. Ask questions that have well-defined answers (*scoring is reversed*)

7. Have students make conjectures in response to mathematical or scientific questions
8. Feel challenged by a student's question
9. Incorporate content based on students' social, cultural, or ethnic backgrounds into mathematics or science lessons

The following alpha reliabilities emerged from these results:

	1997	1998	1999
Teaching for understanding beliefs	.78	.59	.72
Teaching for understanding practices	.75	.77	.76

This paper was presented at the Conference Honoring the Career of Charles E. Bidwell at the University of Chicago, October 2001. The chapter was prepared at the National Center for Improving Student Learning and Achievement in Mathematics and Science, supported by funds from the U.S. Department of Education, Office of Educational Research and Improvement (grant R305A60007). Findings and conclusions are those of the authors and do not necessarily reflect the views of the supporting agencies.

NOTES

1. By "powerful content," we mean content that reflects core scientific and mathematical ideas and that draws connections between important areas of knowledge in science and mathematics.
2. "Technology" in this context refers to the materials and activities of the school's central organizational enterprise, that is, teaching and learning. To say that teaching is an uncertain technology means that relations of cause and effect are ambiguous and that different approaches may work out differently with different participants.
3. All names of persons, places, and programs are pseudonyms.
4. For these comparisons, other's membership and year in SAMM are set to one, as are same grade and school membership; other variables are set to their means, while teaching-for-understanding practices are set to low or high values as indicated.

Part III

The Microsociology of Schools and Classrooms

Chapter 7

The Normative Culture of a School and Student Socialization

Maureen T. Hallinan

For several decades, American schools have concentrated efforts and re-sources on improving students' academic achievement. Recent events in the United States, however, are leading schools to pay closer attention to the so-cializing function of education. Ongoing media coverage of situations endanger-ing American youth has raised public awareness of the problems they face. The American public has been sobered by school crime and violence, the rising inci-dence of adolescent suicide, and the destructive effects of drugs, alcohol, and sex-ual abuse. Business and community leaders are alarmed by secondary school dropout rates and the incidence of both unemployment and low-wage employ-ment among youth. Society as a whole is wrestling with persistent racial and eth-nic conflict.

In response to these situations, Americans are asking questions about how young people are socialized in today's society. In particular, attention is being fo-cused on the school, which, along with the family, is a primary socializing agent of children. Schools are being asked to reexamine the effectiveness of their efforts to train students to live and work together in school and later in a complex and di-verse society. In their attempts to respond to the challenge, schools are placing greater emphasis on preparing students to counter the negative pressures they face both in and outside of school. The goal of educators is to train students to con-tribute to the social and moral order of their school and prepare them for their fu-ture responsibility to maintain the moral order of society.

Despite the considerable goodwill evidenced by school personnel, their efforts to socialize students may not be as successful as the times require. Existing pro-grams, while adequate in the past, fall short of current demands on schools to pre-pare students to live in a complex, diverse environment. As a microcosm of soci-ety, the school reflects the stresses, strains, and dysfunctions of the adult world. The task of socializing students in this kind of complex and challenging environ-ment requires a better understanding of ways to influence students.

In a powerful heuristic essay in the *Handbook of the Sociology of Education*, Charles Bidwell (2000) states that little is known about the processes through which schools socialize students for adulthood. To address this need, he calls for a social psychology of schooling that would identify and explicate the socialization processes that occur in school. A theory is needed that explains contextual effects on individual behavior. The focus of the theory would be an individual's thoughts and sentiments. These states serve as crucial links between context and outcome. Following Bidwell's lead, this chapter examines the social psychological processes that link school context to student socialization. It focuses on how the normative culture of a school affects student cognitions and emotions and how these responses affect students' academic achievement, social participation, and moral development.

THE NORMATIVE CULTURE OF SCHOOLS: DIMENSIONS AND VARIATIONS

Émile Durkheim (1973) states that the cultural norms and values of the dominant members of society are embedded in the social practices and institutions of society. This is particularly true of educational institutions, since they aim to prepare students for adult life in society. The normative culture of a school typically reflects the norms of the wider society. Durkheim points out that a normative culture is comparable to a collective conscience and is part of the apparatus of social control. Group conscience interacts with individual volition. By influencing individuals to think and act in certain ways, a normative culture has significant social consequences. One of these consequences may be social solidarity, though other less desirable consequences also are possible.

The normative culture of a school is the set of norms, values, and meanings that are endorsed by significant members of the school community. As a key dimension of the social context of a school, normative culture is a major socializing agent. Previous research shows that the normative culture of a school influences students' attitudes and behaviors during their school years. Moreover, its influence on a student's civic participation and moral judgment continues into adulthood.

How the normative climate of the school affects student outcomes is one of the most vexing questions facing educators and researchers. If this process were better understood, educators might be able to create a normative culture that fosters positive student cognitive and social development. A theory that focuses on the mechanisms that link the normative climate of a school to student behavior should shed light on this complex and important process.

The Dimensions of the Normative Culture of a School

A school's normative culture typically has three components: norms governing students' academic performance, social behavior, and moral behavior. Norms related to academic achievement are defined by standards of excellence and expectations for performance. Norms governing social behavior encourage social participation and civic engagement. Norms regulating moral behavior ensure the moral order of the school community.

The set of norms most readily recognized in a school are expressed in the academic standards and performance expectations a faculty holds for student achievement. Since student learning is a central purpose of schooling, nearly all schools hold academic achievement high among their priorities. Schools encourage learning overtly through the curriculum, instruction, and a reward system. The curriculum defines the knowledge that students must attain in order to earn a diploma, and teachers convey that information through instruction. A reward structure motivates students to strive for academic excellence.

Schools also encourage learning covertly. Teachers indirectly communicate the value of learning and its impact on students' future lives in several ways. For example, faculty may have informal conversations with students about books they enjoyed reading, about their love of teaching as a profession, or about the opportunities their education provided for them. These covert messages may influence a student's attitude toward learning. When teachers show intellectual curiosity and enjoyment of learning, students may be drawn to appreciate the life of the mind and the satisfaction of learning. This may lead them to increase their own efforts to learn.

Norms related to student social and civic responsibility are seen in the rules and standards governing student participation in the social life of the school. While in school, students learn how to interact with adults and peers in various settings and under different contextual conditions. They learn interpersonal skills, such as negotiation, consensus-building, and strategizing. They are taught organizational skills and are given opportunities to be leaders, team players, and followers.

Schools also set norms regarding appropriate engagement in the community. Faculty teach students the value of pluralism, tolerance, diversity, and democracy. They instruct students in how to balance individualism, self-determination, meritocratic ideals, and personal rights with a concern for the common good. Schools provide the opportunity for students to observe the unequal distribution of societal resources and to understand the effects of social class. Students learn about authority and observe the ways in which adults use power. They discover what it means to be loyal to peers, to experience solidarity with a group, and to make a commitment to an institution. The lengthy social apprenticeship that occurs during school prepares students to live as responsible adults in the diverse communities of which they will be members.

Moreover, the social climate of a school influences students' attitudes toward social class, race, ethnicity, religion, sexuality, and politics. It is through social interactions that students learn the importance of individual rights and freedoms as well as community responsibilities. They also begin to understand that participation in the political process of a democracy is their right and duty. Ultimately, social participation in school is one of the mechanisms through which schools transmit to students their cultural heritage.

A third set of norms contributing to the normative culture of a school pertains to students' moral judgment and behavior. Durkheim (1973, 59–60) claims that "to act morally is to act in terms of the collective interest. . . . The domain of the moral begins where the domain of the social begins." Most schools teach students moral behavior based on a sense of justice and community responsibility. They also teach the personal and social consequences of amoral or immoral behavior. Norms governing social interactions are meant to prepare students to assume their adult responsibilities for safeguarding the moral order of society.

Norms related to moral judgment also extend to students' symbolic expression of their attitudes and values. Adolescents typically adopt a style of dress and behavior that reflects a set of shared meanings and messages, mostly related to independence and autonomy. Many schools place boundaries on these and other forms of student self-expression, establishing rules governing dress and behavior. Other schools grant students considerable leeway in this regard in an effort to teach them the value of political and social expression based on reason, discussion, and negotiation.

The Normative Culture of Schools in Practice

Differences in normative cultures occur both between and within schools. Theoretically, all schools set high standards for students' academic performance, social participation, and moral behavior. In practice, schools place more or less emphasis on each of these student outcomes. Differences in priorities create variation in normative environments across schools. As a result, not all students are socialized in the same way for higher education, the work world, and adult society.

When a school is founded, the administration and faculty define its mission in terms of general educational ideals and goals. A typical mission statement refers to academic excellence, social responsibility, and moral behavior. Mission statements usually prioritize these values, primarily in response to the characteristics and needs of the community in which a school is located. The mission statement in turn becomes a blueprint for the normative culture of the school.

The mission of a school tends to persist over time. Bidwell (2000) claims that the structural characteristics of a school, especially departmentalization and specialization, support faculty commitment to a school's norms and values. By giving teachers the autonomy and independence they desire for their work, schools are likely to reduce faculty disagreement and promote a sense of community. Of course, in some schools faculty independence and autonomy foster conflict and controversy rather than consensus. More typically, however, faculty view themselves as professionals and consider independence and autonomy to be requisites for their work. When faculty are recognized as experts in their field, their morale increases, as does their willingness to work together to achieve the school's mission. Ongoing commitment to a mission produces a stable normative culture. Given that schools differ in their missions, differences in normative culture persist across schools.

Differences in the priority that schools assign to academic achievement are related to characteristics of the student body that the school serves. Schools founded to educate high-ability students tend to hold high expectations for the academic achievement of all their students. Comprehensive high schools, established to educate a more diverse student population, have different academic expectations for various subsets of students, depending on their abilities and career goals. Schools that specialize in the arts or in the sciences, such as academies and magnet schools, tend to hold higher expectations for student performance in these subjects than in other academic areas. Vocational schools expect students to learn a set of job-related skills and may place less emphasis on outstanding performance in academic subjects.

A major part of schooling, especially at the middle and secondary levels, is the extracurriculum. Not all schools attach the same importance to extracurricular activities. Generally, faculty view participation in sports, music, drama, social service, and school clubs as an important dimension of student social development. In some settings, however, faculty perceive the extracurriculum as a threat to academic achievement and discourage students from too much involvement in these activities. Typically, schools encourage students to do well in academics and to participate in extracurricular activities, but they vary in the priority they give to each.

Schools also differ in the norms they establish regarding student civic and social participation. Some faculty place high priority on student involvement in the political life of the school and encourage participation in student government and community activities. In other schools, faculty emphasize the importance of student social behavior and stress the values of inclusiveness, tolerance, and respect for other students. Many, but not all, schools stress multiculturalism and encourage positive interracial and interethnic interactions and friendships among students with different demographic characteristics. Religiously oriented schools tend to prioritize student involvement in issues of social justice and equity, civil rights, and peace.

Finally, schools vary in how explicitly they teach moral values to students. Although most schools recognize the importance of moral training, they differ in how they present moral ideals. Some schools teach moral values directly—for example, by discussing justice issues and communal responsibility. Others present moral values indirectly, by establishing an honor code, by teaching conflict resolution techniques, or by acknowledging instances of courage, responsibility, and integrity. A more limited approach to moral education is found in schools that concentrate on appropriate behavior, such as deference, courtesy, punctuality, and discipline.

The normative culture of a school plays a major role in the socialization of students. Different normative cultures create different socializing experiences for youth. In schools that attach high priority to academic achievement, students are taught to be intellectually focused, studious, and competitive. Academic achievement is rewarded more readily than effort and self-mastery. Students learn to be intellectually aggressive, independent, and goal-oriented. In schools that try to integrate academic and social learning, students learn to balance academic accomplishments with social participation and are rewarded for positive social behavior as well as high grades and test scores. In religious schools, students are taught the primary value of faith and morality. They learn that they must assume responsibility for maintaining moral order in their school and later in society.

The question arises as to how much latitude a school has in setting its own normative climate. The founders of a school establish its normative culture through the school's mission statement. Schools, like most large social institutions, embrace change slowly and often reluctantly. Hence, a catalyst is usually needed to change a school's norms and values. In many cases, a new principal will be able to modify the climate of a school by exerting strong leadership. Another opportunity for change occurs when faculty turnover is high and a critical mass of new faculty introduce their ideas, norms, and values to the school. Vocal, involved students also may be able to shape school policy and practice and, in so doing, modify school norms. Typically, one or more of these catalysts is sufficient to produce some change, although at times not even the involvement of principal, faculty, and students can effect significant change in the normative climate of a school.

A social crisis also provides an opportunity for a school to change its normative climate. The tragedy at Columbine High School led to the establishment of programs to promote social tolerance among students and establish sanctions for destructive behavior, such as bullying. Recent follow-ups on these efforts indicate considerable success. Some schools have introduced curriculum units on civility, respect, and other forms of positive social behavior in response to acts of violence and incivility, and these too show positive results. The magnitude of crises such as these seems sufficient to motivate and mobilize a school community to change both adult and student norms.

Differences in norms and values may be found within as well as between schools. Teachers hold different assumptions about student learning and have different expectations for student performance. Within the same school, one may find teachers who believe that all students can learn and hold all pupils to a high standard of academic achievement; those who maintain high academic standards for students who show intellectual promise but lower standards for lower-ability students; and teachers who have low expectations for the achievement of those students who show little interest in academic work, create disturbances, or performed poorly in the past.

Similarly, teachers in the same school may differ in the emphasis they place on social behavior. While some teachers encourage students to participate in school activities in order to develop their leadership and organizational skills, others stress positive interpersonal relations in order to create a congenial social atmosphere in school and minimize interpersonal conflict. Politically oriented teachers stress the importance of civic involvement to prepare students for their future roles as citizens and community members. Other faculty attach low priority to non-academic achievements and resent their intrusion on instructional time.

Teachers in the same school also may differ in the emphasis they place on moral development. Even in religiously oriented schools, some teachers attach higher priority to moral training than others and devote more instructional time to discussing moral issues. In many schools, moral training is considered the domain of the administration or the counseling department. Teachers concern themselves with student moral development only to the extent that they sanction moral violations. Even teachers who are committed to moral education differ in the amount of instructional or informal time they devote to the issue.

When faculty and students adhere to the same set of norms, within-school conflict tends to be minor and school spirit and morale high. When a school does not have normative consensus, the likelihood of conflict is considerable. For example, if students ignore or violate norms governing academic performance, they obstruct teachers' efforts to promote learning. If students disagree among themselves about their priorities, student subcultures emerge, each with its own normative climate. As James Coleman (1961a) demonstrated, an adolescent subculture can exert a powerful influence on student behavior and weaken if not eradicate the positive influence of a school faculty. In general, schools with a dominant normative culture are most likely to channel the energies of students toward academic achievement and social and moral development.

Empirical Examples of High School Normative Cultures

Similarities and differences in the normative culture of American schools can be seen in several ethnographic studies. Empirical research by Bidwell (2000), Barbara Schneider and David Stevenson (1999), Anthony Bryk, Valerie Lee, and Peter Holland (1993), and John Devine (2000) is illustrative. In some of these schools, academic achievement is the single most important value that influences the formal and informal organization of the school and the behavior of its students. In other schools, faculty and students place considerable emphasis on co-curricular and extracurricular activities. Excellence in these activities provides an alternative to academic achievement as a way to attain faculty and peer respect. In some schools, religious values are stressed as the motivation for academic and non-academic efforts. Specifying differences in normative cultures across schools provides the groundwork for analyzing how normative culture influences students' cognitions and emotions.

Bidwell (2000) describes the normative culture of two midwestern high schools: Meriwether Lewis and St. Aloysius. Lewis High School was established in the early 1930s to serve the children of highly educated parents who worked in the research laboratory of a major company. The mission of the school was to prepare these students for selective colleges in anticipation of high-level careers. An array of extracurricular activities provided additional opportunities for excellence. Given its mission, the normative culture of the school required teachers to offer rigorous instruction, to be competent in their subject area, and to show concern about students' academic progress. Students were expected to strive for academic excellence and to practice personal discipline and sociability.

St. Aloysius High School, a Roman Catholic diocesan school, was founded in the early twentieth century to educate the children of Eastern European immigrants. The mission of the school was to create opportunities for students to become upwardly mobile by preparing them for admission to competitive colleges and universities. Like Lewis High, the school held strong norms of excellence for academic achievement and athletic performance. The reputation of the school enabled it to be selective and to enroll students who were academically capable and serious about their education.

In the 1980s, economic and demographic change dramatically influenced the normative cultures of these two high schools, weakening their strong orientation toward academic excellence. In the Lewis High School community a severe reduction in employment opportunities for professionals led many well-educated families to leave the area, leaving behind lower-middle- and working-class families. The children of these families had weaker academic preparation for high school and lower educational aspirations. This change in the student population directly affected the ability of the faculty to fulfill its mission and to uphold their high standards of academic excellence.

Despite the fact that they found the transition difficult, most teachers at Lewis had too much invested in the school to transfer elsewhere. They reacted to the change by faulting the students for failing to meet the high standards of the faculty. Students responded with disengagement and apathy. Their attitudes further reinforced the faculty perception of their inadequacies. By holding rigidly to its original mission, the faculty evoked student resistance that in turn had serious negative consequences for student learning. The powerful academic culture that had previously characterized the school disintegrated and was replaced by a more diffuse normative culture that had less power to motivate students to strive for academic excellence.

Demographic and labor market changes affected St. Aloysius in a similar manner. When budget deficits forced significant increases in tuition, enrollment in St. Aloysius dropped. The community and school faced an influx of Hispanic students who knew little English and were ill prepared for schooling. During this transitional period, some older faculty resigned and a younger, more diverse group of teachers was hired. The older faculty who remained in the school tried to uphold its original mission. Like their counterparts at Lewis High, these teachers accused students of a lack of discipline when student performance failed to meet their expectations. The newer teachers realized, however, that many of the students were ill prepared for the St. Aloysius curriculum and began offering new courses geared toward expanding life experiences and readying students for community colleges rather than competitive four-year colleges. Two normative cultures emerged in the school. In the first, academic achievement was of primary importance, and students gained recognition for their academic successes. In the other, life experiences were recognized and respected as building blocks for future educational and vocational decisions. The students were exposed to both of these somewhat conflicting sets of norms as they took classes from different teachers. Over time, the normative culture of the school became less clear, and the school began to have a more tenuous hold on student commitment and effort.

In an insightful analysis of the educational ambitions of high school students, Schneider and Stevenson (1999) describe the normative culture of three contemporary high schools: Maple Wood, Middle Brook, and Del Vista. Although each of these schools encourages student achievement, they represent three distinct normative cultures. The schools differ dramatically in the emphasis they place on academic excellence, college aspirations, and career preparation.

Maple Wood High School places heavy emphasis on students' career goals. Its clearly defined mission is to help students identify an occupational objective and take the necessary educational steps to attain it. The normative culture of Maple Wood High School includes the firm expectation that students and their families will plan for the students' future and make academic choices that further their goals. The curriculum consists of a wide array of courses that expose students to various career options. Counselors offer systematic and frequent advice about course selection and choice of college. The value of career planning is the most dominant component of the school's normative culture.

Middle Brook High School has strong norms of academic excellence. Its aim is to prepare students for admission to a highly prestigious college. The focus of the school is on educational attainment and academic prestige rather than career preparation. All students are encouraged to apply to at least one highly competitive college. This "reach strategy" underscores the value the school places on academic achievement. The school offers honors and advanced placement courses. Since extra credit is not awarded for these classes, some students select less rigorous courses to ensure a high GPA for college admissions purposes. In contrast to Maple Wood High, Middle Brook emphasizes strategies for admission to prestigious colleges rather than enrollment in courses that would advance a student's career goals.

Known as a "forgiving school," the aim of Del Vista High School is to graduate all of its students. The curriculum is designed to include courses that all students are likely to pass. Faculty focus on ensuring that students do not drop out of school, and both teachers and counselors direct their efforts to helping students obtain a sufficient number of credits to earn a high school diploma. Del Vista encourages its students to enroll in college, but the emphasis is on two-year colleges rather than four-year colleges. The faculty recognizes the flexibility provided by a community college system as an advantage for their students. If students fail in one community college, they can simply enroll in another to continue their career training.

Each of these three high schools values academic achievement, but in different ways and for different reasons. Maple Wood provides students with the best possible preparation for their specific career choices. Counselors and teachers guide students toward the colleges that would best prepare them to meet their career objectives rather than those with the greatest academic prestige. Middle Brook emphasizes the importance of admission to the most prestigious colleges and devotes little time to discussing specific career objectives with students. Del Vista's aim is to help all students attain a high school diploma and then to attend a career-oriented community college.

Bryk, Lee, and Holland's (1993) research on contemporary Catholic schools provides examples of secondary schools with strong academic norms supported by a religious belief system that motivates student adherence to these norms. The seven high schools in their study varied by socioeconomic status, racial and ethnic composition, ability composition, and percent Catholic. The sample included urban, suburban, and rural schools, of varying sizes and resources. Despite these considerable differences, each of the schools emphasized academic achievement, as evidenced by the quality of the curriculum and the fact that virtually all students were enrolled in college preparatory classes. The schools also exhibited strong social norms and a sense of community. Students were taught to respect each other, to take responsibility for the common good, and to be loyal to their school. Supported by a set of religious beliefs, high academic standards, and a caring school community, the schools motivated and sustained students' efforts to learn and had a positive influence on their social behavior and moral judgment.

Devine's (2000) ethnographic research provides an example of a school with a dramatically different normative culture. The 126 public high schools in New York City are divided into a three-tiered hierarchy. At the top are four prestigious, specialized high schools that admit only those students who pass a competitive examination. The middle tier includes dozens of academic-comprehensive high schools that offer a curriculum that prepares students for college or a specialized career. Other middle-tier schools are regular high schools that offer a few college preparatory courses. In the bottom tier are forty to fifty schools characterized by low test scores, poor attendance, and, most significantly, high rates of violence.

Devine's (2000) study focuses on students who began ninth grade in one of the low-tier schools. He finds that new students are faced with peers who have belligerent attitudes, may carry weapons, and are fearful for their safety. On entering school each day, students pass through security devices and are frisked. During the school day disorder and violence reign in the form of alarms, gang activity, gunfire, and threats. Frequently the violence is camouflaged or ignored by adults and students. In general, the school may be characterized as having a culture of violence. Academic expectations are low, since the students are poorly prepared for and uninterested in high school work and distracted by the school atmosphere.

The normative culture of this low-tier school is influenced by many factors. First, the educational policy that created and continues the hierarchical structure of New York City schools and assigns students to these schools is insensitive to the greater needs of educationally disadvantaged students. Second, the faculty is demoralized by the futility of their efforts to educate. Third, the students feel defeated and have little hope for improvement of their life chances. Fourth, the students who enroll in the school may begin high school with attitudes and behaviors that shape the negative environment of the school. The resulting normative culture perpetuates the academic, social, and moral disorder of the school and its students.

These ethnographic studies are illustrative of the variety of normative cultures that exist in U.S. schools today. Some schools have a single, pervasive normative culture, typically one that stresses academic achievement. Other schools promote both academic goals and extracurricular participation. Still other schools view religious or moral training as their primary mission. Finally, while some schools try to promote academic achievement, they are forced to prioritize other values, such as student safety and control of student deviance.

Transmittal of School Norms to Students

Bidwell (1972) states that a normative culture is transmitted through channels to which an individual attaches significance. When the normative culture of a school is determined primarily by the faculty, it is transmitted to students in several ways. In general, norms governing academic performance, social development, and moral behavior are conveyed through school practices and policies.

Norms pertaining to the academic performance of students are communicated through the curriculum, the organization of instruction, school admission policies, written documents, verbal exchanges, rewards and punishments, and modeling. A school with a rich and diverse curriculum that meets the needs of all students underscores the high priority it attaches to academic achievement. The same is true of a school that assigns students to instructional groups that facilitate their understanding of the curriculum. Similarly, a school that maximizes the amount of time allocated to instruction while minimizing competing demands on students' time conveys the school's academic priorities.

The qualifications required for admission to a school are a clear statement of its values. While public schools must admit all students who apply, private schools can be more selective. Schools reveal their priorities, such as high achievement or religious affiliation, in their admission policies. The mission statement or philosophy of the school also provides a broad vision of the school's aims and goals, as do other written documents, such as the school paper, the yearbook, and the student handbook. These documents convey social and behavioral norms and provide examples of acceptable moral behavior.

A school also communicates its norms and values through the emphasis it places on non-academic activities. Schools convey the importance of social development by establishing co-curricular and extracurricular programs and by encouraging students to participate in them. They promote civic participation by establishing a student government and by allowing students to participate in decisionmaking with respect to school issues. They communicate the value of social service and community involvement by creating opportunities for students to participate in these activities.

The normative culture of a school is also transmitted to students through the school's reward system. Schools reward students for outstanding performance in different areas. The basis on which awards are made reveals the school's priorities. Most schools recognize academic excellence and award medals, trophies, and certificates for academic achievement. Schools also may recognize student effort even when high achievement levels are not attained. In doing so, the school teaches students the importance of working hard to reach their maximum potential. Schools also reward exceptional performance in athletics, music, drama, and other activities, indicating the value of social participation and teamwork. The importance of adhering to school norms is reinforced when a student violates a rule or regulation and the school imposes a penalty.

Other ways in which a school transmits its normative culture to students are through verbal exchanges between teachers and students and through modeling. Teachers communicate their expectations for student academic, social, and moral behavior through their own exhortations, encouragement, and reprimands. Students typically respond to teacher encouragement by increasing their motivation and effort. Teachers also convey school norms by modeling appropriate behavior. For example, when students see that teachers are serious about scholarship and eager not only to teach but also to learn, they receive a powerful message about the value the faculty attaches to education. Similarly, if teachers participate in social and civic activities, become involved in issues of social justice, and themselves live up to a moral code, students are given direct evidence of the norms and values that the school endorses.

THE EFFECT OF NORMATIVE CULTURE ON STUDENTS' COGNITIONS AND EMOTIONS

The potential of a school's normative culture to influence a student's cognitive, social, and moral development highlights the importance of understanding how a student responds to a school's norms and values. In other words, how do students hear a school's messages about academic achievement, social participation, and moral behavior, and why do students respond to these messages as they do?

Bidwell (2000) argues that the normative culture of a school acts on students by affecting their intellectual and psychological states. That is, he sees students' thoughts and feelings as the link between the normative culture of the school and their responses to that culture. To predict whether students will internalize a school's normative culture, it is necessary to understand how the normative culture affects their cognitions, including their thoughts, judgments, evaluations, and analyses, as well as their emotional responses, such as pride, guilt, anger, and satisfaction.

Students vary in their intellectual and socioemotional needs, owing to their widely disparate backgrounds, cultural influences, intellectual abilities, career aspirations, and life goals. As a result, compliance with the normative culture of a school satisfies the needs of some students better than others. Similarly, since schools differ in their normative cultures, one school may meet a student's intellectual and psychological needs better than another. Academically oriented students are likely to comply easily with school norms of academic excellence because those norms satisfy these students' intellectual needs. Schools that value both extracurricular achievements and academic performance are likely to meet the needs of a wider set of students for recognition and status. Neither of these types of schools is likely to meet the intellectual and emotional needs of students who find learning difficult or who are reluctant to participate in the extracurriculum. Better correspondence between the normative culture of a school and the intellectual and psychological needs of students results in a wider acceptance of the school's normative climate.

Social science theories provide insight into how the normative culture of a school affects a student's intellectual and psychological states. Normative reference group theory (Bidwell 1972; Kelley 1947; Merton 1957a) states that a normative reference group is one that sets standards for an individual's behavior. An individual may aspire to membership in a normative reference group or wish to maintain existing membership. The group sets and enforces standards for that individual's behavior.

A school performs the function of a normative reference group for students. When they first enter a new school, students must learn how to navigate in a new environment. They recognize the importance of engaging in normative behavior in order to become integrated into the school. Further, to maintain the rewards of recognition and status that accrue to membership in the school community, they need to continue complying with school norms.

If students accept as legitimate the authority of the school to set norms of conduct, they are likely to internalize the school's normative culture. Compliance with school norms is greater when students recognize that it promotes their intellectual and emotional growth. On the other hand, if the norms of a school do not meet students' intellectual and psychological needs, or if students feel that school norms are ill conceived or outdated, they are likely to search for cognitive stimulation and emotional satisfaction in some other group.

Student peer groups may or may not provide a powerful challenge to the authority of the school in enforcing its norms. Members of a peer group are expected to comply with the norms established by the group. Although many peer groups have norms that are consistent with school norms and reinforce or complement those norms, others endorse norms that conflict with the school's normative culture. When school and peer group norms conflict, a student must choose between the two. The norms that are most attractive to students are those that define behaviors that best meet their own intellectual and emotional needs. If a student peer group is better able than a school to provide a student with respect, status, and a sense of belonging, then students are more likely to comply with the norms of the peer group than those of the school.

Coleman's (1961a) landmark research on the adolescent subculture makes clear that student norms can hinder academic achievement by supporting behaviors that are guided by non-academic goals. Athletic skills and physical attractiveness are among the most common bases for student popularity, and norms governing student interactions and behaviors are influenced by these personal characteristics. Seymour Spilerman (1971) and Coleman (1961a) recommend that schools create a status system that is based on social as well as academic goals. In this way, they argue, students may choose not to reject the normative culture of the school while modeling their behavior on that of peer group members. Further, school efforts to build students' self-esteem by rewarding them for working toward social and academic goals might lessen the attraction of deviant peer groups and weaken their negative influence.

Organization theory sheds further light on how the normative culture of a school influences a student's cognitive and psychological states. Alvin Gouldner (1960) claims that organizations increase employee cooperation and productivity through rewards. Peter Blau and Richard Schoenherr (1971) link rewards to loyalty to the organization; greater cooperation and loyalty increase productivity. Similarly in schools, rewards have a direct influence on students' thoughts and feelings and their subsequent behavior. When a school rewards students for compliance with school norms, they feel like valued members of the school community. This increases their loyalty to the school and their willingness to comply with school norms. Students whose efforts and achievements are not recognized or appreciated will have unmet intellectual and emotional needs, resulting in resistance to school norms and disengagement from the school's academic and social activities.

One organizational characteristic of a school that conditions the impact of the normative culture on students' thoughts and feelings is the arrangement of students for instruction. Most contemporary middle and secondary schools assign students to instructional groups on the basis of their ability. Students experience the normative culture of a school differently depending on the ability group level to which they have been assigned. Students placed in the highest-ability groups are most likely to have personal goals that are consistent with the school's norms. The challenging curriculum provided in high-ability groups and the affirmation that students receive for their academic accomplishments increase their intellectual and emotional satisfaction, thus reinforcing their compliance with the school's norms. Students in lower-ability groups may question whether they can meet the school's academic standards. If they are not offered a challenging curriculum or fail to receive recognition for their efforts to learn, they are likely to reject the school culture because it provides few channels for them to attain intellectual and emotional satisfaction.

Teachers may meet the intellectual and emotional needs of students in different ability groups by tailoring instructional materials, pedagogical practices, and student rewards to the ability level of the group. In so doing, a distinct classroom subculture may emerge with rules and regulations that fit the intellectual abilities and maturation level of the students in the class. Teacher expectations and teacher-student interactions during instruction have an impact on students' thoughts and feelings. This is particularly true in middle and secondary schools where students are prone to embarrassment and feelings of inadequacy when they do not perform well before their teacher and peers. Regardless of ability group level, a teacher who presents a clear, organized lesson and encourages students' efforts to learn has a positive effect on students' confidence and feelings of self-worth. Teachers who are critical of student efforts or who communicate low expectations for student performance are likely to instill feelings of failure in their students. In a classroom in which positive learning experiences and rewarding social exchanges are the norm, students' intellectual and emotional needs are apt to be met.

Social psychological theories of interpersonal relations provide additional insights into how normative culture affects an individual's cognitive and emotional states. Symbolic interactionism is concerned with how an individual's self-image is shaped in interaction with others. Symbolic interactionists claim that during social interaction, individuals evaluate their own abilities and worth and form their identity through the feedback they receive from others. Social interactions also help them evaluate other people, events, and objects in their environment.

Applied to a school setting, symbolic interactionism suggests that students develop an understanding of themselves as they interact with teachers and peers. Students measure themselves against the norms established by the school and the abilities of their peers. If teachers convince students that they are capable of attaining school goals, students are likely to form a positive self-image. Similarly, if students meet academic challenges, they come to believe in their intellectual abilities. Positive social experiences with teachers and friends give a student a sense of being a valued member of the school community. Students who develop a feeling of intellectual competence and social adequacy are likely to be satisfied with school, while those who develop a weak self-image are apt to become alienated from school.

Psychological theories of human development shed further light on how the normative climate of a school affects a student's psychological state. Abraham Maslow (1943) proposed a hierarchy of psychological needs that individuals strive to satisfy. He claimed that once an individual's basic need for survival (food, shelter, safety) is met, higher-level psychological needs are satisfied through interpersonal interactions. According to Maslow, individuals first seek a sense of affiliation with a group, then strive for self-esteem, and finally, endeavor to attain self-actualization. Maslow's theory suggests that if a school's norms and values lead students to engage in behaviors that satisfy their need for affiliation, self-esteem, and self-fulfillment, they are likely to comply with the school's rules and regulations.

A social cognitive perspective (Connell and Wellborn 1991; Ryan 1995) on human maturation suggests that social context influences whether the cognitive and emotional needs of an individual are met. Applying this perspective to schools, Gail Furman (1998) argues that schools need to meet a student's need for social acceptance, trust, and safety. By providing experiences in which students learn to trust others and feel secure in a safe environment, and by supporting positive social relations and healthy interpersonal relations, a school helps students to grow intellectually and emotionally. When students' cognitive and social needs are met, they are more likely to have a positive self-image and a positive attitude toward school values.

These social science theories linking the normative climate of a school to students' cognitive and emotional development point to the importance of a good fit between students' intellectual and psychological needs and the norms and values of their school. Students whose school environment supports their desire to know and their need for self-fulfillment are likely to have a more positive attitude toward the school than those whose cognitive and emotional needs remain unmet. A normative culture that is characterized by a supportive learning and interpersonal environment is likely to produce satisfied and cooperative students engaged in cognitive and social growth.

STUDENT RESPONSES TO THE NORMATIVE CULTURE OF A SCHOOL

Students' responses to the normative culture of a school depend on the extent to which the school meets their cognitive and emotional needs. Students whose values are consistent with those reflected in the school's normative culture are likely to have a positive attitude toward the school and comply with its rules and regulations. If their values differ from or are inconsistent with those promoted by the school, then they are likely to resist the school's socializing efforts.

Teachers and students benefit from student compliance. For teachers, instruction is easier when students are cooperative and engaged in learning. Teachers' sense of efficacy increases when students are learning. Student academic progress raises teacher morale and increases teachers' commitment to the school. Teacher turnover tends to be lower in a school where teachers are satisfied with their teaching experience. Students also benefit from compliance with school norms. When students obey the rules governing their academic work, their performance improves. Students who participate in school activities are better integrated into the school community and develop a sense of pride in their school. Students also benefit from conformity to school norms by experiencing the orderliness and satisfaction of adherence to a moral code that regulates ethical and social behavior.

When a school fails to meet the intellectual and psychological needs of students, they become critical of the school's normative culture. Students may judge that the school's academic standards are too high and not appropriate for them, that participation in school and community activities is unimportant, or that the school's norms are irrelevant or outdated. The more detached or dissatisfied students become, the greater their alienation from the school and the more likely they are to disregard or defy school rules and regulations. If student resistance is widespread, it weakens the spirit of community that faculty and students strive to develop in their school.

When students resist the normative culture of the school, the faculty is faced with the difficult task of changing students' attitudes and behavior. They need to convince students that they will benefit from compliance with the school's code of behavior. Several mechanisms may be useful, such as rewards for compliance, negotiation, joint student academic and social projects, student modeling, peer tutoring, cooperative learning methods, and training in conflict resolution. If these efforts are unsuccessful, both teachers and students are less satisfied with the schooling experience. Teachers are less efficacious in promoting student learning and social development, and students are less successful academically and in terms of social integration into the school community.

In most schools, even students who generally comply with school rules and regulations occasionally challenge school authority. Interestingly, limited deviation from the norms of the school may be beneficial to students. Bidwell (2000) argues that complete compliance with school norms and standards deprives students of opportunities to make moral judgments and effect social change. Schools that are characterized by a certain amount of student resistance provide opportunities for students to reflect on their own goals and objectives and determine how to attain them. In the process, they are required to think about such issues as authority, equity, and democratic processes. Social conflict challenges students to make moral judgments and participate in social and political processes.

In schools with more than one dominant normative culture, such as St. Aloysius or Lewis High School, students may have to choose the norms and values they find most appropriate for their own particular situations. Interaction with teachers and peers whose views are similar to their own reduces normative conflict. The opportunity to observe faculty and peers with different norms and values can be a learning experience for students and help them better define their own values. In multicultural schools in particular, where student background, culture, language, home experience, and educational background differ widely and where the faculty endorse different values, students may come to respect other value systems and understand why people think and act differently. If they learn to accept and value diversity, they are better prepared to live in a diverse adult society.

CONCLUSION

The normative culture of a school plays a major role in socializing students for adulthood. School norms aim to encourage students to develop their cognitive abilities, engage in positive social interactions, develop a sense of responsibility for their school and community, and follow a moral code. Students who comply with the rules and regulations of their school are more likely to cooperate in the learning process and to act as responsible members of their school community. In the process, they become better prepared for future educational and occupational opportunities and for the social and civic responsibilities they must assume as adults.

The potential for the normative culture of a school to foster student intellectual, social, and moral development makes it critical to understand how students respond to the normative climate of their school and how it affects their attitudes and behaviors. Building on Bidwell's (2000) insights, this chapter has examined the effects of the normative culture of a school on student behavior as mediated through students' cognitions and emotions. As Bidwell suggests, students have basic cognitive and emotional needs that must be met before they will cooperate with a school's efforts to socialize them. On a cognitive level, students need intellectual stimulation, a challenging curriculum, motivation to study, and a sense of accomplishment. On an emotional level, they need to have a sense of self-worth, of belonging to a group, and of trusting and being trusted by teachers and peers.

A school can meet these intellectual and psychological needs of students by establishing norms and standards that support students' cognitive and emotional growth. In a supportive learning and social climate, students develop a positive attitude toward school and are predisposed to obey its rules and regulations. If the intellectual challenges and social relationships that students experience in school fail to meet their developmental needs, they are likely to resist school norms and risk becoming alienated from their school.

Understanding that a school's normative culture is linked to student outcomes through the students' cognitive and emotional needs should encourage school personnel to examine whether their efforts to socialize students take this linkage into account. A normative culture that promotes learning for all students and rewards participation in school activities should meet students' cognitive and emotional needs. When students are intellectually challenged and emotionally satisfied, they are more likely to comply with school policies. Student compliance in turn makes classrooms and schools easier to manage, allowing teachers to further promote student cognitive and social development. In the end, students grow intellectually and socially and become better prepared to assume future responsibilities in adult society.

This chapter was prepared for a conference in honor of Charles E. Bidwell at the University of Chicago, October 6, 2001. The author is grateful to the Institute for Educational Initiatives at the University of Notre Dame for research support and to Warren Kubitschek, Stephanie Arnett, and Cheryl Pauley for research and editorial assistance.

Chapter 8

Why Work When You Can Play? Dynamics of Formal and Informal Organization in Classrooms

Daniel A. McFarland

During the 1990s, Charles Bidwell began to focus on the nature of faculty networks and how properties of these networks define instructional practice within schools (Bidwell, Frank, and Quiroz 1997; Bidwell and Yasumoto 1999). While his current work furthers this effort, he has also started to think about the student's world of learning and how it is related to the teacher's world of instruction. In effect, he has begun to reconceptualize schools as organizations to focus on explaining the actual work and interaction that occur within the technical core of schools. His recent integration of social psychology and actors' definitions of situations into his theoretical accounts of organizations is a sign of this reconceptualization. This move can partly be seen in his use of particular concepts and themes—formal *and* informal organization, social networks, school and classroom regimes, participation and interaction. Most recently, Bidwell (2000, 2001) has called for research on classrooms and detailed study of individual schools. Such research would catalog and describe various social processes, practices, and interactions that affect how the work of schools gets done.

This chapter follows Bidwell's call and presents a study of high school classrooms that integrates elements of both organizational theory and social psychology. In substantive terms, this chapter asks and answers a series of questions: Why are some classrooms "madhouses" and others calm and work-focused? Why are some individuals much more vocal than others in tasks and/or sociable forms of participation? And what distinguishes task and sociable forms of participation? What characteristics of classrooms and students matter for participation? What types of relations among students and teachers facilitate or inhibit such actions or inaction?

Empirically, these questions are concerned with educational settings and the behaviors within them. Theoretically, however, they are concerned with the determinants of definitional claims or dominance within informal and formal dimensions of organizational life. What leads certain classrooms and students to stake active definitional claims of a formal or informal nature? What are the levers of task (work) and sociable (play) forms of conduct?

The interplay of the formal and informal dimensions of schools has long been described in the sociology of education. Beginning with Willard Waller (1932), we find early descriptions of how the world of youth is always beyond the reach and comprehension of educators and all too often acts at odds with educational aims. Later work by James Coleman (1961a) and Arthur Stinchcombe (1965) picks up on this theme and describes how informal and formal dimensions of high schools become oppositional, the former acting as the "under-life" of the latter (Eisenstadt 1956; Goffman 1961). Bidwell's (1965) seminal chapter on the school as a formal organization summarizes this literature, contending that most arguments draw attention to structural characteristics of schools and their environments. Remiss in these accounts is a characterization of classroom life and how such oppositions manifest within them. This chapter seeks to contribute to this body of literature by describing how organizational features at multiple levels of analysis influence classroom behavior.

This chapter argues that classroom participation is greatly influenced by various structural characteristics of classroom settings and individuals' status resources. Particular characteristics of classrooms and individuals within them create rigid or porous normative boundaries to formal and informal organizational conduct. On the one hand, an intuitive finding emerges from this chapter: forms of conduct, types of status, and classroom relational structures all have dimensional specificity such that formal and informal organizational dimensions are recognized and maintained. On the other hand, there is a subplot: the informal world of adolescents is brought to bear on almost every classroom task, while the formal world of academic work is often ignored and rejected in the sociable affairs of youth (Coleman 1961a). Thus, while boundaries of formal and informal organization are present, the social world's boundary is rigid and the academic world's boundary is porous, thereby creating a somewhat unidirectional flow of influence on classroom participation. The sections that follow present a series of conceptualizations and research efforts to describe and explain this story of classroom participation.

DIFFERING QUALITIES OF TASK AND SOCIAL PARTICIPATION

Traditional experimental work in sociology makes a distinction between task and socioemotional behavior. Task behavior is value-neutral and concerns the instrumental goals of a collective activity, while socioemotional behavior expresses positive or negative emotions (Bales 1947, 1950/1970; Bales and Slater 1955; Burke 1967, 1971). Early organizational theorists rely a great deal on the distinction between task and socioemotional behavior as a basis for differentiating formal from informal organization (Argyris 1957; Barnard 1938; Lawrence and Seiler 1965; Sayles 1963).

Conversation analysis of workplace communication and sociolinguistic studies of schools, however, suggest a slightly different picture. Such analyses find that, at work, discourse can be concerned with either the completion of formal tasks or informal non-task-oriented situations (Edelsky 1981; James and Drakich 1993). Informal social discourse is seen to arise when subjects "talk about anything" or "just get to know one another." Similarly, sociolinguistic studies of school discourse make a similar claim and distinguish task and social interaction.

According to these analyses, what matters is the *form* and *content* of discourse (Alton-Lee, Nuthall, and Patrick 1993; Mehan 1980; Sieber 1979; Streeck 1984), not necessarily the presence of "socioemotions." With respect to content, task discourse is described as teacher-centered and concerned with school topics. In contrast, social discourse is described as decentralized and concerned with movies, TV, music, dating, gossip, parties, shopping, rock concerts, and sporting events (Doyle 1986; Sieber 1979). With respect to form, informal social discourse is even identified with certain activities that have interaction rules distinct from those used in class tasks, such as gossip, collaborative storytelling, and ritual teasing (Eder 1988, 1991, 1995; Eder and Enke 1991; Goodwin 1980).

The problem remains, then, of identifying the distinguishing characteristics of informal social conduct. Recent work in status characteristics theory has already revisited and attempted to revise the traditional distinction between task and socioemotional behavior, and between formal and informal situations. Cecilia Ridgeway and Cathryn Johnson (1990) argue that socioemotional behaviors often arise as part and parcel of completing a task. Therefore, they classify certain agreements and disagreements as task behaviors because the emotions observed are entirely elicited by task concerns. This reconceptualization suggests that task behaviors entail emotional responses insofar as the behavior is motivated by tasks and/or has work as its content. As such, it is the content or purpose of an act (that is, if it concerns tasks) that makes it identifiable as a form of conduct, not the correspondence with the action's latent functions of goal attainment or integration.

In light of relatively new research in sociolinguistics, this chapter takes Ridgeway and Johnson's (1990) argument one step further. Within the activities of gossip, teasing, and "getting to know one another," persons interact with informal sociable concerns in mind (Huizinga 1950; Simmel 1949), and they may or may not express emotions in the process. In this chapter, formal task conduct is regarded as turns of interaction that are concerned with the completion of tasks prescribed by the organization and its agents. In contrast, informal social conduct is regarded as turns of interaction that pertain not to the completion of prescribed tasks but rather to personal or external topics and more sociable affairs of play (Garvey 1990). According to this conceptualization, socioemotional behavior can pertain to tasks and/or social affairs, and actors express anger, frustration, joy, and criticism in their efforts to control both work and play activities (Ridgeway and Johnson 1990). Thus, the "socioemotional" is not the criterion for categorizing as formal versus informal. Granted, emotive behavior is more overt in sociable affairs since action is given looser reign (see McLaren 1986). Nonetheless, task and sociable behaviors are regarded as distinct dimensions of organizational conduct with different topics and styles of discourse.

TWO LEVERS OF PARTICIPATION: CONTEXTS AND STATUSES

What are the causal levers that make some classrooms and students more vocal in task and/or sociable affairs? When actors enter organizational settings like classrooms, they make decisions about how to act, and these decisions are framed by the definition of the classroom situation (Bidwell 2000, 2001; Thomas 1923). Such definitions are partly characterized by the classroom context, or the social opportunities, political climate, and status resources that individuals have at their discretion.

Contexts and Participation

Descriptions of *formal and informal contexts*, and particularly of relational channels, have long been the forte of organizational studies of work settings. For the most part, these studies describe how work gets accomplished through formally prescribed role relations and emergent friendship relations (Blau 1963; DiMaggio 1992; Gouldner 1954; Ibarra 1992; Krackhardt 1992, 1993; Selznick 1949). A common finding is that work often gets accomplished outside the prescribed roles and relations of tasks and that workers rely on their friends to achieve organizational goals. Hence, studies of organizations suggest that there are distinct organizational contexts (of formal and informal relational channels) through which tasks and social affairs are enacted.

Classroom contexts have sets of work routines that are prescribed by the teacher and define students' *social opportunities*, or access to public discourse in tasks. Moreover, repeated tasks establish a pattern of work relations that entail certain expectations and norms of conduct. In teacher-centered classes, the persistent use of lecture, recitation, and other didactic forms of instruction renders students passive participants—or at most, co-participants following the teacher's lead (Goffman 1981). In student-centered classes, the persistent use of group work, collaborations, and discussions renders students active participants—or co-authors who direct their own learning experiences (Bossert 1979; Doyle 1986; Metz 1978; Stodolsky 1988). Student-centered tasks demand active task participation, while closed task structures focus interactions on the teacher and particular students and therefore create very different opportunities for task involvement and patterns of work relations.

Classrooms also entail friendship relations that define the *political climate* of the setting. Some friendship structures are sparse and centered on certain individuals. These contexts tend to be contentious and judgmental and to inhibit socializing except between close friends (Fine 1987; Giordano 1995). Other networks have wide reach and entail dense sets of interrelated friends. These contexts not only provide students with interpersonal support but make interpersonal demands—that friends socialize with one another and maintain that role relation in spite of the demands of class tasks (DiMaggio 1992).

The structure of tasks and of friendships defines different role expectations and relational channels through which work and play are enacted. Clearly, work routines establish expectations for task participation, and primary group relations establish expectations for sociable participation. As such, these routines and relationships act as structural anchors to different types of conduct and establish a degree of *dimensional specificity* across structure and conduct. However, the organizational literature suggests that informal relations can affect task behaviors and that formal work routines can affect informal social conduct (Krackhardt 1993; Roethlisberger and Dickson 1939). That is, there is *translation across formal and informal organizational boundaries*—where formal relational channels become avenues to play and informal relational channels become avenues to getting work done (Bidwell 2000; Powell 1990). This makes sense if we assume that natural settings entail multiple situations and that participants have multiple identities and role relations with respect to one another (McFarland 2004).

If we construct a table that cross-classifies the types of conduct with the types of relational channels, we acquire a property space with which to describe work and play as they become enacted in different relational dimensions of the classroom. In table 8.1, some cells identify channels and forms of conduct that are consistent with traditional boundaries of formal and informal organization (for example, dimensional specificity is identified in the upper left and lower right cells), while others identify interdimensional translations, where the structure of work routines alters the affairs of play and where friendship networks mediate the conduct of work. A central empirical question of this chapter is when and where dimensional

TABLE 8.1 / Cross-Classification of Organizational Contexts with Types of Conduct

Types of Conduct	Organizational Contexts	
	Formal or Prescribed Relational Channels	Informal or Emergent Relational Channels
Task or work	Formal relations used in work. Example: staying within prescribed channels to get work done (for example, following task rules).	Informal relations used in work. Example: going outside prescribed channels to get work done (for example, using friends).
Sociable or play	Formal relations used in play. Example: staying within prescribed channels to socialize about topics unrelated to work.	Informal relations used in play. Example: going outside prescribed channels to socialize about topics unrelated to work.

Source: Author's compilation.

specificity and interdimensional translation occurs across structural contexts and forms of conduct (work and play).

Status and Participation

While organizational research informs us about different contexts for action, status characteristics research informs us about the *resources* that actors use to dominate interactions (McFarland 2001). When actors have certain status characteristics, such as a reputation for being smart or popular, they are given access to discourse. When actors lack those status characteristics, they are perceived as illegitimate participants. In the research on classrooms, two local status characteristics are repeatedly described as highly salient to dominance behaviors: local academic and peer status (Cohen and Lotan 1997a).[1] Local statuses are described as being quasi-independent of the diffuse status characteristics of race, class, and gender, which are found to be salient in controlled laboratory experiments (Berger, Cohen, and Zelditch 1972).

Even though research on classrooms has identified academic and peer bases of status, researchers almost always collapse them into a single status measure for their statistical models (Cohen and Lotan 1997a). In her work on elementary school classrooms, Cohen collapses these types of status because she finds academic and peer status to be highly aligned. However, recent work on middle school classrooms has found that these types of status can be unrelated or even opposed to one another (Chiu 2000; Cohen and Lotan 1997b). Ming Ming Chiu (2000) finds these status characteristics to be distinct from one another and also finds them to have independent effects on student outcomes.

Nevertheless, research on expectation states has not expanded the scope conditions beyond collaborative group activities. Moreover, it has repeatedly ignored the sociable behaviors that arise within such activities. Even though peer and academic status are viewed as quasi-independent, they are not hypothesized to have different behavioral referents. This chapter argues that when status dimensions diverge, dimensional specificity of status and conduct occurs. Students with highly regarded academic reputations are considered more appropriate participants in tasks because they reputedly have high competence in schoolwork. In contrast, students with a great deal of social rapport are considered more appropriate participants in social affairs because they are better liked and are considered social leaders by their peers. In either type of activity, there are distinct notions of reputation, competence, and legitimacy that define active participants. When academic and peer status oppose one another, participation in one type of interaction undermines the actor's legitimate participation in the other type of interaction.

Table 8.2 cross-classifies the types of conduct with peer and academic status and defines a property space with which to describe status effects on classroom participation. In the table, some cells (for example, the top left and bottom right cells)

TABLE 8.2 / Cross-Classification of Types of Status with Types of Conduct

	Types of Status	
Types of Conduct	Academic-Status Political Resources	Peer-Status Political Resources
Task or work	Academic status salient in work. Example: formal leader dominates work.	Peer status salient in work. Example: informal leader dominates work.
Sociable or play	Academic status salient in play. Example: formal leader dominates play.	Peer status salient in play. Example: informal leader dominates play.

Source: Author's compilation.

identify the expected relationship between types of status and types of conduct—dimensionally specific correspondences between play and peer status and between work and academic status. Other cells identify more surprising relations between types of status and types of conduct—interdimensional translations, where academic status can alter the affairs of play and where peer status can mediate the conduct of work. Whether dimensional specificity or interdimensional translation occurs between types of status and conduct is another question addressed in this chapter.

I argue that participation in classroom tasks and sociable situations is partly dictated by the structure of work activities and friendship relations, as well as by a student's academic and social status within the setting. Clearly, classrooms can be composed of both dense networks and student-centered tasks, each having similar effects on student conduct. Likewise for status: peer status and academic status may encourage task and/or sociable participation. By analytically distinguishing these types of contexts and statuses, I attempt to identify their independent effects on task and sociable forms of participation in classrooms. By devising a statistical model that includes separate variables for each of these contexts and statuses (and controls for diffuse statuses), I can identify which types of organizational contexts and statuses have additive, independent effects on participation in academic and social affairs and thus determine why some classes and individuals are more academically and socially vocal than others.

Settings

The data analyzed were collected in a yearlong field study of task and sociable participation in thirty-six classrooms (for details, see McFarland 1999, 2001). Two schools serve as the settings for the analyses in this chapter: River High and Magnet High. River High is a traditional, tracked high school located in "River Town," a small midwestern town with 17,500 residents, located approximately 100 miles from a large metropolitan area. The high school has around 1,600 students and serves a community population of approximately 25,000 residents. Most students are from River Town, but one-third come from significantly smaller towns and outlying rural areas. Almost all of the residents are white, and only 3 percent of the population consists of racial minorities.

Many River Town students and faculty regard students from the outlying regions and small towns as provincial and regard themselves as more cosmopolitan. This status distinction is somewhat solidified by feeder patterns into the high school. Within River Town, students attend the same large middle schools, while other residents of the region are spread out across multiple smaller middle schools. Upon entering River High, the rural residents are at a social disadvantage in terms of familiar others (Schiller 1999). They begin the year with less extensive social networks to buffer them from the "hick" status attributed to them by classmates and teachers.

Magnet High is very different from River High. It is located over 500 miles away from River Town in a dilapidated neighborhood of a large city. Magnet High has around 900 students enrolled in grades eight through twelve. The student body is racially and economically heterogeneous and is bused in from all over the city. The student population is 50 percent white, 35 percent African American, 10 percent Latino, and 5 percent Asian American. Magnet High is, as the name implies, the school district's arts and sciences magnet school that admits students on the basis of test scores. Hence, while its population may be economically and racially diverse, it is homogeneous in terms of ability. Students and faculty at Magnet distinguish one another according to race and wealth. Race is a salient characteristic at Magnet primarily because of residential segregation. Whites often live on the outskirts of the city, while African Americans and Latinos live in the center.

Data

I use several sources of data for the study of student participation within classrooms: classroom observations, surveys, and school records. At each school, classroom observations focused on tenth- and twelfth-grade core subjects (English, math, history, and science). An effort was made to span the different course ability levels in tenth and twelfth grade. Core subjects were selected for observation because they were more readily comparable across schools. Moreover, in a policy climate that stresses increasing standards in core subjects, it was thought important to understand the learning process that takes place within the "canon" of American high schools. Tenth and twelfth grades were observed for more pragmatic reasons as well. It was apparent that a single researcher could not observe the entire population of students at these schools, and tenth- and twelfth-grade students had been the focus of a prior study that took place at both sites (for a description of the earlier study, see Csikszentmihalyi and Schneider 2000).

In all, an average of twelve class periods for each of thirty-six classes were observed over the course of the 1996 to 1997 school year. This focal set of thirty-six classes entailed a sample of 751 students who were observed during the first semester. Only twenty-five of these classes persisted into the second semester, providing a sample of 467 students for longitudinal surveys and observation. There are thus two samples: one larger cross-sectional sample and a longitudinal subsample.

CLASSROOM OBSERVATIONS   Each class's use of different activities (Stodolsky 1988) was recorded, and exchanges among classroom participants were enumerated. Instead of videotapes, a shorthand method of coding interaction turns was used with a great deal of accuracy in the more controlled classroom environments. In more open classrooms, several turns of interaction sometimes arose simultaneously and in a less sequential fashion. This made full enumeration difficult even though patterns of interaction were recorded accurately. To compensate for this discrepancy the observer estimated the proportion of interaction exchanges recorded for that segment; later, the rate of interaction was adjusted accordingly. The observation data used in quantitative analyses rely on the coding of student-initiated turns at interaction in either task or social activities. The coding of student-initiated turns at interaction is preferable to initiate-reply sequences since replies are often implicit. Student-initiated turns are observable claims.

SURVEYS   Two different surveys were administered to students during the school year, and one was administered to teachers. The first student survey was classroom-specific and administered to students in the thirty-six focal classrooms (95 percent response rate). The survey included a sociometric form that asked students to nominate classmates whom they hung around with as friends (McFarland 1999). This classroom survey was administered in November and again in April. The second survey, administered only once in April 1997, did not focus on the particular classroom setting but asked students about their lives in general. This form asked students to describe their family and their parents' occupations. In addition, it included a sociometric form that asked students to list the friends whom they hung around with outside of class and on weekends (Csikszentmihalyi and Schneider 2000). It acquired information on the student's social network outside of the classroom, whereas the sociometric surveys asked about friendships specific to the classroom setting.[2]

SCHOOL RECORDS   School records provided an array of information. Course schedules and transcripts list information on student courses, grades, and grade levels. The names of guardians and addresses were used for identifying family types and census block tracts (both were checked for reliability with survey information). Yearbooks were used to obtain reliable information on students' voluntary associations in clubs and sports. Yearbook pictures, coupled with observation, and school records provided reliable information on race and gender.

Academic and Social Participation

Multilevel regression models were used to predict the rate of task and sociable participation and to distinguish the effects of classroom contexts from individuals' status characteristics. Rates of participation were operationalized as ego-initiated turns at interaction with other persons or groups within the classroom (out-degree centrality by semester; see Freeman 1979). These acts were observable communications expressed by classroom participants. Rates of participation were commonly used in expectation-states theory as an indicator of the prestige and power order of groups (Cohen and Lotan 1997a) and as an indicator of dominance (Edelsky 1981; James and Drakich 1993).

Two types of participation were analyzed: task (academic affairs) and social (non-academic sociable affairs). Academic participation was defined as those turns of interaction that pertain to the concerns of class tasks (Borgatta and Bales 1953a, 1953b). When teachers gave directions or information, made declarations, and elicited comments during tasks, they were viewed as engaged in task-related interactions; similarly, when students discussed, replied, and asked questions while performing academic tasks, they were viewed as engaged in task-related behavior. Of course, students and teachers could engage in other dyadic encounters as well, such as when a teacher assisted an individual student or the student solicited the help of a neighbor. As already mentioned, task behaviors can also take socioemotional forms (Ridgeway and Johnson 1990). Examples of this would be a student complaining about a task or a teacher praising appropriate behaviors.

When socializing, actors engage in a range of different loosely structured activities unrelated to tasks, such as "getting to know one another" (James and Drakich 1993), games or contests (Corsaro 1994; Corsaro and Rizzo 1988; Maynard 1985), teasing (Sanford and Eder 1984; Eder 1991), collaborative storytelling (Eder 1988), and gossip (Eder and Enke 1991; Goodwin 1980), to name but a few. The topics of social interaction frequently refer to adolescents' lives outside the class, such as sports, dating, jobs, parties, fights, social occasions, TV and movies, music, and generally "fun" or exceptional experiences they had during the day (Sieber 1979). Like task interaction, social interaction can entail socioemotional forms of behavior, such as personal insults and praise.

Rates of participation in tasks and social events were measured as the number of outwardly directed interactions that a student performed in a classroom per hour (as averaged for each semester).[3] Note that the unit of analysis was a student within a classroom, not the student's behavior across classrooms. Also note that rates of participation have a skewed distribution across students and classrooms. Clearly, some classrooms and students are far more vocal than others. To predict rates of participation, a log transformation was used in predictive models. The log of the rate of participation made the dependent variable normally distributed so that it acquired more reliable standard errors in statistical models.[4] (A more detailed description of variable construction and descriptive statistics for each variable are available from the author.)

Explanatory Variables

The substantive question addressed by this research is: which classroom and student characteristics are associated with which types and rates of participation in classrooms? Four sets of variables were hypothesized to influence classroom behaviors: status (resources), social opportunities (task structures), political climates (networks), and habit.

Students have different *status resources*, or status characteristics, that enable them to be accepted participants in classroom affairs. A large body of research describes how the status characteristics of actors bias perceptions such that unequal levels of competence in tasks are attributed to persons holding such characteristics (Berger, Rosenholtz, and Zelditch 1980; Cohen and Lotan 1997a). I defined status at three levels of specificity: societal, school, and classroom. Diffuse status characteristics are the most abstract characteristics of a student and have societal-level referents. I argue that *diffuse statuses* like race, gender, and socioeconomic class are translated into more *specific statuses* within social settings like classrooms. The logic here is that students with higher status ranking (whether diffuse or specific) are viewed as more legitimate participants and are afforded greater rights to discourse. Some of this work even suggests that physical attractiveness acts as a diffuse status characteristic affecting the expectations attributed to actors in tasks (Patzer 1985; Webster and Driskell 1983). In this analysis, certain measures refer to diffuse statuses acquired in and across various domains of social life. Diffuse status characteristics were measured by the student's racial background (minority for Magnet High), urban or rural residence (for River High), gender (female), maturity level (grade level), type of family (traditional nuclear family or not; see Astone and McLanahan 1991), the family's occupational status, and the student's physical attractiveness.[5]

A more specific status characteristic pertains to the student's standing within the school. For example, a student's *academic standing in the school* was defined by grade point average (akin to class rankings). Students enter classes with cumulative grade point averages and class rankings that define an academic biography and rank-position in relation to their peers. Those with high G.P.A.s and rankings are generally known as good students, and such characterizations may lead them to perform well across all classes, regardless of the classroom context. This measure was developed as a relative G.P.A. rank within each school.

While academic status is one characteristic that might increase academic participation, *social status or popularity* among peers may have a different effect altogether (Bidwell 1965; Coleman 1961a; Cusick 1973; Gordon 1957). Certain students enter classrooms as highly regarded in the school and are generally more sought after as friends than other students. We can hypothesize that prominence in the school gives students greater self-esteem and willingness to participate in every class setting. The measure for popularity in the school is the number of selections a student received as a friend outside of school.[6]

A third level of status specificity, *local status in the classroom*, is distinct from societal and school levels (Cohen and Lotan 1997a). Status in the classroom setting depends in part on the external statuses that students possess in society and the school, but they are also highly defined by the composition of the class and events that arise within the classroom itself. As status becomes more specific, its value is more constructed by the local context and emergent processes therein.

At this level, *local academic status* is the relative academic rank a student possesses in a class. For example, when everyone in a class gets a D except for one student who gets a C, then that student's local academic status is relatively high, but his or her academic status in the school is relatively low (assuming the student has a C average). Similarly, *local social status* is the relative popularity rank a student possesses in a class. Just because someone is highly regarded in school does not mean he or she is well regarded in a particular classroom setting. A classroom may be composed of twenty thespians and one externally popular cheerleader whom the thespians intensely dislike. In such a setting, popularity in the school carries little weight.

By differentiating classroom status from school status, it is possible to test whether school or classroom standing brings the student the most legitimacy as a dominant player in academic or social affairs. Moreover, including both levels of status reveals the effect of being popular in school net of being popular in class. Similarly, for academic status we can discern the effect of being a good student in school net of being a good student in class.[7] By distinguishing status characteristics by such levels of specificity, we can determine which status characteristics are salient and how they are used. The basic idea of status resources, whether diffuse or locally specific, and whether translated or emergent, is that they enable actors to take advantage of the classroom social context.

Even though they have different status resources at their discretion, students are influenced by a definition of the classroom situation that may make those resources more or less salient. In particular, the *social opportunities* of tasks and the *political climate* of student friendships create a context wherein greater or lesser amounts of participation occur. These characteristics of the classroom setting have uniform effects on learning experiences and are therefore classroom-level phenomena.

Social opportunities to take the floor are partly determined by the *instructional format* used (Doyle 1986). Centralized tasks like lectures and recitations limit access to the floor. In contrast, decentralized tasks like group work allow greater access at the expense of monitoring and control. These rules of access and levels of monitoring are presented equally to all participants in a classroom activity. Repeated use of certain activities leads actors to expect certain social opportunities and norms of appropriate behavior.

The availability of these social opportunities was defined by the proportion of time that classes spend in more centralized formats of instruction (Bossert 1979; Doyle 1986; Metz 1978; Stodolsky 1988). These controlled activities consist of lectures, recitation, films, and exams. During such segments, access to peers and the public stage is very constrained. Other activities also entail controlled behaviors but are more loosely monitored, such as seatwork. There, student behavior is partly contained but given some degree of freedom in most settings, such that neighbors can quietly talk with each other. Given that these types of instructional formats constrain interaction, I constructed a measure of *teacher-controlled instruction*,

$$\text{Teacher-controlled} = \text{Lecture} + \text{Recitation} + \text{Films} + \text{Exams} + (.5) \times (\text{Seatwork}), \tag{8.1}$$

that was designed to capture task constraints on access to public discourse.

Unfortunately, giving students the social opportunity to interact does not always result in greater participation (Stein, Grover, and Henningsen 1996). A teacher may use the same format all day, but each class reacts somewhat differently. Some classes will take advantage of social opportunities more readily than others because of the political climate among peers. Within classrooms, the political climate is defined by the *pattern of friendship relations* (Diani 1996). If friendships become more densely interwoven and feelings of positive sentiment are evenly distributed, then the climate is friendlier and allows more students to take advantage of social opportunities without fear of reprimand or ridicule (Fischer 1977; Giordano 1995). If friendships are sparse and centralized, then the climate seems somewhat unfriendly and more uncertain to participants, thereby discouraging the participation of all except select individuals. The mobilization potential, or the participation capacity of a classroom, is thus partly a function of the overall shape of the informal social network (DiMaggio 1992). A diffuse or centralized relational structure can block collective participation, while a densely interwoven and egalitarian structure can facilitate it.

The mobilization potential of a classroom network was operationalized as the linear combination of the *density* of classroom friendships and the *spread* of positive sentiments. The density of a network was measured by the total number of friendship ties divided by the number possible. The spread of positive sentiments was calculated as one minus the Gini coefficient for student centralities in a classroom (that is, in-degree centrality; see Freeman 1979). The Gini coefficient was a measure of status inequality ranging in value from zero to one (McFarland 1999; Plank 2000a). Subtracting it from one provided a measure of status equality. These two variables were combined (friendly classroom relations = density plus [one minus Gini in-degree]),[8] thereby capturing the extent to which an informal friendship network was interconnected and equal.

Distinct from status but relevant to social standing is the density of friendships a student experiences within the classroom (Borgatti, Everett, and Freeman 1999). This notion of *egocentric density* is somewhat different from the friendliness of a classroom setting as it pertains to the local relational set of a particular student. As more of a student's friends select each other as friends, the ego becomes more situated in a tight clique where norms and behaviors are reinforced. These closed local networks can place demands on students to recognize and cater to his or her friends. It is expected that dense egocentric networks will hinder task participation and facilitate sociable participation, net of the classroom's political climate.

A final social mechanism salient to participation concerns *habit*. The inertia or stability in presentations of self, or the tendency of prior action to reinforce similar future behavior, is often overlooked in current sociological research. However, George Herbert Mead (1934) and other pragmatists regarded habituation a central mechanism guiding much of human behavior. This work suggests that past patterns of interaction will become routine and that the actor will often behave on "autopilot." To ascertain the effect of past behaviors, a simple measure for first-semester rates of task and sociable participation was used as a control in the longitudinal models.

Multilevel Framework

This chapter employs a multilevel framework to predict rates of student participation in task and sociable affairs (Bryk and Raudenbush 1992; Frank 1998). A multilevel framework fits not only the substantive question but also the data structure, and it overcomes biases that would occur in typical OLS analysis. Participation is nested within students and classrooms, so a multilevel framework is appropriate. Standard regression analysis is not an adequate method because it assumes that coefficients are fixed between groups and that error terms are uncorrelated. To achieve unbiased parameter estimates, I developed multilevel regression models using SAS statistical software (see Littell et al. 1996; Singer 1998).[9] A two-level model overcomes aggregation bias and the mis-estimation of standard errors common to traditional OLS analysis and helps to accurately discern group-level (classroom-level) and individual-level (student- by classroom-level) effects on task and social participation in classes. I report estimates of the effects of classroom characteristics on the log-transformed rate of participation, controlling for a number of independent variables. For these estimates, I specified a two-level, random intercept model where level two consists of classrooms and level one consists of students in classrooms:

$$\log (y_{ij} + 1) = \beta_{0j} + \beta_1 x_{ij1} + \beta_2 x_{ij2} + \ldots \beta_{kj} x_{ijk} + \varepsilon_{ij} \tag{8.2}$$

$$\beta_{0j} = \gamma_{00} + \gamma_{01}(\text{classroom characteristic}) + \ldots + \delta_{01} \tag{8.3}$$

Instead of treating β_{0j} as representing a set of fixed constants, I assumed that each β_{0j} is a random variable with a specified probability distribution.

In sum, multilevel regression models predict whether characteristics of status (be they diffuse or at the school or class level) and classroom organizational characteristics (the social opportunities of prescribed tasks and political climates of informal networks) are associated with heightened participation in task and social affairs of classrooms.

RESULTS

The first set of analyses ascertains whether the variance in task and social participation can be explained by classroom characteristics as distinct from individual

TABLE 8.3 / Decomposition of Variance for Task and Social Participation

Variance Components	First Semester	Second Semester	Second Semester Net of First
Task participation			
Classroom-level variance τ_{00}	.14	.14	.06
Individual-level variance σ^2	.39	.42	.16
Intraclass correlation ρ	.27	.25	.16
Social participation			
Classroom-level variance τ_{00}	.23	.30	.15
Individual-level variance σ^2	.62	.61	.44
Intraclass correlation ρ	.27	.33	.25

Source: Author's compilation.
Note: ρ indicates the proportion of total variance that occurs between classrooms: $\rho = \tau_{00}/(\tau_{00} + \sigma^2)$.

properties. By partitioning the variance within and between classrooms, it is possible to demonstrate the proportion of variance in participation attributable to individual or contextual characteristics (Sampson, Morenoff, and Earls 1999).

The variance decomposition is illustrated in table 8.3 for an unconditional model of first- and second-semester participation. Intraclass correlations reveal the proportion of total variance explained between classrooms.[10] In every model, the variance in rates of participation (first semester, second semester, and net increase) is substantially attributed to classroom-level variation. Anywhere between 6 and 30 percent of the total variation in participation can be attributed to classroom characteristics. In short, student participation is only partly influenced by their characteristics and their particular situations.

Tables 8.4 through 8.7 present results of multilevel regression models. Tables 8.4 and 8.6 present cross-sectional results for the first semester, or the factors initially associated with higher rates of task and sociable forms of participation. Tables 8.5 and 8.7 present longitudinal results, or factors associated with increased rates of task and sociable participation in classrooms.[11] As such, the tables reveal initial associations and then slopes for growth. Within each table, standardized coefficients are listed to allow for comparison of the magnitude of effects across different variables.[12]

Background Effects

Several general findings emerge from the results in tables 8.4 through 8.7. The first set concerns the effects of student background and diffuse status characteristics on participation. In general, students' diffuse status characteristics play a larger role in sociable interactions than task interactions. In tables 8.4 and 8.5, background variables fail to significantly improve the models of task participation. Surprisingly, minority race at Magnet and family structure more generally have no signif-

TABLE 8.4 / Cross-Sectional First-Semester Models: Multilevel Coefficients from the Regression of First-Semester Task Participation (Log) on Selected Predictors

Explanatory Variables (N = 751)	Model 1 b*	Model 2 b*	Model 3 b*	Model 4 b*
Intercept	___***	___***	___***	___**
Background variables				
Magnet minority[a]	.04	.05	.05	.05
River town[a]	−.23**	−.23**	−.24**	−.18*
River rural[a]	−.16*	−.16*	−.17**	−.12
Female gender	.02	.01	.00	.00
Lower grade level	.02	.01	−.01	.00
Non-nuclear family	−.02	−.01	.00	.00
Highest parent occupational status	.04	.04	.03	.03
Missing occupational status	.00	.04	.03	.03
Physical attractiveness[b]	.12***	.11**	.06	.06
Standing in school[b]				
Academic standing in school		.11**	.08	.07
Social standing in school		.03	−.04	−.04
Standing in class[c]				
Academic standing in class			.07*	.07*
Social standing in class			.20***	.20***
Density of ego's network			.03	.02
Classroom characteristics[d]				
Teacher-controlled instruction				−.17*
Friendly classroom relations				.14
Likelihood ratio χ^2				
Unconditional model comparison (df)	−8 (9)ns	−9 (11)ns	16 (14)ns	23 (16)ns
Prior model comparison (df)	−8 (9)ns	−1 (2)ns	25 (3)***	7 (2)*
Log likelihood	1,508.7	1,509.3	1,484.7	1,477.6

Source: Author's compilation.
Note: b* = β (s_x/s_y). Percentage change = exp (b*) −1. To get raw data, b = exp (b* (s_x/s_y)) −1.
[a]Magnet majority is the baseline comparison group for regional variables.
[b]These variables are mean-centered within each school.
[c]These variables are mean-centered within each classroom.
[d]Classroom characteristics are level-two variables with N = 36.
*p < .05; **p < .01; ***p < .001

icant effect on classroom behaviors. However, there are significant effects of diffuse status characteristics for place of residence, gender, occupational status, and physical attractiveness.

River High students start the year less vocal in task and sociable affairs than Magnet youth, but then their participation grows at a steeper rate over the course

TABLE 8.5 / Longitudinal Models: Multilevel Coefficients from the Regression of Second-Semester Task Participation (Log) on Selected Lagged Predictors

Explanatory Variables (N = 467)	Model 1 b*	Model 2 b*	Model 3 b*	Model 4 b*
Intercept	—***	—***	—***	—
Past participation				
Task interaction (log)	.47***	.43***	.42***	.40***
Social interaction (log)	.01	.04	.02	.00
Background variables				
Magnet minority[a]	.06	.08	.08	.07
River town[a]	−.02	−.01	−.02	.10
River rural[a]	.07	.07	.07	.14*
Female gender	−.05	−.08*	−.08*	−.08*
Lower grade level	.02	−.01	−.01	.04
Non-nuclear family	.04	.05	.05	.05
Highest parent occupational status	.07	.05	.06	.06
Missing occupational status	−.16***	−.14***	−.13***	−.13***
Physical attractiveness[b]	.10*	.09*	.07	.08*
Standing in school[b]				
Academic standing in school		.18***	.18***	.18***
Social standing in school		.08*	.06	.06
Standing in class[c]				
Academic standing in class			.01	.00
Social standing in class			.10*	.10*
Density of ego's network			−.07+	−.08*
Classroom characteristics[d]				
Teacher-controlled instruction				−.30**
Friendly classroom relations				.18+
Likelihood ratio χ^2				
Unconditional model comparison (df)	5 (9)ns	17 (11)*	14 (14)ns	27 (16)*
Prior model comparison (df)	5 (9)ns	13 (2)**	−4 (3)ns	13 (2)**
Log likelihood	864.1	851.5	855.1	842.4

Source: Author's compilation.
Note: $b^* = \beta\,(s_x/s_y)$. Percentage change = exp $(b^*) - 1$. To get raw data, b = exp $(b^*\,(s_x/s_y)) - 1$.
[a]Magnet majority is the baseline comparison group for regional variables.
[b]These variables are mean-centered within each school.
[c]These variables are mean-centered within each classroom.
[d]Classroom characteristics are level-two variables with N = 36.
+$p < .10$ (for classroom level only); *$p < .05$; **$p < .01$; ***$p < .001$

TABLE 8.6 / Cross-Sectional First-Semester Models: Multilevel Coefficients from the Regression of First-Semester Social Participation (Log) on Selected Predictors

Explanatory Variables (N = 751)	Model 1 b*	Model 2 b*	Model 3 b*	Model 4 b*
Intercept	—***	—***	—***	—
Background variables				
Magnet minority[a]	.04	.04	.03	.03
River town[a]	−.19*	−.18	−.19*	−.10
River rural[a]	−.14	−.13	−.14*	−.08
Female gender	.06*	.07*	.05	.05
Lower grade level	.08	.07	.02	.03
Non-nuclear family	.04	.04	.05	.06
Highest parent occupational status	.04	.05	.04	.04
Missing occupational status	.03	.02	.01	.01
Physical attractiveness[b]	.19***	.17***	.10**	.10**
Standing in school[b]				
Academic standing in school		−.08*	−.03	−.04
Social standing in school		.09*	.00	.00
Standing in class[c]				
Academic standing in class			−.08*	−.08*
Social standing in class			.32***	.32***
Density of ego's network			.10**	.09**
Classroom characteristics[d]				
Teacher-controlled instruction				−.17*
Friendly classroom relations				.25**
Likelihood ratio χ^2				
Unconditional model comparison (df)	23 (9)**	30 (11)**	127 (14)***	145 (16)***
Prior model comparison (df)	23 (9)**	22 (2)***	96 (3)***	19 (2)***
Log likelihood	1,816.6	1,809.4	1,713.1	1,693.9

Source: Author's compilation.
Note: b* = β (s_x/s_y). Percentage change = exp (b*) −1. To get raw data, b = exp (b* (s_x/s_y)) −1.
[a]Magnet majority is the baseline comparison group for regional variables.
[b]These variables are mean-centered within each school.
[c]These variables are mean-centered within each classroom.
[d]Classroom characteristics are level-two variables with N = 36.
*p < .05; **p < .01; ***p < .001

of the year than that of Magnet students. The rate of growth in River's participation is not steep enough to catch up to the initial advantage that Magnet students have, but it is worth asking why the schools differ in this way. Magnet High contains smaller cohorts of students who take more of the same classes than do River students. Hence, many Magnet students know each other at the start of the year,

TABLE 8.7 / Longitudinal Models: Multilevel Coefficients from the Regression of Second-Semester Social Participation (Log) on Selected Lagged Predictors

Explanatory Variables (N = 467)	Model 1 b*	Model 2 b*	Model 3 b*	Model 4 b*
Intercept	—***	—***	—***	—
Past participation				
Social interaction (log)	.41***	.40***	.38***	.38***
Task interaction (log)	.12**	.12**	.11*	.10*
Background variables				
Magnet minority[a]	.00	.01	.01	.01
River town[a]	−.07	−.06	−.07	.00
River rural[a]	.11	.12	.11	.16*
Female gender	.00	.00	.00	.00
Lower grade level	.02	.00	.00	.04
Non-nuclear family	.06	.06	.06	.06
Highest parent occupational status	.07*	.08*	.09**	.09**
Missing occupational status	−.11***	−.11**	−.10**	−.10**
Physical attractiveness[b]	.15***	.13***	.12***	.12***
Standing in school[b]				
Academic standing in school		−.02	−.03	−.04
Social standing in school		.10**	.07*	.07*
Standing in class[c]				
Academic standing in class			.03	.03
Social standing in class			.09**	.09**
Density of ego's network			−.04	−.05
Classroom characteristics[d]				
Teacher-controlled instruction				−.15
Friendly classroom relations				.22*
Likelihood ratio χ^2				
Unconditional model comparison (df)	30 (9)***	28 (11)**	24 (14)*	33 (16)**
Prior model comparison (df)	30 (9)***	−2 (2)ns	−4 (3)ns	9 (2)*
Log likelihood	959.1	961.3	964.9	955.9

Source: Author's compilation.
Note: $b^* = \beta \, (s_x/s_y)$. Percentage change = exp (b*) −1. To get raw data, b = exp (b* (s_x/s_y)) −1.
[a]Magnet majority is the baseline comparison group for regional variables.
[b]These variables are mean-centered within each school.
[c]These variables are mean-centered within each classroom.
[d]Classroom characteristics are level-two variables with N = 36.
*p < .05; **p < .01; ***p < .001

while students at River often start out with a lot of strangers in the classroom. When the school year commences, River students are uncertain of their surroundings and more cautious when participating than their Magnet peers. As the year gets going, however, acquaintances become friends and River students start to interact more.

Even though gender has no association with initial rates of task participation, males tend to become slightly more vocal in tasks over the course of the school year. Much of the literature on gender and dominance suggests that boys are more vocal in tasks (Lockheed, Harris, and Nemceff 1983; Ridgeway and Diekema 1989), and perhaps more so in the second semester after social ties and classroom norms have been learned (McFarland 2001). After students "learn the ropes" and come to understand the rules of the game, they are more inclined to adopt learned strategies of action that fit their individual dispositions (for example, boys become more aggressive). Why this does not also arise with respect to sociable participation is unclear and requires further analysis.

Interestingly, students who did not provide information on their parents' occupational status are less involved in tasks and sociable affairs over time. Moreover, this effect occurs net of their absences, suggesting that they lessen their participation even when they do show up for class. These students did not provide complete survey responses because they attended class less and less often as the year progressed. Owing to their absence, their membership in the setting and familiarity with daily affairs diminished, and in turn so did their efforts to participate.

Students with parents of higher occupational status tend to become more sociable as the year progresses. These are wealthier students who can afford nice clothes, the "in" haircut, a car, and who have money for social events. Much of the literature on social crowds makes much of social class distinctions in relation to the adolescent world, so it is of little surprise here (Brown 1986, 1989; Canaan 1987; Eckert 1989; Kinney 1993). Since these resources are more salient to the adolescent society than formal tasks, it makes sense that they encourage sociability.

In comparison to other diffuse status characteristics, physical attractiveness is the most salient to classroom affairs. Physical attractiveness is especially associated with sociable behavior and increased involvement in playlike endeavors. Students who are physically attractive have a status resource that enables them to enter conversations (as attractive) and defuse tense situations they encounter (for example, translating them from task to flirting routines). The relevance of physical attractiveness and sexuality to adolescent relations and adolescent-adult interaction is no surprise to most anyone who observes American secondary schools (Webster and Driskell 1983).

School and Classroom Standing

By themselves, background characteristics do not afford the best model of task and sociable participation (see likelihood ratio χ^2). Local status positions in the school and classroom greatly define who can and cannot take a dominant part in the aca-

demic and sociable affairs of classrooms. A student's academic and sociable standing in the classroom plays an important role in defining his or her initial access to
discourse.[13] In particular, popular students in the class are more vocal in both work
and play routines in the first semester. As such, popularity is a versatile resource
that enables the youth to enter any public stage that arises in the setting. In contrast, high academic standing in the class inhibits a student's access to the play activities around them.[14]

Over time, being a good student in the school (high G.P.A. rank) has a greater relation to increased task participation than merely being a good student in that specific classroom setting. Academic standing in the school becomes more relevant
over time as teachers and peers learn of a student's academic reputation. Although
it is true that students achieve at similar levels across school years, teachers initially know very little about a student's past performance. By second semester,
general expectations are established and transferred across particular settings.
Local perceptions of ability, focus, and performance are salient during the first semester, but by second semester the G.P.A. rank of a student is more established as
a salient status characteristic.

Accompanying the effect of G.P.A. rank in the school is the effect of local social
standing in the classroom. Locally popular kids, not "big men on campus" or
"homecoming queens," are more likely to engage in tasks and social activities. This
seems like an odd result, since G.P.A. rank in the school is more related to task participation than local academic standing. Why is popularity in the school less relevant
to task and social dominance than local social status in the classroom? G.P.A. rank is
more salient because it is a standardized measure that can be transposed across settings for use. Teachers and students in one class know just as well as those in another
what an A means. In contrast, there is little consensus on which social crowds are
liked and disliked within the adolescent society. Therefore, local peer support is
more salient to task and social participation than popularity in the school.

A final characteristic of students' individual situations concerns their social networks. The density of an egocentric network has an interesting relation to participation and increased dominance in classroom affairs. Students whose friends are
also friends with one another seem to be less participatory in tasks over time and
initially more vocal in the play activities around them. This effect is thought to
arise because dense friendship relations place social demands on students that remain fairly consistent over the course of the year, owing to the network's closure.
A closed social network, however, demands that the student show allegiance to
friends and therefore makes increased participation in competitive tasks undesir-
able and possibly contradictory to the logic of the group norm (that is, the student
feels pressured to not be a rate-buster; see Homans 1950).

Classroom Characteristics

Thus far, I have discussed only the effects of students' individual characteristics
and their egocentric situations. However, the fitness of the multilevel regression

models significantly improves with the inclusion of two classroom characteristics reflective of the formal and informal organizational contexts that students uniformly encounter in a classroom setting. Results in tables 8.4 through 8.7 indicate that activity structures are more salient to levels of classroom task participation, while the degree of equality and interrelatedness of friendship relations is more salient to sociable affairs, both cross-sectionally and over time. Hence, there is a degree of dimensional specificity. However, the structure of work initially influences play behavior in the classroom, defining its bounds. Over time, task structures become less salient as students learn to maneuver norms and expectations to socialize in spite of them. Similarly, the structure of informal relations has a causal influence on task behavior over time. Friendly contexts encourage increased interaction, especially after students become familiar with the setting. Overall, the more student-centered work routines become, and the more egalitarian and developed friendly classroom relations become, the more vocal a class becomes in general. As work becomes centralized and interpersonal relations become diffuse and centralized, the level of participation diminishes.

Task Participation

Results in causal models (tables 8.5 and 8.7) show the obvious: task participation begets task participation, and social participation begets social participation. However, the models also show that task participation can result in increased social participation, but not vice versa. This result suggests that tasks act like ice-breakers for future socializing. It also suggests that sociable activities become increasingly more vocal and important over the course of the school year.

The results reported in tables 8.4 through 8.7 reveal that there is dimensional specificity across relational channels, types of status, and forms of conduct. However, certain relations, statuses, and behaviors can be used to pirate and translate meanings across organizational dimensions. Recounting the main causes of task and sociable behavior clearly tells such a story. The analyses of task participation in tables 8.4 and 8.5 can be summarized as follows:

- Classrooms are more task-vocal when the activities are open and student-centered.
- Individual students are more task-vocal when they are popular among classmates and academically successful in the specific class.
- Classrooms grow increasingly vocal in tasks when work routines are student-centered and classroom relations are dense and egalitarian.
- Individual students grow increasingly vocal in tasks when they have high G.P.A.s and have been task-vocal in the past. In addition, they grow increasingly vocal in tasks when they are attractive and popular among classmates and unhindered by membership in a dense friendship clique.

Taken as a whole, these results reveal a larger story. First, context matters greatly for high rates of task participation. Student-centered instructional formats and dense egalitarian friendships enable students to be more vocal in tasks, especially as the year progresses. Second, particular status resources enable students to participate in tasks. Popular students and A students in the classroom are more vocal in tasks and become increasingly so over time. In particular, good academic standing in the school generates greater task participation, most likely because youth identify with and attach themselves to the roles in which they excel. However, locally popular students are more vocal at the start of the school year (see model 3 in table 8.4, $b^* = .20$), and they become increasingly so at a rate approaching that of G.P.A. rank (see table 8.5).

Most of these results are straightforward, but the surprising finding is that the informal organization of social relations and social standing therein affect the vitality of formal classroom affairs net of formal organizational characteristics and academic forms of status. Thus, while there is dimensional specificity (task structures and academic standing affect rates of task participation), there is also inter-dimensional causation (characteristics of adolescents' social lives permeate and influence academic affairs).

Social Participation

The analyses of social participation in tables 8.6 and 8.7 can be summarized as follows:

- Classrooms are more sociable when tasks are student-centered and entail developed classroom networks.

- Individual students are more sociable when they are physically attractive, when they are popular among classmates, and when they have dense personal friendship relations in the class, but not when they are academically successful.

- Classrooms grow increasingly sociable if classroom relations are dense and egalitarian.

- Individual students grow increasingly sociable when they are physically attractive, when they are popular among classmates, and when they have been socially and academically vocal in the past.

Taken as a whole, the results for sociable participation also reveal a larger story. Like task behavior, social behavior is highly influenced by characteristics of the classroom context. Instructional formats influence play only at the start of the year, while the overall quality of the classroom friendship network encourages high rates of play early on and causes sociable behavior to grow increasingly vocal as the year progresses. Second, particular status resources enable students to participate in the play routines around them, while others inhibit such participation.

Popular students with dense friendships find many opportunities for sociable interactions. However, academically astute youth find that there are barriers or incentives not to participate in these interactions. There is to some extent a "status barrier," which suggests a unidirectional translation of status into participation. Peer status legitimates the student as a participant in academic affairs, but academic status mildly delegitimates the student in sociable activities.

From the results, we can conclude that conduct in formal and informal organizational dimensions is facilitated by certain classroom and individual characteristics. Successful participation in tasks mainly requires access to the floor and legitimacy as a good student (achievement logic). Successful participation in social affairs primarily requires a context of dense friendship ties and legitimacy as a "likable" boy or girl. Results suggest that social and academic forms of interaction have distinct causal anchors and that the formal and informal organization of classrooms has recognizable boundaries.

At the same time, these results reveal that certain relations and status characteristics can translate across formal and informal organizational boundaries. Task participation arises not only from the formal organizational characteristics of academic status but from social standing in the classroom and the nature of friendship relations in the setting. The formal organization of instruction and learning is altered by the context of informal relations and adolescent conceptions of informal status. This *interdimensional* effect nearly equals that occurring within the formal organizational dimension of task structures and academic definitions of status. In contrast, social participation arises almost exclusively from friendship relations and peer status. The organization of tasks has a mild association with social behavior, but only when the tasks are difficult to monitor, thereby enabling the social world of adolescents to pour forth into classroom affairs. Therefore, the results indicate that the social world permeates formal work routines, while the academic world serves only as an avenue to sociable interactions where academic values are shunned and seldom brought to bear.

CONCLUSION

The answer to the initial research question—what makes some classes and students more academically and/or sociably vocal than others?—should be clear. Some classes are more vocal than others because they have students with friendly interpersonal relations who are given the opportunity to interact with one another through group work and discussion.[15] Moreover, some students are more vocal than others because they have various status resources that make them legitimate participants in various classroom endeavors. In general, status characteristics have greater dimensional specificity than classroom characteristics. However, social standing among classmates and physical attractiveness afford legitimacy in both work and play activities. In contrast, academic status appears to have relevance only for academic affairs and even acts as a mild stigma in social activities. Last, student participation is greatly defined by past levels of participation. However, this too has a degree of dimensional specificity. Sociable play interactions do not lead to greater work involvement, but task interactions do become a basis for future play interactions. As such, classroom participation is characterized by behavioral drift from work to play affairs over time. In short, formal and informal organization have a degree of boundary definition, but the pattern of translation is such that the informal world of adolescents permeates and somewhat supplants the work routines in high school classrooms.

The policy implications of this chapter are somewhat limited, since its sample is limited to thirty-six classrooms from two high schools. Nevertheless, certain hypotheses about classroom organization are suggested by this work. First, opening up task structures increases not only task participation but social participation unrelated to work. However, the opposite strategy is possibly more problematic. Closing task structures inhibits task participation more over time than sociable participation. That is, students will eventually socialize even though the tasks may not allow it. Second, a friendly classroom setting encourages sociable interactions and the digression of tasks into play routines. Some treatment or prescribed organization of adolescent relations may prove to have great returns on active involvement in tasks. Friendliness among students is not a problem per se, but it can become one if left undirected and unmanaged. Third, this research makes status treatments seem more relevant than ever, regardless of the type of activity structure used (McFarland 2001). In particular, the main treatment needs to be peer status, since it has the greatest sway over classroom discourse in general. Popular youth appear to be loci of interaction in classrooms. Whether these students need to be co-opted (McFarland 2003) or circumvented (Cohen and Lotan 1997a) is still a point of debate. Removing popular students from the class often serves to undermine processes of mobilization and consensus among adolescents. Last, further research is needed to explain why academic and peer status are uncorrelated in middle school and high school but positively associated in grade school (Lloyd and Cohen 1999; Chiu 2000). Why does this divergence of academic and social worlds arise?

This chapter has also tried to make a theoretical contribution to sociology and the sociology of education, weaving together status characteristics theory and micro-organizational theory in an effort to explain the different forms and variations of classroom conduct. Status characteristics are regarded as political resources that confer a degree of legitimacy on the adolescent actors (Berger et al. 1980). Micro-organizational theory helps describe relational channels and activities that uniformly affect all actors in the setting, thereby creating opportunities and constraints that affect overall levels of classroom participation (Homans 1950; Roethlisberger and Dickson 1939). The end product is the extension of status characteristics theory and a revival of old institutionalist theories that describe the behaviors and interactions associated with an organization's technical core.[16] Both are relevant to the development of a social psychology of schooling and the study of classrooms that Bidwell's (2000, 2001) most recent work encourages sociologists of education to study.

Portions of this research have been supported by grants and fellowships from the National Science Foundation, the Spencer Foundation, and the Institute for Educational Initiatives at the University of Notre Dame. I would like to thank Charles Bidwell, Elizabeth Cohen, Robert Dreeben, Billie Gastic, Warren Kubitschek, Walter Powell, and Francisco Ramirez for their helpful comments on earlier drafts.

NOTES

1. Academic status and peer status are measured as rankings within the classroom. Students are asked who receives the best grades and who is the most popular. The researcher sums the number of selections each student receives, then sorts students in each classroom into quintiles, thereby creating an ordinal rank out of the number of selections students receive. Students in higher quintiles are viewed as having status characteristics that enable them to be more dominant participants in tasks (Cohen and Lotan 1997a).

2. The friends nominated on general and setting-specific forms are correlated but not multicollinear (.38). Many of the friends listed in class are not friends the student hangs out with outside of school (McFarland 1999). These friends were therefore quite different from the "fair-weather" friends many students had in class.

3. Hugh Mehan (1979) finds that some utterances by teachers and students are indirect and aimed at the entire class. Rendering the dependent variable a rate of outwardly directed utterances makes indirect and direct utterances equal. I started with sociolinguistic coding of sequences of interaction within classrooms (as does Mehan). I then made a series of reasonable abstractions to acquire count-data that were rendered as rate per hour (akin to the "process-product" tradition), thus obtaining a measure of participation that was more useful for predictive analyses.

4. Some actors are nonvocal. Since taking the log of zero afforded negative values, I logged the rate of interaction plus one.

5. Physical attractiveness is considered a diffuse status characteristic (Webster and Driskell 1983). In this study, I evaluated the physical attractiveness of students on a four-point scale. In an effort to assess the reliability of my observations, I asked fifteen college students and professors of differing genders and ages to evaluate the attractiveness of forty-two students in a yearbook. The average correlation of evaluations was .60; for my own coding, the average correlation was .68. The reliability is not ideal (.90 is), but the respondents had not seen the students in person and could not discern height, curves, and so forth, from the yearbook pictures.

6. I initially thought that track placement and extracurricular involvement would matter for participation (following McNeal 1995; Oakes, Gamoran, and Page 1992). However, I found no such effect and, in the interest of parsimony, removed these controls.

7. Academic standing in the class and academic standing in the school are correlated at .52 but are not multicollinear.

8. Another reason to add the term one minus the Gini coefficient is that density was highly

associated with class size (small classes being more dense). In an effort to define network effects as distinct from class size, I saw the density and equality of tie distribution as affording the best measures of trust and rights to discourse.

9. I used the SAS PROC MIXED procedure. The syntax is available from the author.

10. One way to think about the sources of variation in increased rates of participation is to estimate the intraclass correlation, ρ. This is equivalent to expressing the variance-covariance matrix in correlation form. For first-semester task participation: $\rho = \tau_{00} / (\tau_{00}+\sigma^2) = .14 / (.14 + .39) = .27$.

11. Heckman sample selection tests were performed to see whether the longitudinal subsample was significantly different from the larger cross-sectional first-semester sample. Although the probit model found the smaller sample to be composed of more Magnet students and more honors students than the first-semester sample, no significant effect was found for the Inverse Mills Ratio on any outcome variable used in the results section (at $p < .10$ level). A greater number of honors classes are in the longitudinal sample than the cross-sectional sample because honors classes are more likely to be yearlong courses than are other courses.

12. Standardized coefficients of $b^* = B$ (s_x / s_y) where B is the raw coefficient and s is the standard deviation (level specific). Interpreting the effects of each standardized variable requires further transformation, since the dependent variables are log-transformed. Looking ahead to table 8.4, model 5, we see that first-semester task participation is significantly associated with teacher-controlled instruction ($b^* = -.17$). By transforming the raw result (exp (x) $- 1 =$ exp ($-.17$) $- 1 = -.16\%$), I undo the log-transformation and learn the percentage decline in task participation that results with a one-standard-deviation increase in the use of teacher-centered tasks. A one-standard-deviation increase in teacher-controlled instruction translates into a 16 percent decrease in task participation.

13. The regression models in tables 8.4 through 8.7 do not reveal the manner in which diffuse statuses and school status effects on participation translate into local classroom status effects on participation. I performed a series of multiple regressions to determine the direct and indirect effects of diffuse statuses and school status variables. Few diffuse status variables have direct effects on participation (besides attractiveness and occupational status). Some diffuse statuses translate mildly into school standing. Parents' occupational status and family background affect students' G.P.A. ranking. And occupational status affects students' physical appearance (income can be used to buy clothes, haircuts, and so on). Appearance, in turn, very mildly affects popularity in the school and class. More substantial were the effects that school standing has on classroom standing. Popularity in the school affects popularity in the class (correlation .38), and G.P.A. ranking affects academic rank in a class (correlation at .52, but not significantly multicollinear in tests of each model). Status in the school to some extent explains the strong effect of status in the classroom. However, in longitudinal models of task participation, the direct effects of academic rank in the school tend to eclipse local academic rank in a class, while the inverse holds true for the relation of social statuses to social participation.

14. The interaction of academic standing in the school with academic standing in the classroom has a significant positive effect, suggesting that these statuses have a compound-

ing effect. The interaction is less substantial than the additive effects, however, so it was not included in the results.

15. I tested interactions of classroom characteristics and found that they have additive effects, not compounding effects. It is not an either/or story with regard to volume of discourse.

16. The scope of status characteristics theory has been expanded in several ways. The analysis of classrooms is an application of the theory to a natural setting. By using a variety of task structures, the theory has been extended beyond collaborative group situations. And last, by predicting sociable participation, status characteristics theory has been used to explain behaviors emblematic of informal organization.

Chapter 9

School Organization, Curricular Structure, and the Distribution and Effects of Instruction for Tenth-Grade Science

Robert A. Petrin

Sociological research on instruction has produced two important propositions. The first is that different types of instruction depend on distinct organizational contexts for their effective development and implementation (Bidwell, Frank, and Quiroz 1997; Elliott 1998; Lee, Smith, and Croninger 1997; Louis and Marks 1998; Newmann, Marks, and Gamoran 1996; see also Gamoran 1989). The second is that more progressive or participative forms of instruction (sometimes referred to as student-centered, "authentic," or student-agentic instruction) promote the achievement of all students regardless of their grade or ability level while overcoming differences in students' social backgrounds that contribute to inequalities in learning (Lee et al. 1997; Louis and Marks 1998; Newmann, Marks, and Gamoran 1996; Yair 2000).

Recent research has reexamined these claims with regard to high school mathematics and found that while school organization is related to classroom pedagogy, students' instructional experiences can vary greatly within subject-matter curricula (Bidwell et al. 1997; Petrin, forthcoming) and that more participative forms of instruction may not always have the effects that prior research suggests (McFarland 2001; Petrin, forthcoming). This research explains such discrepancies by pointing to the fact that analyses of instruction often neglect the structure of the curriculum as well as variation in the distribution of resources within schools and curricula essential to its production (McFarland 2001; Petrin, forthcoming). In light of these recent findings, it remains an open question as to whether similar omissions influence researchers' understanding of the distribution and effects of instruction for high school science, where hands-on pedagogical activity is traditionally more common than is the case for mathematics, where instructional activity of almost any type is apt to be more resource-intensive and where the subject matter itself is more fragmented and therefore may be especially dependent on particular forms of pedagogy for the effective integration of course material.

This chapter seeks to contribute to the understanding of instruction by examining whether students' instructional experiences are qualitatively similar across courses in the tenth-grade science curriculum, and whether similar types of instruction are generated in the same way and have the same effects on student outcomes across courses in this curriculum. It does so by building on prior research identifying instruction as a resource essential to learning, while placing particular emphasis on the role that intracurricular contexts play in regulating students' educational experiences. Evaluating instruction in this manner requires investigating its distribution and effects in light of what is known about schools as formal organizations and the influence the curriculum has on teaching and learning.

INTRAORGANIZATIONAL CONTEXTS, RESOURCES, AND INSTRUCTION

Schools can be thought of as influencing individual actions and outcomes by creating "contexts" wherein goals are established, resources are assembled, and social exchanges occur (Bidwell 1965, 2000; Bidwell et al. 1997; Coleman 1988; Coleman and Hoffer 1987; Lucas 1999; see also Firestone 1985; Swidler and Arditti 1994). From this perspective, courses represent important units of analysis since they mediate between schools and classrooms, shape teachers' goals and mandates, and reflect the distribution of human capital and other resources within schools and curricula. Courses are also amenable to "structuralist" analyses of educational phenomena, which emphasize the relational aspects of academic and social positions in schools and schooling and call attention to the ways in which students' educational experiences are shaped by their progression through these positions (see, for example, Friedkin and Thomas 1997; Lucas 1999; Stevenson, Schiller, and Schneider 1994; see also Schneider, Swanson, and Riegle-Crumb 1998). This structuralist conception of schools and schooling is in many respects inherent to the Opportunity to Learn (OTL) paradigm of Aage Sørenson and the organizational perspective on schools, both of which inform much of the sociological research on instruction (Bidwell 1965, 2000; Bidwell et al. 1997; Firestone 1985; Ingersoll 1993; Kilgore 1991; Kilgore and Pendleton 1993; Sørenson 1970, 1987).

Drawing on the OTL and organizational approaches, researchers have identified instruction as the core technology of schools and classrooms and an important factor in the stratification of student outcomes (see, for example, Dreeben and Gamoran 1986; Gamoran and Berends 1988; Gamoran 1989; Lee et al. 1997). Yet in spite of repeated reference to the OTL and organizational traditions, and perhaps owing to particular notions of equality of educational opportunity, researchers often treat instruction as a resource bearing a limited relationship to important features of schools and curricula. As a result, measures of pedagogical exposure incorporated into analyses of instruction are often developed for student populations as a whole, and instructional effects are evaluated at the school or track levels (see, for example, Elliott 1998; Lee and Smith 1995; Lee et al. 1997; Louis and Marks 1998).

There are at least three shortcomings to these approaches. First, they assume that a given type of instruction is equally effective for all students. This assumption is not always supported by findings from other social science disciplines, which confirm that instruction is a resource essential to learning but also suggest that pedagogy must be appropriately matched to the needs and abilities of students (Cronbach 2002; Cronbach and Webb 1975; see also Loveless 2003). Second, researchers often neglect the possibility that correlates of instructional practices observed at highly aggregate units of analysis are confounded with structural features of the curriculum, as well as with the distribution of human capital and other resources within schools and curricula (Kilgore 1991; Kilgore and Pendleton 1993; Rowan, Correnti, and Miller 2002; Sørenson 1970, 1987). Sally Kilgore (1991), for example, demonstrates that school size and school academic environment, both of which are hypothesized to be negatively correlated with more progressive types of instruction in other research, also influence students' chances of enrolling in more rigorous courses (see also Kilgore and Pendleton 1993; Oakes 1985; Powell, Farrar, and Cohen 1985). Third, many of the attempts to incorporate the curriculum into analyses of instruction have used students' overall curricular "track" (that is, vocational, college preparatory, general academic, et cetera). Doing so, however, is problematic, since tracks are often heterogenous (see, for example, Gamoran 1992b; Lee and Bryk 1989) and may not provide robust or even intuitive indicators of students' positions within subject-specific curricula (Garet and DeLany 1988; Lucas 1999; Schneider et al. 1998; Stevenson et al. 1994). As a result, aggregate administrative descriptors of students' high school programs may reveal little about the academic material to which pedagogical activity is matched, and may be of limited value in shedding light on the the midlevel phenomena essential to understanding the relationship of instruction to social stratification in education.

For these reasons, it would appear to be important to evaluate the distribution and effects of instruction at the more proximate locations within schools and curricula where learning is produced and the bulk of variation in student outcomes occurs. In doing so, researchers can better match the structuralist assumptions underlying key sociological perspectives on schools and schooling, as well as recent empirical research on the ways in which students negotiate high school curricula.

Structure, Agency, and Instruction

In seeking a broader sociological understanding of the distribution and effects of instruction, it may be useful to think of instruction as a resource that is *generated* within contexts defined by courses representing distinct positions in curricula, rather than as a resource that is necessarily *produced* as a result of school-level resources or organizational configurations. Indeed, both the OTL and organizational perspectives on schools and schooling suggest that the distribution and effects of instruction are likely governed by more of an "ecological" logic than the top-down "production function" logic inherent to many analyses of instruction (see, for example, Bidwell 2001; Firestone 1985; Friedkin and Thomas 1997). If this is the case, evaluating instruction and its relationship to stratification in education requires more explicitly accounting for structure and agency than is currently done in educational research.

To the extent that instruction is an essential resource in education it makes sense to question whether its distribution and effects are influenced by *the structure of the curriculum itself*. This possibility is suggested by both sociotechnical models of schools as well as institutionalist accounts of school functioning (Bidwell 1965, 2001; Firestone 1985; Ingersoll 1993). As is the case for other important resources in education, instruction can be differentiated along both qualitative and quantitative dimensions. Current research recognizes qualitative variation in students' instructional experiences to a degree by specifying, in broad terms, different modes of instruction (such as teacher-centered, inquiry-based, "authentic," or student-centered instruction, and so on; see Lee et al. 1997; McFarland 2001; Newmann, Marks, and Gamoran 1996). However, this research often does not explicitly account for the fact that particular modes of instructional activity may *themselves* display variation across courses in subject-specific curricula, owing to variation in the task environments defining inquiry in these courses. This latter type of qualitative variation is likely to be particularly salient in less hierarchically organized curricula such as science, where the academic material covered in different courses may vary widely and may not build on material covered in students' previous courses in a direct or concrete way (Stodolsky and Grossman 1995). In addition, since the skills required for student-based inquiry can vary across science courses as a function of the academic material they cover, as can the amount of time required by teachers to put in place the conceptual scaffolding necessary for maximizing returns to independent or group-based inquiry, the optimum balance between conventional (that is, teacher-agentic) and progressive (that is, student-agentic) modes of instruction can vary across courses as well, even if no qualitative variation in particular modes of instruction exists across these courses. Therefore, it is likely that instruction is structured by curricula themselves, even before variation in the availability of other important "precursor" resources is accounted for (such as, class size, teacher qualifications, material resources, student human capital, and so on).

Since instruction is the product of social interactions (Bidwell 1965, 2003; McFarland 2001; Waller 1932; Yasumoto, Uekawa, and Bidwell 2001), it is not just variation in the substantive aspects of curricula but variation in *teacher and student agency* that regulate the ways in which instruction is organized across courses in curricula. Teacher agency influences student instructional experiences because different understandings of teachers' professional goals and mandates, and different teachers' professional beliefs influence the types of interactions introduced or permitted in the classroom. Indeed, the autonomy of teachers' work has long been noted as an important feature of schools (Bidwell 1965; Dreeben 2001; Firestone 1985; Ingersoll 1993, 1996). To the extent that teacher agency is related to teacher human capital (for example, years of experience, formal academic preparation, gender) and becomes "matched" to distinct courses in curricula in systematic ways, teachers' goals, mandates, and beliefs could be expected to display different relationships to students' instructional experiences across positions in curricula. Evidence of this matching can be found in Merrilee Finley's (1985) account of curricular structuration at a comprehensive public high school. Finley suggests that teachers' perceptions of appropriate classroom exchanges, as well as their goals and expectations for students, become mapped onto courses in curricula through the intraorganizational politics of teacher course assignments (see also Bourdieu 1996; Bourdieu, Passeron, and de Saint Martin 1994; Firestone 1985; Goodson 1992; Ingersoll 1993; Powell et al. 1985).

Student agency likewise contributes to variation in the distribution and effects of instruction within schools and curricula since students' attitudes and motivations influence the latitude that teachers have in adopting pedagogical strategies in the classroom. Charles Bidwell, for example, argues that instruction depends on a degree of goodwill between students and teachers as well as the elective participation of students (Bidwell 2001; see also Dreeben and Barr 1988; McFarland 2001). In addition, the OTL paradigm states that learning is a function of student effort as well as the resources commonly examined in sociological analyses of achievement (Sørenson 1970, 1987). Indeed, prior research has shown that students' motivation, effort, and efficacy are related to their positions in curricula (Friedkin and Thomas 1997; Heyns 1974) as well as their instructional experiences in tenth grade mathematics (Petrin, forthcoming).[1]

Ultimately it is not just students' attitudes and motivations but their aptitudes that differentiate curricular positions from one another and likely influence the distribution and effects of instruction across positions in curricula. Thus, even in the unlikely event that intracurricular contexts are defined only by variation in students' abilities, there would still be reason to expect variation in the distribution and effects of instruction within schools and curricula due to variation in the aptitudes and pedagogical requirements of students. Contemporary sociological research has uncovered evidence of such "aptitude-treatment interactions" (Cronbach 2002; Cronbach and Webb 1975), attributing them to the organization of curricula or contextual effects (Gamoran and Kelly 2003; see also results discussed in Rowan et al. 2002).

In sum, variations in the distribution and effects of instruction are likely *structural effects*. First, they reflect the ease or difficulty with which teachers faced with particular levels of human capital, material resources, and curricular constraints either choose to or are able to implement various pedagogical practices in the classroom. Second, they provide an indication of the influence of particular types of pedagogical activities on students' achievement and engagement with class material, given the nature of that material and the types of students enrolled in the associated course. Therefore, by drawing the microstructures of curricula directly into analyses of instruction, researchers can control for the effects of school organizational characteristics on the allocation of students to positions in curricula and thus isolate the true relationship of these characteristics to pedagogical practice. By recognizing cross-curricular position variation in student instructional experiences, they can also better understand the influence of classroom pedagogical activities on students' educational outcomes and stratification in education.

A GENERAL STRATEGY FOR ANALYZING THE DISTRIBUTION AND EFFECTS OF INSTRUCTION

A general strategy for evaluating variation in the distribution and effects of instruction can be thought of as entailing four steps. First, researchers must isolate courses within subject-specific curricula capable of serving as proxies for the type and level of material covered in students' classes. Second, measures of classroom pedagogical contents must be developed for each of these courses that provide not only accurate descriptions of students' actual instructional experiences but also insight into variation in pedagogical practices across courses in subject-specific curricula. Third, researchers must isolate those courses for which student instructional experiences are substantively the same and thus comparable with respect to the distribution and effects of instruction. Finally, parallel statistical models relating student, school, and classroom resources to students' instructional experiences as well as to student engagement with class material must be generated for those courses for which students' instructional experiences are comparable.

For the present analyses, students' instructional experiences are viewed as mediating between student, school, and classroom characteristics and students' engagement with science. Although students' actual instructional experiences must be determined empirically, they are posited at the outset as consisting of more conventional, teacher-centered or teacher-agentic instruction and more progressive, inquiry-based, student-centered or student-agentic instruction. In accord with the literature noted earlier, courses within subject-specific curricula are hypothesized to constitute a structure determined by the formal and informal aspects of curricula. In order to highlight the emphasis placed on the relational aspects of courses in the present analysis, the term *curricular position* is adopted here to refer to students' location in the tenth-grade science curriculum. From this perspective, it is not just the causal relationships between exogenous (predictor) and endogenous (outcome) variables that are of interest in analyses of instruction, but also variation in these relationships across curricular positions.

To the extent that variation in the effects of *school variables* on student instructional experiences is found across curricular positions characterized by identical forms of instruction, the data provide evidence suggesting that courses represent distinct, midlevel contexts in the broader institutional environments of schools and schooling that are important to the analysis of instruction. Variation in the effects of organizational resources—noted in prior research as being important to the generation of various types of instruction (school academic press, school professional environment, school curricular revision programs)—is of particular interest since it suggests variation in the implementation and/or operationalization of organizational resources across distinct positions in the curriculum. To the extent that the effects of *teacher variables* on student instructional experiences vary across curricular positions, the data provide evidence suggesting that students respond to identical teacher contributions to the classroom in different ways across different positions in curricula, or that teachers act on identical goals, mandates, and beliefs in different ways across curricular positions, perhaps reflecting the academic or social structure of the curriculum. To the extent that the effects of identical *student instructional experiences* vary across curricular positions in science, the data provide evidence suggesting that particular modes of instruction have different effects on identical student outcomes across distinct positions in the curriculum.

DATA AND METHODS

The data used here are drawn from the student, school, transcript, teacher, and parent components of the National Educational Longitudinal Study of 1988 to 1994 (NELS:88–94). For the present analysis, a sample of 7,170 public high school sophomores enrolled in one of four curricular positions was isolated.[2] These curricular positions, defined as earth and environmental science, biology, chemistry, and physics, were generated by aggregating students by the topical coverage of the science course they were enrolled in at the time of the first follow-up survey administration.[3]

Multigroup confirmatory factor analysis (MGCFA; see Muthén and Christoffersson 1981) was used to develop separate curricular position-specific measures of student instructional experiences and examine qualitative variation in these measures across curricular positions.[4] After curricular positions that are comparable with respect to the student instructional experience measurement models were identified and isolated, a multigroup structural equation model (MGSEM; see Bollen 1989) was used to specify a series of hypothesized causal relationships between student, classroom, and school variables and these instructional experience measures, as well as between student, classroom, and school variables, the student instructional experiences, and student-reported engagement with science, while controlling and/or testing for variation in effects across curricular positions.[5] The variables used in the MGSEM portion of the analysis are described in the next section.[6]

School Variables

School size is included in the MGSEM since it is hypothesized to influence the production of instruction by eroding school professional communities. Specifically, large schools where it is difficult for faculty to interact are believed to pose challenges to the development and implementation of innovative curricula (Corwin and Herriott 1988; Lee and Smith 1995; Louis and Marks 1998; see also Ingersoll 1996). In some situations, however, school size has also been noted as providing favorable economies of scale for certain curricula (Lee and Smith 1997), which may promote certain types of student-centered pedagogy. In the present context, school size is measured using the natural log of the number of full-time teachers at students' schools.

School professionalism is believed to be essential to problem-solving in the non-standardized task environments with which progressive instruction is often associated (Bidwell and Yasumoto 1999; Corwin and Herriott 1988; Lee and Smith 1995; Louis and Marks 1998; Yasumoto et al. 2001). The school professional environment variable included in the present analysis is a derived measure based on school administrators' reports on the following: the proportion of teachers at students' schools holding postbaccalaureate degrees; the extent to which staff members are responsible for solving school problems; the degree to which the school makes use of interdisciplinary teaching teams; the level of the school's commitment to staff development; the extent to which the school groups students on ability in science; the degree to which class activities are highly structured; and the amount of influence students have in selecting courses.[7] This measure is intended to be consistent with concepts of professionalism found elsewhere in the literature that emphasize that professions are characterized not only by higher levels of credentialism and greater autonomy and collegial interdependence in performing work duties in general (Abbott 1988) but also by teacher (versus school) discretion in influencing students' curricular placement and resolving school issues more specifically (Ingersoll 1993; Yasumoto et al. 2001).

The school academic environment variables consist of three separate variables. The first is *school academic press*. High academic press schools are often characterized by highly structured classroom activities, minimal teacher involvement in designing course materials, high levels of student competitiveness, and large numbers of required academic courses (Battistich et al. 1995; Phillips 1997; Shouse 1996). Although high academic press schools are noted as having positive effects on achievement in general (Coleman 1988; Coleman and Hoffer 1987; Wenglinsky 1997), they are sometimes thought to inhibit the development of the creative pedagogical strategies important for maximizing returns to time spent in class (Lee et al. 1997). For the present analyses, school academic press is a derived measure based on school administrators' reports on the following: the percentage of 1990 graduates who attended four-year colleges; the extent to which students are encouraged to compete for grades; the percentage of 1990 tenth-graders enrolled in the school's academic program; the extent to which students have a say in deciding which courses they take; and the extent to which class activities are highly structured.[8] Although school academic press is included in the final MGSEM to isolate the normative effects of school's academic environment on students' instructional experiences and students' engagement with science, an additional variable, indicating whether students' *schools required three or more years of science to graduate*, was included in the model to isolate the influence of schools' formal academic environments on the outcomes of interest.

School financial resources are believed to be essential to students' academic success to the extent they enable schools to hire sufficient numbers of well-trained teachers and keep classroom materials up-to-date (Greenwald, Hedges, and Lane 1996a, 1996b). In addition, special curricular reforms and pedagogical interventions often target poorer schools and schools "at risk" (Padilla and Knapp 1995). For the present analyses, school minority composition (a dichotomous indicator of whether more than 20 percent of students at the school are black or Hispanic), school urbanicity (urban or non-urban), and school poverty level (percentage of students receiving free lunch) are included in the MGSEM to control for various aspects of schools' financial and community resources. Prior research suggests that these variables are suitable for this purpose and capture aspects of school environments not evident in district-level data (Condron and Roscigno 2003).

The school variables also include a dichotomous variable indicating whether students' schools had a *curricular revision program for critical thinking* in place at the time the NELS:88–94 first follow-up questionnaire was administered. This was done to isolate the unique effects of the aforementioned school resources on students' instructional experiences after specific pedagogical programs at students' schools were accounted for.

Classroom and Teacher Variables

Three *classroom resources and constraints* variables were used in these analyses: class enrollment, class achievement level (high versus average, mixed, or low), and level of teachers' highest degree (B.A.,B.S., or less versus master's, professional, or Ph.D.).[9] The *teacher goals* variables included in the MGSEM are the emphasis individual teachers report on preparing students to do well on tests and on enabling students to enjoy course subject matter and become independent thinkers. The *teacher mandate* variable represents teachers' reports of the extent to which they feel encouraged to experiment and innovate in the classroom. The *teacher belief* variable is taken from teachers' reports of the extent to which they believe instruction can influence achievement.

Student Variables

Student demographic variables include students' socioeconomic background (race, gender, parent education level, natural log of parent income); student motivation (student educational aspirations, primary reason student was taking science in grade ten); and student academic ability (grade eight NELS:88–94 science achievement test scores). In accord with the OTL paradigm, student aptitude and motivations are essential controls in analyses of social stratification and structural effects in education (Sørenson 1970, 1987).

Outcome Variables

Two different sets of outcome variables are of interest in the MGSEM. The first is *students' instructional experiences*. Given the centrality of students' instructional experiences to the present analysis, it is useful to highlight some of the important aspects of classroom pedagogy noted in prior research.

Sociological research on instruction often describes students' pedagogical experiences as falling on some point along a continuum (Louis and Marks 1998; McFarland 2001; Newmann, Marks, and Gamoran 1996). On one end of this continuum, teachers maintain exclusive control of class activity. This can be referred to as *teacher-agentic instruction*. On the opposite end, students predominate in directing classroom discourse. This can be referred to as *student-agentic instruction*. It has been argued that classrooms emphasizing review, repetition, and rote problem-solving characteristic of teacher-agentic instruction can work against student achievement by limiting the range of experiences through which students interact with course material (Lee and Smith 1999; Lee et al. 1997; Newmann, Marks, and Gamoran 1996). It has also been suggested that student-agentic instruction increases student engagement with class material while providing means of improving school performance (Lee et al. 1997; Louis and Marks 1998; Newmann, Marks, and Gamoran 1996; Padilla and Knapp 1995; Yair 2000).

For the present analyses, students' instructional experiences are operationalized as manifest in their responses to questionnaire items pertaining to the frequency with which they encountered the following pedagogical practices in their (then) current science courses: reviewing work from the previous day, taking notes in class, listening to the teacher lecture, watching teacher demonstrations, using books to do experiments, conducting an experiment on one's own, writing reports on experiments, choosing one's own topic of study, discussing careers in science, and making up methods to solve problems. Muthén's MGCFA for categorical indicators (see Muthén and Christoffersson 1981) was used to determine the relation of these items to students' overall instructional experiences, as well as the similarity of these instructional experiences across curricular positions (results of this analysis are presented in the next section). Whereas prior research has relied on teacher-reported or observational indicators of pedagogical emphases as proxies for student pedagogical exposure, student reports of participation in classroom environments are used in these analyses since they look beyond teacher intentions to *actual student experiences* in tenth-grade science.[10]

The second outcome of interest in the MGSEM is student engagement with science.[11] For the present analyses, *engagement* pertains to a student-level measure derived from the factor-weighted average of the NELS:88–94 student questionnaire items "How often do you feel challenged in science class?" (a few times a week or less versus every day) and "How often are you asked to show you understand science?" (a few times a week or less versus every day). The engagement measure was constructed using Muthén's MGCFA for ordered categorical indicators, allowing for variation in the mean and variance of student engagement across curricular positions. To reduce the number of parameters in the MGSEM, the factor scores from the engagement measurement model were included in the final analysis.

RESULTS

In accordance with the general strategy for examining the distribution and effects of instruction presented earlier, two sets of empirical results are of interest in this chapter. The first pertains to similarities in students' instructional experiences across distinct curricular positions in tenth-grade science. The second pertains to the differential effects (if any) of specific school, teacher, classroom, and student characteristics on students' instructional experiences *for those curricular positions for which instruction can be judged to be qualitatively the same*, as well as the differential effects (if any) specific aspects of instruction have on students' engagement with science. Both sets of results are now considered in turn.

Student Instructional Experiences in Tenth-Grade Science

In the framework outlined earlier, qualitative variation in student instructional experience measures across curricular positions provides evidence suggesting that instruction has structural features that need to be taken into account in research on school organization and instructional effects.[12] To examine qualitative variation in student instructional experiences, the ten NELS:88–94 student instructional experience items were fit to separate CFA models for ordered categorical data for each of the four science curricular positions noted earlier. These preliminary CFAs revealed that the latent variable measurement models for all four curricular positions were similar in form and that the simplest model that would fit any of the four curricular positions was a three-factor model. The measurement models obtained from these initial CFA models bore a strong resemblance across curricular positions, and a composite model form was developed based on these cross-group similarities.[13]

The findings from subsequent statistical comparisons revealed that the strongest cross-group similarities occurred for the biology and chemistry students. Thus, biology and chemistry students' responses were re-fit to a second composite model.[14] Experimentation with different model forms (including higher-order factor models) revealed that student reports of classroom instructional contents could not be reduced to a single, unidimensional scale. Thus, the three-factor model is the one that was used to generate proxy measures of biology and chemistry students' instructional experiences. This model is presented in table 9.1.[15]

The three latent factors in the final MGCFA can be interpreted as indicating student-reported exposure to teacher-agentic, shared-agentic, and student-agentic instruction. *Teacher-agentic instruction*, so-called because it is the teacher who dominates classroom discourse and inquiry, represents those activities generally associated with conventional pedagogical practice: reviewing work from the previous day, taking notes in class, listening to teacher lectures, and watching teacher demonstrations. *Shared-agentic instruction* relates to those activities that require students to play an active part in the classroom by doing experiments as specified in books, making up methods to solve problems, and writing reports based on results obtained from experiments. Here teachers and students both play active but shared roles in directing classroom discourse. As shown in table 9.1, this factor has a *negative* relationship with the "listen to teacher lecture" item ($\lambda = -.272$), but a positive relationship with student reports of watching their teachers do experiments ($\lambda = .487$). Thus, while students play a more active role in shared-agentic instructional activity than is the case for teacher-agentic activity, the associated classroom pedagogical contents remain heavily influenced by the teacher and formal classroom materials, and resemble conventional ideas of what occurs in laboratory science classes. *Student-agentic instruction*, in contrast, is characterized by more

TABLE 9.1 / Selected MGCFA Measurement Model Parameters for Tenth-Grade Biology and Chemistry Students, Derived from Reports of How Often They Participated in Noted Activities in Their Current Science Classes (Unstandardized Coefficients)

	Biology			Chemistry		
FA Model Parameters	Teacher Agentic	Shared Agentic	Student Agentic	Teacher Agentic	Shared Agentic	Student Agentic
Actor loadings						
Review work from previous day	0.269***	#	0.318***	0.269+	#	0.318+
Take notes in class	0.645***	#	#	0.645+	#	#
Listen to teacher lecture	1.000+	−0.272***	#	1.000+	−0.272+	#
Watch teacher demonstration	0.368***	0.487***	#	0.368+	0.487+	#
Use books to do experiment	#	1.000+	−0.309***	#	1.000+	−0.309+
Conduct own experiment	#	#	1.031***	#	#	1.031+
Write reports on experiments	#	0.673***	#	#	0.673+	#
Choose own topic to study	#	#	1.000+	#	#	1.000+
Discuss careers in science	0.218***	#	0.566***	0.218+	#	0.566+
Make up methods to solve problems	#	0.183***	1.035***	#	0.183+	1.035+
Item probit thresholds						
Review work from previous day—1	−0.663***			−0.663+		
Review work from previous day—2	0.024			0.024+		
Take notes in class—1	−0.919***			−0.919+		
Take notes in class—2	−0.290***			−0.290+		
Take notes in class—3	0.619***			0.619+		
Listen to teacher lecture—1	−0.682***			−0.682+		
Listen to teacher lecture—2	0.251***			0.251+		
Watch teacher demonstration—1	0.048***			0.048+		
Watch teacher demonstration—2	0.972***			0.972+		
Use books to do experiments—1	−0.076***			−0.076+		
Use books to do experiments—2	0.841***			0.841+		
Conduct own experiment—1	0.819***			0.819+		

TABLE 9.1 / *Continued*

FA Model Parameters	Biology			Chemistry		
	Teacher Agentic	Shared Agentic	Student Agentic	Teacher Agentic	Shared Agentic	Student Agentic
Conduct own experiment—2	1.368***			1.368+		
Write reports on experiments—1	0.374***			−0.946***		
Write reports on experiments—2	0.226***			−0.225***		
Choose own topic to study—1	0.778***			0.778+		
Choose own topic to study—2	1.160***			1.160+		
Discuss careers in science	0.346***			0.346+		
Discuss careers in science	1.000***			1.000+		
Make up methods to solve problems—1	0.819***			0.819+		
Make up methods to solve problems—2	1.259***			1.259+		
Factor variances and covariances						
Teacher agentic	0.671***			0.648***		
Shared agentic	0.289***	0.750***		0.353***	0.733***	
Student agentic	0.111***	0.403***	0.491***	0.171***	0.320***	0.431***
Factor means	0.000+	0.000+	0.000+	0.285***	0.272***	0.000+
Multigroup model fit information (robust weighted least squares)						
Chi-square/df				407.54 / 62		
RMSE				0.042		
CFI				0.954		
TLI				0.960		
Number of cases in combined sub-sample				6,367		

Source: U. S. Department of Education (1996).
Notes: Data weighted to be representative of 1990 public high school sophomores enrolled in biology or chemistry in grade ten. The sample analyzed here is a teacher-matched sample for biology and chemistry students. All item scale factors—"delta parameters" in the parameterization of Muthén (Muthén and Christoffersson 1981)—restricted to 1.0 for both biology and chemistry respondents. Factors scaled to the same item for both subgroups to facilitate cross-group comparison of factor loadings and item thresholds.
***$\alpha < .01$; **$\alpha < .05$; *$\alpha < .10$ (two-tailed tests); # parameter set to zero; +parameter value fixed (within or across groups)

genuine, student-directed, independent inquiry. It is in fact *negatively* correlated with using books to do experiments and positively (and strongly) correlated with student-reported frequency of choosing their own topics to study, conducting their own experiments, and making up methods to solve problems (λ's are −.309, 1.000, 1.031, and 1.035, respectively). This factor also has a positive correlation with student reports of the frequency with which they review work from the previous day, suggesting that student-agentic instruction, rather than amounting to a "free-for-all in the lab," includes regular, structured input from biology and chemistry teachers.

Predictors of Students' Instructional Experiences

Results from the MGSEM portion of the analysis are presented in table 9.2. Here the preceding student instructional experience measurement model is directly incorporated into the MGSEM. Parameter estimates, model fit statistics, and coefficient standard errors have all been adjusted for the NELS:88–94 sample design; missing data were treated via multiple imputation (MI) using forty independently imputed datasets.[16] Coefficients are left unstandardized to facilitate comparisons across curricular positions (across adjacent columns in table 9.2).[17] In addition, coefficients whose cross-curricular position differences are statistically significant at the α = .10 level or better are enclosed in shaded cells.

The fitted curricular position–specific means presented in the last row of coefficients in table 9.2 suggest that after accounting for student, school, teacher, and classroom characteristics, biology and chemistry students' mean levels of teacher-agentic instruction, shared-agentic instruction, and engagement with science are equal across curricular position, while the mean level of student-agentic instruction is lower for chemistry students than for biology students (b = −1.67, with a t-ratio of −1.87).

Turning to the *student background and motivations* variables presented at the top of table 9.2, it can be seen that student socioeconomic characteristics and students' attitudes and motivations play sizable roles in the generation of their instructional experiences. Minority students report higher levels of exposure to all three types of instructional experiences in both biology and chemistry, while female students report higher levels of teacher-agentic instruction but lower levels of student-agentic instruction than do male students for both curricular positions. The latter finding is consistent with prior research suggesting that some aspects of inquiry-based instruction may work against the participation of female students in class (see, for example, Burkam et al. 1997; Jovanovic and King 1998).

After school financial and community resources are accounted for, parent education level plays a minor role in students' access to instruction. Parent education levels are associated with higher levels of teacher-agentic instruction and student-agentic instruction in biology (b = .082 and .130, respectively), while the corresponding effect for student-agentic instruction is not statistically significant for

TABLE 9.2 / Selected Parameters from the MGSEM Regressing Student Instructional Experiences and Engagement on Various Student, Classroom, and School Covariates: Simultaneous Outcome Measures for Public High School Students Enrolled in Biology or Chemistry in Grade Ten (Unstandardized Coefficients)

Variable or Parameter	Teacher-Agentic Instruction		Shared-Agentic Instruction		Student-Agentic Instruction		Student Engagement	
	Biology	Chemistry	Biology	Chemistry	Biology	Chemistry	Biology	Chemistry
Student background and motivations								
Minority student	0.134**	+	0.209**	0.428***	0.101*	0.252***	0.011	+
Female	0.200***	0.116*	−0.085	−0.009	−0.241***	+	0.065**	0.007
Parent education (college versus none)	0.082*	+	0.031	+	0.130**	−0.101	−0.003	−0.155***
Ln parent income	0.000+	+	0.082**	−0.010	−0.038	0.004	0.008	+
Grade eight test score	0.002	+	0.000+	+	−0.008***	+	−0.005***	+
Educational expectations: less than college	0.112**	−0.074	0.092*	−0.045	−0.010	0.072	0.027	+
Taking science because wants to (not assigned or required)	0.281***	0.176**	0.317***	0.364***	0.297***	+	0.044	0.092**
School demographic context								
Urban school	−0.023	+	−0.040	+	−0.049	+	0.059	−0.080
School size (ln number of full-time faculty)	0.000+	+	0.055*	−0.079***	0.012	−0.055**	−0.011	0.015
More than 15 percent students black or Hispanic	−0.097	−0.206*	0.141	−0.043	0.040	+	0.055	−0.154**

(Table continues on p. 190.)

TABLE 9.2 / Continued

Variable or Parameter	Teacher-Agentic Instruction		Shared-Agentic Instruction		Student-Agentic Instruction		Student Engagement	
	Biology	Chemistry	Biology	Chemistry	Biology	Chemistry	Biology	Chemistry
Ln percentage of students receiving free lunch	0.000+	+	0.014**	+	0.007	+	0.001+	+
School academic and professional context								
Academic press	-0.046	+	0.151*	-0.030	-0.048	-0.132	0.008	-0.163**
Teacher professional environment	-0.078	0.035	0.068 ...	0.514***	-0.007	0.215(*)	0.110(*)	0.048
Three or more years of science required	0.000+	+	-0.164**	+	0.177** ...	-0.012	-0.019	+
Curricular revision program for critical thinking	0.033	+	0.057	+	-0.023	0.031	0.019	+
Classroom resources or constraints								
Ln of class enrollment	0.023	0.110	-0.237*** ...	0.131	-0.133(**) ...	0.231*	0.002	-0.047
Class achievement level	-0.065	0.099	-0.129* ...	0.225*	-0.019	0.008	-0.109	0.029
Teacher degree level	0.008	+	-0.015 ...	0.249**	-0.003	0.139	-0.023	0.027
Teacher goals, mandates, beliefs								
Goal: students enjoy, become independent	0.074	-0.078	-0.094	0.016	-0.070(*)	+	-0.108	0.009
Goal: students do well on tests	0.077	+	-0.089	-0.158	-0.107*	0.057	0.070*	-0.037

Teacher mandate: experiment, innovate	0.161***	0.018	0.093	0.190*	0.020	…	0.232**	0.015	+
Belief: instruction can influence achievement	−0.045	0.082	0.069	−0.035	0.121**		−0.010	−0.070*	−0.025
Student instructional experiences									
Teacher agentic instruction	—	—	—	—	—		—	0.356***	+
Shared agentic instruction	—	—	—	—	—		—	−0.021	0.079**
Student agentic instruction	—	—	—	—	—		—	0.165***	−0.085*
Outcome variable means	0.000+	+	0.000+	+	0.000+	…	−1.670(**)	0.000+	+
Model fit information									
CFI/standard deviation of CFIs	0.929 / 0.003								
TLI/standard deviation of TLIs	0.921 / 0.004								
RMSE/standard deviation of RMSEs	0.024 / 0.001								
Number of free parameters	192								

Soruce: U.S. Department of Education (1996).

Notes: Data weighted to be representative of 1992 public high school sophomores enrolled in biology (N = 2,195) or chemistry (N = 1,119). Standard errors are robust standard errors adjusted for NELS:88–94 sample design. Estimation is:via a robust WLS algorithm. Coefficients and model fit statistics are combined results from forty independent imputations using the method of Rubin (1987). The three instructional experience measures are posited as mediating between the student, school, and classroom predictor variables and student engagement and are incorporated into the MGSEM as a multigroup CFA measurement model.
***α < .01; **α < .05; *α < .10; + parameter fixed within or across curricular positions; boxed coefficients are statistically significant across curricular positions after parameter covariances are taken into account (α < .10)

chemistry students. The influence of parent education level on students' exposure to student-agentic instruction is greater in biology than in chemistry ($\alpha < .10$). Student prior achievement level has a negative and statistically significant effect on student-agentic instruction that is identical for both biology and chemistry, suggesting that higher-ability students in both curricular positions are taught differently or choose to participate in class differently than lower-ability students. Finally, students' educational expectations and primary reason for taking science in grade ten are also correlated with student instructional experiences. Students with lower educational expectations report higher levels of teacher-agentic instruction and shared-agentic instruction in biology. Neither of the corresponding effects is statistically significant for chemistry students. Cross-curricular position significance tests reveal that the effect of educational expectations on teacher-agentic instruction is statistically different across curricular positions at the $\alpha = .05$ level.

The majority of the *school demographic context* variables in table 9.2 are not statistically significant. Nevertheless, the data provide some indication that economies of scale for organizing instruction may vary across positions in the science curriculum, since school size is positively correlated with shared-agentic instruction in biology while the opposite is the case for chemistry (the difference is statistically significant at the $\alpha = .01$ level). School size is also negatively correlated with student-agentic instruction in chemistry ($b = -.055$), while the effect for biology students is not statistically significant at the $\alpha = .10$ level or better. The corresponding cross-curricular position difference in effects is statistically significant at the $\alpha = .10$ level (t-ratio $= 1.88$). School poverty level (the percentage of students receiving free lunch) has no statistically significant relationship with either teacher-agentic instruction or student-agentic instruction, although it does have a modest, positive correlation with shared-agentic instruction that is identical across curricular positions.

The *school academic and professional context* variables display no statistically significant relationship to teacher-agentic instruction in either biology or chemistry. However, academic press is associated with higher levels of shared-agentic instruction in biology. Teacher professional environment is positively associated with shared-agentic instruction in chemistry, while no corresponding statistically significant relationship exists for biology. Cross-curricular position tests for the corresponding coefficients reveal that the latter difference in effects is statistically significant at the $\alpha = .05$ level. Based on the curricular positions examined here, it appears that schools' teacher professional environments contribute to the stratification of students' instructional experiences across curricular positions. Schools' formal science requirements are positively correlated with student-agentic instruction in biology; and while the corresponding effect is not statistically significant for chemistry, the cross-curricular position difference in effects is statistically significant at the $\alpha = .10$ level. This finding, along with the effects for academic press noted earlier, suggests that highly structured academic environments are not necessarily opposed to inquiry-based instruction, although the effects of rigorous academic environments on instructional experiences may vary by curricular position.

The effects associated with the *classroom resources and constraints* variables for the student instructional experiences outcomes portion of the model indicate that, at the more proximate locations within schools and curricula where pedagogical activity is organized and educational exchanges occur, instruction is generated in different ways across different positions in the curriculum. Class enrollment, for example, is negatively correlated with shared-agentic instruction and student-agentic instruction in biology (the latter effect just misses attaining statistical significance at the $\alpha = .05$ level with a t-ratio of 1.91), while the *opposite* effects are observed for chemistry. Both of these effects display cross-curricular position differences that are statistically significant at the $\alpha = .05$ level. Class achievement level is positively correlated with shared-agentic instruction in chemistry, while the opposite is the case for biology (the difference in effects is statistically significant at the $\alpha = .05$ level). In addition, teacher degree level is positively correlated with higher levels of shared-agentic instruction in chemistry, but not in biology. These findings suggest that the social environments of classrooms tend to differentiate curricular positions from one another at the level of the tenth-grade science curriculum examined here. Formal teacher qualifications play a role in this differentiation as well and point to an increased reliance on inquiry-based instruction on the part of more highly educated teachers that is particularly evident for chemistry (but not biology) classrooms.

The remaining block of variables for the instructional experiences portion of the MGSEM indicates that *teachers' goals, mandates, and beliefs* are either operationalized differently across different curricular positions or responded to differently by students in different curricular positions. The teacher goal of having students do well on tests has a negative association with student-agentic instruction in biology that does not exist for chemistry. (The corresponding effects for teacher-agentic instruction and shared-agentic instruction are in the expected direction but are not statistically significant after cross-imputation variation in standard errors is accounted for.) Teacher mandates to experiment and innovate in the classroom are positively associated with teacher-agentic instruction in biology (but not in chemistry) and with shared-agentic instruction and student-agentic instruction in chemistry (but not in biology). The cross-curricular position difference for student-agentic instruction is statistically significant across curricular positions ($\alpha = .10$ level). This finding indicates that teachers' perceptions or operationalizations of pedagogical innovation vary across courses in the tenth-grade science curriculum, at least at the level of the curriculum examined here. Finally, teachers' belief that instruction can influence achievement has a positive association with student-agentic instruction for biology that does not exist for chemistry.

Overall, these findings suggest that shared-agentic instruction is more strongly influenced by classroom resources and constraints than is teacher-agentic instruction or student-agentic instruction, while student-agentic instruction is more strongly influenced by teachers' goals, mandates, and beliefs than is teacher-agentic instruction and shared-agentic instruction.

Predictors of Student Engagement with Science

The last pair of columns in table 9.2 pertain to the coefficients for the student engagement portion of the MGSEM. From the *student instructional experiences* coefficients at the lower right-hand corner of the table, it can be seen that higher levels of teacher-agentic instruction are correlated with higher levels of engagement for both biology and chemistry students. In spite of this, shared-agentic instruction has a *negative* and nonstatistically significant correlation with engagement for biology students (b = −.021), but a *positive* and statistically significant relationship for chemistry students (b = .079). Student-agentic instruction, on the other hand, has a *positive* and statistically significant correlation with engagement for biology students (b = .165), but a *negative* correlation with engagement for chemistry students (b = −.085). The cross-curricular position differences in effects for shared-agentic instruction and student-agentic instruction are both statistically significant at the α = .05 level or better. Thus, the data suggest that different forms of inquiry-based instruction have different effects on student engagement depending on their position in the curriculum, even after students' prior ability and primary motivation for taking science have been taken into account.[18]

Many of the remaining coefficients in the engagement outcome portion of the model are not statistically significant, no doubt owing to collinearities in the model. In spite of this, the results provide further indication that students' learning experiences are stratified by the interpenetration of school, classroom, and curricular structures. For example, students in higher academic press schools are likely to feel less engaged in chemistry (b = −.163), while the corresponding effect is not sizable or statistically significant for biology students. (The cross-curricular position difference in effects is, however, statistically significant at the α = .05 level.) In addition, teachers' goals, mandates, and beliefs have direct effects on students' reported engagement with science that vary somewhat by curricular position. Teachers' goal of having students do well on tests is positively correlated with engagement for biology (b = .070), while the corresponding effect is negative (and nonstatistically significant) for chemistry. In addition, teachers' belief that instruction can influence achievement is negatively correlated with student engagement in both biology and chemistry, although the effect is only statistically significant for biology students (b = −.070, with a t-ratio of −1.81). While neither the biology nor chemistry effects for teachers' emphasis on students enjoying class and becoming independent learners has a statistically significant relationship to student engagement, the cross-curricular position difference in these effects is statistically significant at the α = .10 level.

DISCUSSION AND CONCLUSION

This chapter examined the relationship between student and school resources, curricular structure, student instructional experiences, and student engagement in order to generate a fuller understanding of factors influencing the distribution and effects of instruction for tenth-grade science. It was found that student instructional experiences have sizable effects on student engagement in tenth-grade biology and chemistry even after school resources, classroom constraints, teachers' goals, mandates, and professional beliefs, and students' prior ability and motivations are taken into account. In addition, the data suggest that student instructional experiences do not always have the effects that proponents of pedagogical reform often suggest, even in an area of the curriculum where student-centered instruction typically constitutes a significant portion of classroom activity. Indeed, at the levels of the science curriculum examined here, students benefit from different aspects of inquiry-based instruction depending on their positions in the curriculum. Given the influence of school and curricular organization on the stratification of educational experiences within curricula, it appears that relying on aggregate measures of curricula in analyses of instruction obscures important structural effects in education and misspecifies the relationship between school organization, classroom resources, and the stratification of student outcomes. Two main implications follow.

First, instruction is a structural resource central to stratification in education. This is seen not only in qualitative variation in student instructional experiences across curricular positions but in variation in the mean levels of instructional experiences, variation in the way identical types of instruction are generated across positions in curricula, and variation in the effects of identical types of instruction on student engagement with science. Thus, it can be concluded that a given type of instruction is not equally effective for all students within a given curricular area and that the teacher strategies and organizational characteristics correlated with particular types of classroom pedagogical contents vary by curricular position. In light of these findings, instruction is perhaps best analyzed as a resource derived from diverse aspects of students' positions in curricula rather than as an input into schools and classrooms whose production and effects can be taken for granted in analyses of stratification in education or efforts at curricular reform.

Second, analyses of educational reform and related initiatives should adopt bottom-up rather than top-down approaches that are sensitive to the formal aspects of secondary education. Richard Ingersoll (1993) suggests that this can be achieved by reexamining the loose-coupling model of educational institutions and adopting research agendas that more explicitly acknowledge the formal aspects of schools. To this it could be added that an essential step in analyzing stratification in education is identifying the distribution and effects of instruction within curricula as elementary "social facts" that should inform subsequent theory and research on teaching, school organization, and stratification in education. Proceeding in this manner, analyses of the distribution and effects of instruction can lend much not only to the understanding of stratification in education but to current debates on curricular and school reform by pointing first to the most effective classroom pedagogical contents, so that then, from these facts, the organizational and professional forms essential to ensuring their equitable and effective distribution within schools and curricula can be derived.

With these implications in mind, it may be useful to pursue the following research and policy questions. First, researchers and policymakers may wish to expand existing ideas of "effective instruction" to take into account variation in course material as well as variation in the distribution of human capital within schools and curricula. At the same time, they need to obtain a better understanding of the causes of variation in the effects of instruction. For example, what proportion of this variation is due to the availability of adequate curricular materials (texts, lesson guides, laboratory equipment, teacher training), the social structure of the curriculum (the allocation of student human capital, effort, and motivation within schools and curricula), or the substantive demands of the academic material itself (the number of class hours necessary to lay the conceptual groundwork and develop the basic laboratory skills necessary for rewarding and productive inquiry-based instruction)? The findings reported here suggest that answering these questions will require "systematizing" subject-specific curricula in a way that does not legitimate the inequalities curricular differentiation often promotes.

After addressing these questions, researchers should move toward embedding this systematized model of curricula in models of "actually existing schools" to understand the ways educational institutions contribute to the stratification of instruction. For example, in what instances are higher levels of teacher professionalism associated with greater differentiation of student instructional experiences? To what extent does the career structure of teaching (career progression, advanced training and teacher specialization) contribute to the allocation of instructional resources within schools? Are there specific positions in curricula that, owing to demographic or overarching institutional forces, create barriers to the implementation of pedagogical or curricular reforms?

The broader implication of the preceding findings for the sociological study of schools and schooling is that analyzing instruction as the core technology of schools requires explicitly treating curricula as systems embedded within the larger system of schools themselves. The empirical tools for this enterprise are well established in recent work on instruction (see Bidwell and Yasumoto 1999; Petrin, forthcoming; Yasumoto et al. 2001; see also Friedkin and Thomas 1997). In addition, with respect to social stratification in general and the role of schools and schooling in such processes, it may be worthwhile to investigate recent trends in the sociology of knowledge (for example, Bourdieu 1996; Swidler and Arditti 1999) that attempt to link stratification, structure, and agency to distinct phenomenological locations within institutions and organizations.

NOTES

1. Additional evidence on the relationship between student agency and student instructional experiences can be found in the literature identifying the role of gender in regulating students' pedagogical experiences in high school science (see, for example, Burkam, Lee, and Smerdon 1997, as well as Jovanovic and King 1998).

2. Analysis was further limited to non–American Indian students enrolled in comprehensive public high schools at grade ten who did not change schools between the first (grade ten) and second (grade twelve) follow-up surveys.

3. The curricular positions used here are defined as follows:

   Earth and environmental science (274 respondents): environmental science, earth science, earth science–college prep, geology

   Biology (5,248 respondents): biology–basic, biology–general 1, biology–general 2

   Chemistry (1,119 respondents): chemistry–introduction, chemistry 1, chemistry 2

   Physics (529 respondents): physical science, physical science–applied, physics–general, physics 1

4. Confirmatory factor analysis (CFA) was used to develop measures of students' instructional experiences, since it bears a direct correspondence to the two-parameter item response theory (2-P IRT) models commonly used to develop latent variable measures in sociological and educational research (Muthén and Christoffersson 1981) and is readily available in structural equation modeling applications. Multigroup CFA models allow separate models to be fit to two or more distinct groups of respondents simultaneously (in this case, students grouped by curricular position), so that difference-in-chi-square tests can be used to test for statistically significant variation in key parameters across groups (Bollen 1989).

   A special variant of the standard MGCFA model, Muthén's MGCFA for ordered categorical indicators (Muthén 1984, 1989; Muthén and Christoffersson 1981), was used in these analyses, since conventional MGCFA is not appropriate for categorical indicator variables with fewer than five categories (Bollen 1989; Muthén 1989). As in conventional CFA, Muthén's model defines latent factor constructs as the unobserved variables explaining the correlation between a set of observed indicator variables. Because the indicator variables are categorical in this instance, however, the factor loadings (lambda parameters) from the Muthén model are the regression coefficients obtained from performing a set of simultaneous probit regressions of the categorical indicator items on the specified latent variables (yielding a set of probit threshold parameters). The Muthén model does not include conventional error terms for the indicator items but rather scale factors, which are necessary to identify the model and are related to the inverse of the error terms featured in conventional CFA (Muthén 1989; Muthén and Christoffersson 1981).

   MGCFA was also used to generate the school-level measures of school academic press and school professionalism. All latent variable models developed for these analyses were constructed applying the method that Karl Jøreskog (1969) described as exploratory factor analysis in a confirmatory factor analytic framework.

5. MGSEMs provide a convenient means of simultaneously fitting identical (in form) yet separate (with respect to parameter estimates) SEMs to two or more distinct subsets of a sample (Bollen 1989). In this situation, the use of MGSEMs is akin to allowing group-specific (curricular position-specific in the present context) interaction effects for all of the predictor variables in a model. MGSEMs are particularly useful in the present analyses since the interaction effects of interest include those for continuous latent vari-

ables (which are difficult to estimate without the use of special computationally intensive estimators) and since modeling a large number of interaction effects by more conventional means is problematic (owing, for example, to excessive collinearity). Cross-group differences in population composition were controlled for by including a host of student- and school-level variables in the MGSEM that are associated with the selection of students into one population versus another (in this case, one curricular position versus another), as is recommended by Bollen (1989).

6. Descriptive statistics for the variables included in the analysis are available from the author upon request.

7. Each of these items, with the exception of the "class activities are highly structured" item, is positively correlated with the school professionalism measure.

8. The school academic press measure was developed simultaneously with the school professionalism measure using Muthén's MGCFA for categorical indicators (Muthén and Christoffersson 1981). Each of the academic press indicator items was positively correlated with the final academic press measure, with the exception of the item pertaining to students' influence over deciding which courses they would like to take. To allow the school academic press and school professional environment variables to remain comparable across curricular positions, the same measurement model was used to fit all students regardless of their curricular position.

9. Teachers' degree fields are not included in the model since for the final MGSEM samples more than 90 percent of teachers majored or minored in science in either college or graduate school.

10. This approach isolates important aspects of the phenomenological environment of the classroom and brings the actual focus of pedagogical practice (the students) to the forefront of analysis (Yair 2000).

11. Although it would be desirable to estimate the influence of students' instructional experiences on their gains in achievement, it is not possible to do so with the present data, since NELS:88–94 only measures achievement at two-year intervals and is therefore not suitable for assessing the effects of instructional interventions on gains between survey waves (see Rowan et al. 2002). The engagement measure is similar to that used in analyses by Yair (2000).

12. In the present context, qualitative variation refers to substantial variation in the MGCFA measurement model parameters described in note 4.

13. These curricular position-specific CFA models are available from the author upon request.

14. For the biology and chemistry MGCFA model, it was found that in order to achieve a good fit to the data, it was necessary to allow the "write reports" probit item thresholds to vary across curricular positions. The resulting model provided good fit to the data (RMSE = .042, CFI = .954, TLI = .960). The "write reports" item thresholds indicate that tenth-grade chemistry students reported writing reports in class less often than did biology students. In the subsequent MGSEM analyses, these terms were restricted to be equal across curricular positions. Additional analyses revealed that restricting or freeing these terms had no effect on model fit or the findings presented here.

15. To identify the multigroup variant of the Muthén CFA model, it is typical to set the latent variable means to zero and scale factors to one for a reference group and allows the

remaining terms to vary for all other groups (Muthén and Christoffersson 1981). Only when the parameters relating the indicator variables to the latent variable (the loadings, indicator item thresholds, and indicator item scale factors) can be restricted to be identical across groups can the corresponding measures be said to be identical (see note 4).

16. Although the overall response rate for most of the variables included in these analyses was robust, several respondents were missing information for one or more variables essential to the analysis. The loss of cases that would result from listwise deletion would reduce the analysis samples by roughly 50 percent and limit the representation of minority students in the analysis. This rate of missingness is *not* unusual (in fact, it is quite common; see, for example, King et al. 2001; Rubin 1996), and in general omitting data discards important survey design information and risks biasing parameter estimates (King et al. 2001). In addition, Gary King and his colleagues (2001) demonstrate that analyses performed on incomplete, listwise-deletion samples can produce parameter estimates that have the *opposite* signs of the actual relationships they represent. For these reasons, the present analysis incorporates multiple imputation to ensure the validity and generalizability of results (Little and Rubin 1987). Donald Rubin (1996) argues that MI is superior to all other methods for treating missing data (see also King et al. 2001 and Meng 1994). The software used for imputing data was the stand-alone Windows application Amelia (Honaker et al. 1999).

    The NELS:88–94 first follow-up teacher data were collected only for a random subset of the NELS:88–94 student sample. The missing teacher data are therefore MAR (missing at random)–MBD (missing by design). Although the teacher-matched student sample can be analyzed without incurring any sample selection bias provided the appropriate NELS:88–94 weight is used, the missing teacher data were imputed for the chemistry subsample to achieve convergence of the chemistry subgroup imputation model. The full imputed chemistry sample was then used in the subsequent MGSEM. This imputation strategy is consistent with the NELS:88–94 sample design (refer to Raghunathan and Erizzie 1995). Analyses revealed that the inclusion of cases with imputed teacher data in the MGSEM, in spite of increasing the standard errors, produces parameter estimates that are highly consistent with those obtained from the reduced, complete-teacher-data sample. Given the high rate of missing data for the teacher data in the chemistry sample, forty independent imputations were used in the final MGSEMs.

17. Given the high degree of parameterization of the model, the RMSE criterion is given preference in judging model fit (Hu and Bentler 1995) and reveals that the final model provides good fit to the data. The small variation in the MGSEM fit statistics across imputations provides an indication that the imputations were of good quality. During the fitting of the model, coefficients whose values were identical or nearly identical across curricular positions were restricted to be equal. In addition, coefficients with extremely small values were restricted to zero. Nested chi-square tests of fit revealed that these restrictions did not significantly reduce the quality of model fit (p > .99).

18. The preceding effects are robust to alternative parameterizations of the CFA portion of the MGSEM (such as the partial invariance condition discussed by Muthén and Christoffersson 1981).

Chapter 10

Subgroups as Meso-Level Entities in the Social Organization of Schools

Kenneth A. Frank and Yong Zhao

Charles Bidwell has helped us to look cold and hard at the social organization of schools. Early on, Bidwell (1965) appreciated the complexity of the organization of schools, with its implication that teachers are only loosely coupled to one another. With Jack Kasarda, Bidwell explored a key theoretical implication of loose coupling: that schooling is organized in multiple levels, with interplay within and between levels affecting the allocation of resources that fuel educational experiences (Bidwell and Kasarda 1980). Also with Jack Kasarda, Bidwell characterized how schools participate in open systems, influenced by federal and state mandates but also changing the systems in which they are embedded (Bidwell and Kasarda 1985, 1987). Most recently, Bidwell has drawn on the classic mechanisms of competition, authority, collective action, and institutionalized policies to characterize school decisionmaking in terms of markets, autocracies, collegia, or bureaucracies (Bidwell and Quiroz 1991; Bidwell, Frank, and Quiroz 1997).

Though there are clear and enduring themes in Bidwell's work, it is up to us to determine which of his ideas apply in a particular context. Should we focus on the internal decisionmaking of schools or the relationship of schools to external systems? Should we be thinking of schools as functioning on multiple levels or as a loosely coupled horizontal structure of teachers? In this chapter, we attempt to integrate many of Bidwell's theoretical ideas through the structuring of relationships among school actors (for example, students, teachers, and administrators) within and between collegial subgroups.

A condensed form of our argument is as follows: many of Bidwell's theoretical contributions coalesce in the role of subgroups in structuring informal relations among school actors. These ideas can then be applied to study the diffusion of technology innovations in schools, a critical issue for schools today. For such a study, one can employ graphical representations of networks to understand case studies, and statistical models of networks to quantify patterns within and across schools. Such techniques make important contributions to the identification and analysis of subgroups, and how such subgroups inform organizational theory.

INTEGRATING THEORETICAL THEMES: THE STRUCTURING OF INTERACTION IN SCHOOLS

Bidwell's ideas regarding loose coupling, multiple levels, and open systems have consistently been at the vanguard of theory in the sociology of education. Others, in particular John Meyer (1977), have described how the loose coupling of teachers to principals, schools to communities, and education to societal demands allows educators to acknowledge and partially respond to external demands without drastically altering educational practices on a daily basis. Together with the insights of Rebecca Barr and Robert Dreeben (Barr and Dreeben 1977, 1983), Bidwell and Kasarda's writing on the multiple levels of schooling anticipated the prevalence of multilevel modeling in current educational research, as evidenced in almost any recent issue of *Sociology of Education, American Educational Research Journal, American Journal of Education, Educational Evaluation, and Policy Analysis*. Recent demands for accountability make it clear that schools operate in open systems, and responses to such demands demonstrate the agency of schools as they contribute to defining standards, measures, and policy implications.

Bidwell's theories about schools as organizations have appeal beyond education because schools are typical or prototypical of other organizations (for reviews, see Bolman and Heller 1995 and Perrow 1986). The epitome is Bidwell's chapter in James March's *Handbook of Organizations* (1965). More generally, as reviewed by Bidwell and Kasarda (1985), in each stage of the evolution of organizational theory there were early and prescient examples in education, from control theory (Callahan 1962) to contingency theory (Greenfield 1975) and then the new institutionalism (Meyer and Rowan 1977; Rowan 1995). Thus, when Bidwell writes about loose coupling, multiple levels, open systems, or decisionmaking, think broadly. The ideas are as likely to apply to nonprofit organizations or Fortune 500 companies or Starbucks franchises.

Most recently, Bidwell has implored sociologists of education to attend to social psychological processes and networks within schools (Bidwell 2000, 2001). School actors inform one another, persuade one another, and exert social pressure through their relationships. Thus, by conveying attitudes and information, these relationships shape individual actions that accumulate in school decisionmaking. For example, teachers' orientations to teaching emerge as they are socialized by their peers and students (see, for example, Rowan 1990a; Trent 1992; Wilson and Ball 1991; Zeichner and Gore 1989), and of course students' social organization reflects the structures of the school and community (Quiroz, Gonzalez, and Frank 1996; Coleman 1961b).

Quintessentially drawing on Willard Waller, Bidwell notes that the social psychological aspect of schools was an early and important theme in the sociology of education, helping us understand the social structures and processes that are co-incidental with education in schools. This theme faded as researchers focused on the stratification that occurred in broad areas of education and through broad processes of schooling. In this regard, the sociology of education paralleled general sociology, which moved from the small systems of organizations to the macro processes of stratification by race, gender, and ethnicity that currently dominate issues of the *American Sociological Review*. (Business and organizational psychology, meanwhile, have eagerly embraced the study of interpersonal processes within organizations.)

Given Bidwell's track record of anticipating trends in the study of schooling, we would do well to heed his call to attend to social psychological processes within schools. Although multilevel models have helped educational researchers differentiate the effects of the individual from those of the school as an organization, one of the most striking and robust results is that 66 to 90 percent of the variation in student or teacher outcomes is within schools. This applies across levels of schools and countries (see Frank 1998). Characteristics of students and teachers, such as socioeconomic background, gender, race, and seniority or age, explain a portion of the variation within schools. But what accounts for the remaining variation? Ethnographies and case studies often point to the social psychological processes through which school actors influence each other's beliefs and attitudes (Coleman 1961b; Grant 1988; Johnson 1990; Mehan, Hertweck, and Meihls 1986; Zeichner and Gore 1989). These social psychological processes are what differentiate interactions within schools from other interactions; they are what make schools *social* organizations.

Studying the social psychology of schools means attending to relationships among school actors. At different times, Bidwell has analyzed various sets of relations. With Noah Friedkin, Bidwell described the inherent tensions in relationships between students and teachers (Bidwell and Friedkin 1988), a theme that reappears in Daniel McFarland's (1999) dissertation. Bidwell and Pamela Quiroz (1991) explicitly attended to the relationship between teachers and administrators in each of four decisionmaking forms. In a forthcoming book with Quiroz, Jeffrey Yasumoto, Kazuaki Uekawa, and Kenneth Frank, Bidwell has focused on relationships among teachers, with implications for relationships between teachers and students; this is a recent example of the interplay of levels in the multilevel processes of schooling (Bidwell et al., in preparation).

Clearly, the importance of relationships implies that school actors do not act independently. Indeed, some form of coordination, emerging from underlying social processes, is inherent in voluntary participation in the common organization of the school. But relations are not merely piled together in an unstructured heap (Wellman and Frank 2001), with actors randomly forming and using ties to obtain information and influence others. School actors, like members of most other social systems, organize themselves into formal units and subgroups in which relations, or ties, are concentrated (see Frank 1995, 1996, 1998; Homans 1950; Roethlisberger and Dickson 1939; Simmel 1955; Simon 1965; for a review, see Freeman 1992).

A critical feature of the subgroup is that it is defined in terms of informal ties. Teachers may be organized by subject field, department, or grade. These units may appear on a formal organizational chart and thus may be an enduring, important structuring of interaction in an organization. But the informal processes that shape many school decisions also are structured by subgroup boundaries: "Do we really have to change our attendance record-keeping?" "How can we integrate the new emphasis on technology with our current approach to social studies?" "How can we organize demand for a new course sequence?" Like the members of other organizations, teachers are likely to turn to subgroup members as well as members of the same department or division to make sense of competing demands. But as in other organizations, subgroups are not isolated: actors may gain access to expertise throughout the organization through a direct tie with a nonsubgroup member or through an indirect tie mediated by a subgroup member (Granovetter 1973; Selznick 1961; Simmel 1955).

As in other areas, when Bidwell focused on the social psychology of schools, he brought important theory to the structuring of relationships within formal and informal boundaries. Along with Anthony Bryk and many others at the University of Chicago, Bidwell's contribution was critical to the development of Frank's software KliqueFinder (applications of which are presented later in this chapter). The research team started by relating teachers' orientations to teaching to their departmental affiliation; it then constructed crude sociograms that represented interactions within and between departments. The team then realized the limitations of such an organization: departments and subject fields differed from school to school, and fieldwork revealed idiosyncratic patterns of interaction that were artifacts of history or architecture or personal preferences (for example, the smokers' lounge).

KliqueFinder was developed through an incremental process. Typically, Bidwell would identify a limitation: Are ties concentrated equally within each subgroup? Where is information about ties spanning between subgroups? Can we identify regions of subgroups? Can these ties be represented in a two-dimensional graph rather than as a table of associations? Behind each question were Bidwell's keen instincts to represent a social structure that contextualizes the social psychological processes of school decisionmaking.

Bryk, Yasumoto, and Frank tried to address Bidwell's concerns. The result was a robust procedure that identifies non-overlapping cohesive subgroups and embeds the subgroup boundaries in a sociogram. These sociograms represent a social structure consistent with long-standing theory (Blau 1977; Durkheim 1933; Homans 1950; Roethlisberger and Dickson 1939; Simmel 1955; Simon 1965). Not surprisingly, the software has been applied to an array of social networks, from the referral patterns of community service agencies (Foster-Fishman et al. 2001) to friendships among the French financial elite (Frank and Yasumoto 1998), mobility patterns among schools (Kerbow 1996), organizational ties focused on watershed management (Lynch, Taylor, and Frank 2001), food webs (Krause et al. 2003), and friendships among students in schools (Plank 2000b; McFarland 1999).

The study presented in this chapter is a return to the original motivation and application of KliqueFinder—relations among school actors in schools—but it draws on two extensions of the methodology. First, as in Frank and Yasumoto (1998), we establish the social structure in terms of stable ties (for example, collegial relations among school actors) and then overlay the pattern of interaction (talk about computer technology, for instance) on the stable structure. This links specific decisionmaking action to enduring, underlying social structure. We also model these tendencies using social network techniques. Second, in a new feature, we graphically represent *changes* in actors' reported levels of behaviors. Although not definitively causal, representing change through longitudinal data establishes more of a basis for linking social structure to decisionmaking than do inferences from cross-sectional data.

We focus on three questions. First, do interactions affect school actor beliefs and behaviors? A positive answer reaffirms Bidwell's focus on social psychological processes. Second, how does the structuring of interactions help us understand organizational decisionmaking? Third, to what extent are interactions structured by formal categorizations and subgroup membership? The answers should help us characterize the meso-level structures of interaction that affect decisionmaking and through which schools react to external forces.

THE IMPLEMENTATION OF COMPUTER TECHNOLOGY IN ELEMENTARY SCHOOLS

We have chosen to study the diffusion of innovations because much of Bidwell's work either implicitly or explicitly applies to how schools adopt and implement change. Loose coupling, especially as developed by Meyer but in Bidwell's conceptualization as well, can be understood as a limitation of diffusion from administrator to teacher or from one school actor to another. Participation in an open system can be recast as schools' adaptation to externally generated innovations. The adoption process typically involves multiple levels, since implementation requires support from central administrators down through action from a school actor. Once within the school, decisionmaking processes allocate resources to competing demands, many of which emerge during the implementation of innovations. In fact, the decisionmaking process often is a reconciliation of past practices and current innovations.

We have focused on technological (such as computer, Internet, digital camera) innovations because there is strong pressure on schools to implement such innovations (Budin 1999; Cuban 1999; Loveless 1996; Norris, Smolka, and Soloway 1999; President's Committee of Advisers on Science and Technology 1997).[1] Several studies have already investigated how "early adopters" of educational technology compare to those who may be more reluctant to adopt and use technology in the classroom (Becker 1994; Hadley and Sheingold 1993; Wells and Anderson 1997). Even without strong links to student achievement, school actors are being asked to get students online, word processing, and otherwise expressing themselves with computers.

Generally, the diffusion of innovations within organizations is a complex process, involving the interaction of the innovation, the individuals, and the organizational context (Bayer and Melone 1989; Yetton, Sharma, and Southon 1999). As such, diverse literatures have addressed the diffusion of innovations. Engineering-based descriptions emphasize the technical characteristics of the innovation (Ramamurthy and Premkumar 1995) or the interaction of technology and task (Cooper and Zmud 1990) and deemphasize the human component. The organizational psychology literature attends to the beliefs and perceptions of organizational members but is constrained by a survey research paradigm (Agarwal and Prasad 1998; Ajzen and Fishbein 1980; Igbaria and Iivari 1995); individual action is responsive only to individual beliefs, as though actors are independent, and organizations are characterized merely in terms of the aggregate of beliefs. Absent are direct representations of interpersonal relations. The management literature has identified the role of the manager in the diffusion process, as well as antecedents of successful diffusion, but typically the management literature focuses on the level of the organization, often without a strong theoretical underpinning in the action of organizational members (Bayer and Melone 1989; Borton and Brancheau 1994; Brancheau and Wetherbe 1990; Kwon and Zmud 1987; Meyer and Goes 1988; Rogers 1995; Yetton et al. 1999; Zmud 1983; Zmud and Apple 1992).

In complex organizations like schools (Etzioni 1961; Hage 1999), it is not a simple matter of a few key decisionmakers making a collective decision to adopt and implement an innovation (Pfeffer 1981; Tornatzky et al. 1983). Instead, the process is more one of diffusion of innovation within the organization, since each actor has some autonomy to make her own decision and implement it, partly in response to the ideas, information, and other social forces to which she is exposed. Thus, most innovations are unevenly implemented throughout the organization (Tornatzky and Fleischer 1990).

If the technology itself is complex, with a range of possible applications and contexts, then organizational members may benefit from informal interactions with colleagues (Eveland and Tornatzky 1990). The question "Who can I talk to about this?" is critical to implementation. Of course, the formal organizational chart may identify a centralized department responsible for supporting technological innovations (Attewell 1992), but much help may also come through the informal organization (Aiken, Bacharach, and French 1980; Ibarra 1993; Kanter 1983).

Do Interactions Affect School Actor Beliefs and Behaviors? A Review of Recent Evidence

To address how school actors' technology use changes as a function of their interactions, we draw on recent studies we have conducted of school actors' use of technology. Based on longitudinal social network data in six elementary schools, Kenneth Frank (2002) and Frank, Yong Zhao, and Kathryn Borman (2004) have found that the more a school actor receives help and talks to highly expert school actors, the more the school actor increases her use of computers. Frank and his colleagues also found that the more school actors perceive social pressure to use computers, the more likely they are to use computers. In Zhao and Frank (2003), we linked social pressure to school actors' uses of computers and the provision of help more directly to student uses of computers.

These results validate Bidwell's recent attention to the social psychological processes in schools. In fact, effects mediated by the social structure were comparable to those of long-standing diffusion theory associated with school actor perceptions regarding the value of technology or the technological resources available to implement technology. This implies that the implementation of technological innovations is as much a function of social structure as of the distribution of individual perceptions and resources.

In addition to evidence of social psychological processes, we found that technology implementation was affected by several structural factors. In particular, school actors are more likely to use computers if they have small classes and access to computer resources. Interestingly, school actors are less likely to use computer technology if they perceive an increase in standardized tests, perhaps because technology and standardized tests compete with each other for the resource of school actor time. These effects emphasize the location of the school in a multi-level, open system.

A Social History of Diffusion in One School as Structured by Collegial-Based Subgroups

Our recent findings establish that school actors' talk about technology affects their use of technology. Thus, social psychological processes are important for school actor behavior. But the analyses do not reveal the structure of talk. One might be inclined to structure talk by relying on the boundaries defined by the formal organization. Teachers in elementary schools could be expected to talk within grades, and teachers in high schools could be expected to talk within departments or subject fields (see, for example, Johnson 1990; Siskin 1991). But units of the formal organization vary from school to school. Furthermore, formal categories may not be mutually exclusive. High school teachers may teach more than one subject, and elementary school teachers may teach more than one grade. In fact, about 50 percent of the respondents in our previous analyses (including regular class teachers, support staff, and administrators) could not be categorized as teaching in a single grade. Correspondingly, we seek to relate the diffusion process to the informal structure of a school, defined by subgroups of collegial ties.

To graphically represent the informal structure of school actor collegial ties, we used Frank's (Frank 1995, 1996) KliqueFinder algorithm for identifying cohesive subgroups based on the pattern of ties among actors, and then for embedding the subgroup boundaries in a crystallized sociogram. Frank's algorithm employs a stochastic definition of cohesion, focusing on ties within subgroups *relative to* actors' propensities for engaging in ties and sizes of subgroups.[2]

Typically, the criteria used to define cohesiveness are fixed (in terms of the absolute number of ties present or absent in a subgroup), and the corresponding structures accommodate variation in the data by allowing the subgroup boundaries to overlap, producing what Kadushin (1995, 212) refers to as "several overlapping small clusters" (see also Frank 1993; Freeman 1992). Such overlapping clusters are inconsistent with many of the theoretical characterizations of systems composed of *non-overlapping* subgroups. In particular, overlapping boundaries fail to establish "an inside and an outside" (Abbott 1996, 872) necessary to define a sociological entity. How can we differentiate action within subgroups from that between subgroups if two actors can simultaneously be members of the same subgroup and members of different subgroups? At the more macro level, though ties between members of different subgroups can and must exist, systemic processes cannot be characterized in terms of components if the components are not distinct.

DATA AND METHODS   We analyze data from one of the six schools studied by Frank and his colleagues and reported on earlier. As a set, the schools represent a range with respect to ethnicity and socioeconomic status. Westville, the school that is the focus of these analyses, is a suburban elementary school located about five miles from a city of over 500,000. It was chosen because it underwent a dramatic change in technology resources and use during the time of the study.

From January to June 2000, Frank interviewed ten school actors in the school as well as the principal and district technology coordinator. In April and May 2001, Frank returned and conducted five to ten more interviews (ranging in formality and length), three of which were reinterviews of subjects from the first wave. The interviews were based on a simple protocol ("How do you use technology?" "How do you make the decisions about technology?" "What is the social context in which you make those decisions?") to learn about the processes through which diffusion occurred and how diffusion was related to relationships among faculty. These interviews (as well as those from other schools) not only provided basic phenomenological-level data regarding technology use but also informed the development of a questionnaire to assess school actors' use of technology, perceptions regarding the potential of technology, background information, and so forth.[3] The questionnaire also included sociometric questions regarding close colleagues, providers of help in using computers, talk about computers, and influences on computer use. Thus, each school actor indicated those others who were close colleagues, most influential, helpful, and so forth.

To achieve a high response rate at each time point, Westville was offered $500 compensation for an 85 percent response rate or greater.[4] Frank administered the survey at faculty meetings and then followed up with the principal and a contact teacher to identify and solicit those school actors who had not yet responded. This was necessary to capture information on school actors who might marginally identify with the school and therefore were less likely to participate in a school survey. Eighty percent of the school actors responded at each wave. To obtain longitudinal survey data, Frank first surveyed school actors in the spring of 2000 (time 1) and then again in the spring of 2001 (time 2).

ANALYSES OF SUBGROUPS   To represent an example of a stable, enduring structure, we applied Frank's algorithm to collegial ties among faculty and staff. Then, following Frank (1996), we embedded the subgroup boundaries in the crystallized sociogram, as shown in figure 10.1. We refer to the sociogram as crystallized because it reveals an isomorphic nesting of structures. Within each subgroup there is a structure of people and ties, and between subgroups there is a structure of subgroup boundaries and bridging ties. Thus, the boundaries differentiate regions of dense and sparse concentrations of collegial ties. Ultimately, the technique reorganizes the data to generate a clearer and more accessible image of the social structure that is consistent with characterizations of systemic social structures.

Before interpreting the crystallized sociogram in figure 10.1, we use Frank's (1995) simulations to address two specific questions regarding the identified subgroups. First, because the application of KliqueFinder would reveal a concentration of ties within subgroups in data in which the ties were generated at random, we must ask whether the ties are more concentrated within the subgroup boundaries in figure 10.1 than is likely to have occurred by chance alone.[5] In this case, the predicted probability of obtaining the concentration of ties within the subgroup boundaries in figure 10.1, *after employing KliqueFinder*, was less than one in one hundred. Thus, there is strong evidence that the subgroups are salient in terms of capturing concentrations of collegial ties.

Second, we ask whether KliqueFinder accurately recovered the "true" subgroup memberships.[6] For networks of comparable size and concentration of ties within subgroups as in figure 10.1, Frank's simulations indicate that the odds that two actors in the same known subgroup would be assigned by KliqueFinder to the same observed subgroup were almost nine times greater than they were for two actors in different known subgroups. This finding, taken together with the evidence that ties are concentrated within subgroups, supports a conclusion that the subgroups were not imposed on a fluid pattern of ties but represent an empirical tendency for collegial ties among the school actors in Westville to be concentrated within the subgroup boundaries displayed in figure 10.1.

In figure 10.1, each number represents a school actor. The text following the number indicates the grade in which the teacher teaches (for example, G3 indicates grade 3, MG indicates multiple grades, and GX indicates unknown grade). The subgroup boundaries are represented by circles around subsets of actors. The lines connecting pairs of school actors indicate that at least one school actor listed the other as a close colleague (solid lines within subgroups, dotted lines between subgroups).

There is a clear alignment of grade and subgroup boundaries embedded in the sociogram in figure 10.1. Subgroup A consists of mostly third-grade teachers, subgroup B consists of mostly second-grade teachers, and there is a dense concentration of collegial ties in each subgroup.[7] But the subgroup structure also characterizes those faculty, administrators, and staff who do not neatly fit into the categories of the formal organization. For example, subgroup C contains the physical education teacher, a special education teacher, the principal, and two teachers who do not have extensive ties with others in their grades. The members of subgroup C are not unaffiliated: they are members of a cross-grade subgroup within which roughly 50 percent of the possible collegial ties are realized. This is enough to distinguish the density of ties within subgroup C from all of the between-subgroup densities (which range from 0 to 29 percent).

FIGURE 10.1 / Crystallized Sociogram of Collegial Ties at Westville Elementary School

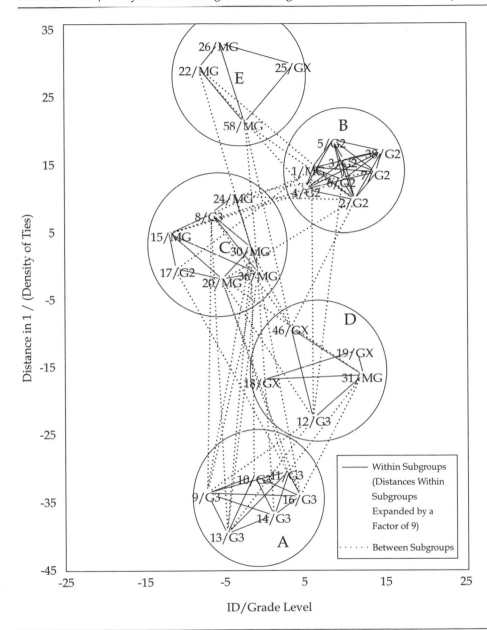

Source: Authors' compilation.

TALK ABOUT TECHNOLOGY Following the methodology of Frank and Yasumoto (1998), in figure 10.2 we have overlaid talk about technology between time 1 and time 2 on the geography defined by the collegial ties in figure 10.1. We generally observe that technology talk is concentrated within subgroups, especially the grade-based subgroups A and B. (Again, solid lines are within subgroups and dotted are between subgroups.) Now we extend the methodology of Frank and Yasumoto by representing *change* in school actors' use of technology. To begin, each school actor's identification number has been replaced with a dot proportional to his or her use of technology at time 1 (with an * indicating no information available). The larger the dot, the more the school actor used technology as reported at time 1. The ripples indicate increases in the use of technology from time 1 to time 2.[8]

The interpretation of figures 10.1 and 10.2 can be understood relative to the historical context of technology at Westville. Westville's commitment to technology goes back to a state-of-the-art Macintosh computer lab established in the early 1990s. But recently Westville lost considerable decisionmaking control to the district, especially regarding technology. In particular, the central administration made a commitment to use the Windows platform. This was based on a recommendation from a business consultant. The basic argument provided by the district was that many businesses would be using Windows, and thus students needed to learn Windows. Furthermore, district administrators felt they would be able to obtain more support and software for the more prevalent Windows platform. This decision was for the most part not supported by the school actors at Westville, who were more familiar with the Macintosh platform at the time the decision was made.[9]

Within the school, some actors who were comfortable with Macintoshes resisted the Windows technology. Furthermore, the most technology-oriented actor in the school, teacher 20 of subgroup B, was much more proficient with the Macintosh than with Windows. Thus, the change in platform rendered much of her knowledge useless. Furthermore, like most elementary schools, Westville did not have a full-time support person for technology, and district support was only minimally available. The problem for the school then was how to gain access to the technical knowledge to implement the new technology.

It was clear that the school would have to draw on internal resources, but there was no source of Windows expertise in the school. Some school actors responded by taking outside courses in the summer. The district responded by assigning a Windows expert, teacher 2 (a second-grade teacher in subgroup B), to Westville. (This action is represented by the arrow on the far right of figure 10.2.) Although this teacher had knowledge of Windows, she did not have extensive collegial ties within the school. The problem then became one of integrating teacher 2 into this fragmented school.

Teacher 2 immediately established collegial ties with the other teachers in subgroup B, and she followed up on those ties by talking with and helping others in subgroup B regarding computer technology. Thus, she generated extensive discussion regarding technology in her subgroup, resulting in a few small

FIGURE 10.2 / Talk About Technology Within and Between Subgroups at Westville,
Including Changes in Levels of Technology Use

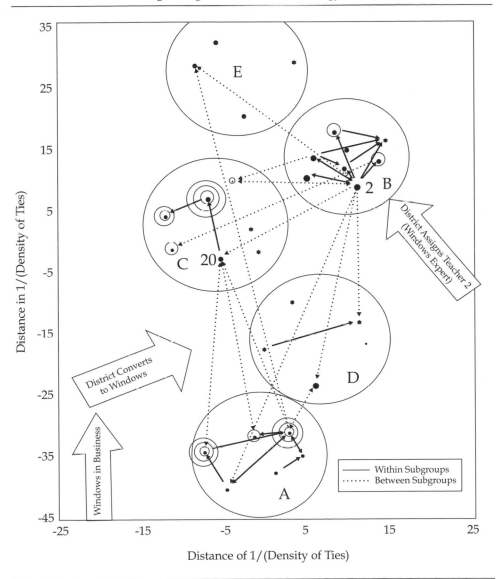

Source: Authors' compilation.
Note: • = base level use (* is unknown); circles indicate increases.

increments in technology use. But the fragmented nature of the school confined her expertise within subgroup B.

The key to extending teacher 2's knowledge beyond her subgroup was the collegial tie that teacher 2 formed with teacher 20. Though these teachers did not know each other prior to teacher 2's assignment to Westville, perhaps out of professionalism or a commitment to technology, the two formed a collegial tie, as shown in figures 10.1 and 10.2. Teacher 2's knowledge of Windows spread primarily through her connection with teacher 20. Teacher 20 talked about computers with members of her subgroup, C, resulting in substantial changes in use (as can be observed in the ripples around school actors in subgroup C), and teacher 20 talked about technology with members of subgroup A, also resulting in considerable increases in use of technology.

Many of the theoretical processes detailed in the writing of Bidwell and others are represented in figure 10.2—in particular, the open system of schools, the response of schools to external institutions, the multiple levels of schools, loose coupling within schools, school decisionmaking, and social psychological processes among school actors. The district's decision to adopt Windows (represented by the arrows on the left in figure 10.2) is an example of the school conforming to external institutions. This external influence then permeated the school because the district controlled the purchase of hardware and software, including the machines in the school lab and classrooms (represented by the arrow pointing from left to right).[10] In a sense, this dynamic pushed the openness of schools to the district level; in this case the district adopted the institution of the Windows platform.

According to both Meyer's and Bidwell's descriptions, processes in the school and district were loosely coupled. The district's decision to implement Windows was originally only loosely coupled with action because the school actors had more expertise with Macintoshs. Then the district's assignment of teacher 2 was only loosely coupled to changes in the school because teacher 2 did not have extensive collegial ties throughout the school. Finally, as in Bidwell's sense, the action of the teachers in subgroup B was only loosely coupled with the action of others in the school, particularly those in subgroup A, because of the dearth of collegial ties between members of subgroup B and other school actors.

School actors addressed the problem of the platform change through their own talk. As a social psychological process, this talk affected their access to information and perceptions regarding how computers work. This talk then affected their behavior, since their talk often resulted in changes in how they used computers. In the aggregate, these classroom behaviors defined school decisionmaking as much as or more than the district's decision to adopt the Windows platform. Finally, as hypothesized in Frank (1996) and Frank and Yasumoto (1996), these same subgroup boundaries also structured the spread of the diffusion at the level of the organization: information and influence circulated within subgroup B, then spanned to subgroup C (through the tie between teacher 2 and teacher 20), circulated a little in subgroup C, and then spanned to subgroup A. The power of cohesive subgroups to characterize both individual contexts and systemic diffusion is deceptively simple, but critical. Ultimately, it is only because the same subgroup boundaries are relevant to individual and organizational functions that the subgroups become salient meso-level entities in the organization of the school.

Analysis of Talk About Technology Across Schools

The crystallized sociograms represent the value of structuring collegial ties and interactions in a single school. To explore whether talk about technology was similarly structured across many schools, we analyzed data in a second, larger, but cross-sectional dataset. Note that these cross-sectional data were adequate for describing how talk is structured, since grade levels and subgroups (defined in terms of collegial ties) can be taken as stable, and therefore as given, relative to talk about technology. These data also afforded the opportunity to compare talk about computer technology ("With whom do you talk about new uses for computers in your teaching?") with a paired question regarding talk about the curriculum ("With whom do you talk about new ideas for the curriculum?"). Thus, we could establish the extent to which talk about the recent innovation of technology compared with talk about the core issue of curriculum.

This dataset consisted of approximately 430 school actors in nineteen elementary schools in four districts in Michigan. The criteria used to select districts for participation in the study included recent passage (within the last two to three years) of a bond referendum or receipt of a community foundation grant for implementation of technology, the willingness of the superintendent of schools to participate in the study, and the presence of at least three elementary schools in the district. These were essential criteria for selection and resulted in a school sample slightly more advantaged than the average school in Michigan. Procedures for administering the survey were similar to those followed for the first dataset (see Zhao and Frank 2002).

To describe the structuring of technology talk, we estimated multilevel cross-nested models, with pairs of school actors nested within the nominators and nominees of ties. These are p_2-like social network models that control for individual tendencies to nominate and be nominated, providing a new alternative to modeling social network relations with their inherent dependencies. Rather than ignoring sets of dependencies, as in the initial p_1 social network models (Holland and Leinhardt 1981), or reducing dependencies to a set of characteristics of network structure, as in the p* models (Wasserman and Pattison 1996), the p_2 framework uses multilevel models to capture dependencies with random effects for nominators and nominees and then models the dependencies as functions of individual characteristics (Lazega and Van Duijn 1997).[11] Thus, only the *variances* of nominator and nominee effects are specified. Correspondingly, estimation is more tractable because the number of parameters does not increase with network size.

Formally, whether i indicates talking to i' is a function of the tendency of i' to be talked to regarding technology ($\alpha_{i'}$) and the tendency of i to indicate talking to others (β_i). The model at level 1 for the pair of actors i and i' is:

level 1 (pair):

$$\log\left(\frac{P[\text{Talk}_{ii'} = 1]}{1\ P[\text{Talk}_{ii'}]}\right) = \alpha_{i'} + \beta_i \tag{10.1}$$

Note that for ease of interpretation, the occurrence of technology talk was dichotomized from original data indicating frequency of talk, with $\text{talk}_{ii'}$ taking a value of one if i indicated talking at all to i', and zero otherwise. Therefore, a logistic model is specified at level 1.

To capture the effects of ascriptive characteristics as well as ascriptive formal and informal structuring, we included dummy variables indicating whether school actors were the same gender, taught in the same grade, or were in the same subgroup. Subgroup membership was determined by application of KliqueFinder to collegial ties in each of the nineteen schools. In two of the schools collegial ties were not strongly enough concentrated within subgroups to reject the null hypothesis that ties were unstructured by subgroup. Therefore, in these schools all school actors were considered members of one common subgroup.

To capture a balance effect (Davis 1967; Heider 1958; Newcomb 1961), we included a term indicating the absolute value of the difference between i and i' in perceptions regarding the value of computers. We then included two predictors at level 1 to capture the link between the stable structure, defined in terms of collegial ties, and specific talk about technology. First, we included whether i indicated that i' was a close colleague. Second, we included the structural similarity of i and i' defined in terms of the number of common others whom i and i' indicated were close colleagues. The theory here is that school actors who were structurally similar might have been more aware of each other's needs and strengths and felt more inclined to talk to one another (Burt 1987; Frank and Yasumoto 1998). Drawing on theories of power (Blau 1967), we also included a term indicating the difference in the number of close colleagues listed by i and i'. The theory was that prominent school actors would be more likely to talk with other prominent school actors who could command their attention. Following the p_2 models, we included a reciprocity effect, signifying whether i' indicated talking to i. The final level 1 model is:

$$\log\left(\frac{P[\text{Talk}_{ii'} = 1]}{1\ P[\text{Talk}_{ii'}]}\right) = \alpha_{i'} + \beta_i +$$

$\delta_1 \ (\text{same grade})_{ii'} +$

$\delta_2 \ (\text{same subgroup})_{ii'} +$

$\delta_3 \ (\text{same gender})_{ii'} +$

$\delta_4 \ (\text{difference in beliefs about value of computers for teachers})_{ii'} +$

$\delta_5 \ (\text{difference in beliefs about value of computers for students})_{ii'} +$

$\delta_6 \ (\text{direct colleagues})_{ii'} +$

δ_7 (structural similarity of collegial ties) $_{ii'}$ +

δ_8 (difference in number of colleagues) $_{ii'}$ +

δ_9 (talk from i' to i) $_{ii}$ 　　　　　　　　　　　　　　　(10.2)

The tendencies of school actors to report talking to others and for others to list them are then modeled at a separate level:

level 2a(i': nominee):

$\alpha_{i'} = \gamma_{00} + u_{0i'}$

level 2b(i: nominator):

$\beta_i = \gamma_{10} + v_{0i}$ 　　　　　　　　　　　　　　　　　(10.3)

Thus, the random effects, $u_{0i'}$ and v_{0i}, account for dependencies in the data that can be attributed to the fact that each individual contributes to more than one pair.[12] Estimating the variances using models 10.1 and 10.3, an unconditional model, there is eight times more variation in the frequency with which school actors were nominated as the recipients of talk about technology than there is for school actors' tendencies to nominate others (.85 versus .1). That is, there were a few actors who were highly central in talk about technology.[13]

Finally, we included three measures of stress for school actor i: whether i indicated that the school introduced many new things; average class size of i; and whether i was teaching a new subject. We reasoned that each of these factors might place time demands on school actors and therefore limit the extent to which they could engage others in talk about an innovation. We also included fixed effects through dummy variables to account for school membership. Thus, the final level 2a model was:

level 2a(nominee):

$\alpha_{i'} = \gamma_{00} + \gamma_{01}$ many new things$_{i'} + \gamma_{02}$ class size$_{i'}$
　　　$+ \gamma_{03}$ new subject$_{i'} + \gamma'_{04-21}$
　　　[dummy school 1, dummy school 2, . . . ,
　　　dummy school 18] $+ u_{0i'}$ 　　　　　　　　　　(10.4)

We did not model the tendencies of school actors to be nominated for talk; thus, the final model 2b is as in equation 10.3.

Even with the use of multilevel models, the interpretation of standard errors is controversial. Emmanuel Lazega and Maritjte Van Duijn (1997) report standard errors and use them as a basis for interpretation, although they indicate that t-tests are approximate. More generally, Stanley Wasserman and Philippa Pattison (1996) and Paul Holland and Samuel Leinhardt (1981) express extensive concern about standard errors and significance tests due to dependencies in the data, and so we report and interpret t-ratios (and rough p-values) with caution.

The results from the estimated model are presented in table 10.1. Not surprisingly, the strongest predictors of whether i reported talking with i' about technology were whether the school actors were colleagues, whether they taught the same grade, and whether i' indicated talking to i. The direct effect of collegiality establishes the importance of the strong pairwise tie, membership in the same grade establishes the effect of the formal organization, and i' indicating talking to i represents reciprocity. Beyond these, there is a moderate balance effect—the more similar two school actors were in their perceptions of the potential of computers for teachers, the more likely they were to interact. (The negative sign for the coefficient for difference in perceptions implies that the smaller the difference, the more likely two actors were to talk.) Note that with cross-sectional data we cannot determine whether school actors who held similar perceptions chose to talk to one another or whether school actors generated similar perceptions through their talk. The two mechanisms need not be separated from the balance perspective—it is enough to know that there is alignment. (In the discussion section, we comment more on whether school actors influenced one another's perceptions.)

There was an effect of membership in the same subgroup (barely statistically significant at $p \leq .049$, recalling the tenuous nature of statistical inferences in these models). Though the coefficient is only moderate, it indicates that the odds that two school actors talked were about 30 percent greater if they were members of the same subgroup than if they were not. Critically, this effect is net of the effect of the formal structuring of grade membership. Thus, there is moderate evidence of informal structuring as well as strong evidence of formal structuring of talk.

There is moderate evidence that school actors who reported their school introducing many new things engaged in more talk than others. Contrary to the stress hypothesis, this finding is more consistent with the argument that school actors use talk to implement innovations. Neither class size nor new subjects taught are strongly related to the tendency to engage in talk. Thus, overall, there is limited evidence for the hypothesis that time demands inhibit opportunities for talk. There is little support for the effects of structural similarity or differences in number of collegial ties (representing differences in power or prominence).

To evaluate whether talk about new technology was similar to other types of talk, we analyzed a second model identical to the first except with curricular talk as the outcome. Results are reported in table 10.2. The coefficients in table 10.2 are similar to those in table 10.1, suggesting that factors that affected the core interactions regarding curriculum were similar to those regarding talk about technology. Most interesting is the fact that curricular talk is about 22 percent more strongly nested within the formal and informal structures than is technology.[14] Thus, descriptively, technology talk was moderately more likely to transcend the formal and informal structures than was curricular talk. In this sense, technology talk has the potential to integrate relatively disconnected components of the organization.

To determine whether talk about technology changed collegial structures, we returned to our longitudinal dataset and modeled change in collegial ties as a function of talk about technology across six schools. Change in collegial ties was defined by two dichotomous variables: one indicating the emergence of new col-

TABLE 10.1 / Cross-Nested Multilevel Logistic Regression (p_2-Like Social Network Model) of Talk with i' About Technology Reported by i

Independent Variable	Coefficient	Approximate Standard Error	t-Ratio	Odds Ratio
Pair level				
Formal: same grade	1.390	.129	10.78	4.015
Informal: same subgroup	.270	.137	1.971	1.31
Ascriptive: same gender	.204	.163	1.252	1.226
Balance: difference in perceptions regarding value for teachers	−.217	.090	−2.41	0.805
Balance: difference in perceptions regarding value for students	.162	.101	1.604	1.176
Social: colleague	2.756	.137	20.12	15.74
Social: collegial structural similarity	.004	.055	0.07	1.004
Social: number of i' colleagues minus number of i colleagues	−.010	.030	−0.33	0.99
Reciprocity: talk from i' to i	1.271	.141	9.014	3.564
Characteristics of school actor i				
School introduces many new things	.245	.060	4.083	1.278
Class size	−.005	.008	−0.63	0.995
New subject taught	−.208	.151	−1.38	0.812

Variance Components

	Unconditional	Unconditional as Percentage
Nominator (i)	.10	10.53
Nominee (i')	.85	89.47

Source: Authors' compilation.
Notes: School effects are not reported. The data analyzed are for 433 school actors. The total number of pairs = 10,322 (only pairs within schools were analyzed).

legial ties where none had existed before, and the other indicating the dissolution of a previously existing collegial tie.

The models followed the p_2 format, with the following variables modeled at the pair level: teaching in the same grade; membership in the same subgroup; talk about technology as reported either at time 1 or time 2; the extent of structural similarity in terms of collegial ties shared by i and i'; the difference in the number of

TABLE 10.2 / Cross-Nested Multilevel Logistic Regression (p_2-Like Social Network Model) of Talk with i' About Curriculum Reported by i

Independent Variable	Coefficient	Approximate Standard Error	t-Ratio	Odds Ratio
Pair level				
Formal: same grade	1.793	.123	14.58	6.007
Informal: same subgroup	.346	.126	2.746	1.413
Ascriptive: same gender	.348	.156	2.231	1.416
Balance: difference in perceptions regarding value for teachers	−.147	.084	−1.75	0.863
Balance: difference in perceptions regarding value for students	.175	.097	1.804	1.191
Social: colleague	2.685	.119	22.56	14.66
Social: collegial structural similarity	.093	.052	1.788	1.097
Social: number of i' colleagues – number of i colleagues	−.016	.029	−0.55	0.984
Reciprocity: talk from i' to i	1.443	.131	11.02	4.233
Characteristics of school actor i				
School introduces many new things	.248	.072	3.444	1.281
Class size	−.017	.009	−1.89	0.983
New subject taught	−.421	.188	−2.24	0.656

Source: Authors' compilation.
Notes: School effects are not reported. The data analyzed are for 433 school actors. The total number of pairs = 10,322 (only pairs within schools were analyzed).

colleagues between i and i', reasoning that people seek colleagues who are more prominent than themselves; and whether i reported technology help from i', either at time 1 or time 2. We included dummy variables to account for school effects in level 2a of the model.

The results for the emergence of new collegial ties are reported in table 10.3. Generally, new collegial ties emerged from the existing structure. Thus, school actors who were structurally similar, who taught in the same grade, or who were members of the same subgroup were more likely to form new collegial ties than others. In addition, new collegial ties were linked to the general social structure: school actors reported new collegial ties with others who were more prominent. Most interestingly, talk about technology, during either time interval, predicted the emergence of collegial ties. (The effect of the help provided was in the same di-

TABLE 10.3 / Cross-Nested Multilevel Logistic Regression (p_2-Like Social Network Model) of Emergence of New Collegial Ties Reported by i with i′

Independent Variable	Coefficient	Approximate Standard Error	t-Ratio	Odds Ratio
Pair level				
Formal: same grade	.810	.207	3.913	2.248
Informal: same subgroup	.660	.153	4.314	1.935
Technology talk (reported by i with i′), time 1	.535	.066	8.106	1.707
Technology talk (reported by i with i′), time 2	.292	.092	3.174	1.339
Social: collegial structural similarity	.075	.017	4.412	1.078
Social: number of i′ colleagues—number of i colleagues	.143	.031	4.613	1.154
i′ provided technology help to i, time 1	.004	.0063	0.635	1.004
i′ provided technology help to i, time 2	.004	.0067	0.597	1.004

Source: Authors' compilation.
Notes: School effects are not reported. The data analyzed are for 101 school actors. The total number of pairs = 2,831 (only pairs within schools were analyzed).

rection, but not as strong.) In fact, the effect was especially strong for talk about technology up until time 1, for which the stronger causal argument can be made: talk about technology prior to time 1 clearly occurred prior to the emergence of new collegial ties from time 1 to time 2. This represents a lagged effect, which seems natural, since collegial ties form slowly. Effects on the loss of collegial ties were similar (with most predictors being negative, preventing the loss of a collegial tie) and are not reported here.

CONCLUSION: THE STRUCTURING OF SOCIAL PSYCHOLOGICAL PROCESSES AND THE SOCIAL ORGANIZATION OF SCHOOLS

Just as Bidwell and Kasarda's call for attention to the multiple levels of schooling demonstrated the need for multilevel models, so Bidwell's call for attention to social psychological processes demonstrates the need for social network tools and models. In this chapter, we have referred to two of the fundamental social network models. Our recent models of change in school actors' use of technology employed talk about technology as an independent variable in a "network effects" model (Marsden and Friedkin 1994). The models of who talks to whom and who forms collegial ties with whom treated ties as outcomes in models of selection, employing the new p_2 approach for specification and estimation. Though much needs to be learned about specifying and estimating these models (see, for example, Frank 1998; Frank and Fahrbach 1999; Lazega and Van Duijn 1997; Wasserman and Pattison 1996), they are already developed enough to explore theoretical propositions and help researchers develop new theory. But social network processes are tricky, and thus graphical representations of data, such as the crystallized sociogram we used here, contribute to theory development and model specification.

Results from the statistical models confirm many of the theories of Bidwell and others regarding the organization of schools. Our recent findings indicate that school actors' use of computers is influenced at multiple levels. Districts and schools determine class size, access to resources, and emphasis on standardized tests, while perceptions regarding the value of computers characterize the school actors. Of course, many of these factors are affected by institutions that call for standardized tests or for tomorrow's workforce to be proficient with computers. Processes at multiple and potentially competing levels almost ensure that action at any one level will be only loosely coupled with action at other levels. Amid these other processes, the social psychological element is clearly present: school actors who talk with other experts are more likely to increase their computer usage. Thus, Bidwell's call for attention to social psychological processes is justified.

Attending to social psychology in terms of the social organization of schools means attending to the structure of interaction. In this chapter, we used subgroup memberships to characterize how an external change affected a school. The process began when the school's district responded to external institutional pressure to install the Windows platform, and the social issue emerged when the district assigned a new second-grade teacher who was an expert in Windows. The new problem for the school became finding a way to circulate the expertise of the new teacher from subgroup to subgroup. In this case, the problem was addressed through the social structure: one key senior bridging teacher formed a collegial tie with the new teacher and was able to convey the expertise to her subgroup and then to others.

Applications of the p_2 models demonstrate that talk about technology was concentrated within the formal organization defined by grades, and less so within informal subgroups. Though the stronger effect is for grade, recall that 50 percent of school actors could not be categorized by grade, thus necessitating the informally defined subgroups. The effects of grades and subgroups are in addition to links between specific technology talk and general collegial ties and the balance effects associated with differences in perceptions.

In its structuring, technology talk is very similar to curricular talk, although the two are not coincidental. Thus, the formal and informal structuring is more robust than tendencies among specific pairs of school actors. A given pair of school actors who talk about technology may not necessarily talk about curriculum, but the subgroups and grade assignments that structure talk about technology are the same as those that structure talk about the curriculum. Thus, formal categories and informal collegial subgroups define meso-level entities that generally structure interaction.

Generally, the new dynamic feature of the sociograms reveals many of the processes of schools as organizations. We observe that institutions or external forces penetrate a school first by influencing a small number of actors, who then influence members of their subgroups, who then influence others in the school. Transitions between levels are accomplished as school actors are influenced by, and influence, other subgroup members. School actors are only loosely coupled because their collegial ties and their interactions specific to technology are concentrated within formal and informal boundaries. Thus, information about an innovation may diffuse slowly throughout a school as it circulates within subgroups, then spans between subgroups. Correspondingly, the implementation of an innovation, constituting a schoolwide "decision," is likely to be uneven at any given time.

Results of models of the evolution of collegial ties indicate just how fundamentally schools are open to the external influences of technology. At the very least, technology talk anticipates new collegial ties. At most, technology talk generates new collegial ties as school actors develop strong, general relationships through their specific interactions. This finding casts a different light on the fact that technology talk transcends grades more than curricular talk. As technology talk anticipates new collegial ties, the pressure to adopt new technology could be increasing the separation between the formal and informal organizations of schools. The results could be profound: the press for technology may be integrating school actors across previously segregated formal barriers, generating new alliances and factions associated with technology use or disconnecting school actors from their grade affiliations. Of course, no change is likely to be dramatic, since collegial ties evolve slowly, influenced by structural similarity and prominence as well as by previous direct collegial ties.

Two processes are conspicuously absent in the data. First, there is little evidence to support Ronald Burt's (1987) finding that adoption of an innovation is influenced by the adoption of structurally similar actors. Most likely, as Bidwell (2000) notes, power and competition are not as strongly evident in schools as they are in other organizations and systems. Correspondingly, school actors may be more motivated by others with whom they directly interact than by the need to keep up with a reference group (Merton 1957b).

Second, in separate analyses, there was little evidence that school actors influenced each other's perceptions regarding the potential to use computers through talk about computers (the standardized effect for log of talk with experts on change in perceptions was .11 with t-ratio 1.0). Thus, it is unlikely that school actors are inducing one another to conform in perceptions, as is implied by Noah Friedkin's (1998) process models. Instead, when school actors talk, they may well be sharing information that directly increases the capacity for implementing computers (for example, sharing technical expertise regarding digital cameras) without changing perceptions regarding the potential for computers (for example, the value of digital cameras for displaying student work).

When we pair the hypothesis that school actors are sharing information in their talk about technology with the finding that school actors are highly variable in the extent to which they are listed as being talked to, we are motivated to ask: why do some school actors take the time to talk with others and share information about technology use? Why wouldn't they merely operate within their own classroom (see Lortie 1975)? Are they motivated to educate a common set of students, or to fulfill faculty obligations, or to enhance their prestige? Turning the question around, are there differences in school actors' capacities to access knowledgeable others? Are there reciprocal arrangements, or is there a more general exchange process (Cook and Whitmeyer 1992; Emerson 1972)? These questions become questions about the distribution of social capital (Bourdieu 1986; Coleman 1988; Lin 2001; Portes 1998), that is, actors' capacities to attract resources through informal ties. We address these questions in other contexts (Frank 2002; Frank, Zhao, and Borman 2004), and we urge other researchers to address this theoretical issue as well.

NOTES

1. We are aware that this almost colloquial definition of "technology" differs from the classic sociological definition (see, for example, Woodward 1965), which refers more generally to any means of production. We use it here because "technology" has become synonymous with "computer technology" in the modern classroom and administrative offices.
2. Kenneth Frank's criterion can be defined as the increase in the odds that there will be a tie between two actors (as opposed to the absence of a tie) associated with membership in a common subgroup. The odds ratio is large to the extent that actors engage in ties within subgroups and do not engage in ties between subgroups. The ratio is small to the extent that actors do not engage in ties within subgroups and engage in ties between subgroups. Balancing the two effectively accounts for subgroup sizes and the propensities of actors to engage in ties. Maximization of the criterion described by Frank also satisfies Charles Kadushin's (1995, 212) call for an algorithm that "maximizes both in-[sub]group density and minimizes out-[sub]group relations."
3. Frank also initially conducted a pilot study of the questionnaire (with colleagues Andrew Topper and Yong Zhao), establishing the reliability of several of the measures of perceptions regarding technology (see Frank, Topper, and Zhao 2000).
4. Owing to accounting constraints, Westville was prepaid in June 2000 for their participation in 2001.
5. For this type of simulation, Frank (1995) recorded odds ratios of the association between membership in a common subgroup and the presence of a tie after repeated applications of KliqueFinder to networks of the same size and distribution of row marginals (the out-degrees are considered fixed) as in figure 10.1, but in which the ties among the actors were randomly assigned.

6. To allow others to address this question, Frank (1995) applied KliqueFinder to multiple simulated networks in which the subgroup memberships were known. Frank then estimated a model to predict the extent to which subgroup memberships identified by KliqueFinder were consistent with the known subgroup memberships.

7. This school represents one of the strongest alignments of subgroups and grades because it was recently reconfigured, drawing most of the second-grade teachers from one school and most of the third-grade teachers from another. Furthermore, the teachers' room assignments reinforced grade assignments: all but one of the second-grade teachers were on one wing, and all but one of the third-grade teachers were on another wing.

8. Because the metrics varied slightly between administrations of the instrument, each measure of use was standardized, and then the difference was taken from the standardized measures. Each ring represents an increase of .2 standardized units.

9. In fact, the Windows platform was incompatible with the software featured in the grant proposal that originally attracted us to the school, and the software was not functionally available during the time of this study.

10. This is typical of many elementary schools. In fact, in research based on nineteen elementary schools in Michigan, 99 percent of the variation in technology use between schools could be attributed to district membership.

11. The Hierarchical Generalized Linear Model (HGLM) (Bryk, Raudenbush, and Congdon 2002) software with cross-nested effects was used to estimate the models. This software maximizes a penalized quasi-likelihood in the random effects (and so may slightly underestimate some random effects).

12. By including parameters for individual effects, this model is similar to the earlier p_1 models and can be considered a special case of $p*$ (see Wasserman and Pattison 1996, 410).

13. After modeling, the variances were 1.5 and .02, respectively, but the goal was to incorporate variation into individual-level differences more than to model it.

14. These differences were tested for statistical significance by modeling the occurrence of curricular talk in the absence of technology talk, and technology talk in the absence of curricular talk. Statistically, the tendency for curricular talk to occur within grade was significantly greater than for technology talk, but the difference between curricular talk within subgroups and technology talk within subgroups was not statistically significant, recalling the tenuous nature of statistical inference for these models.

Part IV

Change in Social Organizations

Chapter 11

The Cross-National Context of the Gender Gap in Math and Science

Catherine Riegle-Crumb

The broadly defined role that schools play in influencing student achievement has been a central focus of sociological research on education. Whether focusing on school factors that promote or discourage the learning and attainment of students in general or highlighting how schools can contribute to the reproduction of social inequality, such research underscores the importance of considering the organizational context of the educational experiences of individuals (see, for example, Bidwell and Kasarda 1975; Bowles and Gintis 1976). Yet when examining instances of the educational inequality common across societies, it is relevant to expand the consideration of context beyond organizations or institutions within a society and to instead view societies themselves as the relevant context in which inequality occurs.

Specifically, a gender gap in math and science achievement and attitudes, where on average male students outscore female students on tests and express more favorable attitudes toward the subjects, is evident not only in the United States but in countries across the world (Benavot 1989; Biraimah 1989; Harnisch 1984; Williams et al. 2000). This gender gap is a worldwide concern, not only because it signifies inequality during students' school years, but also because of its consequences for women's lives beyond their schooling. The lower achievement and interest of girls can lead to the relative exclusion of women from degrees in math and science, and subsequently lower-income and lower-status jobs in economies throughout the world that are increasingly based on science and technology (Oakes 1990; Stage and Maple 1996; Tabar 1992).

The gender gap in math and science achievement and attitudes is not a phenomenon that occurs exclusively within the confines of a classroom or school. Rather, the academic experiences of boys and girls are situated within and influenced by the larger social context in which they live. Much of the previous research on this gender gap focuses on determinants of inequality such as teacher bias in the classroom, differential parental expectations, or the academic abilities of individuals (American Association of University Women 1992, 1998). This chapter marks a departure from such a proximate focus and instead poses the question of whether variation in the extent of gender stratification at the societal or national level helps to explain differences among countries in the extent of the gender gap in math and science.

Within a given society, the gender roles that adult men and women occupy can have a great influence on the behaviors and attitudes of young people, as well as the choices they eventually make. In other words, there is a feedback loop between the gender-stratified outcomes of one generation and the real and perceived opportunities available to the next generation. Predominant societal gender roles are likely to affect the educational experiences of young people directly, through socialization or rationalization of behavior, as well as indirectly by influencing the actors and institutions that educate and support them. This chapter examines the relationship between national levels of gender stratification in the family, labor force, and government, and gender inequality in math and science educational outcomes.

GENDER STRATIFICATION ACROSS TIME AND PLACE

In large part because of the spread of Western institutions and ideologies to the developing world through industrialization and the growth of a world economy in which national boundaries are becoming less salient, women's lives across much of the world are characterized by the sexual division of labor into private and public spheres (see, for example, Boserup 1970; Pampel and Taneka 1986). The maintenance of the private sphere of the home remains predominantly the responsibility of women (Milkman and Townsley 1994). This is not simply another equally viable domain for human fulfillment, but rather an area where women are economically dependent on men and attributed lower societal status and prestige (Hartmann 1981; Ware 1988).

Additionally, factors such as restrictive gender norms, employer discrimination, unequal pay, and role conflict all operate to discourage women's employment and other public roles in favor of their domestic role (Brinton 1993; Connelly, DeGraff, and Levinson 1996; Ware 1988). Consequently, women's domestic responsibilities substantially impede them from gaining a significant degree of economic and social power and independence, whether by ideological or more tangible means. Thus, the sexual division of labor is a clear instance of gender stratification, where women disproportionately occupy the societal strata of lower prestige and greater dependency (Chafetz 1984; Milkman and Townsley 1994; Okin 1995). While the limited opportunities of adult women in a society are an important problem in their own right, such limits also have consequences for the experiences of subsequent generations.

Specifically, it is likely that gender stratification at the national or societal level influences the perceptions and actions of youth, as well as those of the adults who are involved in their socialization and/or academic training. For instance, while the general underrepresentation of women in the labor force is a cross-national phenomenon, some countries have less equitable employment patterns than others (Charles 1992). Countries with higher levels of gender stratification in the labor force are likely to convey stronger societal messages about the link between gender and opportunity; when young people and those around them receive these messages, ideas about gender inequality are reinforced.

This idea is consistent with research on the reproduction of gender inequality at the individual level within a society. A central empirical finding of this literature is that children learn gender roles and attitudes from the people and places around them and from the educational and occupational opportunities they see in their families and communities (Eccles, Barber, and Jozefowicz 1999; Eder and Parker 1987). Because the labor force is visibly segregated with regard to gender, children learn to view some occupations as appropriate for their gender and others as inappropriate (Marini and Brinton 1984). Children who are exposed to a more gender-stratified family or school are more likely to see their future opportunities as constrained and are more likely to be encouraged by others to maintain the status quo of predominant gender roles (Ayalon 2002; Cunningham 2001; Jacobs et al. 1998; Riegle-Crumb 1996).

CROSS-NATIONAL INFLUENCES ON GENDER INEQUALITY IN MATH AND SCIENCE

To examine whether countries with less equitable roles for adult men and women in society also exhibit more prominent national patterns of inequality in the lives of young people, it is logical to focus on students' educational experiences. Specifically, there is considerable variation among countries in the magnitude of the gender gap in math and science educational outcomes for middle and high school students. In an effort to explain this cross-national variation, David Baker and Deborah Jones (1993) examined the relationship between national trends in gender stratification and the extent of gender inequality in math performance using data from the Second International Mathematics Survey (SIMS). After finding that there is less of a gender gap for math achievement in countries where women have more equal access to jobs and higher education, Baker and Jones suggest that the anticipation of future opportunities can shape current performance.

Pushing the argument further, educational achievement and attitudes in the subjects of math and science may be particularly vulnerable to gender-differentiated future role expectations given the stereotype of these subjects as a male domain and the perception that they are the most difficult and competitive courses in school, as well as the ones most directly related to future labor force participation (Ayalon 2002; Oakes 1990). In a gender-stratified society where girls are confronted with the prospect of limited opportunities for their future, they may invest less effort in their education, perceive it as less relevant, and be more susceptible to discouraging stereotypes related to academic performance. Specifically, if girls accept the prevailing gender roles in a society as legitimate and valid, they may not even meaningfully consider other alternatives. In addition to the socializing effect on younger generations of visible gender stratification patterns, girls may also make decisions about their education and future life choices based on a rational analysis of their opportunities. They may choose not to work toward occupational or public-sector roles that they have little expectation of attaining. Therefore, the perceived economic returns of educational investments may explain gender differences in achievement and other outcomes.

Furthermore, while sex segregation is likely to have a direct effect on young people's perceptions of available future opportunities, it is also likely to influence the support given to them by other actors and institutions. The idea that schools may reproduce existing patterns of social inequality through differential treatment of students is not new to sociological research on education (see, for example, Bowles and Gintis 1976). With regard to gender differences in math and science, schools in more sex-segregated societies may endorse different curricular focuses for girls and boys, or they may select gender-biased textbooks, tests, and other educational materials (Ayalon 2002). Furthermore, in a more gender-stratified societal context, teachers may be less inclined to function as mentors or to encourage girls' academic work in math and science. Furthermore, prior research suggests that in countries where women have lower levels of labor force participation, parents are less likely to encourage and assist girls in math- and science-related endeavors (Baker and Jones 1992).

In summary, by creating a perceived opportunity structure of future limitations, prevailing patterns of gender stratification are likely to influence girls' relative math and science educational experiences. The mechanism through which this occurs may be socialization or rationalization of current behavior, which may influence girls' observations directly as well as more indirectly by influencing the educational support offered by schools and parents. If these hypothesized patterns of influence are accurate, girls will have lower performance and less favorable attitudes toward math and science compared to boys in countries that are characterized by more gender stratification. Conversely, countries with more equitable experiences for women and men in areas such as the labor force are likely to have a more equitable distribution of math and science outcomes by gender. Thus, by focusing on the larger societal context of gender stratification, we may be able to answer the question of why gendered outcomes in math and science are more equitable in some countries than others.

DATA AND ANALYSES

The analyses in this chapter explore the relationship between national levels of gender stratification and the gender gap in math and science educational outcomes. To establish the larger context of national gender stratification, the analyses begin with an examination of several indicators of women's representation in the family, labor force, and government and continue with an examination of the relationship between these indicators and national levels of economic development. I then present an empirical test of the cross-national relationship between gender stratification and the gap in math and science achievement and attitudes. Using test scores, the traditional marker of performance and ability, I examine the gender gap in achievement, as well as the gender gap in favorable attitudes toward math and science. This is a less-studied but important component of the gender gap because it is indicative of the extent to which girls are likely to pursue further education and careers in math and science, somewhat independently of ability level (Benbow and Minor 1986; Catsambis 1994; Seymour and Hewitt 1997).

Indicators of Gender Stratification at the National Level

The home, labor force, and government are interrelated domains of gender stratification across the world. As discussed earlier, women's domestic obligations prevent or discourage them from participating equally in the formal labor force, where they can gain some degree of economic and social power. Women's under-representation in government is another important indicator of stratification, since this is the component of the public sphere that can redress issues of inequality. For example, legislation can alleviate some of the conflict between the domestic sphere and the labor market by addressing problems such as lower pay and lack of child-care options. Progressive governments are also able to counteract societal gender norms—for example, by legislating equality in the labor force (Chang 2000; Connelly et al. 1996; Orloff 1993).

Data from the United Nations Women's Indicators and Statistics Database (WISTAT) provide an opportunity to examine gender stratification in these three areas for forty countries around the world during the early 1990s.[1] I chose two indicators to represent the amount of gender stratification in each of the three domains. For the area of the home and family, the first indicator is the *total fertility rate*, or the national average number of children born to women of childbearing age. In general, women with more children have stronger responsibilities within the home. I also included a variable for the *availability of legal abortion* for economic or social reasons, or on request. Access to abortion is an important indicator of stratification because it is indicative of the extent to which women have real decisionmaking power over their childbearing and thus have control over the extent of their domestic responsibility. This variable is dichotomous, with a score of one representing legal availability of abortion and a score of zero otherwise.

For gender stratification in the labor force, the first indicator is *women's share of the labor force*. For this variable, a score of close to fifty means that women make up an equal share of the labor force. The second indicator refers to the *percentage of women age fifteen years and older who are considered economically active*. The definition of the economically active population includes individuals who are self-employed as well as unpaid family workers. While these variables do not capture the quality and context of women's employment, they do indicate women's presence in the public sphere and their subsequent opportunity for financial gain that is not dependent on others.

I also selected two variables from WISTAT to measure gender stratification in government representation. The first is the *total percentage of government positions filled by women*, regardless of level. The second indicator is the *percentage of submin-*

isterial positions filled by women, which includes deputy and vice ministers, permanent secretaries, and deputy permanent secretaries. To the extent that countries have lower representation of women in the government, gender stratification exists with regard to access to positions of power and authority.

Gender Stratification by Level of Economic Development

It is often assumed that countries that have attained higher levels of economic progress are also more progressive in terms of social issues (Chang 2000). This more equitable social ideology would likely be associated with a decrease in the gender gap in math and science achievement. It is therefore important to determine whether the most economically developed countries have the lowest levels of gender stratification and how this stratification affects academic attitudes and performance. However, before treating gender stratification as an influential national phenomenon in its own right, I first present evidence that gender stratification is not simply a manifestation of the level of economic development.

Table 11.1 displays the means for each of the six indicators of gender stratification by level of economic development, categorized as three levels ranging from low to high.[2] Beginning with the area of gender stratification in the home and family, a general negative linear trend is apparent between fertility rates and economic development. The average total fertility rate for countries in the lowest economic development group is 2.46 children. By comparison, the fertility rate for the medium development group is 2.0 children, and the average for the highest group is 1.87, or below replacement levels. In general, then, countries at higher levels of development have lower fertility. However, focusing on differences between levels of development obscures substantial variation within categories. For instance, the high mean fertility rate for the lowest economic group is in large part due to the high fertility rates of two countries, the Philippines and Iran.[3] Turning to the indicator for the availability of abortion, the lowest mean is observed for countries in the category of lowest national development. Yet the group mean is over 0.5 for all groups, indicating that over half of the countries in each category provide legal access to abortion.

Table 11.1 also presents the means for gender stratification in employment by level of economic development. Both the means for women's share of the adult labor force and their economic activity rate are highest in countries with low levels of development. Thus, it appears that women in countries with low development are slightly more likely to work. However, the means for women's economic rate reveal a U-shaped pattern consistent with previous literature on the subject, where higher levels of employment are found at the high and low ends of economic development, compared to the middle (Pampel and Taneka 1986).

Finally, the means for gender stratification in government suggest that countries at the highest level of development have greater female representation. The mean percentage of women in government is highest for the high economic group, compared to the other two groups. Although the percentage of women in government

TABLE 11.1 / Gender Stratification in Forty Countries by Level of Economic Development

	Level 1: Low Economic Development	Level 2: Medium Economic Development	Level 3: High Economic Development
Gender stratification in the home			
Total fertility rate	2.46	2.00	1.87
	(1.25)	(1.04)	(.45)
Access to abortion	.60	.67	.67
	(.52)	(.52)	(.48)
Gender stratification in employment			
Women's share of the labor force	43.00	41.50	41.21
	(8.11)	(3.73)	(4.17)
Women's economic rate	54.8	48.33	50.75
	(13.31)	(7.09)	(8.70)
Gender stratification in government			
Women's representation in government	10.28	9.60	13.44
	(8.33)	(6.35)	(8.49)
Women's representation at sub-ministerial level of government	11.18	11.03	12.46
	(9.09)	(7.30)	(8.96)

Source: WISTAT, version 4.

at the subministerial level shows less variation across all three classifications of economic development, it is still slightly higher for countries in the highest economic group. However, examining the individual averages for the countries within each development category reveals that several countries at low levels of development, such as Colombia and the Philippines, have comparatively high female representation in government. Thus, while there may be more of a tendency for high-development countries to have more women in government, it is also important to note that women have a stronger voice in some low-development countries.

Overall, the descriptive statistics reveal that even though the extent of gender equity varies somewhat according to level of national development, it is not the case that progress for women is synonymous with issues of economic or even social progress. Moreover, despite the fact that gender stratification in the home, labor force, and government is apparent in all countries, there is considerable variation between countries in the extent of gender inequality in power, resources, opportunities, and experiences. It is thus relevant to investigate whether countries with higher levels of gender stratification in these areas, or with less equitable outcomes for adult women at the societal level, are also characterized by greater gender gaps in the math and science outcomes of younger generations.

Predicting the Gender Gap in Math and Science Achievement

To examine the cross-national relationship between levels of gender stratification and the math and science achievement gap, I used data from the Third International Mathematics and Science Survey (TIMSS). Conducted in 1995, TIMSS is the largest national database on education, with data from over forty countries. It consists of surveys administered to principals, teachers, and students at three different age groups. Math and science achievement tests were also administered to students. The analyses in this chapter focus on the population 2 students, which include respondents from seventh and eighth grade.

Consistent with prior research that finds evidence of a cross-national gender gap in math and science achievement test scores, an analysis of the TIMSS data also finds such patterns.[4] Boys have higher average math test scores than girls in thirty-two of the countries, or 80 percent of the sample. Boys outscore girls in thirty-six of the countries (90 percent of the sample). Additionally, the average gender difference in science achievement test scores is higher than for math. Although the predominant trend is definitely one of male advantage in math and science achievement, there is substantial variation in the magnitude of difference.

To investigate whether the gender gap in students' math and science achievement varies based on national levels of gender stratification in the home, labor force, and government, two-level hierarchical linear models (HLMs) were conducted. This statistical method has the advantage of estimating coefficients and partitioning variance into different levels, in this case both the student and country level (Bryk and Raudenbush 1992). The level 1 or student model in the analysis is represented by the following equation:

$$Y_{ij} = B_{0j} + B_{1j} \text{ (female)} + B_{2j} \text{ (maternal education)} + B_{3j} \text{ (SES)} + r_{ij} \qquad (11.1)$$

The dependent variable, Y_{ij}, is the individual student's math or science achievement test score. The student-level variables used to predict achievement are gender, maternal education level, and family socioeconomic status (see appendix for a description of the variables). B_{0j} is the intercept, which is defined as the mean achievement for boys of low socioeconomic status (SES) and maternal education.[5]

The specific purpose of this analysis is determining how the gender gap in achievement varies according to the extent of gender stratification. Thus, national indicators of gender stratification at level 2 are used to predict the slope between gender and achievement at level 1. The main level 2 model is presented in equation 11.2:

$$B_{1j} = y_{10} + y_{11}W_j \text{ (level of development)}$$
$$+ y_{12}W_j \text{ (national test average)}$$
$$+ y_{13}W_j \text{ (home and work status)}$$
$$+ y_{14}W_j \text{ (government status)} + u_{1j} \tag{11.2}$$

Control variables at level 2 include national level of economic development, coded one for high development and zero otherwise. Additionally, a control for the national achievement score in either math or science makes it possible to determine whether the effects of gender stratification exist independently of the country's overall achievement level.

The variables home and work status and government status are factor scores from principal components analyses of the six gender stratification variables discussed earlier.[6] The analyses resulted in two factors accounting for approximately 75 percent of the variance: one with high loadings for the family and labor force indicators and one with high loadings only for the two indicators of women's representation in government. The existence of two distinct dimensions of gender stratification speaks to the connection between women's roles in the home and the labor force, while women's relative power in the government appears to be a related but separate issue. For both variables, a high score indicates higher status for women, or less gender stratification. Thus, a high score on the first factor indicates a low degree of domestic responsibility together with a high degree of labor force participation, and a high score on the second factor indicates a high level of female representation in government.

Table 11.2 displays the results of the HLM analysis for math achievement in the first column of coefficients. The level 1 model indicates a negative effect of gender on achievement, and thus the level 2 effects indicate which variables have a significant effect on this negative relationship. The level 2 coefficients reveal that countries with higher math test averages overall have smaller gender gaps in math. However, the gender gap in math does not vary significantly by level of economic development. With regard to the effects of gender stratification on the gender gap in math, there is a positive and statistically significant relationship between women's representation in the government and the slope of gender on math test scores. In other words, controlling on the other variables in the model, countries where more women are employed in government have smaller gender gaps in math achievement. Women's relative status in the home and family does not have a significant effect.[7]

Table 11.2 also displays the results of an HLM analysis where the science achievement test is the dependent variable. Overall, the patterns found are similar to those observed for math. Once again, the factor representing women's representation in government has a positive and statistically significant effect on the slope of gender on achievement. Thus, countries with higher women's representation in the government have lower gender gaps in science achievement. Countries with higher overall levels of science achievement also have smaller gender gaps, while economic development has no significant effect.

TABLE 11.2 / The Effects of Gender Stratification on the Gap in Math and Science Achievement: HLM Analyses

	Math Coefficients	Science Coefficients
Level 2 models (N = 36)		
Model predicting B_1 (female slope)		
Women's status in government	2.864**	3.777*
Women's status in home and at work	.456	−5.451
National average test score	.075**	.331***
Level of economic development	−2.268	.044
Intercept	−2.136	−12.428***
Level 1 models (N = 184,290)		
Female, B_1	−3.492***	−12.962***
Maternal education level, B_2	10.538***	9.361***
Socioeconomic status, B_3	15.104***	13.982***
Intercept, B_0	470.030***	479.099***
Partition of variance (unconditional model)		
Level 2 (between countries)	25%	16%
Level 1 (between students)	75%	84%

	Variance	Degrees of Freedom	Chi-Square
Random effects (math model)			
Intercept, U_0	1,471.35	32	4,258.48***
SES slope, U_1	112.35	35	519.583***
Female slope, U_2	54.40	31	260.68***
Mated slope	8.86	35	472.07***
Random effects (science model)			
Intercept, U_0	1,236.86	32	2,764.30***
SES slope, U_1	126.54	35	571.43***
Female slope, U_2	264.38	31	926.92***
Mated slope	9.66	35	439.63***

Source: TIMSS, population 2 student data, and WISTAT, version 4.
Notes: Student-level data are weighted to account for the multistage sampling design. Table displays selected coefficients from complete model which also estimated level 2 effects on B_0. Level 2 controls for average math and science test score in B_1 models are grand-mean centered.
*p < .10; **p < .05; ***p < .01 (two-tailed tests with robust standard errors)

Predicting the Gender Gap in Math and Science Attitudes

The next analysis addresses the question of whether gender stratification in the home, labor force, and government is related to the gender gap in math and science attitudes. Four questions were chosen from the TIMSS questionnaire to measure gender differences in students' attitudes toward math and science: How much did they enjoy math or science class? How much did they like both subjects? How good did they perceive themselves to be in both subjects? And did they want to obtain a job someday that uses math or science?[8] Available categories of responses were coded on a four-point scale from strongly disagree to strongly agree. A summed scale was created as the dependent variable with a minimum value of four and a maximum value of sixteen.[9]

Descriptive analysis confirms that, on average, boys have more positive attitudes toward math in the majority of countries.[10] However, there are four countries where girls' positive math attitudes significantly eclipse those of boys. Interestingly, for science, in almost 40 percent of countries girls' national averages were higher than those for boys. This somewhat surprising result may be related to the fact that girls in population 2 were interviewed when they were in seventh or eighth grade, a time when they were just being introduced to real science subjects such as biology. Although there is already a gender gap in science achievement at this point, middle school girls may nevertheless have a level of interest and excitement in these subjects that does not begin to dissipate until high school.

To investigate the effect of gender stratification in the lives of adult women on the gender gap in math and science attitudes, I conducted two-level HLM analyses. The dependent variable at level 1 is the math or science attitude scale.[11] For the level 2 model predicting B_1, or the negative slope between gender and the math attitude scale, I observed a positive and statistically significant effect of women's status in the home and family (see table 11.3). This means that countries where women have more domestic freedom and higher labor force representation have smaller gender gaps in favorable math attitudes. The indicator for women's status in the government does not have a significant effect. Additionally, the table reveals that the gender gap in math attitudes does not vary significantly by level of economic development and that countries with more positive math attitudes overall are likely to have smaller gender gaps in attitudes.

Table 11.3 also displays the results of an HLM analysis where the science attitude scale is the dependent variable. The model predicting the slope between gender and scores on the science attitude scale indicates that the same component of gender stratification, women's status in the home and labor force, has a significant effect on the gender gap in science. Thus, in countries where women have more domestic freedom and participate more in the labor force, girls are more like boys with respect to favorable science attitudes. Additionally, the level of economic development has a positive effect, meaning that countries at the highest level of development have smaller gender gaps in science attitudes. Finally, countries with higher average science attitudes also have smaller differentials in gender attitudes.

CONCLUSION

The gender gap in math and science has been the topic of a vast body of research in the United States as well as in many other countries. Previous studies have highlighted factors such as girls' lower levels of ability and preparation, reduced

TABLE 11.3 / The Effects of Gender Stratification on the Gap in Math and Science
Attitudes: HLM Analyses

	Math Coefficients	Science Coefficients
Level 2 models (N = 34)		
Model predicting B_1 (female slope)		
Women's status in government	−.005	−.065
Women's status in home and at work	.463***	.909***
National average attitude score	1.035***	1.386***
Level of economic development	−.258	.778***
Intercept	−.213	−.514**
Level 1 models (N = 157,140)		
Female, B_1	−.351***	−.030
Maternal education level, B_2	.100***	.109***
Socioeconomic status, B_3	.261***	.167***
Intercept, B_0	7.86***	7.91***
Partition of variance (unconditional model)		
Level 2 (between countries)	8%	9%
Level 1 (between students)	92%	91%

	Variance	Degree of Freedom	Chi-Square
Random effects (math model)			
Intercept, U_0	.551	30	1,864.84***
SES slope, U_1	.019	33	99.43***
Female slope, U_2	.505	29	2,526.87***
Mated slope, U_3	.002	33	142.64***
Random effects (science model)			
Intercept, U_0	.531	30	2,177.60***
SES slope, U_1	.027	29	199.44***
Female slope, U_2	.502	29	5,160.67***
Mated slope, U_3	.004	33	201.94***

Source: TIMSS, population 2 student data and WISTAT, version 4.
Notes: Student-level data are weighted to account for the multistage sampling design. Table displays selected coefficients from complete model, which also estimated level 2 effects on B_0. Level 2 controls for average attitude score in B_1 model are grand-mean centered.
**p < .05; ***p < .01 (two-tailed tests with robust standard errors)

self-confidence, or lower access to mentors as predictors of gender differences in math and science achievement and attitudes (Catsambis 1994; Eccles 1987; Seymour and Hewitt 1997). However, few researchers have examined why gender outcomes in math and science are more equitable in some countries than others. Such a focus is consistent with educational research that examines how student achievement is influenced by the organizational context of schools. By taking an even broader perspective and considering national contexts, comparative research can offer insights into why some countries are more successful in promoting equity and consequently suggest ways in which equity in other countries can be increased.

The main argument presented in this chapter is that the gender-related outcomes in the lives of one generation largely create the perception of opportunities available to younger generations. The result is socialization to maintain the status quo of gender stratification or, at the very least, to lower the expectations of girls, parents, and schools that less traditional behavior might be rewarded. A vicious cycle exists whereby gender stratification in one generation is passed to the next in a dysfunctional inheritance of gender roles. School walls are permeable, and young people's academic decisions and the support offered by school personnel and family members are influenced both overtly and more subtly by the broader society in which they live.

These analyses cannot explicitly test the mechanism by which gender stratification influences the gap in math and science outcomes, but the results are nevertheless suggestive of likely processes. For example, the results presented in table 11.2 are consistent with the argument that in societies characterized by the relative absence of women from positions of power, girls may be less motivated to perform and less encouraged by others to invest in their education, particularly in the competitive and high-status subjects of math and science. Also, countries with a stronger female presence in government are probably more committed to issues of gender equity. Such governments may be promoting gender equity in math and science education by developing programs and increasing the resources directed toward education. This would very likely establish a societal gender norm that performance in these subjects is important for all individuals and that expectations are not related to a person's gender. Additionally, in such an atmosphere parents and teachers would be more motivated to encourage their daughters' academic investments in math and science.

Girls' attitudes toward math and science are partly determined by the roles held by women in both the public and private spheres of their country. For example, girls who live in families where the average number of children is high probably expect a future of high fertility for themselves and perceive education as less useful for their later lives. Furthermore, if girls know few women who are employed in the formal labor force, then they have little reason to plan for their own future employment. This attitude could subsequently influence their interest in difficult school subjects that are linked to labor force opportunities. In countries with more gender stratification in the home and labor force, girls are also likely to be encouraged by their families and others to maintain the status quo of traditional gender attitudes.

Thus, a primary goal of this chapter has been to demonstrate how systems of national gender inequality are maintained by the connection between perceived opportunities and real outcomes. While the results of the analysis suggest that changes at the macro level would influence perceptions at the individual level, there are nonetheless tangible ways to encourage gender equity in math and science. For example, highlighting successful female mathematicians, scientists, and legislators in textbooks and lessons could alter girls' perceptions of future opportunities. Schools that choose to endorse more gender-equitable programs of study and academic counseling, as well as educational materials, could counteract stratified gender patterns within the society. Thus, education systems could interrupt the feedback loop between patterns of stratification at the societal level and gender inequality in education that is still present in most countries.

APPENDIX: DESCRIPTIONS AND CALCULATION OF VARIABLES IN TABLES 11.2 AND 11.3

1. *Level 2 Variable: National Average Math Score and Science Score*: Taken from TIMSS variable BIMATSCR and BISCISCR in population 2 student background file. This variable represents the national means, which are calculated from the student scores in each country, weighted with student weight, SENWGT.

2. *Level 2 Variables: Gender Stratification Factors* (derived from WISTAT statistics):

   a. *Gender stratification in the home and labor force factor*: This variable represents high factor loadings (above an absolute value of 0.5) for total fertility rate, access to legal abortion, women's share of the labor force, and women's economic activity rate.

   b. *Gender stratification in the government factor*: This variable represents high factor loadings (above an absolute value of 0.5) for women's total representation in government and women's representation in the subministerial level of government.

3. *Level 2 Variable: Level of Economic Development Indicator*: Calculated from World Bank category designations. This variable is coded 1 for countries at the highest level of economic development and 0 for countries in the medium and low categories of economic development.

4. *Level 1 Variable: Female*: Derived from TIMSS variable ITSEX in population 2. This variable is coded 1 for female and 0 for male.

5. *Level 1 Variable: Maternal Education Level*: Derived from TIMSS variable BSBGEDUM in population 2. This variable is coded from 1 to 6, with the following categories: 1 = finish primary school; 2 = finish some secondary school; 3 = finish secondary school; 4 = some vocational education; 5 = some university education; 6 = finish university education.

6. *Level 1 Variable: SES*: Derived from TIMSS variable BSDGPSA in population 2 student background file. This variable is coded 1 for students who report having all of the following in the home: computer, calculator, and dictionary. It is coded 0 for students who do not report having all three items.

7. *Descriptions of Individual Items for Math and Science Attitude Variables*:

   a. *Good at math or science*: Taken from TIMSS variable BSBMGOOD (math) and BSBSGOOD (science) in population 2. The wording was "I usually do well in mathematics (science)." Response categories from 1 ("strongly agree") to 4 ("strongly disagree") were reverse-coded. For countries with a specialized science questionnaire, "I usually do well in biology," or BSBBGOOD, was used.

   b. *Want to work in math or science*: Taken from TIMSS variable BSBMWORK (math) and BSBSWORK (science) in population 2. The wording was "I would like a job that involves using mathematics (science)." Response categories from 1 ("strongly agree") to 4 ("strongly disagree") were reverse-coded. For countries with a specialized science questionnaire, "I would like a job that involved using biology," or BSBBWORK, was used.

   c. *Enjoy math or science*: Taken from TIMSS variable BSBMENJY (math) and BSBSENJY (science) in population 2. The wording was "I enjoy learning mathematics (science)." Response categories from 1 ("strongly agree") to 4 ("strongly disagree") were reverse-coded. For countries with a specialized science questionnaire, "I enjoy learning biology," or BSBBENJY, was used.

   d. *Like math or science*: Taken from TIMSS variable BSBMLIKE (math) and BSBSLIKE (science) in population 2 file. The wording was "How much do you like mathematics (science)?" Response categories ranged from 1 ("dislike a lot") to 4 ("like a lot"). For countries with a specialized science questionnaire, "How much do you like biology?" or BSBBLIKE, was used.

This research was supported by a grant from the American Educational Research Association, which receives funds for its grants program from the National Science Foundation and the U.S. Department of Education's National Center for Education Statistics and Office of Educational Research and Improvement under NSF grant RED-9452861. Opinions reflect those of the author and do not necessarily reflect those of the granting agencies.

NOTES

1. Data on the gender stratification variables discussed here were limited to the forty countries that participated in the population 2 sample of the Third International Mathematics and Science Survey (TIMSS), the dataset that provides the dependent variables of gender inequity in math and science achievement and attitudes. Additionally, the gender stratification variables discussed are representative of the extent of stratification

that existed at approximately the same time that the TIMSS surveys were being administered to students.

2. The World Bank designates a country's level of economic development as low, lower middle, upper middle, or high. No countries in the publicly released TIMSS database qualified for the category of low. Thus, all of the countries in the sample are in the lower middle, upper middle, or high category of economic development. Because of the small sample size considered here (forty countries), I do not discuss the statistical significance of differences between means.

3. A complete list of values on all of the variables for the countries considered is available at http://unstats.un.org/unsd/demographic/gender/wistat/ (accessed January 18, 2005).

4. These analyses are not shown here but are available on request from the author.

5. HLM analyses were also conducted where maternal education level was centered on both the group mean and the grand mean, so that the intercept could be interpreted as the score for boys with mothers of average education level. However, this model took many more iterations to converge and did not change the substantive meaning of any of the results.

6. Principal components analysis is a data reduction technique that allows the researcher to examine whether the observed relationships between several manifest or observed variables can be explained in terms of one or more underlying or latent dimensions (Kleinbaum, Kupper, and Muller 1988).

7. Although not displayed, level 2 models were also conducted to predict B_0 or the intercept, with the same level 2 equation as that used for B_1 (with the exception of the control for national test average). The results of these models for both math and science indicate that gender stratification does not consistently and significantly influence boys' mean achievement.

8. Two different versions of the survey sections about science attitudes were administered based on whether the country had an educational system in which students in the seventh and eighth grades were taught general or integrated science and whether students were taking specific courses such as biology, chemistry, earth science, or physics. The latter survey, referred to as the "specialized science" questionnaire, was administered in seventeen countries. There were separate attitude questions for each of the four specific science subjects. However, most of the specialized science countries had the highest numbers of students enrolled in biology, compared to the other three subjects. Thus, I substituted the biology attitude questions for the general science attitude questions for all of the science variables used. (For complete information on this issue, go to http://timss.bc.edu/timss1995.html.)

9. I also conducted factor analysis. Although one factor emerged from the principal components analysis, it accounted for only 60 percent of the variation among the four items. Thus, the simple summed scale was retained as the dependent variable. However, I also performed all of the subsequent HLM analyses using the math and science factor variables as the dependent variables, and the overall findings were the same as when I used the summed scale as the dependent variable.

10. These analyses are not shown but are available on request from the author.

11. Although not presented, models identical to the level 2 model predicting B_1, or the gender-attitude slope (with the exception of the control for national attitude score), were also conducted for B_O, the intercept, where the dependent variable is boys' average math or science attitude score when the other variables in the model are set to zero. Results for these models did not show consistent and significant effects of gender stratification.

Chapter 12

Organizational Coupling, Control, and Change: The Role of Higher-Order Models of Control in Educational Reform

Christopher B. Swanson

It has now been almost four decades since organizational theory first started to systematically consider the nature of educational organizations. The now-familiar tension between the elements of a classic Weberian bureaucracy and the actually existing arrangements of schooling were evident from the beginning. In one of the seminal works in this field, Charles Bidwell (1965) analyzed the structures, processes, and functions of schools, describing the coexistence of both bureaucratic and professional modes of educational organization. This dual arrangement arises from the competing imperatives of imposing some minimal degree of uniformity over the quality of schooling outcomes and allowing classroom teachers the flexibility to accommodate their practices to difficult-to-anticipate variability in schooling inputs (such as the ability of students) and classroom conditions (for example, teacher and student interactions). This substantial autonomy of classroom activities is a prime example of what Bidwell (1965, 976) terms "structural looseness" among organizational subunits. Similar dynamics can also be found at other levels of the educational system among the interactions of governmental agencies, school districts, superintendents, and principals.

These types of loose organizational connections have been observed in subsequent studies of the social organization of schooling and teaching, as well as in domains of social life other than education (Dreeben 1973; Lortie 1973; Orton and Weick 1990). The same basic phenomenon has also become known by a variety of names. A study by Jeffrey Pressman and Aaron Wildavsky (1984), for instance, describes the "complexity of joint action" that characterized the implementation of an economic development program as it passed through a long stream of actors and decisionmaking junctures from its origination in the federal government to its destination in a local community. Organizations that display such characteristic looseness, however, have been most generally and most commonly referred to in organizational theory as "loosely coupled" systems.

Karl Weick (1976) describes loose-coupling in its broadest sense as connoting weak linkages between elements of organizational systems, which might include sets of actors, departments or other subunits, means and ends, intentions and actions, or hierarchical positions. Although these linkages may lack the strength and rigidity implied by a classic bureaucratic model of organization, the elements of loosely coupled systems nevertheless maintain some degree of interdependence and therefore their integrity as an organizational system. The concept of loose-coupling also occupied a central place in the development of the new institutional perspective in organizational theory, which devotes considerable attention to the relationship between organizational configurations and the properties of their larger institutional environments (see Powell and DiMaggio 1991; Scott and Meyer 1994).

The malleability of the loose-coupling logic and its possible application to a wide variety of situations have made it an attractive explanation for all sorts of organizational phenomena. Weick (1976, 5) provides a sense of the richness of this concept by delineating fifteen distinct connotations of loose-coupling in organizational systems, ranging from slack resources to causal independence to a lack of correspondence between organizational structure and activity. He also discusses a variety of ways in which loose-coupling can be alternately beneficial or detrimental for organizational functioning and survival, depending on the circumstances (6–9). It may be no exaggeration, therefore, to suggest that one could craft a loose-coupling interpretation custom-fit for nearly any organizational occasion.

Applications of loose-coupling ideas have been especially prominent in explorations of educational organizations. Much of the early support for the loose-coupling perspective, in fact, was derived from examples of the weak connections between the administrative apparatus of schooling and the activities of teaching and student learning in the classroom, activities that constitute the technical core of production for the education system. The popularity and widespread use of loose-coupling explanations can largely be attributed to a combination of conceptual appeal and the ability to account for a variety of frequently observed organizational dysfunctions, including the perceived chronic ineffectiveness of educational reform.

As is often the case for concepts that strike an especially resonant cognitive chord, the popularization of the loose-coupling idea has come at a price. The tendency of much past research to demonstrate the presence of a loosely coupled organization rather than to analytically probe the essential properties of organizational coupling has resulted in a lack of conceptual clarity (Firestone 1985; Orton and Weick 1990). This problem, of course, has only been exacerbated by the almost offhanded way in which loose-coupling has sometimes been evoked as an all-purpose explanation for the ailments of organizational systems. One consequence has been a tendency to conflate loose-coupling as a theoretical construct with one of its oft-observed empirical manifestations—weak structural relationships between organizational elements. A prominent structural component can undoubtedly be recognized in many instances of loosely coupled systems. Given the complexity of these organizational phenomena, however, it is also unlikely that structural arrangements are in themselves sufficient as a general explanation. Put another way, organizational coupling is almost certainly a multidimensional construct, although past theory and research have typically addressed only its most prominent, structural component.

Rather than focusing on structure, this chapter considers a different dimension of coupling that captures variations in abstract models of organizational control. This consideration may be especially salient when we are dealing with the higher-order elements of institutional systems, such as the national and state levels of the educational system. It may also be a critical factor during periods of change when implicit standard operating procedures are redesigned and made explicit in the form of models, visions, or blueprints for organizational reform and institutional change. To explicate these concepts, I contrast two general models of organizational control that respectively revolve around issues of process management and the regulation of system inputs and outputs. When applied with the intention to promote systemwide change, these models of control imply the implementation of very different kinds of intervention into the productive activities of an organizational system.

The empirical part of this chapter searches for evidence that distinctive models of organization control actually exist in higher-order institutional systems. Using formal statistical measurement models, I conduct an in-depth analysis of the standards-based and accountability reforms in education during the 1990s, movements that exemplify process and regulatory models of organization control, respectively. The analysis specifically focuses on the dynamics of higher-order system elements, such as the internal coherence of policymaking activities. I argue, however, that the particular models of administrative control adopted at higher institutional levels should have important and formerly neglected implications for the implementation of substantive changes in productive activities at the local levels of an organizational system.

MODELS OF ORGANIZATIONAL CONTROL: REGULATION AND PROCESS

Structural arrangements exert an important influence on the coordination of individual units within an organizational system. In addition, the abstract models of organizational process and reform developed by higher-order administrative agents to direct the actions of lower-order line-level subunits may also contribute to the coupling (or decoupling) of elements within organizational systems. A distinction can be drawn between two fundamental approaches to organizational control by first illustrating the production process in its most basic terms. The top panel of figure 12.1 presents a highly simplified and conventional view of production in an organization: depicted there are linkages between system inputs (resources), process (technical work activities), and outputs (products). In educational organizations inputs might include students as well as fiscal and material resources, teaching and learning are the main production activities, and student knowledge and performance would be examples of important outcomes.

The second panel introduces the influence of higher-order organizational agents

FIGURE 12.1 / Models of Organizational Control

A: Line Production in an Organization

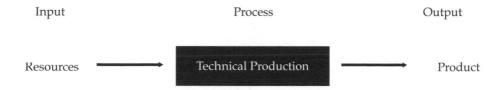

Input   Process   Output

Resources   Technical Production   Product

B: Administrative Control over an Organization or System

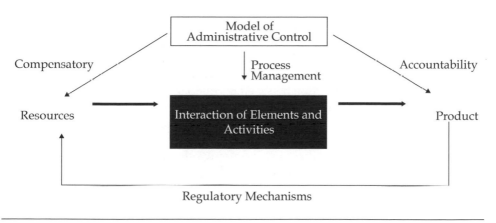

Model of
Administrative Control

Compensatory   Process   Accountability
                           Management

Resources   Interaction of Elements and   Product
                            Activities

Regulatory Mechanisms

Source: Author's compilation.

over the administration of the production activities that occur in lower-order sub-units. This happens through the imposition of administrative or organizational control models. These models or designs can be thought of as abstract mappings of organizational operations that may include: representations of key actors or organizational elements; their interrelationships to one another; productive methods for the arrangements of materials and work techniques; and regulatory mechanisms by which system outputs and inputs are connected through monitoring arrangements like quality assurance procedures. Of course, models of organizational control may be more or less explicit and visible to the lower-order units themselves. Some forms of control may also involve stronger and more directive methods than others. In educational systems, for example, it has been suggested that efforts to implement planned change are made through methods of control that resemble persuasion more than mandates (McDonnell 1994).

In general terms, purposive attempts to enact institutional change come about by introducing new models of operation that target certain organizational components or connections. As the term is used in this study, *regulatory* approaches to control and change are those that target system inputs and outputs. Within this category, compensatory models of change seek to alter the quantity or quality of system inputs. On the other hand, accountability models monitor system outputs and generate information that may feed back into decisions regarding the subsequent allocation of system resources. Rather than attempting to intervene directly into the technical core of production activities, regulatory approaches manipulate system inputs and production goals while devolving decisions about specific alterations to the production process to the lower-order subunits and actors. From the point of view of the higher-order agent, technical production is essentially treated as a "black box" in regulatory forms of administration.

Process management models of control, by contrast, are not primarily concerned with altering the amount or condition of the system inputs or with establishing goals for production outputs. Instead, they specify changes to the methods, techniques, and activities through which inputs are brought together and manipulated, transforming raw materials into finished product. Process-oriented models attempt to peer inside the black box of production and tinker with its internal workings as a means of rectifying shortcomings in system operations.

Certainly this basic distinction between regulatory control and process management oversimplifies the nature of organizational production and change and only hints at its complexity. For instance, models of organizational administration may be more or less comprehensive to the extent that they incorporate elements of multiple modes of control. Even these basic considerations, however, provide a useful foundation for a more critical examination of organizational coupling and coordination as revealed through a comparative examination of two prominent educational reform movements—standards-based reform and accountability reform. These movements represent examples of a predominantly process-oriented model of control over curriculum and instruction (standards-based reform) and a regulatory approach focused primarily on enacting minimum standards for system outputs (accountability reform).

STANDARDS AND ACCOUNTABILITY: ALTERNATIVE APPROACHES TO EDUCATIONAL CONTROL

Efforts to bring higher standards and greater accountability to education characterized much school reform activism of the 1990s. These standards and accountability movements are described in the following section.

Elements of Standards-Based Reform: Aligning Policies for Educational Process

Standards-based reform became a major force in the national policy arena during the 1990s. A number of reform leaders articulated a vision for high educational standards and outlined the more concrete steps required to implement such a vision. As early as the mid-1980s, national professional associations had started calling for the kinds of deep changes in curriculum and instruction that would become central tenets of the standards movement. Separate subject-specific academic standards, for instance, have since been published by national organizations of educators and scholars across a number of disciplines.

This professionally driven movement relied on the strategy of building consensus for change among members of academic communities as a foundation for reform. An emphasis on professional consensus also characterized most federal efforts to promote higher standards for academic content, at least during the 1990s. In some cases (for example, in math and science), this approach has helped to provide a reasonable measure of legitimacy for the proposed reforms in the eyes of the principals, teachers, and other educators who would be called to put the standards into action. In other subject areas (for example, language arts and history), curriculum wars erupted over controversial attempts to define a recognized canon or body of valued knowledge, effectively stalling reform efforts (see Loveless 2001; Ravitch 1995).

Often characterized by the slogan "high standards for all students," the standards movement has several key features that distinguish it from other approaches to improving American education. Most prominently, standards-based reform is a process-driven reform. It espouses a renewed model of curriculum, instruction, and student learning founded on rigorous academic subject matter that establishes challenging expectations for student performance, emphasizes the acquisition of higher-order skills, and values the application of student knowledge to real-world situations (McLaughlin and Shepard 1995). The curriculum and instructional reforms led by major discipline-based professional organizations like the National Council of Teachers in Mathematics (NCTM) and the American Association for the Advancement of Science (AAAS) have been instrumental in shaping the national agenda of the standards movement and providing concrete models of reformed educational content and practice that can serve as guides for state-level policymaking. Standards-based reform also maintains a strong commitment to educational equity. The vision of standards-based schooling is an inclusive one intended to apply to all students, even (and perhaps especially) to groups that historically have been poorly served by the public education system (O'Day and Smith 1993). The impact of the movement, therefore, is expected to be far-reaching with respect to the practical changes sought for instruction and learning as well as the scope of the student population intended to benefit from a standards-based education.

The standards movement is also notable for the high degree of cohesiveness it appears to display compared to many earlier educational reforms. This coherence extends both to strong theoretical models that envision the change process and to the relatively favorable political context in which the movement for standards emerged during the 1990s. Although several prominent models of reform centering on the development of high academic standards emerged, they held in common many key elements of their educational visions and typically drew upon similar profession-driven models of curriculum and instruction. Further, standards-based reform explicitly sought to remedy one of the problems often cited as a main factor contributing to the ineffectiveness of prior federal and state efforts to reform schooling—a lack of coordination among specific policy drivers and supporting programs. Systemic approaches to standards-based reform in particular have stressed that the successful implementation of the reform depends on maintaining functional linkages between the broader set of policy elements (Smith and O'Day 1991).

Agenda-setting efforts for standards-based reform and reports on the progress of the movement both commonly cite three coordinated policy drivers used by the states to promote rigorous academic subject matter in their schools: content standards, performance standards, and alignment of assessment systems with content standards. *Content standards and curriculum frameworks* form the foundation of the standards-based strategy. Since states have pursued somewhat different routes to standards development, the level of detail with which they specify the envisioned high-quality academic content varies from state to state (Council of Chief State School Officers 1995, 1997). At a minimum, however, these content standards are statements that articulate in broad terms the knowledge and skills that all students are expected to learn. These standards are typically developed for particular academic subjects (mathematics, science, language arts, social studies) and delineate subject matter appropriate for certain grades or grade ranges (elementary, middle grades, high school). Some frameworks also address broader learning themes that cut across subjects and grade levels, such as cultivating higher-order thinking and developing problem-solving skills.

Performance standards are "concrete examples of what students have to know and be able to do to demonstrate that such students are proficient in the skills and knowledge framed by content standards" (U.S. Congress 1994, sect. 3). In essence, this element of standards-based reform builds on content standards by further establishing acceptable levels of student mastery over the academic subject matter elaborated in the curriculum frameworks. Much as with content standards, the implementation of performance benchmarks has not followed a single path across the states. Some states pursue an integrated approach by combining performance standards with detailed curriculum frameworks, while others establish performance standards as relatively independent policy elements. Performance standards are also described using different terminology from state to state: they may be referred to as performance benchmarks, achievement indicators or levels, learning outcomes, or instructional goals. Regardless of the particular form performance standards take or the language in which they are couched, these reform elements provide specific criteria upon which progress toward implementing a standards-based education can be measured and monitored over time.

The third central component of standards-based reform models, *aligned assessments*, involves coordinating high-quality curricular content with assessment methods capable of measuring the acquisition of higher-order skills. Marking a departure from traditional instructional styles, which rely on drill and practice of basic skills and concepts, progressive, cognitively oriented theories of learning propose that more performance-based strategies for evaluating students' academic progress are needed. They argue that higher-order thinking and flexible problem-solving cannot be adequately captured using conventional tests consisting entirely of multiple choice or simple fill-in-the-blank responses. Under a standards-based model of schooling, teachers are expected to incorporate into classroom instruction the use of "authentic" techniques, such as interactive exercises, discussion and writing about the process of problem-solving, individual and group projects, demonstrations, and cumulative portfolios of student work. State reform efforts incorporate principles of standards-based reform into assessment systems in two primary ways—by linking the domains assessed in state tests to a specific vision of valued content knowledge and by introducing innovative performance tasks into state testing programs.

Some systemic versions of standards-based reform highlight the alignment of curriculum-centered efforts with other supporting policy instruments (Smith and O'Day 1991; Goertz, Floden, and O'Day 1996). A reform's overall success, it is argued, may depend heavily on facilitative policy measures such as the provision of necessary instructional and curricular materials, systems of assessment and accountability, and professional standards for teachers. Raising *professional standards*, for instance, would help to ensure that teachers have the requisite subject matter knowledge and pedagogical skills to effectively instruct a new high-standards curriculum. Specific policy drivers in this area might involve changes to pre-service teacher education, the conditions for licensure of new teachers, requirements for the recertification of practicing teachers, or continuing in-service training to familiarize teachers with the state's educational priorities and the challenges associated with implementing a reformed curriculum. To some extent, systemic reform can be viewed as embodying a more comprehensive model of organizational control that links both a specific vision of educational process with the regulation of system inputs and outputs.

Elements of Accountability Reform:
An Output-Driven Strategy

Accountability-focused reform strategies came to the forefront of national debates on education during the mid-1980s, largely in response to the National Commission on Excellence in Education's *A Nation at Risk* (NCEE 1983) and a series of other reports that highlighted the poor academic performance of America's students, especially compared to their peers in other nations. In addition to drawing a tremendous amount of public attention to the apparently lamentable state of American schooling, these reports also prompted an impressive array of state-led educational reforms (U.S. Department of Education 1984). These regulatory instruments remained a fixture of state policymaking repertoires through the 1990s and have been greatly reinvigorated as a result of the emphasis placed on assessment-based accountability by the No Child Left Behind Act of 2001 and other initiatives of the (George W.) Bush administration's educational agenda.

A Nation at Risk is often viewed as a primary impetus and in some cases a model for regulatory reforms in education, although the report has not always been cast in a favorable light (see Berliner and Biddle 1995). While the standards-based re-form efforts outlined earlier are founded on models of learning and teaching processes, the improvement strategies featured in A Nation at Risk spring from a diagnosis of national educational shortcomings and the rearticulation of these deficits as areas to target for improvement. In particular, A Nation at Risk draws up general goals in five main areas. *Content* recommendations lay out broad mini-mum guidelines for academic course-taking that should be required for a high school diploma, termed the "New Basics." *Standards and expectations* address the need for higher standards of achievement (including college entrance criteria), more rigorous and extensive standardized testing, and improved textbooks and materials. The report also calls for increasing the amount of *time* devoted to pro-ductive academic work. *Teaching* recommendations highlight the need to raise standards for teacher qualifications and compensation rather than addressing classroom instructional practices. In the area of *leadership*, the report calls for states and local actors to adhere to and fiscally support federally identified educational priorities.

In keeping with the broadly defined areas targeted by A Nation at Risk, the en-suing wave of state-led reform efforts enacted increases in course-taking require-ments for high school graduation, expansions of statewide student testing pro-grams, and utilizations of assessment results in performance-based accountability systems for schools and students (Fuhrman, Clune, and Elmore 1988; Stevenson and Schiller 1999). These reform efforts have often been described as "output-driven" because they attempt to improve the quality of education by raising the standards for critical outcomes of schooling rather than by manipulating the inter-nal productive processes of schools. Specifically, these accountability initiatives es-tablish more rigorous standards of *minimum* competency in areas such as the num-ber of academic courses required to qualify for a high school diploma, the score a student must obtain on a test of academic achievement to be promoted to the next grade, and the level of performance a school must reach to avoid sanctions. This strategy attempts to raise system performance by shoring up the floor of perfor-mance expectations rather than by raising the ceiling, the latter strategy being one that would be more attuned with the philosophy underlying standards-based reform.

Regulatory models of control, such as those guiding accountability reforms, typ-ically operate by imposing formal requirements and goals for system outputs *with-out* aligning these outputs to a specific vision of educational content or process.

Students, for instance, may be required to take three years of mathematics in order to graduate from high school, but there may be no explicit guidelines for the subject matter these courses should cover. Similarly, student performance may be evaluated using traditional achievement tests that are not tightly linked with any particular vision of a high-quality curriculum. In fact, such standardized tests are often specifically designed to be curriculum-neutral. As discussed earlier, regulatory reforms concentrate on formalized definitions of organizational outputs and may be especially susceptible to decoupling efforts aimed at preserving the localized autonomy of organizational actors (Meyer and Rowan 1978). For instance, the intent of a policy requiring students to take three years of high school mathematics may be effectively circumvented or "gamed" by districts or schools. Such actors might choose to creatively interpret the rules (for example, by allowing students to take the same course three times) or to manipulate the formalized definitions (for example, by offering essentially the same class under the guise of multiple course titles).

The process-oriented model of standards-based reform could be represented as a network of coordinated policy drivers. Each element in this constellation of policies plays a necessary and specialized role in supporting a broader reform process that revolves around a core vision of curriculum and instruction. The roles of individual standards–based policies are, in essence, differentiated from one another in a planned division of labor. By contrast, accountability-focused reforms of the past have typically lacked a unifying vision or conceptualization of the educational production process that might articulate distinct roles for or functional relationships among a set of individual policy drivers. Rather, accountability-based systems employ an equivalent regulatory technique (establishing formal requirements for minimal levels of acceptable performance) to monitor and (ideally) control a variety of educational outputs for students and schools. States or other organizational entities might also apply a similar strategy of monitoring the quality of system inputs.

Standards, Accountability, and the States: Bringing National Reform Closer to Home

As they have been articulated in the national reform arena, accountability- and standards-based approaches to educational reform diverge on a number of dimensions that include their substantive focus, the mechanism through which they seek to drive educational change, and the level of coordination intended to be maintained among individual policy drivers. Taken together, these differences illustrate the basic characteristics of process management and regulatory control models for organizational administration. Despite these distinctions, both reforms held prominent places in policy circles during the 1990s, and both enjoyed considerable support from influential actors at various levels of the government and educational system.

In an institutional environment with a federalized system of governance and administration, however, even support from key quarters provides no guarantee that a national movement for reform will result in the systematic implementation of a desired policy by the responsible local decisionmaking parties—in this case, the states. Because states enjoy constitutionally defined autonomy over many aspects of public schooling, they have traditionally been free to chart their own individual courses for reform. States may adhere closely to a reform model as promoted by national advocates, implement a modified (perhaps very different) version of that reform, or choose not to pursue that particular strategy at all. Far from being unique to educational policy and reform, the conditions that might promote loose-coupling or organizational looseness are also found in other domains of social life characterized by decentralized governance and pockets of localized autonomy.

Moving from a Theoretical to an Empirical Perspective on Coupling

In addition to engaging in an analysis of loose-coupling as a theoretical concept, this study also aims to analyze empirically the administrative control models underlying institutional reform strategies in practice. The next portion of the chapter investigates the state-level adoption of policies associated with the standards-based reform and accountability movements during the 1990s. These statistical analyses attempt to provide a firm empirical basis for addressing several critical issues surrounding the nature of coupling in large organizational systems, particularly in the context of purposive attempts to promote institutional change.

First, we consider coupling in its most basic sense of loose or tight connections in the actions of organizational agents. Given a pool of individual policies that prima facie appear to be associated with a recognized national reform movement (in theory), we empirically test the proposition that these policies are adopted in a systematic fashion by the state-level authorities (in practice). Another guiding question asks whether states pursue a set of nominally related policies in a coherent, internally consistent manner. Put another way, are there any "misfits" in the pool of policies that we suspect represent a nascent reform strategy? The concern here is the presence or absence of regularities in the way the states adopt the individual policies that constitute a broader reform. Finally, assuming that some kind of systematic patterning is observed, we ask whether the particular internal organization or configuration of constituent policy activities conforms to the broader designs of national models for reform, particularly with respect to their distinctive modes of administrative control.

METHODOLOGY

This study analyzes data on state-level adoption of thirty-three distinct education policies. The following section describes this extensive set of policy indicators. I also provide a brief overview of the statistical method used to characterize broader patterns of state policy activism around standards-based and accountability-based reforms.

Data

Unlike most empirical studies of institutional coupling or educational policy, the present investigation is comparative. Examining two reform strategies at the same point in time has the distinctive advantage of holding constant many aspects of the larger institutional environment that will be common to both reforms. This then allows us to devote greater attention to the dimensions along which these reforms differ, in particular their models of administrative control. Using the account of the standards and accountability movements outlined here as a guide, we can identify two pools of state-level policies that could be aligned with these respective visions for educational change. Taking 1996 as the point of reference, we will consider eighteen policies as possible constituents of a standards-based reform strategy, eleven policies for accountability, and four policies related to teacher professional standards. As noted earlier, professional standards could be an element of either a standards-based or accountability initiative.

These state policy indicators have been constructed primarily from information published by the Council of Chief State School Officers (1995, 1996a, 1996b, 1997; see also National Center for Education Statistics 1998). Since the 1980s, the CCSSO has been active in developing empirical indicators for state education policy as part of a larger effort to provide reliable reporting on trends in policymaking, reform, and educational practice across the states. The group has tracked key state policies associated with accountability reforms since the 1980s and has followed standards-based reform since the early 1990s.

The policy information employed in this study is sufficiently detailed to construct ordinal measures specifying three distinct levels or stages of adoption for each policy. The use of ordinal data on implementation provides a more subtle insight into policy activity than we would obtain from a simple binary distinction between adopting versus not adopting a policy. The coding criteria for these policy activity levels are defined separately for specific sets of items, although most variables fall into one of two general definitions: policy not pursued, under development, or adopted; and policy not pursued, adopted at a low level, or adopted at a high level. Table 12.1 provides additional information on these variables and their coding.

Methods

This study employs a statistical technique known as item response theory (IRT) measurement analysis to investigate empirically the degree to which discrete state policies coalesce into an identifiable movement or take the form of concerted policy

TABLE 12.1 / Standards and Accountability Policy Indicators

Reform Elements and Policies	Description of Policy (Coding Categories)
Standards-based reform	
Content standards	
Curriculum frameworks (math, science, language arts, social studies)	Statements of content areas and curriculum topics are included in instruction for specific academic areas (not pursued; in development; adopted)
Content guides (math, science)	Published documents present a state's vision of desired content knowledge for academic subject areas (not pursued; in development; adopted)
Curriculum innovativeness (math, science)	Timing of state's introduction of academic content standards (no standards; 1990 to 1996 to 1989 or earlier)
Performance standards	
Performance benchmarks (math, science)	Guidelines establish formal performance expectations for mastery over academic content knowledge (not pursued; in development; adopted)
Performance levels (math, science)	Specific performance benchmarks are incorporated into state assessments (none; pass-fail; multiple levels)
Benchmark innovativeness (math, science)	Timing of state's introduction of academic performance standards (no standards; 1995 to 1996; 1994 or earlier)
Assessment standards	
Aligned assessments (math, science)	Statewide assessment program aligns content knowledge domains of tests with state content standards (no linkage or assessment; in development; completed)
Innovative assessments (items, tests)	Performance-based tasks or tests are incorporated into the state assessment program (none; combination of traditional and performance-based elements; all performance-based elements)
Accountability reform	
High school graduation requirements	
Subject-specific course-taking (math, science, English, social studies)	Minimum number of course credits (Carnegie units) in each of four academic subject areas are required by state for high school diploma (English: two and a half units or less; three; four or more) (Other: one and a half units or less; two; three or more)
Academic intensity of course-taking	Proportion of total course credits required for high school graduation that must be in taken core academic subjects (English, social studies, math, and science) (less than half; 50 to 59 percent; 60 percent or more)

TABLE 12.1 / *Continued*

Reform Elements and Policies	Description of Policy (Coding Categories)
Assessment program scope	
Population coverage	Extent to which state assessment program components test students on a census basis at targeted grade levels (no components; some; all)
Subject coverage	Number of major academic subject areas (reading, writing, math, science, history/social studies) tested by statewide assessment program (two or fewer subjects; three to four; all five)
Grade coverage	Number of elementary and secondary grade levels tested by statewide assessment program (three or fewer grades; four to six; seven to twelve)
Accountability systems	
Instructional improvement	Statewide assessment results used for instructional purposes: diagnosis or placement of students, instructional improvement, and program evaluation (not used; used in one area; used in multiple areas)
School accountability	Statewide assessment results used for school accountability purposes: evaluating school performance, enforcing accreditation requirements, and issuing awards to schools (not used; used in one area; used in multiple areas)
Student accountability	Statewide assessment results used for student accountability purposes: grade promotion, high school graduation, issuing student awards (not used; used in one area; used in multiple areas)
Professional standards	
Major in field	State requirements for undergraduate major in an academic field for new teacher licensure (none; secondary-level teachers only; all levels)
Licensure testing	State requirements for testing applicants for new teacher license in the following skill areas: basic skills, professional skills, subject knowledge, and in-class observation (none; some areas tested; all areas)
Recertification requirements	State requirements for recertification or renewal of teacher license (none; one-time renewal; periodic renewal)
Licensure-standards linkage	State requirements for teacher licensure are linked to state academic standards; used in standards-based reform analyses only (not pursued; in development; adopted)

Source: Author's compilation.

activism. Similar to statistical methods like factor analysis, IRT analyses are used to generate a composite variable (or measurement scale) that empirically characterizes an *unobserved* latent trait based on a pattern of *observed* responses to a larger set of items that are related to the trait of interest (Embretson and Reise 2000). Factor analysis is another example of a scaling technique used to develop composite variables. Item response theory is most often applied to the development and scoring of psychometric assessments such as standardized achievement tests and psychological inventories. Recently, however, IRT has been employed to study more unconventional topics like policy adoption and classroom instructional practices (see Lee 1997; Swanson, Plank, and Hewes 2003; Swanson and Stevenson 2002). In this study, we use the WINSTEPS program to estimate a one-parameter partial credit IRT model, sometimes referred to as a Rasch analysis (Andrich 1988; Linacre and Wright 2000; Masters 1982; Muraki 1992; Wright and Masters 1982).

A full exposition of IRT methods lies far beyond the scope of this chapter. However, a brief analogy using the familiar example of achievement testing helps to introduce some key IRT concepts relevant to this study's application of the method to policy analysis. In the present study, for example, states take the place of student test-takers, and education policies correspond to test items or problems. Instead of test score, this study generates a score for the state's level of policy activism, our unobserved trait of interest. The items that comprise an IRT measurement scale have a property (or parameter) commonly referred to as "difficulty." For achievement test items, difficulty relates to the percentage of students who get the right answer. Difficulty for a policy is associated with how often it is adopted (a difficult policy will be adopted by fewer states). IRT models also assume that item difficulty produces a distinctive patterning of responses across the entire set of items comprising the measurement scale. On a well-designed test, then, we would expect that a student who correctly answers a difficult question will also be very likely to get easier questions right. Similarly, if a particular educational reform exists as a coherent policymaking strategy, only the most activist states should be adopting the most difficult policies related to that reform.

RESULTS

IRT analysis proves to be a very flexible tool for delving into the internal organization or substructuring of measurement scales, as the three-stage analysis later in the chapter demonstrates. First, we test whether states systematically adopt individual standards and accountability policies in a manner that suggests broader reform strategies. The concern here lies with the coupling of policies to reforms, such as whether professional standards policies are best viewed as part of a standards or accountability approach, as part of both, or as part of neither. Second, we examine the reliability of the estimated measurement models for standards-based and accountability policymaking. These analyses indicate how loosely (or tightly) coupled these reforms are as higher-order models of institutional change. Finally, we examine policy difficulty patterns to determine whether state policymaking displays more subtle forms of internal organization or substructuring. In particular, we consider whether the patterning of standard and accountability policies are distinctive from one another and consistent with their respective guiding models of administrative control.

The Coupling of Policies to Reforms: The Case of Professional Standards

As a first step in developing a reliable empirical measure of policy activism, we must determine whether all of the policies initially identified as potential elements of a larger reform strategy are actually part of the same underlying reform in practice. We begin by estimating a preliminary IRT measurement model for standards-based reform that employs the complete set of twenty-two individual policies distributed across four distinct reform domains—content standards, performance standards, aligned assessments, and professional standards. This first stage of analysis determines whether certain policies or clusters of policies display systematically poor alignment with the estimated measurement scale for standards activism.

This IRT analysis produces two closely related statistics that capture the fit of an item (policy) to the measurement scale for the construct of interest (standards activism). Both of these diagnostic measures capture the mean differences between the observed policy adoption data and the patterns that would be predicted by the IRT measurement model. The *infit* statistic places greater weight on unexpected responses to items that have a difficulty close to a case's estimated trait level (for example, a moderately activist state fails to adopt a policy of moderate difficulty). By contrast, the *outfit* statistic is more sensitive to outlier patterns (for example, a generally low-activism state adopts a very difficult policy). These scores are expressed as policy fit indices on a standard normal scale with an expected value of zero and standard deviation of one. Index values significantly greater than the expected value (for example, +2.0 or greater) suggest that a policy is not adopted in an orderly manner across the states. This in turn signals a lack of alignment (or a loose coupling) between that policy and the larger reform strategy.

The first panel of figure 12.2 plots the infit and outfit indices for the set of twenty-two standards-based reform policies. We find that the majority of items cluster tightly around expected values for the indices. This graph also provides clear evidence of systematically poorer fit among the policies relating to professional standards, with large statistically significant discrepancies between observed and expected values found for three of the four policies in this area. In other words, policies associated with professional standards are poorly aligned or loosely coupled with the broader standards-based reform strategy.

Two distinctive patterns of nonconforming policy adoption account for this result. On the one hand, some states with low overall levels of standards activism do adopt professional standards (which are relatively "difficult" policies) at unexpectedly high levels. At the other extreme, some states did not adopt professional standards despite their generally high activism across the full set of policies. Both

FIGURE 12.2   /   Alignment of Policies to Standards-Based and Accountability Reforms

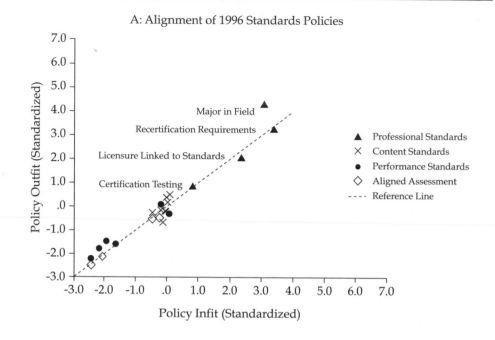

A: Alignment of 1996 Standards Policies

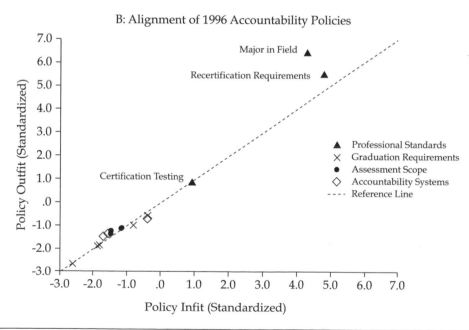

B: Alignment of 1996 Accountability Policies

Source: Author's compilation.

scenarios, however, are consistent with the interpretation that professional standards do not cohere with the other standards policy drivers.

Increasing the professional capacity of teachers has often been cited as an important goal of implementing standards-based education. Nevertheless, the empirical patterns of state policy activity suggest that the processes governing the adoption of professional standards differ substantially from those driving other elements of this reform. These preliminary analyses provide strong grounds for concluding that regulation-oriented professional standards policy does not empirically conform to the higher-order organization of standards-based reform as it has been enacted in state policy. Recalling the forms of organizational control discussed earlier, standards-based reform, as it exists in practice, appears to embody a narrowly process-oriented model of organizational change rather than the more integrated combination of process and regulatory control advocated in some systemic visions of the reform.

Although professional standards policies do not fit with standards-based reform, it might be the case that these policies instead align with a competing reform strategy. In the second panel of figure 12.2, we explore the possibility that professional standards are better aligned with an accountability-oriented model of educational reform. The results of this IRT analysis reveal that professional standards policies also have a poorer fit with accountability reform than any of the other policies examined. In fact, two of the three professional standards policies display extremely large and statistically significant levels of misalignment. By contrast, all but one of the remaining policy items cluster closely together, with fit indices statistically indistinguishable from the expected value. Based on these results, we conclude that input-oriented professional standards do not couple tightly with this otherwise largely output-oriented regulatory strategy of accountability reform.

On the one hand, professional standards may fail to align with the two distinct reform approaches examined here because states do not follow any kind of systematic pattern of policy adoption as far as teacher standards are concerned. On the other hand, it is also possible that states pursue professional standards in a coherent fashion, but that teacher-oriented policies constitute their own unique reform strategy or that they align more closely with other input-oriented regulatory policies. A more thorough exploration of teacher-oriented policymaking is beyond the scope of the present study. These findings, however, underscore the importance of maintaining a broader comparative perspective on reform that looks beyond a single focal policy movement and considers other competing or complementary strategies that organizational agents like the states might adopt. An overly narrow focus runs the risk of misidentifying the policy elements that constitute a reform movement in practice.

Coupling Between National Reform and State Policies

The low level of misalignment observed earlier for the core policies associated with the standards-based and accountability strategies provides our first indication that patterns of policy adoption are relatively coherent for these reforms. A revised pair of measurement models can be estimated after removing the poorly aligned professional standards policies. From these refined analyses, we obtain a new diagnostic statistic that measures the reliability of the policy activism scales. The value of this model fit statistic ranges from zero to one and can be interpreted in a manner similar to Cronbach's alpha, a measure of inter-item reliability commonly used in scale construction. The magnitude of this reliability statistic captures the proportion of variance in responses to the observed items (policy adoption) that is not attributable to estimation error. Larger values therefore signal greater internal coherence among the state policies.

Model results indicate the presence of a very coherent construct for standards-based reform activism, as evidenced by the estimated measurement scale's high level of reliability (.95). In addition, now that professional standards policies have been removed, none of the eighteen remaining standards policies display a significant degree of misalignment with the overall measurement model. A revised analysis of accountability-oriented policies also produces a measurement scale with a very high degree of inter-item reliability (.92). No significant policy misalignment is found among the eleven accountability policies retained for the final scale.

In technical terms, these findings indicate that it is possible to reliably measure levels of activism in each of these educational reform domains across the fifty states using a pool of discrete policy indicators and formal statistical measurement techniques. Substantively, we have found evidence to support the proposition that the states have pursued coherent strategies of reform activity with respect to these policy areas. These results also show signs of organizational coupling. Based on prior research and theory, we would expect there to be great potential for structural looseness. Nevertheless, a systematic connection exists between the higher-order models of reform promoted by national-level actors and the productive activities of the lower-order state-level decisionmakers who translate these models into the (relatively more) concrete form of enacted policies.

Internal Coupling of Reform Activities: Process Management and Regulatory Control

Having demonstrated that state policy adoption shows evidence of a broader structuring, this final section explores the internal patternings that characterize activism in standards-based and accountability reforms across the states. In particular, we seek to assess whether the observed patternings of state policy adoption are characteristic of the process and regulatory models of organizational control embodied in these two approaches to reform. The policy difficulty parameters generated by the final measurement models are reported in table 12.2. Policies are ranked within each reform element by increasing level of difficulty. As noted earlier, more difficult policies are less frequently adopted and receive larger (more positive) scores. We report difficulty scores here in roughly standard normal units called *logits*, although they could also be rescaled to other more intuitive metrics.

TABLE 12.2 / Policy Difficulty Scores from IRT Measurement Models:
Standards and Accountability

Reform	Policy Difficulty
Standards-based	
Content standards	
Math guide	−2.745
Science guide	−1.965
Language arts framework	−1.580
Social studies framework	−1.460
Math framework	−1.026
Science framework	−.895
Math curriculum innovation	−.428
Science curriculum innovation	−.191
Performance standards	
Math benchmarks	.211
Math performance levels	.383
Science benchmarks	.512
Science performance levels	.945
Math benchmark innovation	1.239
Science benchmark innovation	1.357
Assessment standards	
Aligned math assessment	.288
Aligned science assessment	.734
Innovative items	1.579
Innovative tests	3.041
Model reliability	.95
Accountability	
High school graduation requirements	
English credits	−1.536
Social studies credits	−1.050
Mathematics credits	−.532
Science credits	.376
Percentage of credits in core subjects	.390
Assessment program	
Population coverage	−1.228
Subject coverage	.688
Grade level coverage	1.244
Accountability systems	
Instructional improvement	−.953
School accountability	.490
Student accountability	2.110
Model reliability	.92

Source: Author's compilation.

The earlier stages of the measurement analysis found that the revised activism scales are highly reliable and contain no misaligned policy elements. By implication, this means that states tend to follow a systematic pattern of adopting progressively more difficult policies. Results for standards-based reform show that policies related to content frameworks are without exception the least difficult of the activities associated with this reform movement. All difficulty scores for content standards policies fall below the mean value for the scale (zero logits). Descriptive analyses of policy adoption patterns indicate that forty-four states had completed a math curriculum guide by 1996, further confirming the IRT result. By comparison, performance standards show moderate to high levels of difficulty, ranging from .211 to 1.357 logits. The most difficult policies to adopt are found among the aligned assessment items, particularly the use of innovative assessment methods. In fact, only one state had a testing program consisting entirely of progressive components like performance-based tasks or portfolios of student work in 1996.

The observed ranking of these three major policy elements mirrors the logical progression of implementation anticipated by national models of reform. In effect, the measurement model suggests a three-stage policy adoption strategy. States typically start by defining high-standards academic content in various subject areas. They proceed to establish the levels of mastery that students are expected to display over this content. Finally, states align their testing programs with content and performance expectations by employing the performance-based assessment techniques required to accurately gauge the acquisition of higher-order standards-based skills and knowledge. Thus, the coupling and internal structuring policy activities closely correspond to standards-based reform's process-oriented model of organizational control over educational production.

By examining policy difficulty rankings *within* these broader domains, we also gain several more subtle insights into the finer structure or internal organization of the standards movement in practice. First, within each of the main reform domains, policies related to science are consistently more difficult than the comparable mathematics policies. This pattern can be found for content frameworks, performance standards, published guides, and levels of curriculum innovativeness (timing of standards adoption) and in the alignment of state assessments. In many cases these differences in math and science policy difficulty are substantial. These findings confirm the perception that more progress has been made toward implementing a standards-based vision of education in mathematics and in other subject areas.

Second, with respect to both the content and performance standards domains, the indicators that reflect the timing of policy adoption are consistently the most difficult. As would be expected, these indicators serve to refine the measurement scale by introducing innovativeness as a distinct dimension of standards activism. At a given point in time, for instance, a number of states may have similar sets of standards policies in place. Among these states, however, the earlier introduction of curriculum-based reform elements should signal a greater degree of reform activism. The high difficulty associated with the early adoption of both content frameworks and performance standards supports this expectation.

Third, the very high difficulty levels associated with incorporating innovative assessment methods into state testing programs probably reflects the convergence of several key challenges. Aligned assessment systems, according to the internal logic of most standards-based reform models, represent one of the final stages in the process of progressively moving toward a state educational system organized around a content-centered vision of high academic standards. The implementation of alternative performance-based assessments is also a technically challenging process that requires a substantial commitment of fiscal resources on the part of the state to develop, administer, and score the assessments (Linn 1993). Finally, the introduction of a nontraditional assessment system often proves to be a politically divisive issue, a rallying point around which opponents of standards-based reform may mobilize support (Cohen and Hill 2001). So, apart from technical considerations of implementation, the adoption of such assessments may prove especially difficult because it requires a substantial commitment of political capital and political will on the part of state educational policymakers. Garnering support for an ambitious reform may also require the cultivation of strong ties or couplings between the state-level actors and other more local constituencies upon whom the ultimate success of the policy initiative will rest.

Just because a coordinated pattern of standards-based policy adoption exists does not mean that all states are at the same place on the road to reform at a given point in time. In fact, as figure 12.3 demonstrates, states displayed considerable variability in their levels of standards activism in 1996. State activism scores are displayed here on a standard normal scale (mean = 0, standard deviation = 1). Their relative rankings, however, prove to be consistent with information from other sources that document state involvement in the standards movement.

Maryland and Kentucky were among the most active states at this point in time. The Maryland State Department of Education has historically taken an active stance toward addressing a variety of educational issues, including curriculum reform. In 1992, for example, the state introduced the Maryland School Performance Assessment Program (since discontinued), which linked a statewide performance-based student assessment to school-level accountability provisions and professional development opportunities for teachers (Firestone, Mayrowetz, and Fairman 1998). In Kentucky the State Supreme Court issued a 1989 ruling declaring the state educational system unconstitutional. This watershed event opened the way for an aggressive and innovative program of state-led standards-based reforms during the 1990s that included the development of high-quality academic curricula, performance standards in core academic subjects, performance-based state assessments, and extensive professional development (Corcoran and Matson 1998). At the opposite end of the spectrum, Nebraska, Iowa, and Wyoming display very low levels of standards activism. In these states, primary responsibility for directing educational policy has traditionally rested with local school boards, with state educational agencies playing a relatively minor role in formulating reform strategies.

Just as the distinctive patterns of internal coordination that characterize a process-oriented model of organizational control are evident in results for standards-based reform, the less differentiated patterning observed for accountability reform

A: State Activism in Standards-Based Reform, 1996

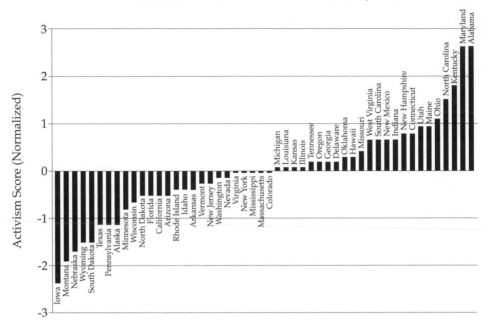

B: State Activism in Accountability, 1996

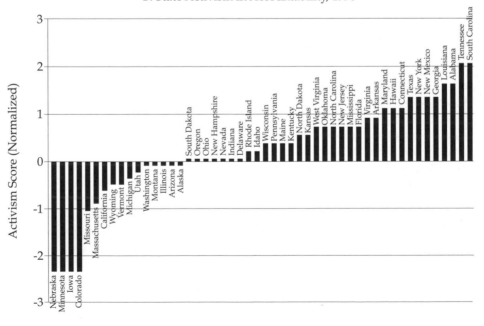

Source: Author's compilation.

belies its regulatory mode of control. Policies associated with each of the major domains of accountability reform (graduation requirements, assessment programs, accountability systems) span a wide range of difficulty levels. In addition, there is considerable overlap in the difficulty distributions of these three domains.

On the whole, the relatively undifferentiated internal configuration of accountability policy elements observed here is consistent with the account of regulatory modes of organizational control presented earlier. There it was noted that, in the context of a regulatory model of organizational control, individual policies could be viewed as largely interchangeable rather than interdependent reform elements. Although recognizable as a coherent reform strategy, the adoption of accountability-focused policies has not been influenced by the kind of organizational control model focused on process management that would promote internally coordinated relationships among a series of policy activities.

In comparing results for standards and accountability, it is interesting to note that we find the same consistent ranking of policy difficulties associated with specific academic subject areas. In particular, graduation credit requirements and curriculum frameworks are easiest to implement for English, followed by social studies, mathematics, and then science, in increasing order of difficulty. Without additional information on a larger set of subject-specific policies, it is difficult to probe this intriguing relationship between individual academic subject areas and policy activity in more depth. It is possible, for example, that these patterns are influenced by differential organization of instructional work or professionalization across academic disciplines. Since such factors have strong connections with issues of organizational coupling and institutional change, they may represent a fruitful avenue for future research.

As was the case for standards-based reform, levels of activism in accountability policy also vary greatly across the fifty states (see figure 12.3). The southeastern part of the country (South Carolina, Tennessee, Alabama, and Georgia) appear to have been at the vanguard of this reform movement in 1996. This finding concurs with the observation that governors from this region showed strong educational leadership during the 1980s, when heightened accountability emerged as a strategy for improving the nation's schools. Similar to results for standards-based reform, we find that states with a strong culture of local control in education (for example, Nebraska, Iowa, and Colorado) also tend to have the lowest levels of state-led policy activism in accountability-oriented reforms.

CONCLUSION

This chapter has paired a refined conceptual critique of loose-coupling theory with a promising statistical technique for investigating higher-order models of organizational control and (ultimately) the mechanisms of large-scale institutional change. Although this study's focus has been educational change, it illustrates a broader conceptual and methodological approach that could be fruitfully applied to other domains of social policymaking—welfare, health care, the environment, national security—where the locus of decisionmaking authority may rest at institutional levels ranging from the municipality to the nation-state. Approaches of this kind offer a means of quantifying social activism in a way that complements and enriches the knowledge gained through more qualitative or analytic studies of planned organizational and institutional change. An empirically grounded strategy may also help to reconcile descriptive accounts of social movements' often-idealized visions for change with the complicated reality of implementing change in its more concrete practical forms.

The insights gained through this study's analysis may be of particular interest to students of organizational theory and especially to those seeking to expand the boundaries of our thinking about organizational coupling, coordination, and control. This chapter has highlighted two distinctive approaches to educational reform with the intention of exploring their internal structuring and coherence as well as quantifying their implementation across the states. Policymaking patterns around both standards and accountability reveal that well-defined strategies have been pursued across the states. This implies some degree of organizational coupling between national- and state-level elements of the educational policy environment.

Given the states' legitimate authority to exercise significant autonomy in charting their own paths for educational reform, we should not consider the study's empirical findings to be in any way inevitable or a foregone conclusion. In fact, a lack of coherence in state-level policymaking has been cited as a long-standing problem for promoting effective educational change. Looking deeper into the internal organization of the standards and accountability reforms, we find signs of distinctive patterning among the individual policies associated with these respective strategies. These differences in substructuring might be attributed, at least in part, to the fact that standards and accountability approaches stem from different models of organizational control. Although accountability reform as a whole has been adopted in a systematic fashion, it displays relatively little differentiation either among or within its three major policy domains. By contrast, standards-based reform exhibits the characteristic signs of strong internal articulation—both within and across policy elements—that are consistent with a movement influenced by a process-oriented model of institutional change.

In attempting to explain unsuccessful educational reform initiatives of the past, organizational theorists tend to call attention to the structural fragmentation of education as an institutional system. Policy analysts, on the other hand, generally focus to a greater extent on the design characteristics of the reform model itself. Taken as a whole, the findings of this study would suggest that these two factors do not operate independently of one another. In fact, we might consider them to represent distinctive forms of coupling that relate to structural relationships and models of organizational control, respectively. The loosely coupled character often attributed to movements for change in education and other areas of social life may be a product of a complex structural and governance relationship as well as the loosely coupled higher-order designs or models for change that guide reform efforts. Focusing exclusively on a single aspect of coupling may therefore result in a rather one-dimensional and perhaps misleading perspective on the dynamics that drive institutional change processes in complex organizational-political environments.

I thank Andrew Abbott, Charles Bidwell, and Barbara Schneider for their helpful comments and suggestions. This research was supported in part by a grant from the National Science Foundation (REC-9987943) and by dissertation and postdoctoral fellowships from the Spencer Foundation. The views expressed here are those of the author and do not represent those of the granting institutions, the Urban Institute, or its board of trustees.

Chapter 13

Achievement and Equity

Chandra Muller and Kathryn S. Schiller

A major aim of public education in the United States has been to give children an opportunity for social mobility and to succeed in American society beyond their parents' status through learning and academic achievement. Equality of opportunity has been a consistent goal, yet the definition of who should have access, the perceived source of inequity, and the means of achieving equality of opportunity have shifted dramatically. Today a focus on equity according to race and family background drives much of the educational policy and rhetoric, yet there is a lack of clarity about what equality actually means, how to achieve it, or even how to measure it. Recently, the most visible and significant initiative, the No Child Left Behind (NCLB) Act of 2001, has mandated testing and school accountability with the dual goals of raising achievement and closing performance gaps according to family background and race.

The study reported in this chapter examines how state variations in testing policies, which are often an important element of accountability programs, shape the educational attainment of public high school students. Using two national datasets, each collected in the early 1990s, we use hierarchical linear modeling (HLM) to study the relationships between state-level testing policies and student-level advanced mathematics course-taking. To gauge the relative impact of family background and school processes on student achievement, we are particularly interested in between-state variations in the associations of students' background and academic preparation with their educational attainment. This multilevel analytic approach allows us to examine the interplay of states' policies with students' characteristics, school processes, and achievement. Although this is not a test of the efficacy of the NCLB policy, the study does take advantage of variations in state policies that foreshadowed NCLB and links those state policies to some of the student outcomes targeted in the legislation.

LEGISLATING EQUITY AND ACHIEVEMENT

The No Child Left Behind Act, coupled with increased accountability and assessments based on standards, captures many of the long-standing historical debates in education policy, including the tension between family and school, the ambiguity inherent in the concept of equity in education, and the fundamental purposes of schooling. One largely ignored aspect of the debate is that standards and accountability practices could actually bring about *larger* performance differences in students' achievement even if they raise the performance levels of most students, as proponents argue that they will. Given the current gaps in performance, lower-performing students, who by definition have more difficulty succeeding in the school system, would have to improve more than higher-performing students. In effect, the gap may not close if the highest-performing and most advantaged students are encouraged to perform to capacity.

This raises provocative questions about how to accomplish the goals of raising achievement and closing the gap. In terms of the formal processes of schooling, more resources would need to be concentrated in bringing up the achievement of the lowest-performing students. In addition, optimal curriculum for reaching low-performing and disadvantaged students would need to be identified. However, internal processes also should be addressed. Schools are highly stratified, with informal processes structuring opportunities to learn and students' successes and failures. Rather than focusing on test score gaps or the attainment of credentials, we examine the number of advanced mathematics courses students take in high school. This indicator captures students' academic progress and opportunities to learn as well as their preparation for elite postsecondary education and access to careers, such as those in the medical, technology, engineering, and science fields that require advanced mathematics knowledge.

MECHANISMS SHAPING OPPORTUNITIES TO LEARN

Occupational opportunities are differently shaped during adolescence when some students take advanced college preparatory courses and others drop out of courses at this level, or out of school altogether (Bidwell and Yasumoto 1999). Curricular differentiation in schools is most clearly observed in students' course enrollment patterns. Typically, the high school curriculum is organized into sequences of courses in which subject knowledge gained from one course prepares a student for the next course (Schneider, Swanson, and Riegle-Crumb 1998; Stevenson, Schiller, and Schneider 1994). Mobility between sequences is restricted and forms the foundation of a stratification system for adolescents. Scheduling requirements (Pallas, Natriello, and Riehl 1994), the homogeneity of course composition based on students' prior achievement (Hallinan 1994; Oakes 1994), and other features of the formal organization shape students' opportunities to learn.

Students' experiences with the formal organization of schools is not monolithic; instead, it is defined by the specific sets of courses in which they participate (Bidwell and Friedkin 1988). In high schools today students taking advanced courses and multiple years of foreign language experience a different social context than those taking vocational education courses or a few basic years of core subjects. These patterns of stratification are similar to an "occupational structure" or status system for high school students in which everyday life and current and future opportunities are shaped by status and position in this structure (Rosenbaum 1986; Sørenson 1987). The course sequences reflect the formal organization of curricula and schools that must be considered if we are to understand the effects of curricular exposure on achievement over time.

Sociologists recognize the gatekeeping functions of school structures and personnel, including teachers' attitudes, which influence differential access to specific courses for some students. In addition to course placement, teachers' expectations can limit students' academic success by imposing self-fulfilling prophecies. Alan Kerckhoff (1993) describes the tendency of teachers' ratings and course placements to remain stable—even when they are not merited by students' performance—as "institutional inertia." Some view these school processes as either the cause or a symptom of unequal opportunity (Oakes 1985), whereas others see them as a mechanism of a meritocracy (Hallinan 1991).

Clearly, the mechanisms that create students' opportunities to learn are complex. Rather than focusing on such mechanisms, accountability and assessment policies target the outcomes of the schooling process. Yet criticism of these policies is often directed at how the system deals with students who are vulnerable to reduced opportunities through a multiplexity of mechanisms that marginalize them. In this chapter, we evaluate the effects of elements of these policies on students' preparation for postsecondary study. Importantly, we evaluate direct effects and how the effects differ according to the background and preparation of the students. Taken together, this chapter addresses the debate about whether the policies act as an engine of social mobility and opportunity or as one more way in which inequality is reproduced and legitimated in our society. We also elaborate on two possibly conflicting aspects of these effects by analyzing the levels of attainment (in the form of the number of advanced credits accumulated), as well as the possible closing or widening of gaps in race and socioeconomic status (SES).

DATA AND METHOD

The analyses in this chapter required the use of two datasets: one to provide longitudinal information on students' social backgrounds and academic experiences, and the other to provide information on states' assessment and accountability policies. Both of the studies we used were conducted in the early 1990s. We use a multilevel modeling strategy to estimate the policy effects on the amount of advanced math credits students accumulate.

Sample

Information on students' backgrounds and academic progress come from the National Education Longitudinal Study of 1988 to 1992 (NELS:88–92), which followed a nationally representative sample of eighth-graders in 1988 through their high school careers and beyond (Ingels et al. 1992). The panel used for these analyses consisted of 10,046 public school students who participated in the first three waves of data collection (1988, 1990, and 1992) and for whom high school transcripts were collected. All 50 states and the District of Columbia are represented in NELS:88–92, with an average of 196 students and 22 high schools per state. For these analyses, the sample was weighted to be representative of the 1988 eighth-grade cohort and to take into account the complex sample design and nonresponse rates.

Information on states' assessment and accountability policies was obtained from the National Longitudinal Study of Schools (NLSS). One purpose of NLSS was to examine the impact of state policies on school practices (Levine and Stevenson 1997; Stevenson and Schiller 1999). In 1993 state departments of education were asked through the National Cooperative Education Statistics System to answer a lengthy questionnaire concerning their testing and accountability policies. Responses were received from all fifty states and the District of Columbia.

Mathematics Course Enrollments

The measures of students' mathematics course-taking were constructed from the NELS:88–92 course-level transcript file, which includes indicators of the course topic and when the course was taken for each course a student took while in high school. Based on the standard sequences of mathematics courses most students take, courses were classified into one of the following groups, in hierarchical order, from 0 to 9: no math, remedial math, general math, pre-algebra, algebra 1, geometry, algebra 2, advanced math, pre-calculus, and calculus. The analyses in this chapter predict the number of Carnegie units earned in higher-level mathematics courses (defined as geometry and above), which are commonly required for admission to a competitive college or postsecondary academic program. Students earn one Carnegie unit by obtaining a grade of D or better in a one-year academic course taken the equivalent of one period a day, five days a week. The amount of advanced mathematics course work students take has a strong association with achievement (Bryk, Lee, and Smith 1990) and college attendance (Schneider, Swanson, and Riegle-Crumb 1998). On average, the students earned 1.68 units in advanced mathematics, which is a little more than having taken geometry and algebra 2 (Legum et al. 1993). Owing to a highly structured sequence of prerequisites, the number of Carnegie units students accumulate is a good indicator of how far they progress toward calculus. Also, where students start in the sequence is likely to affect how far they progress, so freshman course placement is used as a predictor for this variable in some models. A full description of all student-level variables can be found in table 13A.1.

Student-Level Variables

Analyses focus on differences across states not only in students' freshman mathematics course placements and number of advanced credits earned but also in the relative differences related to socioeconomic status and race or ethnicity. In these analyses, family SES—a composite of parents' education and occupation created by the National Center for Education Statistics (NCES)—is considered a measure of students' financial and social resources outside the school. Using HLM, we evaluate whether the relationship between SES and mathematics course-taking varies across states with differing assessment policies.

Instead of the usual four-group classification of students' race or ethnicity, our HLM models include only indicators for African American and Latino and Latina, with the comparison group being defined as white or Asian American. We choose not to distinguish between white and Asian American students because of the latter group's small sample size and sparse distribution in many states, which resulted in unreliable HLM coefficients. Results concerning the effects of race or ethnicity on mathematics course-taking and their variation across states were not substantively affected by this decision.

To control for prior gatekeeping functions by the school, we take into account students' mathematics course-taking in middle school, a measure that mediates where students were located in the mathematics curricular sequence before they entered high school. The measure of eighth-grade mathematics course-taking is based on eighth-graders' reports of whether they attended remedial, general, or algebra classes at least once a week (Stevenson et al. 1994). Students' position in the mathematics curricular sequence in eighth grade can be considered an indirect measure of teachers' assessments of students' potential to succeed in mathematics in high school (Hallinan 1992; Kerckhoff 1993; Useem 1991).

To control on other individual characteristics that can influence mathematics course enrollments, we include other indicators of students' background characteristics (gender and family structure) and prior academic achievement (middle school mathematics grades). Grades are used rather than test scores because they measure how well students met the expectations of their middle school teachers in their classes and are often used by high schools to place students in freshman mathematics courses. We also include indicators for whether students attended an urban or rural public high school, with suburban as the reference category.

State Policy Measures

Rather than focusing on the details of a particular policy, we use indicators of general strategies that states have adopted to raise expectations and increase accountability for students' academic progress. Our approach to characterizing state policies is midway between general characterizations of policy environments that blur distinctions regarding the purposes of policies (Lee 1997) and analyses of specific policies that have an impact only on some students and schools (Catterall 1989). Our approach, in attempting to capture crucial aspects of the policies related to the implementation of policies and the incentive structures that are inherent in them, is more akin to the general approach of James Coleman and his colleagues (1997). Our goal was to develop indicators of state policies that tap the purpose of policies and the extent to which that type of lever for change is employed. The measures used in our analyses are the state policies reported in 1993, the year most NELS students graduated from high school.

Our measure of the extensiveness of states' testing programs in 1993 was based on states' reports of the number of grade levels and major academic subjects in which they had mandated that students be tested during high school. Only seven states reported no mandated testing of high school students in the major subjects of English, social studies and history, mathematics, and science. On average, states gave four tests to high school students, although two states (Minnesota and Virginia) reported testing students in all four subjects every year. The extensiveness of a state's testing program is an indicator of whether external examinations were used on a regular basis to monitor students' progress through the established curriculum, usually with the intention of raising overall levels of achievement.

Although most states tested high school students, they varied in the extent to which performance on those tests carried meaningful consequences for students or schools. Our measure of consequences for students based on test performance is the sum of states' reports of whether test scores were recommended or required for purposes such as placement in remedial or advanced courses, promotion to the next grade, or the award of a high school diploma. Almost two-thirds of the states had guidelines or mandatory policies specifying how test scores should be used to determine some aspect of students' academic program or success. States with such policies linked test scores to an average of three or four consequences for students.

Fewer states linked students' performance on state tests to rewards and sanctions for schools in 1993. The survey asked about eight types of consequences, such as financial rewards for meeting standards or sanctions like loss of accreditation for failure to do so. Over two-thirds of the states reported that they either did not set performance standards or did not provide incentives for meeting those standards. The remaining third of the states linked aggregate test scores to an average of three to four consequences for schools. Descriptions of each state policy variable can be found in table 13A.2.

Analytic Technique

The question of whether state testing policies are related to students' high school mathematics courses requires a multilevel analytic strategy. Our analyses are concerned not only with variation in students' mathematics course-taking across states with differing policies (direct effects), but also with whether the associations of students' outcomes with their social backgrounds vary across states (interaction effects). A common technique for analyzing hierarchical data (in this case, students nested within states) and cross-level effects is HLM, which allows simultaneous consideration of factors from two levels of analysis (Bryk and Raudenbush 1992).[1]

We used the state policy variables to predict the number of advanced mathematics credits students will earn. The student-level model is shown in the following equation:

$$Y_{ij} = B_{0j} + B_{1j}(SES_{ij}) + B_{2j-3j} \text{ (race-ethnicity}_{ij}) + B_{4j-10j} \text{ (controls)} + e_{ij} \quad (13.1)$$

where ij is the value for a given student in a given state and B_{kj} provides the coefficients for students' SES, race or ethnicity, and the control variables in each state. The effects for some of the student-level factors, such as race or ethnicity, were expressed by several coefficients (for example, B_{2j} one for Latino and Latina, and B_{3j} for African American). The term e_{ij} is a measure of the random error, which includes unmeasured sources of variation in a particular student's outcome. In our analyses, all the student-level variables were centered on the grand mean for the sample, which allows the intercept (B_{0j}) to be interpreted as the mean outcome for each state adjusted for the characteristics of students in that state (Bryk, Raudenbush, and Congdon 1996; Willms and Raudenbush 1989).

Preliminary analyses indicated that the associations between the student control variables and mathematics courses could be characterized as: associations were very similar across most states; variations in the coefficients were not related to state testing policies; or the results for SES and race or ethnicity were not affected by the assumption of no variation in the effects of a given control variable across states. Thus, for the analyses presented here, the coefficients for the student-level control variables were set to be "fixed effects," and our statistical model assumed that the relationship between these student characteristics and mathematics course enrollments were the same for all states (Bryk and Raudenbush 1992). The initial HLM model without any state-level variables provides an estimate of the proportion of variance in mathematics course enrollments between students versus across states. It is also the basis for evaluating the amount of variation at the state level that is explained by the state policy indicators.

The state-level analyses, in essence, examine the extent to which variation in the coefficients for the intercept, SES, and race or ethnicity are related to accountability policies. Equation 13.2 shows the general model for estimating the effects of these state policies:

$$B_{kj} = \gamma_{k0} + \gamma_{k1-k4} \text{ (state policies}_j) + u_{kj} \quad (13.2)$$

Each of the policy variables was centered on its grand mean, which means that γ_{k0} is the average effect of variable k across states, and the other coefficients are adjustments, or interaction effects, to those coefficients for states that differ in their testing policies. The effect of a student-level variable is increased when the coefficient for a state policy variable is in the same direction (plus or minus) as the intercept for the student-level variable, and reduced when the two coefficients are in the opposite direction. The term u_{kj} is the error term for estimation of the student-level coefficient for each state. The combined HLM model is shown in equation 13.3:

$$\begin{aligned}
Y_{ij} = &[\gamma_{00} + \gamma_{01-04} \text{ (state policies}_j) + u_{0j}] \\
&+ [\gamma_{10} + \gamma_{11-14} \text{ (state policies}_j) + u_{1j}] \times SES_{ij} \\
&+ [\gamma_{2-30} + \gamma_{22-34} \text{ (state policies}_j) + u_{2-3j}] \times \text{race-ethnicity}_{ij} \\
&+ \gamma_{4-100} \times \text{control variables}_{ij} + e_{ij} \quad (13.3)
\end{aligned}$$

RESULTS

States vary in their approaches to raising high school students' academic attainment and promoting equality of opportunities for learning, but the impact of these policies on students' achievement and the gap in achievement is uncertain. In this study, we estimate the effects of states' strategies for raising standards and establishing accountability on students' academic progress and future opportunity by modeling the number of advanced mathematics credits they earn in high school and the gap between students according to race and ethnicity, SES, and initial high school course placement. Because of the sequential nature of the high school mathematics curriculum, the mathematics courses that freshmen take provide a strong predictor of how far they will progress in this subject area before graduation. The coefficients for this model are shown in table 13.1.

The top panel of table 13.1 displays the coefficients for the intercept and independent variables modeled at the state level. The first column shows the level-two intercept, or average effect, for the student-level variables of interest; the coefficients for state policy variables are shown in the other three columns. The lower

TABLE 13.1 / Effects of State Policies on Number of Advanced Mathematics Credits Earned

	Average Effect	Extensiveness of Testing	Consequences for Schools	Consequences for Students
Student-level variables				
Intercept	1.631***	.003	.047**	−.026
Socioeconomic status	.323***	.014*	.009	−.008
Race-ethnicity				
Latino and Latina	−.103*	.035	.030	−.016
African American	.039	−.008	.021	−.037
Freshman math level	.448***	−.007	.027**	−.018*
Student-level controls	Coefficient			
Male	−.039			
Living with both parents	.103**			
Middle school math grades	.249***			
Eighth-grade math class				
Remedial	−.107			
Algebra or advanced	.482***			
Urbanicity				
Urban	−.005			
Rural	−.027			

Source: National Education Longitudinal Study of 1988 to 1992 and National Longitudinal Study of Schools.
*p < .05; **p < .01; ***p < .001

panel displays the coefficients for the student-level controls, which were assumed to be constant across states.

Focusing on the control variables, students who lived with both parents, those who had higher mathematics grades in middle school, and those who took algebra in eighth grade tended to earn more advanced mathematics credits in high school. These differences persisted even though the analysis takes into account students' placement as freshmen, which suggests that these differences affect students' progress in high school beyond the effect on their early experiences. Gender and urbanicity were not significantly related to the number of credits that students earned in courses such as geometry, algebra 2, or trigonometry. However, SES was positively associated with the accumulation of mathematics course credits, and Latinos earned slightly fewer advanced mathematics credits.

The top panel of table 13.1 shows that state policies were related to students' advanced mathematics course credits accumulation, both directly in the average number of credits earned and through interactions with students' socioeconomic status and freshman course placement. On average, students tended to earn 1.6 credits in advanced mathematics, approximately equivalent to a year of geometry and over half a year of algebra 2. Students in states with more consequences tended to earn a somewhat greater number of advanced mathematics credits, although the effect is fairly small at about 5 percent ($.052 = .047 \times 1.137$) of a credit more per standard deviation increase in the number of consequences for schools. The number of advanced mathematics credits did not differ according to the number of consequences for students or the extensiveness of testing in a state. African American students earned about the same number of advanced mathematics credits as whites once initial course placement and SES were controlled.

The state policies are also related to differences in the number of advanced mathematics credits based on students' SES or race and ethnicity. The effect of SES tends to be slightly stronger in states with more extensive testing programs. The effect of SES on the number of advanced mathematics credits earned increased by 15 percent [$.15 = (.014 \times 3.461)/.323$] per standard deviation change in the extensiveness of testing. These results suggest that extensive testing had a persisting effect on social stratification, not only through initial placements but also through increasing differences between poor and rich students over the course of their high school careers.

Finally, states' accountability policies appear to have influenced students' trajectories through the high school mathematics curriculum. On average, students tended to accumulate almost .45 of a Carnegie unit more in advanced mathematics for each increase in the level of their freshman mathematics course. The link between freshman course placements and accumulated course credits was stronger in states with more consequences for schools linked to test performance and with a fewer number of consequences for students. These interaction effects were statistically significant but modest, amounting to a 9 to 12 percent change in the effect of freshman course placements per standard deviation increase in a given state policy measure. These results suggest that some state policies may encourage students to persist in taking more advanced level courses; however, greater consequences for schools also result in a larger gap according to freshman year course placement.

CONCLUSION

The state policies examined in this chapter are similar to those currently employed to raise student achievement and close the performance gaps between rich and poor and between white and minority students. Based on data from the early 1990s, our results suggest that these policies are likely to have mixed effects on students' opportunities to learn mathematics in high school. Given the strong link between course work and learning, these effects on student achievement and inequality will probably likewise be interrelated.

Overall, our results indicate that state policies had small but statistically significant effects on students' mathematics course-taking in high school, both on the number of credits earned and on stratification according to social class and earlier course placement. The small size of the effects is not surprising considering that individual students' course-taking patterns are influenced by many factors, such as their educational aspirations, personal preferences, and class schedules (Oakes 1985; Useem 1991). However, even small differences between states are important because they reflect the experiences of large numbers of students.

These findings indicate that increasing school accountability for student test performance was the only strategy that seemed to increase all students' opportunities for learning mathematics in high school. Students in states that linked test performance to a greater number of consequences for schools appeared to persist in taking the advanced-level courses necessary for acceptance into competitive colleges as well as for entry into health care, science, and technology occupations. The effect of this policy was strongest for students who took higher-level courses as freshmen. Essentially, holding schools accountable for students' learning appears to both raise the achievement of all students and increase the gap based on preparation. This suggests the need for coordination of policy at multiple grade levels, as well as in early childhood, to ensure adequate preparation for all students in the early grades.

The formal school structure associated with course-taking opportunities and placement appears stronger in states that hold schools accountable for students' learning (Bidwell, Frank, and Quiroz 1997; Coleman et al. 1997). One possible explanation for this effect of stronger school consequences is that school accountability focuses students and teachers on a common goal of academic excellence, with those students who show potential being particularly encouraged to progress further in the mathematics curriculum. Alternatively, higher rates of advanced mathematics course-taking could also be the result of at-risk students being more likely to drop out of school in these states (Schiller and Muller 2000). More research is needed to determine whether school accountability provides incentives not only to invest in academically able students likely to excel but also to encourage students who are at risk of failing or planning to leave school early.

We also found that extensive testing was related to greater stratification accord-ing to students' socioeconomic status. Low-SES students tended to earn more ad-vanced mathematics credits in states with fewer mandated tests, while advanced mathematics credits for high-SES students varied very little between states. Fre-quent testing may reinforce rather than alleviate academic problems through self-fulfilling prophecies concerning the academic ability of poorer children (Muller and Schiller 2000). The weaker impact of this policy on affluent children is not sur-prising given the additional academic support and encouragement they receive from parents, teachers, and peers focused on college attendance. Extensive testing does not appear to increase students' opportunities for learning and does tend to exacerbate social class inequality.

The gap between rich and poor may widen with clearer standards and more em-phasis on standardized assessment. With a more focused curriculum, students' progress is more easily assessed quantitatively. Accompanying such assessments with expanded ceilings and floors in performance assessment might increase per-formance variation, and the ceiling would most likely expand more than the floor. Better training for teachers and increased resources for both schools and families in support of preparing children to learn would not necessarily accompany stan-dards and assessment. Consequently, the larger and more insidious sources of in-stitutional inequality might remain and could easily contribute to even greater performance differentials once attention to teaching is more focused on a limited set of concepts. This is a major concern of critics of these policies, who also implic-itly fear a wider gap if poor children are held to the same standards as the middle class. The gap between the haves and have-nots could come about even if average performance levels increase over time.

Diane Ravitch (1995) claims that, contrary to popular opinion, "equity" and "excellence" are compatible with each other and with standards reforms. How-ever, if we adequately measure academic achievement, it seems likely that stu-dents with socioeconomic advantages will learn at faster rates than those with fewer advantages, and larger performance gaps will develop. Schools that teach disadvantaged students could compensate for family socioeconomic disadvan-tage to reduce the gap, but they will face greater challenges as a result. Schools alone cannot eliminate the achievement gap based on socioeconomic inequality. Some schools may go to heroic efforts to close the gap, but in the absence of a rad-ical change in social policy, the gap is unlikely to close on the scale necessary to also close the socioeconomic performance gap in the general population. These policies are one step—albeit a step with complex consequences—but they are far from a panacea.

If, in fact, standards, assessments, and the accompanying accountability prac-tices that deliver sanctions to schools do increase the performance of all students but increase the gap between rich and poor as well, then cases can be made in favor of and against these policies as a vehicle for equality of opportunity. Stu-dents may learn more, and they may even acquire skills and knowledge that make them desirable to employers. In addition, our ability to quantify differences and establish a hierarchical order among them will also sharpen; that order will be partially determined by their social class backgrounds.

Will the policy result in increased opportunities for traditionally disadvantaged students? This is possible only if an ordered hierarchy among students is not used to evaluate their merit. If the system rewards the acquisition of skills and knowledge, more course work that results in preparation for college and jobs will lead to greater opportunities. However, if the system uses these courses as a sorting device to legitimate the advantages of privileged family backgrounds, as Randall Collins (1979) argues, then the long-term effects of these courses will be diminished for lower-SES students. Our results on the effects of state policies on how students get ahead suggest a complex system that both rewards performance and legitimates existing ascriptive advantages.

Since there is little doubt that standards and accountability practices are politically popular and becoming more widely implemented, it is important to ask how our social institutions handle the standardization of information about students' performance. Ironically, at the same time that standards and accountability are becoming commonplace in our public schools, there is a trend against the use of standardized test scores as a means to evaluate individuals' applications to college, a major gatekeeper to middle-class opportunity.

Texas is an interesting case in the implementation of standards and accountability and in the ways in which students are sorted, on the one hand, and provided educational opportunity, on the other hand. Texas has a well-developed and growing system of assessment and accountability practices in place for elementary, middle, and high schools. Yet in a reaction to the *Hopwood v. University of Texas* decision, which prevented the University of Texas from using race as an admission criterion, the state legislature mandated that any student with a grade point average in the top 10 percent of his or her high school graduating class must be admitted to any state university. The policy made students' performance on standardized test scores and indicators of their substantive proficiency in academic subjects (except as measured by their grades) virtually irrelevant for college admissions for many students. The admissions policy also compensated for the effects of variations in school quality and performance differences on access to higher education of students. Other states, such as California, have adopted similar practices.

There is little doubt that assessment and accountability practices are becoming commonplace. Setting aside the debate about whether the policies are desirable, we must recognize that testing students more frequently and with more finely tuned instruments will clarify the social inequality inherent in our society and in our schools. The differences between students may become larger and will certainly be more observable. As a consequence, we will need to tackle thorny issues concerning social inequality that have been obscured by less visible and precise means of evaluating differences between students. As a nation, we may be in for a heated debate about social inequality as our standards and assessment policies collide with our social values about what schools can and should do and the opportunities all children deserve.

TABLE 13A.1 / Source, Coding, and Descriptive Statistics for Student-Level Variables

High School Mathematics Course	Mean	Standard Deviation	Source and Coding
Level of freshman mathematics course	3.53	1.27	Obtained from high school transcripts
Advanced mathematics credits	1.68	1.29	Obtained from high school transcripts, number of Carnegie units in algebra 2, geometry, trigonometry, pre-calculus, and calculus
Socioeconomic status	.01	.73	NCES-constructed variable in the second follow-up student file
Race-ethnicity			
African American	.11	.32	Constructed from an NCES variable
Latino and Latina	.08	.28	based on student reports, with European Americans and Asian Americans as the base category and Native Americans excluded from analysis
Male	.49	.50	NCES variable based on student report; coded 1 = male and 0 = female
Living with both parents	.68	.47	Composite based on parents' and students' reports of adults in the household; coded 1 = both parents and 0 = other
Middle school mathematics grades	4.04	.97	Eighth-graders' report of mathematics grades "from the sixth grade until now"
Eighth-grade mathematics courses			
Remedial mathematics	.06	.24	Eighth-graders' report of which mathematics courses they
Algebra	.37	.48	attended that year
Urbanicity			
Urban	.20	.40	Constructed from an NCES variable
Rural	.36	.48	with the suburban as the base category

Source: All information is obtained from the National Educational Longitudinal Study of 1988 to 1994.

TABLE 13A.2 / Sources, Coding, and Descriptive Statistics for State-Level Variables

State Testing Policies	Mean	Standard Deviation	Source and Coding
High school graduation requirements	9.960	3.203	"Please indicate your state's high school graduation requirements for the class of 1992" —The variable is the sum of the number of Carnegie units required for a "regular diploma" in English, mathematics, science, and social studies.
Extensiveness of testing ($\alpha = .8949$)	4.020	3.461	"At what high school grades, and in which content areas, does current state policy require that student performance be assessed?"—Summed across mathematics, reading, science, and history/social studies for ninth through twelfth grades.
Consequences for students ($\alpha = .5976$)	2.066	2.189	"Does your state currently require or set guidelines for high school student testing for any of the following purposes?"—Coded 2 = "state has mandatory policy"; 1 = "state has guidelines"; and 0 = "neither." Summed across high school graduation, placement in remedial (compensatory education) programs, diploma eligibility, and promotion.
Consequences for schools ($\alpha = .8485$)	1.137	1.929	"Does state policy set standards for high school's performance based on student test results?"—Coded 0 if "describes neither acceptable nor unacceptable results." Otherwise, number of rewards for meeting standards (financial incentives, official recognition or publicity, accreditation, waivers from testing or reporting requirements, waivers from other regulations or deregulation) and sanctions for failing to meet standards (negative publicity, loss of accreditation, loss of control to higher educational authority).

Source: National Longitudinal Study of Schools.

NOTE

1. In preliminary analyses, we ran three-level models nesting students within schools within states but decided against using them because we are not interested in school effects per se and the results were substantively similar but more robust with the two-level models.

Chapter 14

School Transition Programs in Organizational Context: Problems of Recruitment, Coordination, and Integration

Kathryn S. Schiller

Perennial problems for all organizations are created by turnover in membership, whether or not the process is predictable and gradual. An organization's failure to replace former members may raise questions of institutional legitimacy and severely hamper its ability to obtain resources (Meyer and Rowan 1977). Whether new members are obtained through conscription or recruitment, organizations are usually required to communicate with the suppliers of these individuals to, at minimum, exchange information concerning them (Stinchcombe 1990) and possibly to provide feedback or coordinate their internal operations (Coleman 1997). The arrival of new members creates the potential for structural and social disruptions of the organization as they are allocated to positions and learn the established norms and values (Coleman and Hoffer 1987). Most organizations have structures, such as personnel departments in businesses or counselors in schools, to systematically address such potential problems and at least partially smooth the transition of new members into their daily operations.

Schools are among those organizations that experience a large, regular turnover of membership each year as graduates depart and novices enter. This latter transition process is potentially problematic for both the new students, regardless of whether they are kindergartners or college freshmen, and the schools they enter. Faced with adjusting to a new social and academic environment, many students experience academic difficulties and report emotional distress following school transitions (Roderick 1993; Tinto 1988). At the secondary and postsecondary levels, these difficulties often lead to students leaving school before completing their courses of study. In addition to helping new freshmen adjust successfully, schools try to predict the resources needed by the new students each year (Delany 1991). Unanticipated changes in the number of students, or of a particular type of student, may require dramatic reallocation of resources such as personnel and classroom space. Communication with feeder schools may reduce uncertainty concerning these issues, but coordination of academic programs between schools is often impractical (Riehl, Pallas, and Natriello 1999).

This chapter focuses on the transition to high school as an institutional feature with various sets of organizational problems related to coordination with other schools, recruitment of new students, and integration of freshmen into the larger student population. Using a national sample of over one thousand high schools attended by the 1990 sophomore cohort, I explore variation relating to institutional type and geographic location in organizational practices designed to facilitate the transition process. These two organizational characteristics reflect the institutional environments of schools that shape the particular problems created by the annual turnover of student membership.

INSTITUTIONAL AND ORGANIZATIONAL FEATURES OF THE TRANSITION TO HIGH SCHOOL

In most nations, secondary school enrollments have dramatically expanded over the last century. The transition to high school is a normative transition that, in contrast to school transfers, involves not only entry into new physical and social settings but also institutionalized changes in students' social roles and the academic environment they negotiate (Felner, Primavera, and Cauce 1981). The institutionalized nature of these transitions is evident in the initiation processes that often mark entry into the new social status as high school students, even when the transition does not involve changing school buildings.

Schools have routinized processes to facilitate the transfer of information and allocation of resources (Cicourel and Kitsuse 1963), but they are also organizations in a state of flux as they absorb freshmen classes (DeLany 1991; Felner, Ginter, and Primavera 1982; Gamoran 1992a; Riehl et al. 1999). Problems inherent in the process of moving individuals across organizational boundaries can disrupt the receiving organization's daily activities and reduce its effectiveness. Because of the numbers involved, even normative transitions can exacerbate organizational problems related to the recruitment of new members and the integration of freshmen into the established social system (Bidwell 1965). This chapter explores the types of uncertainties that high schools are likely to experience during this transition process.

In anticipation of problems related to the transition process, schools have developed ways of reducing the resulting uncertainties (Mac Iver and Epstein 1991). However, the particular techniques and programs adopted are likely to vary based on the particular types and amounts of potential uncertainty. I argue here that, in general, high schools with tight links to middle or junior high schools may find coordination of curriculum with these feeder schools a more efficient way to reduce uncertainty about freshmen's preparation for high school. Those high schools without close ties to feeder schools may find it more important to make freshmen feel a part of their school community as they facilitate a smoother integration of new students.

Problems of Recruitment

As client-serving organizations, high schools must try to predict how many and which students will attend classes because organizational resources depend on these numbers. Public school funding allocations, especially those from states or the national government, are usually based on student enrollment in classes at the beginning of the year. Similarly, most private schools are dependent to a large extent on tuition paid by enrolled students. Having too many students enrolled, however, can be as problematic as too few. As the number of students increases, so does the amount of information that is processed to allocate students to courses (DeLany 1991; Riehl et al. 1999). Significant changes in the size of freshmen cohorts between successive years are also highly problematic for schools, especially if the demands on facilities and personnel vary dramatically from year to year.

Schools, however, differ in how they obtain their students—some do so through conscription and others through recruitment. Traditional public high schools have been described as enjoying a "monopoly" (Chubb and Moe 1990) or as being "domesticated" (Carlson 1964). As such, traditional public schools are viewed as buffered from environmental uncertainty through a steady supply of resources and students. Public high schools can often predict years in advance how many freshmen they will have based on elementary school enrollments, owing to stable feeder patterns established by district central offices. Although neither the student nor the school selects the other, the size and source of the freshman class is predictable for public schools.

In contrast, private schools have no institutionally guaranteed constituency and must be concerned each year with attracting and keeping students, which makes them more responsive to their clientele (Chubb and Moe 1990). Breaking the public school monopoly to introduce more competition for students and encourage increased organizational effectiveness was one rationale behind the school choice movement (Cookson 1992). By design, magnet schools—and more recently, charter schools—must attract sufficient numbers of students to justify their costs because their enrollments are not based on residential assignment. For private and choice public high schools, the sizes of their freshmen cohorts may not be determined, depending on the system, until late spring, or maybe even not until students arrive in the fall.

In addition to institutional type, unstable institutional environments also make predicting enrollments of freshmen each year difficult (DeLany 1991; Riehl et al. 1999). Frequent shifts in district policies and mobile populations create unpredictable environments for urban high schools, which draw freshmen from multiple middle schools, many of which feed different high schools (Schiller 1995). The minority and poor populations in urban areas are more mobile than the more affluent populations in suburban areas (Jarrett 1995). Thus, predicting which students will attend a particular high school is more difficult for urban schools than for rural or suburban ones.

In summary, fixed attendance zones help decrease the organizational uncertainty about students' movements from middle to high school through stable feeder patterns. However, schools with fixed attendance zones have little control over which students enroll, so they must maintain flexibility in their allocation of instructional and other resources. On the other hand, schools without attendance zones face greater uncertainty over how many students will enroll but have more control over the types of students they will receive through their recruitment efforts and the application process. These mechanisms increase the likelihood that students who end up enrolling fit the schools' goals and are suited to their curricula. Thus, as one form of uncertainty is decreased, another increases.

Problems of Coordination

Regardless of whether new students are conscripted or recruited, their movement across organizational boundaries creates potential problems for high schools related to their relationships with feeder schools (Bidwell 1965). The loosely coupled nature of school systems reduces the need to tightly coordinate activities across not only classrooms but also schools (Weick 1976). However, communication with feeder schools can facilitate the processing of information concerning freshmen and provide at least some measure of quality control.

Because most students change schools during the transition to high school, some of the problems encountered by schools result from the process of transferring information across organizational boundaries (Stinchcombe 1990). With the vast amount of information being transferred, details of individual cases are often missed or glossed over. One particularly problematic aspect of information-processing in school transitions is the allocation of students to courses—especially in unstable social and political environments (Useem 1991) with scarce resources (Gamoran 1992a)—and variations in grouping practices among feeder schools (Hallinan 1991). Elizabeth Useem (1991, 240) notes that "details of a system's [tracking] policy often changed from year to year depending on such factors as cohort size, teacher assignments, and changes in administrative personnel and philosophy." The process of allocating students to courses often verges on the chaotic, and adjustments are frequently made well into the school year (DeLany 1991; Riehl et al. 1999; Weiss 2001). To increase the efficiency of this process, most high schools send counselors to meet with middle school students and their counselors to discuss academic programs.

Another way schools might decrease uncertainty concerning the educational preparedness of freshmen would be to coordinate academic programs and curricula across schools. What curricular materials were covered in middle school classes may directly affect the topics that a high school teacher is later able to cover with freshmen (Weick 1976). Although such coordination of teachers' efforts with feeder schools might result in less repetition of the materials taught to some students and not others, each meeting between faculty at different schools is likely to require that teachers spend time away from classrooms and that teachers at the other school cooperate as well. Thus, efforts to build relationships with feeder schools are more likely to be undertaken by principals and counselors, who have more flexible schedules than teachers.

Problems of Integration

The structure of American school systems is such that entry into adolescence coincides with entry into the new physical, social, and pedagogical environments that mark teenagers' transition to high school. On average, eighth-grade classes tend to disperse over three high schools, such that at least one-third of high school freshmen attend a school with few of their earlier classmates (Schiller 1999). Such transitions to a new school disrupt teenagers' relationships with teachers and peers at a time when they are also becoming more independent from their families and experiencing less parental involvement in their schooling (Dornbusch and Ritter 1988). The maintenance of social norms, obligations, and expectations built up during middle school among classmates may contribute to the continued academic success of adolescents (Coleman 1988). Thus, the transition to high school can be a critical turning point in teenagers' social and academic lives.

TRANSITION PROGRAMS IN ORGANIZATIONAL CONTEXT

As described earlier, the movement of students between organizations creates for schools uncertainties about which freshmen will be enrolling and problems of information management. Douglas Mac Iver and Joyce Epstein (1991) suggest that schools' adoption of transition programs for entering students is fairly recent. Some schools may adopt these programs in the best interests of students, while others may do so specifically to address organizational problems.

The analyses presented here take advantage of the diversity in school contexts captured by the National Education Longitudinal Study of 1988 (NELS:88), which followed a nationally representative sample of eighth-graders as they made the transition from middle school to high school. The base year sample was drawn using a multi-stage cluster sampling design to select a sample of about 25,000 eighth-graders in approximately 1,000 schools (Ingels et al. 1992). During the two years between the base year and first follow-up data collections, the initial sample members dispersed among approximately 3,000 high schools. To reduce data collection costs, the National Center for Education Statistics (NCES) approved the subsampling of 1,500 of these high schools, producing a sample of 15,197 students in 1990.[1]

As part of the NELS:88 first follow-up, high school principals were asked to indicate which programs from a list of ten options their schools used to facilitate student transitions into high schools. Over 90 percent of principals reported that their schools used at least one of the programs, with the average being between four and five. Thus, the vast majority of American high schools have some system in

TABLE 14.1   /   Programs to Facilitate Students' Transition to High School

Type of Program	Students in a High School with a Given Program	High Schools with a Given Program
Recruitment programs		
HSSTV: "High school students present information to middle-grade students."	54.4%	56.5%
MSTAS: "Middle-grade students visit the high school for an assembly."	59.1	57.2
MSSTV: "Middle-grade students attend regular classes at high school."	12.7	13.9
MSPV: "Parents visit high school while children are still in middle grades."	52.3	53.5
Coordination programs		
Teachers: "Middle-grade and high school teachers meet together on courses and requirements."	47.0	45.7
Principals: "Middle-grade and high school administrators meet together on articulation and programs."	63.6	61.9
Counselors: "Middle-grade counselors meet with high school counselors or staff."	71.3	66.9
Integration programs		
PfallO: "Parents visit high school for orientation in the fall after children have entered."	51.9	54.7
Smeet: "Summer meetings are held at the high school."	30.7	30.3
Buddy: "Buddy or Big Brother/Sister program (pairs new student with older upon entry) is in place."	16.2	21.0

Source: Author's compilation from NELS:88 first follow-up school questionnaire.

place to facilitate students' transition to high school. The wording of these questions is given in table 14.1, along with the percentage of students and schools whose principals reported that their schools used such programs.

Recruitment Programs

Recruitment programs involve students and parents before the transition to high school and include activities that provide initial contact between high schools and these potential new members. In some cases, such as magnet or private schools, these programs are designed to "sell" the school to prospective students who may also be considering another school. Recruitment efforts may be crucial for these high schools, which may cease to exist if they cannot attract enough new students to replace their graduating classes. For other schools that are assured of a freshman class, these programs may provide students with information about the choices they must make for the next year (Cicourel and Kitsuse 1963), such as required courses or the availability of clubs and other extracurricular activities. In this case, freshmen are being recruited for particular classes or groups.

Most high schools have at least one of the four programs targeted at recruiting students for the school as a whole or activities within the school before freshmen start classes. The most frequently used recruitment program, reported by over 50 percent of principals, is an assembly at the high school for middle school students. Typically, students are ushered into the auditorium to listen to short presentations by departments about their classes and by school clubs about their activities. In many schools, several hundred potential students from several feeder schools visit the campus on this day. High schools also frequently provide opportunities for middle school parents to visit. These events are often similar to student visits, but when they are held at night they are not as disruptive as the daytime student visits. The exchange of information may be minimal or superficial, but the disruption to the normal operation of the high school can be limited.

Disruptions created by student or parent assemblies can be further minimized by sending high school students to visit middle schools to present information, an approach also reported by more than half of the principals. One constraint in this type of program is that the number of schools that participating high school students can visit is limited because they cannot miss their classes.

Very few high schools allow prospective students to attend regular classes before formally beginning their high school experience. The rarity of this program reflects the logistical difficulties in organizing such visits and the resulting disruptions to the daily routine of high school classes. For most schools, these difficulties outweigh the benefits of providing students with a taste of high school life. For others, though, the benefits of having direct and more intense contact with prospective students outweigh the disruption of school routines.

Coordination Programs

The most frequently used types of transition program are those that involve coordination between the middle schools and high schools through meetings with the former's staff concerning topics such as coordination of curricular programs or transfer of student records (Cicourel and Kitsuse 1963; Smith 1997). Principals' reports, however, indicate that staff involvement in these efforts to coordinate with feeder schools varies considerably across positions. Most high schools have their counselors meet with their counterparts at feeder schools, probably to discuss individual students' academic progress and problems so as to provide information for placing them in courses (Cicourel and Kitsuse 1963; Oakes and Guiton 1995). These discussions, along with school records, are usually the basis for counselors' placement of students in courses, which often affects their educational opportunities throughout high school (Schiller and Hunt 2001). Over 60 percent of high school principals meet with their counterparts at feeder schools about improving articulation of their academic programs, which may involve coordination of course content coverage, academic philosophies, and curricular programs. Finally, teachers are the least likely staff members to meet with their counterparts at feeder schools. As discussed earlier, while potentially increasing the efficiency of the transition process, these coordination efforts may interfere with staff and teachers' time with current students.

Integration Programs

The last type of transition program examined here involves integrating freshmen into high school to help them adjust to the social and physical environments in their new school. These programs are often described as being responsive to freshmen's needs by providing higher levels of peer and teacher support to reduce their emotional stress and increase their attachment to school (Felner et al. 1981; Smith 1997). Although integrating freshmen may seem like an important step, these programs are the least likely to be reported by principals. The most frequently used program, with over half of principals reporting its use, is an orientation session for parents in the fall. In contrast, only about 30 percent of high schools hold orientation sessions with students over the summer, which involves arranging time for freshmen and school staff to meet when school is not in session. However, these meetings allow more contact between new students and school personnel than the mass assemblies with middle school students. Pairing new students with older ones is used less than any other transition program with the exception of having middle grade students visit high school classes.

In summary, the distribution of transition programs indicates that, while most high schools have some programs designed to manage the transitions of new students, not all programs are used as frequently as others. In general, programs that focus on coordination with feeder schools are used most frequently, followed by recruitment programs and, finally, those designed to facilitate students' integration into their new schools. The first two types of programs reflect organizational efforts to manage the flow of information between high schools and their feeder schools or prospective students. Meetings between school staffs increase the transfer of information about students and feedback on academic programs across organizational boundaries. However, the use of transition programs also involves organizational trade-offs. Exposing middle school students to high school classes and encouraging teachers to communicate with their middle school counterparts are intensive programs that not only have great potential to facilitate the transition process but also can disrupt classroom activities. Communication between teachers may be difficult because they are operating on varied schedules and subject to professional demands. Depending on district size, there may also be an uneven number of teachers available for potential collaboration, which imposes further demands and stresses on those teachers who do participate. Furthermore, when large numbers of incoming freshmen compromise the efficiency of such programs, schools often rely instead on large-scale orientation programs, which cannot address the needs of individual freshmen and their families.

DIFFERENTIAL USE OF TRANSITION PROGRAMS

While most high schools use transition programs, organizational and environmental factors are likely to influence how many and which programs they use. The remaining analyses explore differences in the number of programs and propensity to use particular programs related to two key school characteristics—institutional type and geographic location.

As discussed earlier, the institutional environments of high schools differ dramatically depending on whether they are located in an urban, suburban, or rural area. For the analyses in this chapter, I use the NCES indicator of school urbanicity based on U.S. census three-level classifications of metropolitan status. One of the strengths of NELS:88 is that the data allow for a finer-grained categorization of institutional type than the usual public-private school distinction. My analyses distinguish between four types of public high schools and two types of private schools (Coleman, Schiller, and Schneider 1993). In addition to the traditional high school to which students are assigned based on residence (assigned schools), indicators are used for whether a student attended a vocational (3.2 percent), magnet (3.9 percent), or other type of "choice" (14.1 percent) public high school.[2] More students were enrolled in these nontraditional public schools than attended either Catholic (6.1 percent) or other types of private schools (3.5 percent).

Number of Transition Programs Used by School Types

Table 14.2 shows some variation in the number of transition programs used by schools across institutional types: patterns are almost identical regardless of whether students or schools are used as the unit of analysis. Although the average number of programs tends to be similar across most institutional types, other private schools use significantly fewer programs and magnet schools have significantly more programs. Principals of "non-Catholic" private schools are not more likely than others to report that their schools assist students in ways not listed in the questionnaire, suggesting that they simply tend to use fewer programs. However, in multivariate analyses (not shown), only the Catholic schools showed a statistically significant tendency to use fewer programs than traditional public schools, controlling for location, cohort size, and a grade configuration including grades eight and twelve.

The use of transition programs is also related to high school location: urban schools tend to use more programs compared to suburban and rural schools.

TABLE 14.2 / Average Number of Transition Programs Used by Type and Location of High School

	Weighted by Number of Students	Averaged Across Schools
Type of high school		
Assigned public	4.60	4.67
Choice public	4.73	4.99
Magnet	5.29	5.42
Vocational or technical	4.44	4.64
Catholic	4.52	4.23
Other private	3.13	3.62
Location of high school		
Urban	4.96	4.88
Suburban	4.82	4.76
Rural	4.00	4.04

Source: Author's compilation from NELS:88 first follow-up school questionnaire.

Urban schools have an average of almost five programs compared to just over four in rural schools. The difference between urban and rural schools remains statistically significant when controlling for institutional type, cohort size, and grade configuration.

Variations in the Types of Programs Used

Despite the prevalence of transition programs across the country, schools may vary in the particular programs they use. To explore such differences, I computed the relative usage of each program by institutional type and geographic location. The tendency of a program to be used by a given group of schools is simply the percentage of schools in group k that have program i (equation 14.1).

$$p_{ik} = \left(\sum_{j=1}^{n_k} \frac{x_{ijk}}{n_k} \right) 100 \qquad (14.1)$$

The propensity with which group k uses any transition program is $\bar{p}_k$ (equation 14.2), which is equivalent to the average number of programs used by that group of schools in table 14.2 multiplied by 10.[3]

$$\bar{p}_k = \frac{\sum_{i=1}^{10} p_{ik}}{10} \qquad (14.2)$$

The relative likelihood that program i is used by school group k is the difference between p_{ik} and $\bar{p}_k$ (equation 14.3).

$$d_{ik} = p_{ik} - \bar{p}_k \qquad (14.3)$$

Table 14.3 shows d_{ik}, which is the percentage of group k using program i above or below what would be expected if all programs were used with the same frequency in that group. In other words, d_{ik} indicates the relative use of a particular program by schools sharing similar organizational characteristics, taking into account their overall propensity to use transition programs.

Although the number of programs used tends to be very similar, schools clearly differ by institutional type in their propensities to use particular types of programs. First, the top two rows of table 14.3 indicate that assigned and choice public schools are very similar in their usage patterns. The greatest emphasis is placed on coordination programs, particularly meetings between middle and high school principals and counselors. These programs are used by 20 to 30 percent more schools than would be expected if all programs were used equally. Recruitment programs, except for having middle school students visit high school classes, are used the next most frequently. The least frequently used programs are those designed to facilitate students' integration into their new schools. Thus, assigned and choice schools are very similar in that they seem to emphasize efforts to coordinate with their feeder schools while giving little attention to special efforts to integrate freshmen.

Second, magnet and vocational schools use transition programs in patterns similar to those of public schools, but they differ in their use of coordination and integration programs. Other than counselors' meetings, coordination efforts are less likely to be emphasized at these schools compared to other public schools. In particular, meetings between middle and high school teachers are used much less frequently than other programs—by 23.6 percent fewer magnet schools and by 17.5 percent fewer vocational schools—than would have been expected based on their general tendency to have programs. Another difference between these and other public schools is that magnet and vocational schools tend to have more integration programs, particularly fall orientation for parents. Magnet and vocational schools do differ slightly from each other in that the former is the only group with a propensity to use summer meetings and the latter are more likely to emphasize sending their students as emissaries to middle schools. Overall, however, magnet and vocational schools tend to be very similar in their tendency to place less emphasis on coordination programs and more on other types of programs, such as promoting direct contact with parents.

Third, Catholic and other private schools tend to emphasize the use of intensive programs, such as having middle school students visit classes and matching new students with older ones. Private schools are the only ones to use buddy programs more frequently than other transition programs: 5.8 percent more for Catholic schools and 3.8 percent more for other private schools than would be expected if all programs were used equally. Though not the most frequently used program,

TABLE 14.3 / Relative Usage of a Particular High School Transition Program by Organizational Characteristics

	Recruitment Programs				Coordination Programs			Integration Programs		
	HSSTV	MSTAS	MSSTV	MSPV	Teachers	Principals	Counselors	PFallO	SMeet	Buddy
School type										
Assigned	8.1	13.4	-37.0	6.0	3.3	21.0	29.7	4.7	-14.6	-34.6
Choice	13.2	13.9	-39.2	10.5	-0.9	17.2	26.6	7.1	-18.4	-30.4
Magnet	8.7	11.9	-38.1	10.3	-23.6	5.5	23.2	20.0	3.9	-21.9
Vocational-technical	26.9	11.4	-44.2	-4.2	-17.5	2.5	35.8	20.3	-13.1	-17.5
Catholic	20.9	1.1	-7.4	20.0	-12.1	-5.5	-28.1	26.6	-21.5	5.8
Independent	2.8	1.8	-10.2	0.8	10.8	14.8	-0.2	2.8	-27.2	3.8
Location										
Urban	16.7	6.5	-31.5	9.2	-9.8	9.5	12.7	18.0	-13.5	-18.1
Suburban	8.1	10.1	-37.7	8.1	5.1	19.0	26.2	7.4	-17.6	-28.3
Rural	4.8	19.4	-25.5	3.4	4.8	19.7	24.4	-3.7	-16.6	-31.1

Source: Author's compilation from NELS:88 first follow-up school questionnaire.

having students visit classrooms is used much more often in private schools compared to public schools. Private schools also place less emphasis than public schools on eighth-graders attending a high school assembly and having middle and high school counselors meet. The more frequent use of the program in which middle school students visit high school classrooms may indicate that private schools tend to give prospective students a more intimate and individualized introduction to high school life. The elevated importance of retaining freshmen may also account for the high usage rate of buddy programs for freshmen in these schools. Catholic and other private schools also differ from each other in that the former are less likely to emphasize coordination programs over recruitment programs compared to other private schools. In general, however, private schools use a configuration of programs that is distinctly different from that of public schools and that emphasizes facilitating students' integration into the school's social and academic community.

Table 14.3 also shows clear differences in the types of programs that urban, suburban, and rural schools tend to use. First, urban (and to a lesser extent, suburban) high schools are more likely than rural schools to send students to feeder schools to make presentations than to have middle school students visit for an assembly. Second, rural and suburban high schools are more likely than urban high schools to have meetings with teachers or principals at feeder schools. Third, high schools in urban and suburban locations appear to institutionalize efforts to have contact with parents of both prospective and new students more than rural schools do. Thus, in general, urban and suburban schools are more likely to emphasize contact with parents than are rural schools, which are more likely to have direct contact with middle school students and their teachers or principals.

DISCUSSION AND CONCLUSION

Results showed that almost all schools have some program to ease students' transitions to high school. Programs that focus on coordination with middle or junior high schools are used most frequently, suggesting that the transfer of information about students between the organizations may be one of the most problematic aspects of the transition process. These programs may also be used more frequently than others because they involve the least amount of disruption to the daily operations of the school. The exception to the pattern of relying on contact between high schools and feeder schools is the program of having meetings between middle and high school teachers, possibly because this infrequently used program would disrupt the daily activities of the school. These patterns may indicate that transition programs involve organizational trade-offs between increasing flows of information and protecting classrooms, the schools' technical core (Weick 1976).

Virtually all schools make some effort to smooth the transition process, but the particular programs schools tend to use vary substantially between institutional types and geographic locations. Institutional type is related to the following program use patterns: emphasis on coordination in assigned and choice schools; less emphasis on coordination and more on the integration of parents in magnet and vocational schools; and reliance on transition programs involving closer or more intense involvement of students in private schools. In addition to using more programs, urban schools make greater efforts to recruit students and ensure their social integration, while rural schools appear to invest in coordination with feeder schools.

The differences by institutional type in schools' usage of transition programs are probably related to organizational problems created by how they acquire their freshmen classes. Assigned and, to a varying extent, choice public schools are assured of freshmen classes but have little or no control over which students they are allotted. The most pressing questions for these schools are how prepared students are for the high school curriculum and how to allocate them to classes (Cicourel and Kitsuse 1963; DeLany 1991; Riehl et al. 1999). The relatively greater emphasis on coordination programs in assigned and choice schools—especially having counselors meet—may be a response to these issues. Meetings between counselors facilitate the transfer of information about particular students—for example, by clarifying transcript information to increase its usefulness for scheduling and other administrative purposes. During meetings between middle and high school principals, issues related to the articulation of instruction and other programs can be discussed. Thus, for traditional public schools these programs address the issue of what instructional resources are needed—a major organizational uncertainty created by the transition of students to high school.

Magnet and vocational schools differ from the other two types of public schools in that they have specialized instructional programs for which they must attract and keep suitable students. The selection process reduces the need for coordination with feeder schools, which are unlikely to have a curriculum designed to interface with that of the high school (Riehl et al. 1999). In addition, because students come in small groups from widely scattered feeder schools, coordination with these middle schools may not be practical. At the same time, these specialized academic programs are likely to be unfamiliar to parents, who may be expected to provide additional support in the form of volunteering or resources. Fall orientation sessions provide opportunities for parents to learn about these expectations and to have direct contact with the school and each other. The relatively high usage of summer meetings by magnet schools may reflect the perceived unfamiliarity of prospective students and parents with the school's specific features and programs.

Problems of attracting and retaining adequate numbers of students who suit the school's mission and program are more vital for private schools than for public ones (Chubb and Moe 1990). If they fail, losing students to either other private or public schools, these schools will cease to exist. Private schools' unusually high usage of transition programs involving disruptions to normal school routines may pay off by providing students and parents with richer and more detailed information. Because prospective students who visit classrooms directly experience what life in the school is like, the match between freshmen and the school may be improved. This benefit may outweigh the costs of having classes disrupted by prospective students. Having students more tightly integrated into the school through the use of a buddy system (matching younger and older students) may similarly provide greater benefits to private schools than to public schools.

The general argument here is that uncertainties over how many and which students will attend a school influence which transition programs the school is likely to use. Coordination programs provide assigned and choice schools with sources of information about their freshman class, which they have little ability to select but are assured of receiving. Collaboration with feeder schools is of less concern for magnet and vocational schools since students enter these schools because they are interested in a particular academic or other specialized program. Private schools' frequent use of transition programs that disrupt its daily functioning (such as prospective students visiting classrooms) may indicate that concerns about attracting and keeping students are more vital for them than for public schools, which use such programs infrequently.

The trends seen in transition program use patterns between urban and rural schools most likely reflect differences in the organizational problems created by their institutional environments. Classmates in urban areas are less likely than those in rural areas to move between middle school and high school as a large group, tending instead to disperse across several schools (Schiller 1995). Coordinating with a small number of feeder schools may make meetings between middle and high school teachers more practical and productive for rural schools than for urban schools. Similarly, having middle school students visit the high school for an assembly is simplest when the high school has few feeder schools. Sending high school students to visit middle schools may be more practical for urban schools than trying to identify prospective students from many feeder schools and arranging transportation in the other direction. Parents' knowledge of a high school is also likely to vary between urban and rural areas (Useem 1991). In smaller communities, middle school parents are more likely to have had contact with the high school either directly or through friends and family members. Urban high schools' emphasis on transition programs involving parents may be a response to a lack of earlier contact.

Regardless of the organizational context and types of programs used, the usual chaos during the first month of each school year suggests that schools' efforts to facilitate the transition process are, at best, only partially effective. Despite efforts to coordinate with feeder schools, high schools frequently have to adjust students' course schedules and shift resources (Delany 1991; Riehl et al. 1999). Freshmen's academic adjustment to high school is not strongly related to the types of transition programs used by their school (Schiller 1995). Thus, schools may indicate that they have transition programs, but their efforts may involve only a small percentage of students needing the services, or they may be too limited in detail or scope to be effective.

Additionally, students and schools may have conflicting interests during the transition process, such as when the former are sorted into courses. In attempting to make efficient use of classroom and faculty resources, schools use students' previous school records as a readily available and standardized, though incomplete and sometimes misleading, source of information about them (Hallinan 1991; Useem 1991). When deciding which classes to sign up for, many freshmen must depend on course descriptions in the student handbook or on counselors' advice (Oakes and Guiton 1995). A few may have contact with older students who offer advice based on their experiences. Conflicts may arise when a student's preference for a course does not correspond with the availability of the course or its perceived appropriateness for the student. What may be considered a successful resolution of the conflict for one party may not be seen as such by the other. For example, if enough students successfully petition for entrance into a course, whether or not justified by ability or preparation, either the school must add another section of the course, which costs money, or a teacher must teach a larger class.

Similarly, schools' efforts to manage students' transitions to high school also affect students' abilities to manage the transition and their subsequent academic careers (Baker and Stevenson 1986). For example, public school attendance zones reduce organizational uncertainty over which students will attend which schools, while also constraining the ability of families to choose which school their children will attend. Minorities and economically disadvantaged students often have limited residential choices and must attend the school to which they are assigned (Coleman et al. 1993). Both the economic and social resources of more educated parents equip them with tools to circumvent organizational and environmental constraints. Educated parents with high educational ambitions for their children may pressure the school system to transfer their children to a better public school in the area, or they may invest in private schooling.

In conclusion, as described by Charles Bidwell (1965) almost forty years ago, schools are formal organizations that are shaped by their environment and the associated potential problems of recruiting members and obtaining resources. Institutionalized procedures and structures reflect efforts to routinize potentially problematic processes, such as students' transition to high school. These efforts, however, are likely to be only partially successful, owing to the competing demands created by organizational complexity (for example, protecting the technical core versus obtaining external legitimacy) and by diverse constituencies—teachers and district personnel as well as students and parents. The analyses presented in this chapter suggest, for example, that charter schools will differ from traditional public schools in their use of various transition programs because of their need to recruit students. However, the recruitment efforts that charter schools are likely to adopt will reflect organizational trade-offs. Although these schools may make greater efforts to improve the integration of freshmen and their parents, they are likely to reduce their efforts to coordinate curriculum or instructional efforts with the increasing number of feeder schools. The effects of such changes on their social structures and on students' educational achievement or attainment are likely to be as complex as schools' organizational structures and environments.

NOTES

1. While the sample of eighth-grade schools in NELS:88 is representative of such schools around the nation, the high schools were sampled based on the probability that students from a base year school attended that school in tenth grade (Ingels et al. 1992). Although the student-level analyses in this chapter were weighted to be representative of the tenth-grade cohort in 1990, NCES did not provide first follow-up school weights, so the school-level analyses are not weighted. However, estimates of transition program distribution show similar patterns regardless of whether students or high schools are used as the unit of analysis.
2. See Coleman and others (1993) for a description of how these schools were identified from the NELS:88 first follow-up school administrators survey. In many respects, these schools were precursors of today's charter schools.
3. Schools are used as the unit of analysis here because the percentage of schools using a particular program can be calculated from information in tables 14.2 and 14.3.

Chapter 15

Mobilizing Community Resources to Reform Failing Schools

Lori Diane Hill

There is a crisis in urban education that nearly two and a half decades of federal, state, and local efforts have not been able to curtail. Achievement levels in inner-city schools continue to fall below national norms, and African American and Latino urban high school students continue to drop out at distressingly high rates. The reality for most students who do graduate from inner-city schools is that "they are often so poorly prepared, they cannot successfully compete in the labor market" (Kantor and Brenzel 1992, 278).

Schools in communities characterized by high concentrations of poverty and high degrees of social isolation are disproportionately affected by this crisis. In the wake of dramatic labor market shifts, continuing changes in social policy, and contentions over urban space, there is an increased sense of urgency that disadvantaged urban communities must arm themselves to face such challenges. One approach that community leaders have taken to address these issues is to try to ensure that youth in their communities have access to quality educational institutions. The expectation is that this approach will prepare young people to succeed in a transformed urban labor market and, in turn, contribute to the future viability of urban communities.

Grassroots initiatives to reform urban schools emerged in the 1960s, partially in response to concerns about the practices and ideology of public schools and the extent to which they were able to address the needs of marginalized groups (Tyack 1974). Those concerns led to a strong push for community control of schools. Nearly two decades later, in the 1980s, a similar sense of urgency was prompted by concerns about the country's ability to maintain its place as a leader in the world economy (Murphy 1992). During this period, approaches to reform were rooted in the belief that poor schooling outcomes "are attributable to the poor quality of school workers and the inadequacy of their tools and that these problems are subject to revision through mandated, top down initiatives" (Murphy 1992, 5). More recent efforts to reform public education have focused on increasing standards and accountability. This policy shift reflects a growing opinion among policymakers that "strong external accountability will impel schools to improve student achievement" (Newmann, King, and Rigdon 1997, 41). However, research has shown that it is difficult to implement practices of strong external accountability. Even when successfully implemented, external accountability measures may undermine a school's organizational capacity. Requirements for increasing student achievement can aggravate the existing vulnerabilities that many urban school administrators and teachers have about their own effectiveness (Bryk and Schneider 2000).

In some respects, the radically decentralized structure of the Chicago public schools holds a great deal of promise as a tool for communities trying to rebuild the capacity of their educational institutions. Despite the potential of locally controlled schools to carry out community-level school improvement initiatives, this characteristic alone is not sufficient for ensuring quality education. The limitations of the decentralized structure—particularly in the poorest communities, where school councils have members from the community who may be unfamiliar with educational practices—are evidenced by the persistent failure of most of Chicago's public high schools.

The Chicago School Reform Act of 1995 emphasized accountability within the framework of reform that had been established in the 1988 school reform legislation (Bryk, Kerbow, and Rollow 1997). The 1995 reform specified a multi-stage progression of interventions for schools in which reform initiatives pursued following the 1988 legislation had not been successful. Reconstitution was the final stage in a progression of interventions and sanctions that included school remediation and probation. Reconstitution occurs when the governing agency determines that the problems (primarily low student performance) cannot be changed by community control. School reconstitution forces incumbent faculty and administration to vacate their positions and reapply for them. This process is viewed by many as destructive to the schools: teachers are displaced, in this view, without sufficient attention to the impact on the community's future educational opportunities.

This chapter focuses on Vernon High School, one of the first Chicago high schools to be recommended for reconstitution. Vernon High School, unlike other schools recommended for reconstitution, was already in the process of reorganizing itself through the actions of local community members, alumni of the school, and school staff. The Vernon High School Collaborative was organized in 1995 (before the 1995 act took effect) to revitalize Vernon High School as a community institution and to improve educational outcomes for students. At the time the Collaborative was organized, the structures for democratic localism were well established: they had been a cornerstone of the 1988 reform. However, the Collaborative emerged in the tradition of the grassroots initiatives of the 1960s in response to the failure of those structures to meaningfully improve educational processes in the school.

This group did not resist but rather advocated reconstitution, despite the prevailing belief that reconstitution further stigmatizes poorly performing schools and holds little promise of success. I employ social capital theory as a framework for analyzing the ways in which the Vernon High School Collaborative has functioned as an institutional agent for school change, how its activities might be understood as purposeful mobilization of social capital resources to influence educational outcomes, and the implications of such activities for school reform in urban communities. I analyze this case in terms of the conceptual framework that links social trust to successful change in urban schools. This study illustrates the way in which the activities of the Collaborative redefined the expectations and obligations traditionally associated with social relations between members of the school community. I argue that building organizational capacity in schools serving disadvantaged urban communities may require a new model for community engagement in schools.

INSTITUTIONAL AGENCY AND RELATIONAL TRUST: RESOURCES FOR SCHOOL CHANGE

The following two sections review relevant literature on social capital and relational trust and discuss, from a sociological perspective, the Collaborative's role as an institutional agent and its focus on relationships inside Vernon High School as components of a capacity building strategy that suggests the need for new models to reform urban schools.

Social Capital

During the past four decades the issue of school resource inequality has been at the center of education policy debates over how to increase educational attainment for disadvantaged students (Coleman et al. 1966; Hanushek 1996; Summers and Wolfe 1977). As the opportunity structure for members of disadvantaged groups has changed, so have ideas about the significance of resource inequality at both the individual and organizational levels. The kinds of resources that are most salient for understanding persistent disparities in educational outcomes have been recognized as well. Social capital theory has played an important role in expanding our understanding of the relationship between social resources and outcome disparities in educational processes (see, for example, Carbonaro 1998; Coleman 1988; Hill 2001; Morgan and Sørenson 1999; Pong 1998).

Social capital consists of resources embedded in social relations that can be mobilized by actors to increase their likelihood of success in pursuing a particular action. This definition represents the convergence of a number of conceptualizations of social capital that have been developed by sociologists and other social scientists in recent decades (for example, Bourdieu 1986; Coleman 1994; Lin 2001; Portes 1998). James Coleman (1988) introduced the concept in the field of sociology of education as a tool for understanding how resources that inhere in the structure of relations between individuals are linked to educational processes such as individual academic achievement and educational attainment. Coleman described several forms of social capital, including obligations and expectations, norms and effective sanctions, authority relations, and intentional organization. His framing of the concept has been extended and refined in ways that better explicate the mechanisms through which specific forms of social capital operate and facilitate a desired outcome. For example, Rebecca Sandefur and Edward Laumann (1998) specify three mechanisms (information, influence and control, and social solidarity) through which social capital can be useful in attaining a particular goal.

Social capital has been defined and analyzed from two perspectives: one focuses on its usefulness for individuals, and the other on its group benefits. The group-level perspective emphasizes the ways in which groups develop and maintain social capital, whereas the individual-level perspective emphasizes the ways in which individuals "capture" resources embedded in social relations (Lin 2001). Both perspectives are relevant for understanding the role the Collaborative played in bringing about change at Vernon High School. My primary interest in this analysis, however, is in the Collaborative's role in pursuing organizational change in Vernon High School. More specifically, I focus on the way in which it was able to mobilize resources embedded in relations between group members and in relations between the group and other entities (such as local universities or the Chicago Public School District) in its pursuit of reform at Vernon High School.

In a study that analyzes the role of social capital in the reproduction of inequality at the individual level, Ricardo Stanton-Salazar and Sanford Dornbusch (1995) define institutional agents as individuals who can transmit or negotiate the transmission of resources and opportunities that lead to successful outcomes for high school youth. Moreover, they argue, for low-income and minority youth whose families and communities are less likely to offer them access to resources that facilitate successful schooling outcomes and adult occupational success, access to institutional agents outside of their family and community networks, such as teachers or counselors, is critical. They argue that the absence of access to such agents reproduces inequalities associated with students' social and economic status positions.

In the present analysis, institutional agency is used to frame the unique role the Vernon High School Collaborative played for the school. Thus, the analysis focuses in part on the Collaborative's emergence as an institutional agent for the school and the way in which the group's collective assets influenced change in the school. It is argued that the activities of the Collaborative have broad implications as a model for community involvement in initiatives to reform schools serving disadvantaged communities.

Relational Trust

In addition to analyzing the Collaborative's pursuit of organizational change at Vernon in terms of its implications as a model for community engagement in school capacity building, this study also examines why—in its capacity as an agent for positive change at Vernon—the Collaborative advocated for reconstitution.

A recent study that examines the role of relational trust in school reform processes (Bryk and Schneider 2000) argues that a school's ability to improve is contingent on the nature of social exchanges between members of a school community (teachers, students, parents, and principals). The theory focuses specifically on relational trust as it exists in role relationships between teachers and students, between fellow teachers, and between teachers and parents. Participants in these role sets understand the obligations that accompany their role and maintain expectations about the obligations of the other member of the role set. Bryk and Schneider assert that maintaining relational trust in a role set depends on the "synchrony" of the expectations and obligations of the parties involved. According to the theory, organizational capacity or organizational function is linked to the degree to which behaviors within primary role sets are consistent with established expectations and obligations.

Relational trust functions as a resource for school improvement in four ways: it moderates the risk to individuals that accompanies organizational change; it reduces the transaction costs associated with reform-related decisionmaking; it facilitates clear understandings of role obligations; and it sustains an ethical imperative among members of the school community to advance the best interests of children (Bryk and Schneider 2000, 33–34). In school contexts characterized by social relations in which trust is absent or significantly diminished, the capacity to reform is limited. As client-serving organizations, public schools are unique in that there is limited recourse for failures of trust in relations, especially between teachers and students (Bidwell 1970).

In this chapter, I argue that the Collaborative's pursuit of reconstitution illustrates the significance of relational trust as a resource for school improvement and the difficulties inherent in rebuilding it when teacher investment is limited. In the absence of relational trust among teachers and staff in the existing school, a new social system—the Vernon High School Collaborative—was formed with the shared goal of rebuilding the high school. I examine the Collaborative's attempts to foster teacher-student and teacher-teacher trust relations and to sustain a commitment among adult participants in the school community to prioritize the students' best interest as they relate to the Collaborative's decision to pursue reconstitution.

DATA

The analysis that follows relies on data that were collected during a three-month period in 1996. The study of Vernon High School was completed as part of a larger MacArthur Foundation initiative that focused on a broad range of community-based activities in several low-income communities in Chicago. The project described here focused on the relationship between the organizational changes occurring at Vernon High School and the activities of a group of community members—Vernon Heights residents, Vernon High School alumni, parents, and current students, local community organizations, and area businesses—who became the Vernon High School Collaborative.

Project data were collected from three main sources: from interviews with members of the Collaborative; from historical information about Vernon Heights and Vernon High School in public and private archival sources; and from organizational records (such as meeting minutes, correspondence, action plans, and funding proposals). Additional data came from sixteen interviews with Collaborative participants, including the Collaborative's main organizers and at least two participants in each of the primary participant categories (teachers, students, parents, alumni, community members). For a more detailed description of data collection and analyses, see Lori Diane Hill (1997).

D. L. Vernon High School

D. L. Vernon High School is situated in Vernon Heights, a low-income African American neighborhood in Chicago. Like many poor urban schools, Vernon is located in a community that is 96 percent African American, with nearly all the students receiving some form of federal assistance such as free lunch. In the past, Vernon Heights was one of the destinations for the many blacks who were among the first wave of migrants to arrive in Chicago in search of employment and other opportunities, including better schools. Vernon High School was once the center of a thriving, racially segregated, but economically heterogeneous neighborhood. Alumni of the school from the late 1930s through the 1960s recall their experiences at Vernon High School and revere its former status as a center of community activity and an institution that offered the youth of Vernon Heights a good education and solid preparation for adulthood and the world of work. As one alumnus put it, the high school was once considered central to the surrounding neighborhood: "Vernon used to be the center of things in the black community. The school was well used by members of the [Vernon Heights] community, and generally people were very pleased with the education their children were getting at Vernon. Many of the students were members of families that recently arrived from the South."

In Vernon Heights, as in many urban neighborhoods, demographic shifts over time have precipitated the erosion of the institutional infrastructure (see Spear 1967; Wilson 1996). Businesses have disappeared from what used to be a thriving business district in Vernon Heights, but schools, on the other hand, have registered this pattern of deterioration in the community's organizational infrastructure not in terms of their absence but in terms of their severely diminished capacity to operate in a way that consistently benefits students and the larger community. The Vernon High School Collaborative emerged in 1995 as a grassroots initiative to help transform the school into a viable community institution. The Collaborative was intended to mobilize a broad range of resources that would increase the school's capacity to serve a community where the realities of economic and social isolation had imposed severe constraints on the structures that otherwise would have offered a forum for community participation and on teaching and learning processes.

THE COLLABORATIVE: FORMATION AND ACTION AGENDA

The Vernon High School Collaborative was organized to bring together parents, teachers, students, and community members to participate in the transformation and revitalization of Vernon High School. The Collaborative grew out of a long-standing discussion among its organizers about the problems Vernon was facing. They decided that something "dramatic" had to be done to change the course of education at the school. The broad agenda for the Collaborative's organizers was to bring together a diverse group of stakeholders possessing a range of skills and assets to deal with problems that had significant implications for the future of the school and the Vernon Heights community. The Collaborative developed from a shared sense among its core organizers that the changes in district structure and practice that were instituted as a result of the 1988 school reform legislation (for example, decentralized school governance) did not adequately consider the connection to the surrounding community or what was going on in the classroom between teachers and students. A motivating factor for many Collaborative participants was a shared memory of Vernon High School's former place in the community structure. An alumnus and longtime resident of Vernon Heights reflected on how the community's high esteem for the school began to fade over time:

> Vernon High school was once very highly regarded by members of the community. Much more so than now. Back then the community had a much more positive sense of itself. . . . People had a strong sense of pride in the community and in themselves. They acted as if they were as good as anyone anywhere. The factor that eliminated all that was economic.

Two members of the Vernon Heights community with long histories of community involvement and two Vernon administrators, in cooperation with a community development collective, worked together to organize the Collaborative. The community development collective included local community organizations, banks, hospitals, and a nearby university. The group's broad planning objectives were to strengthen the organizational capacity of the school by taking steps that would improve teaching and learning and make Vernon High School the center for local economic and community development. The notion of Vernon High School as a hub of economic and community development reflects the Collaborative's view of what the school should be able to offer its students and the larger community. Members of the Collaborative recognized that the impediments to meaningful improvement in Vernon's organizational capacity were complex. Among them were the ways in which Vernon Heights' extreme political, social, and economic isolation had penetrated the school organizational boundary through the limitations of the local school council and the attitudes and behaviors of students and teachers in the school context.

The Chicago school reform legislation of 1988 made the individual school the primary governance unit. As a result, school-level decisionmaking was carried out through local school councils (LSCs), whose members included teachers, parents, community representatives, and, at the high school level, students. Local school councils were vested with academic and fiscal decisionmaking authority as well as authority to hire and fire principals. The Collaborative's organizers conceived of the group as complementing the LSC's function by drawing on a larger set of resources than those that were available in the LSC. Moreover, as an independent body, the Collaborative would be able to take on issues and employ tactics that extended beyond the legitimate domain of the LSC. Although the Collaborative defined itself as a complement to the LSC, the group formed in part as a response to the LSC's ineffectiveness as a vehicle for improving education at Vernon. As one of the Collaborative's main organizers pointed out:

> Leaders in the [public housing development near the school] took over the LSC, so it was being run by people who had already been corrupted by the system of patronage [and] who did not have the academic or professional background to deal with the education issues. The LSC became a political tool, and education was relegated to the background to some extent because the people running it didn't have that kind of experience [or] know-how.

The Collaborative's formation and the agenda for action it pursued was also informed by the participants' clear understanding of the ways in which students' attitudes toward and behaviors in school were influenced by characteristics of the community setting. According to one teacher involved in the effort, students and their attitude toward school and their ability to succeed are influenced by the problems being experienced in the surrounding neighborhood. She made a connection between students' low test scores and low motivation, on the one hand, and

> environmental factors like the education level of the parents. . . . Some of the students have children, there are gangs, students are afraid. There is something going on all the time, some crisis. Students have to deal with living in the housing developments, where there are too many people crowded in one place. Kids are in families with single parents, and some of them are parents themselves. Kids stay out of school because they have children; some of them don't have a place to live. Students come to school unprepared, and each day teachers may have a different group of students.

The community context presented a formidable challenge to teachers at Vernon. However, the attitudes displayed by teachers toward students and toward their fellow teachers were an impediment to the organizational capacity building that helped frame the Collaborative's agenda for action. The Collaborative needed to address the fact that many staff members were not prepared to deal with students coming to school unprepared for learning and with the realities of the problems those students faced.

There is no question that the Collaborative's strategy was to improve educational outcomes for Vernon students, but the group's objectives went beyond a desire to raise students' test scores. Its objectives were much broader in scope than those that might have been set if it had focused narrowly on meeting standards imposed by the school system. Instead, the Collaborative wanted to reintegrate Vernon High School back into the surrounding community as a unifying force. The plans the Collaborative developed reflect a realistic perspective on the context in which the school operates and an optimistic view of the impact that true reform at Vernon would have on the future of the school and the community.

Goals and Strategies

The Collaborative pursued a relationship with Vernon High School that would allow it to advance its goal of building Vernon's capacity to operate as a viable educational and community institution by mobilizing resources and channeling them to the school. As one teacher stated, the group's goal was "to create partnerships between the community and the school [and to] provide resources for the school and the teachers in the form of money and other things. The Collaborative is trying to see to it that kids in the school have a safe environment [and to] make things better for those who are here."

It was clear among Collaborative organizers and participants that as a group they did not want to be the administration or the LSC. One Collaborative member reported, "Given the talents of the group, we wanted to be a force to alter the direction the school was going in and [to] bring the community into the school, support the teachers, and support the principal." Given the role it was organized to play for the school, the Collaborative pursued a strategy for change at Vernon that was distinct from traditional approaches to urban school reform, not only in terms of its scope and content but also in terms of the assumptions upon which the strategy was developed. The group pursued its agenda for school improvement based on the assumption that, in the words of one alumnus, "the school has to operate from the premise that the child's only hope is the school. They're not going to get it from home, or church. The school is their last hope."

The Collaborative also felt it was important that what was going on in the schools be informed by the reality of the children's lives. Thus, the group set out to develop a strategy that would address the way in which "changes in the community" were associated with the school's diminished capacity to educate students in the community. The group identified and appraised five improvement areas: curriculum and instruction, educational facilities, professional development, student life and family, and community development. The five improvement areas were based on a thorough assessment of the range of obstacles to student achievement at Vernon. They also reflected an understanding that both the community and the school system had failed to provide students with the resources and support they needed to succeed.

The Collaborative developed an ambitious strategy to realize the group's initial goals for Vernon High School based on an evaluation of the five improvement areas. The components of the plan were a clear articulation of the kinds of changes that would be necessary in each area if student outcomes were to improve. As a consequence, it translated the resources generated by its formation into some significant accomplishments for the school. The process also yielded important lessons about the obstacles to student achievement that proved resistant to even the most well conceived resource mobilization effort. To understand the position the Collaborative took on reconstitution, it is important to understand the kind of insight its participants and organizers gained from the year and a half of activities that preceded the school board's recommendation that Vernon be reconstituted.

Implementation Successes and Failures

The Collaborative's agenda for capacity-building at Vernon High School was to create a physical, curricular, and social environment that would enable quality teaching and learning. More than fifty attendees at the group's initial meeting were divided into working committees that focused on one of the five improvement areas. The components of their ten-point strategy targeted facilities, curricular change, and student life and illustrated some of the group's significant accomplishments. Improvements in the physical plant emerged as a priority on the Collaborative's agenda because in the group's judgment the condition of the school building did not communicate to students and other members of the school community the value of respect and the importance of education that they saw as necessary to the learning process. Thus, one of the group's most visible accomplishments was securing more than $4 million in capital improvement funds for renovations to the school building and the surrounding landscape.

The school's receipt of capital improvement funds is one of the clearest examples of how the Collaborative helped the school gain access to resources that were available in the district (that is, in the institutional environment) as a result of the school reform legislation. Although the funds were available in the district, the school was able to benefit from those resources to the extent that it did only through the relationships between members of the Collaborative and key district-level decisionmakers. As one of the Collaborative's organizers pointed out, Chicago public schools CEO Paul Vallas "has kept most of the promises he made to Vernon [because] the Collaborative just keeps at it until things get done."

The group also succeeded in meeting some of its objectives for changing the curriculum. The Collaborative was concerned that the curriculum lacked integration across subject areas and that its content was disconnected from the life experiences of the students. They were also concerned that it did not sufficiently communicate the connections between school and work, career, or preparation for higher education. The general mission of the Curriculum and Instruction Committee was to provide a comprehensive curriculum that would meet the needs of the student body. The committee was especially interested in increasing the rigor of the curriculum so that students at Vernon would be prepared for the demands of higher education and the workforce.

One of the issues they faced was that an overwhelming proportion of the entering freshman class was not even prepared to meet the demands of high school. In 1996, more than half of the incoming class of nearly 250 ninth-grade students were reading at the third-grade level or below. The Collaborative proposed a Freshman Academy to address the academic deficits of the incoming students and prepare them to perform at higher levels by their sophomore year. The Freshman Academy had not been established by the start of the 1996 to 1997 academic year, however, because of problems associated with space, staff, and curriculum.

Despite the difficulties encountered with the Freshman Academy, the Curriculum and Instruction Committee was able to add German and several advanced placement (AP) course offerings for 1996 to 1997. Much of the success of the advanced placement program can be attributed to the outside support and resources that were available to both the students and the instructors. The AP physics program received significant support from the Illinois Institute of Technology (IIT), which provided lab space, student tutors, and mentors. Likewise, the AP English course benefited from a weekly writing seminar taught by a professor at another nearby university. Commenting on the kind of support the advanced placement program received from local universities, one of the AP instructors observed that "there's lots of goodwill out there, [and] goodwill is the theme of community. There are lots of informal partnerships going on to help black children succeed." The Collaborative's ability to facilitate the formation of such partnerships between Vernon and outside entities that were willing to lend their support had a significant positive impact on the advanced placement program and on other aspects of the rebuilding process.

The student life issue that emerged as a priority for the Collaborative was security in and around the school. Securing safe passage to and from school for the students was a particular concern for the group. The security problems were amplified by the alleged gang affiliation of some members of the security staff. The Collaborative worked with the school administration to replace some of the existing security personnel with a private security firm, and this arrangement showed a great deal of promise. For the short time it was in place, the private firm proved quite effective. However, the Collaborative's restaffing of the security force was short-lived, in part because the bureaucratic Chicago public school system did not pay the security staff in a timely fashion. Although the private security firm showed promise as an effective response to security problems that impinged on educational processes, the experience is also an example of the Collaborative being less effective in securing resources for which the school still had to rely on the district—in this case, to pay staff salaries.

Despite the group's accomplishments, there was a consensus among members of the Collaborative that a Summer Institute convened in the summer of 1996 was its biggest failure. The Summer Institute was originally designed to be a two-week institute to prepare students, faculty, and staff for the "new" Vernon High School to be opened that fall. The institute was shortened to one week, however, because of limited financial resources. Moreover, the number of faculty committed to participating decreased significantly because the limited resources supported faculty compensation at a rate of only eight dollars per hour. In the end, the institute's focus was narrowed to faculty and curriculum development and included leadership training sessions for the small number of students who participated.

The Summer Institute marked an important turning point for the Collaborative and its implementation strategy. One Collaborative organizer described the Summer Institute as the biggest disappointment of the Collaborative's process, mainly because the education consultant hired to run it failed to meet the group's expectations. Despite the disappointment with the consultant and his handling of the Summer Institute, in some ways the institute was a source of valuable insights about a set of problems whose solutions seemed beyond the scope of the resources available to the Collaborative. The experience with the Summer Institute led Collaborative organizers to conclude that large-scale restructuring of staff, curriculum, and management might not be the best strategy for improving school performance in the short term. As a result, they developed a revised improvement strategy that focused on advanced placement support, security, and the Freshman Academy.

Another important lesson taken from the Summer Institute was about the difficulty of changing the way instruction occurs in the classroom. A report on the Collaborative's progress acknowledged that even though the group's organizers saw the changes proposed at the Summer Institute as positive—particularly those having to do with the school's reorganization—the only way fundamental change would occur would be if the Collaborative's activities generated a change in instructional style, expectations, supervision or monitoring, outcome measures, and teacher coordination in the classroom. It became clear as the Collaborative continued its implementation process that the critical elements of the school that shaped the educational climate—that is, the effectiveness of the school's leadership and the commitment and professionalism of the faculty—would be the most difficult to influence, despite the significant financial and social resources the Collaborative could offer the school's staff (for example, an implementation grant and connections to school district officials).

One of the characteristics that distinguishes the Collaborative as a model for urban school reform is that the group's strategy for improving education reflected its view that parents and other members of the Vernon Heights community had an obligation to take a more active role in the life of the school and the education of its students. However, they operated under the assumption that, at least in the short run, typical expectations about parents' obligations and involvement in promoting their child's education were likely to be unfulfilled for many students. Consequently, the level of relational trust in teacher-teacher and in teacher-student relations would play a more critical role in informing the success of the school improvement strategy.

Thus far, I have focused on the Collaborative's activities and the ways in which it mobilized resources through relationships among members as well as through relationships between the group and other actors. I have also noted the extent to which social exchanges among participants in a school community (teachers, parents, students, administrators) had important implications for the success of school improvement initiatives. The next section examines the impediments to trust that existed at Vernon and their implications for the Collaborative's capacity-building strategy.

Impediments to Relational Trust

An important area of concern for the Collaborative was the way in which relationships between teachers and students, between teachers and other teachers, and between the principal and other members of the school community defined a climate that did not support effective educational processes. As previously indicated, relationships between participants in the school community (role sets) define roles that are characterized by specific expectations and obligations. For example, in the teacher-student role set, teachers are expected to teach students and to continue to challenge them academically. Students, on the other hand, are expected to invest themselves in absorbing the material that teachers present to them. A recent Vernon graduate described the obligations and expectations for teacher-student relations in the following way: "Students have to take advantage of what's there [in school]. Absorb what is available. Teachers have to let students know that they are really there and are willing to help them. Teachers have to show they care and really stay on the students."

Successful school improvement initiatives depend on the high levels of relational trust that result when participants in a school community have a clear understanding of their role obligations and these are demonstrated and reinforced in day-to-day practices (Bryk and Schneider 2000). Successful school reform initiatives also depend on high levels of relational trust as a means for sustaining an ethical imperative among members of the school community to promote the interests of students. The organizational climate characterized by student attitudes, teacher performance and expectations, and the principal's performance was identified as a serious problem by Collaborative participants.

Reflecting on the challenges that teachers face in their relationships with students as a result of the students' attitudes about school, one teacher with seven years' experience at Vernon and thirty-five years' experience as a resident of Vernon Heights pointed out that "energizing and creating interest on the part of students is a big problem. The students are very negative, but they can still be reached. You're not taught to work with these kids, you learn as you go along. The kids need a lot of love, a lot of patience. You can't teach them according to a script, you have to deal with something new every day."

A balanced set of expectations in the student-teacher relationship in which both students and teachers understand their obligations and can forge strong trust relationships must be based on behavior that supports that understanding. However, the teachers' observations about the approach required to "reach" students at Vernon reflect the reality in the school at the time when the Collaborative began to develop its plan. Although the ultimate goal was to pursue a strategy that would build trust on both sides, the success of the Collaborative's strategy depended on the teachers' willingness to not only pursue their standard obligations to teach students but also to make the extra effort often required to reach and teach Vernon's students.

The extent to which a critical mass of teachers were failing to meet their basic obligations in their relations with students is illustrated in a statement from one Collaborative participant whose comments communicate a perspective that was universal in these interviews: "The institutional makeup, the mind-set of much of the teaching staff, and the failure of the leadership [both in the school and in the community] have all contributed to the failure of the high schools. There was very little teaching and learning going on at Vernon."

One of the primary goals of the Summer Institute was to provide a context that would bolster relational trust in student-teacher exchanges as well as relationships between school staff. The Collaborative organizers had concluded early on that the only way the group would be able to foster fundamental change at Vernon would be to change what was going on in the classrooms, including instructional styles, teacher expectations, and supervision of students. Their attempt to address these issues through the Summer Institute's focus on staff development was unsuccessful. The problems related to climate and teacher performance at the classroom level—the level that is central to the education process—were problems that the resources readily available to the Collaborative proved ill equipped to address.

Collaborative participants acknowledged that some of the school's problems resulted from the ineffectiveness of the school's leadership. It was clear to many who respected the principal's commitment that her leadership style would not benefit Vernon in the long run. As a student stated: "Vernon needs someone strong who is sure about what they want the school to become. Discipline is important, but the person should be understanding about what the students are going through, because most students are embarrassed, ashamed to tell about their problems."

This comment was echoed among the adults, as one community member indicated: "Students [at Vernon] need a disciplinarian, nurturer, one who knows curriculum, a true educator. Filling these roles is the real challenge, task for a school leader. . . . [Vernon's former principal was] warm and caring, but not a disciplinarian and not about the task of education."

Before the end of the 1995 to 1996 academic year, illness compelled the principal to resign, giving the Collaborative an opportunity to seek out the kind of leader the school would need to move its agenda forward. Before she left, the principal had encouraged the Collaborative to pursue reconstitution for Vernon. From the school board's perspective, reconstitution for Vernon was the next stage in a continuum of sanctions for schools that failed to raise student achievement to levels established by the school system. For the Collaborative, however, reconstitution was an opportunity to bring additional resources to bear on a process—initiated long before reconstitution was being seriously considered in Chicago—that had been stalled by precisely the kinds of barriers that reconstitution could serve to remove.

Principal Selection and Reconstitution at Vernon

By the spring of the 1996 to 1997 academic year, the Collaborative had been pursuing its strategy for reform at Vernon for a year and a half. The collective assets of the group not only had allowed it to achieve a number of the goals in its broad agenda for change but also had emerged as an effective structure for "capturing" resources that addressed the school's needs. In its role as an agent for the school, the Collaborative was particularly influential in the principal selection process. Because of the Collaborative's involvement with the school up to that point and its perspective on the kind of leadership the school needed, it was in a unique position to influence the principal selection process. As one alumnus reported:

> [The Collaborative] wanted someone who could relate to students, deal with gang members, someone strong and forceful who knew what should be done and would say, this is the way it's going to be. An implementer, not just someone who had rules, but someone who could implement things, who could delegate responsibility. The principal needed to make sure that each teacher had an organized program for stu dents, a clearly laid out curriculum that the teacher followed. A strong counseling program that dealt with the kinds of problems the students were facing. . . . [Someone to] make sure that security was a priority. Someone who would push for whatever the school needed, who would go to the board and fight for the school.

The Collaborative's engagement with the school during the year and a half before the selection of the new principal had allowed it to formulate a clear vision of the kind of leadership that was required to make the school work. As a result, the Collaborative wanted to identify a principal who shared its vision for the school and who could effectively meet the needs of the institution and the students by functioning as both manager and advocate for the school. Helping to identify an effective leader for the school meant that the Collaborative had overcome a significant obstacle to the kind of reform it had envisioned for Vernon. Reconstitution would give the new principal the authority he or she would need to assemble a group of faculty and staff with the more unified sense of mission that would be critical for the success of the rebuilding effort.

The school board's recommendation for reconstitution came after Vernon had selected its new principal. The Collaborative developed a rationale in favor of reconstitution that included the following points:

- Reconstitution under the astute leadership of Vernon's recently appointed principal would begin the next phase of restoring Vernon to its status as one of the leading schools in Chicago.
- Vernon had languished at a very low point for many months, exacerbated by the illness and subsequent retirement of its past principal.
- Vernon served a very special population that needed to be challenged in ways that would ensure they were able to meet and take advantage of the challenges

and opportunities being provided in their community and able to compete with their peers in the twenty-first century.

- Reconstitution would remedy the problems that had arisen because many, if not all, of the faculty members at Vernon had simply lost interest in the children. A student survey found great and widespread student dissatisfaction with the rigor of the curriculum, the quality of instruction, and the overall level of civility in the school environment.

- Reconstitution at this juncture would be very timely given the millions of dollars invested in the capital improvement work at Vernon and the community-wide revitalization and restoration of Vernon Heights. An investment in the students of D. L. Vernon High School, the future adult members of this community, made good business sense to ensure a return on the city's investment.[1]

These insights illustrate the group's understanding of the importance of the selection of the new principal and its belief that the reconstitution of Vernon High School needed to be tied to an agenda to rebuild not only the school but the community. From the Collaborative's perspective, reconstitution would bring dramatic change to an environment in which teachers were distanced from their students. The three main advantages of reconstitution, in the group's view, were that it would demand that students be at the center of reform efforts, it would give the principal power to move the educational agenda forward, and it would give the principal access to resources that never would have been available to him or her under other circumstances. As a group, the Collaborative took a positive position on reconstitution for Vernon because it allowed for a more complete implementation of its strategy for change.

CONCLUSION

Schools serving urban communities with extremely limited social and economic resources are caught in a double bind: the problems of the community often affect both the quality of the school and the extent to which students are able to benefit from school (Hill 2001). Nonetheless, these schools operate in institutional environments where they are expected to respond to ever-increasing standards and accountability expectations without the kinds of resources that are required to build their capacity to meet those standards. An emerging perspective (see Anyon 1997) on the requirements for meaningful improvement in "ghetto" schools is that fundamental social change (change that addresses the root causes of the extreme economic and racial isolation that persists in some urban communities) must take place first. Despite the consensus that fundamental change in the urban social and economic landscape is an essential long-term goal, school districts and communities are faced with the need to "do something now" that will help schools work better for urban youth.

The Vernon High School Collaborative was organized in part to help free Vernon High School from the constraints of this double bind that results from the complex intersection between a school and its community setting. Drawing on its knowledge of Vernon High School, its students, and the surrounding community, the Collaborative developed a strategy that systematically addressed a wide range of issues that consorted to stall the education process at the school. The idea that the most promising strategies for reforming urban schools are those in which local communities take an active role has maintained its currency through several decades of school reform activity. However, there appears to be no clear consensus about the specific ways in which communities, broadly defined, should be involved in schools. Urban communities have tended to become involved in systemic reform by mobilizing political power to influence reform at the district level or by monitoring the implementation of reform and its effects on individual schools (Orr 1996). The activities of the Vernon High School Collaborative address a different issue: in the context of comprehensive district reform (for example, the Chicago School Reform Act), what model for community engagement is needed to advance meaningful change in schools whose community settings define a set of needs that extend beyond the resources provided by public schools and also beyond the resources available from parents and neighborhood infrastructure?

When the Vernon High School Collaborative was organized to reestablish the school as a vital community institution, it created a kind of resource that researchers and policymakers have long recognized as critical for successful educational outcomes but that does not figure prominently in school reform strategies. The Collaborative's formation established a relationship between the school and a set of actors who not only wanted to improve education for youth in the community but collectively possessed a set of skills, knowledge, and ties to networks both inside and outside the community that were essential for meeting the group's objectives. Coordinating members of the community who were committed to the school and whose collective assets would allow the group to be a strong link to a broad complement of resources that were necessary to change the course of the school was a key component of the group's strategy. The resources embedded in the structure of relations among Collaborative participants played an important role in advancing the group's objective. This was particularly apparent in the Collaborative members' cooperative participation in the five work groups. However, this analysis has focused on the Collaborative's role in pursuing change in Vernon High School and the ways in which an array of resources were mobilized that served the interest of the school by responding to the broad range of problems that limited the school's organizational capacity. The Collaborative is an organization whose action was purposefully directed at improving the quality of education at the school as an investment in the community's future. Thus, the Collaborative provided a vital link between the school and the kinds of resources that are essential to making schools work and building strong community institutions.

One of the strongest indications of the Collaborative's function as an agent for the school was the role it assumed in selecting a new principal for Vernon. The group was able to be a strong voice in helping to select the school's new principal in part because it had developed and was able to articulate a clear sense of what the school needed in a leader. Like the priorities the group set for rebuilding the school's organizational capacity, the priorities it set for choosing a principal were defined by a commitment not only to establish a strong academic program but also to create an organizational context that was cognizant of and responsive to the challenges facing the community.

For the Collaborative, school reconstitution, like so many other resources employed in its reform strategy, was a means to an end. The group's attempts to foster the kind of relational trust that is essential for the organizational change it had proposed proved unsuccessful. The negative attitudes and low commitment levels of a significant proportion of the teaching staff proved to be insurmountable obstacles for the group's capacity-building strategy. Reconstitution, which from the district's perspective was a sanction for Vernon's persistent failure to meet district standards for achievement, was an opportunity for the Collaborative, in cooperation with the newly selected principal, to help identify a faculty with a common perspective on their expectations and obligations as members of the Vernon High School community.

If Vernon experiences a sustained increase in achievement following reconstitution, then policymakers are likely to point to Vernon as evidence that reconstitution is sound policy, but little acknowledging the complex causal configuration that influenced what has happened at the school. Components of that configuration include the organizing infrastructure and legacy of community action in Vernon Heights, the determination of the Collaborative organizers and participants, the selection of a principal who has the capacity to get things done, and the opportunity to identify a staff with a common sense of mission and commitment to Vernon and its students.

This case is noteworthy for a number of reasons, but perhaps most importantly because it represents action that is likely to make a significant difference in a school and a community that are both struggling to rebuild. Another important aspect of the case is that it stands as a powerful illustration of why we need to expand our ideas about how to reform urban schools, particularly urban high schools. School reformers have two main options in their pursuit of effective reform strategies. The first is to continue to develop reform models that give little or no attention to the contexts in which schools operate and that as a result are not likely to have any significant impact on student outcomes. The second option is to acknowledge the challenges created by the community contexts, to take what we know about the resources that lead to successful educational outcomes for students, and to figure out how to generate those resources in communities where they are sorely lacking.

Vernon is one of many high schools embedded in a community burdened by the consequences of extreme poverty. Like families in most communities, the families in Vernon Heights want their children to have access to a quality education. Unfortunately, the exigencies of the lives of many of the parents leave them ill equipped to force the kind of action that is needed to effectively reform schools in their communities. As noted previously, education researchers and policymakers acknowledge the importance of social capital resources for educational success.

However, the enduring assumption is that unless those resources are available in relationships that already exist in families and communities, there is little hope for devising interventions that will generate social capital resources in other ways. Reconstitution is often seen as a reform effort that has a negative influence on the community, but it can be a positive solution when it comes from the people on whom it is most likely to have a direct impact. Although extreme in its operation, reconstitution in the Vernon High School community became a mechanism for mobilizing social resources, including a shared vision and plan of action for school improvement. To the extent that the Collaborative's activities can be described as purposeful mobilization of social capital resources, this case provides significant support for a broader conceptualization of the kinds of resources that can be mobilized to fix failing schools. It also suggests that a new model for community engagement in the school reform process may be necessary to move the education reform agenda forward.

The research reported in this chapter was funded by the John D. and Catherine T. MacArthur Foundation. Additional writing support was provided by the Ford Foundation Postdoctoral Fellowship in Poverty, the Underclass, and Public Policy at the University of Michigan.

NOTE

1. These points were abstracted from comments made at a school board meeting.

References

Abbott, Andrew D. 1983. "Sequences of Social Events: Concepts and Methods for the Analysis of Order in Social Processes." *Historical Methods* 16(4): 129–47.

———. 1988. *The System of Professions: An Essay on the Division of Expert Labor*. Chicago: University of Chicago Press.

———. 1996. "Things of Boundaries." *Social Research* 62(4): 857–82.

Abelson, Robert P. 1964. "Mathematical Models of the Distribution of Attitudes Under Controversy." In *Contributions to Mathematical Psychology*, edited by Norman Frederiksen and Harold Gulliksen. New York: Holt, Rinehart and Winston.

Abu-Lughod, Janet L. 1999. *New York, Chicago, Los Angeles: America's Global Cities*. Minneapolis: University of Minnesota Press.

Adams, Robert. 1996. *Paths of Fire: An Anthropologist's Inquiry into Western Technology*. Princeton, N.J.: Princeton University Press.

Agarwal, Rith, and Jayesh Prasad. 1998. "The Antecedents and Consequents of User Perceptions in Information Technology Adoption." *Elsevier Science* 22(1): 15–29.

Aiken, Michael, Samuel B. Bacharach, and J. Lawrence French. 1980. "Organizational Structure, Work Process, and Proposal Making in Administrative Bureaucracies." *Academy of Management Journal* 23(4): 631–52.

Ajzen, Icek, and Martin Fishbein. 1980. *Understanding Attitudes and Predicting Social Behavior*. Englewood Cliffs, N.J.: Prentice-Hall.

Aldrich, Howard. 1978. "Centralization Versus Decentralization in the Design of Human Service Delivery Systems: A Response to Gouldner's Lament." In *The Management of Human Services*, edited by Rosemary C. Sarri and Yeheskel Hasenfeld. New York: Columbia University Press.

———. 1979. *Organizations and Environments*. Englewood Cliffs, N.J.: Prentice-Hall.

———. 1999. *Organizations Evolving*. Thousand Oaks, Calif.: Sage Publications.

Aldrich, Howard, and Jeffrey Pfeffer. 1976. "Environments of Organizations." *Annual Review of Sociology* 2: 79–105.

Alton-Lee, Adrienne, Graham Nuthall, and John Patrick. 1993. "Reframing Classroom Research: A Lesson from the Private World of Children." *Harvard Educational Review* 63(1): 50–85.

American Association of University Women. 1992. *How Schools Shortchange Girls: A Study of Major Findings on Girls and Education*. Washington: American Association of University Women.

———. 1998. *Gender Gaps: Where Schools Still Fail Our Children*. Washington: American Association of University Women.

American Federation of Teachers. 2000. *Survey and Analysis of Teacher Salary Trends 2000*. Washington: American Federation of Teachers.

References

Andrich, David. 1988. *Rasch Models for Measurement*. Newbury Park, Calif.: Sage Publications.

Anyon, Jean. 1997. *Ghetto Schooling: A Political Economy of Urban Educational Reform*. New York: Teachers College Press.

Archer, Margaret S. 1979. *Social Origins of Educational Systems*. Beverly Hills, Calif.: Sage Publications.

———. 1984. *The University Edition of Social Origins of Educational Systems*. Beverly Hills, Calif.: Sage Publications.

Argyris, Chris. 1957. *Personality and Organization: The Conflict Between System and the Individual*. New York: Harper & Row.

Astone, Nan, and Sara McLanahan. 1991. "Family Structure, Parental Practices, and High School Completion." *American Sociological Review* 56(3): 309–20.

Attewell, Paul. 1992. "Technology Diffusion and Organizational Learning: The Case of Business Computing." *Organization Science* 3(1): 1–19.

Ayalon, Hanna 2002. "Mathematics and Science Course-taking Among Arab Students in Israel: A Case of Unexpected Gender Equality." *Educational Evaluation and Policy Analysis* 24(1): 63–80.

Baker, David P., and Deborah Perkins Jones. 1992. "Gender Stratification in the Science Pipeline: A Comparative Analysis of Seven Countries." In *Education and Gender Equality*, edited by Julia Wrigley. London: Falmer Press.

———. 1993. "Creating Gender Equity: Cross-national Gender Stratification and Mathematical Performance." *Sociology of Education* 66(2): 91.

Baker, David P., and David L. Stevenson. 1986. "Mothers' Strategies for Children's School Achievement: Managing the Transition to High School." *Sociology of Education* 59(3): 156–66.

Bales, Robert F. 1947. "Role and Role Conflict: Task Roles and Social Roles in Problem-Solving Groups." In *Readings in Social Psychology*, 3rd ed., edited by Eleanor E. Maccoby, Theodore M. Newcomb, and Eugene L. Hartley. New York: Henry Holt.

———. 1950/1970. *Interaction Process Analysis*. Cambridge, Mass.: Addison-Wesley.

Bales, Robert F., and Philip Slater. 1955. "Role Differentiation in Small Decision Making Groups." In *Family, Socialization, and Interaction Process*, edited by Talcott Parsons and Robert F. Bales. Glencoe, Ill.: Free Press.

Ball, Deborah L. 2001. "Mathematics." In *Handbook of Research on Teaching*, edited by Virginia Richardson. Washington: American Educational Research Association.

Barnard, Chester Irving. 1938. *Functions of the Executive*. Cambridge, Mass.: Harvard University Press.

Barr, Rebecca. 2001. "Research on the Teaching of Reading." In *Handbook of Research on Teaching*, edited by Virginia Richardson. Washington: American Educational Research Association.

Barr, Rebecca, and Robert Dreeben. 1977. "Instruction in Classrooms." In *Review of Research in Education*, vol. 5, edited by Lee Shulman. Itasca, Ill.: Peacock.

———. 1983. *How Schools Work*. Chicago: University of Chicago Press.

Battistich, Victor, David Solomon, Dong-Il Kim, Marilyn Watson, and Eric Schaps. 1995. "Schools as Communities, Poverty Levels of Student Populations, and Students' Attitudes, Motives, and Performance: A Multilevel Analysis." *American Educational Research Journal* 32(3): 627–58.

Baum, Joel. 1996. "Organizational Ecology." In *Handbook of Organization Studies*, edited by Stewart R. Clegg, Cynthia Hardy, and Walter R. Nord. Thousand Oaks, Calif.: Sage Publications.

Bayer, Judy, and Nancy Melone. 1989. "A Critique of Diffusion Theory as a Managerial Framework for Understanding Adoption of Software Engineering Innovations." *Journal of Systems and Software* 9(2): 161–66.

Becker, Henry J. 1994. "How Exemplary Computer-Using Teachers Differ from Other Teachers: Implications for Realizing the Potential of Computers in Schools." *Journal of Research on Computing in Education* 26(3): 291–321.

Becker, Howard S. 1952. "The Career of the Chicago Public School Teacher." *American Journal of Sociology* 57: 470–77.

Benavot, Aaron. 1989. "Education, Gender, and Economic Development: A Cross-National Study." *Sociology of Education* 62(1): 14–32.

Benbow, Camilla, and Lola Minor. 1986. "Mathematically Talented Males and Females and Achievement in the High School Sciences." *American Educational Research Journal* 23: 425.

Ben-David, Joseph. 1977/1992. *Centers of Learning: Britain, France, Germany, the United States*. New Brunswick, N.J.: Transactions Publishing.

Ben-David, Joseph, and Randall Collins. 1966. "Social Factors in the Origins of a New Science: The Case of Psychology." *American Sociological Review* 31(4): 451–65.

Berger, Joseph, Bernard P. Cohen, and Morris Zelditch. 1972. "Status Characteristics and Social Interaction." *American Sociological Review* 37(3): 241–55.

Berger, Joseph, Susan Rosenholtz, and Morris Zelditch. 1980. "Status Organizing Processes." *Annual Review of Sociology* 6: 479–508.

Berger, Peter, and Thomas Luckmann. 1967. *The Social Construction of Reality*. New York: Doubleday.

Berliner, David C., and Bruce J. Biddle. 1995. *The Manufactured Crisis: Myths, Fraud, and the Attack on America's Public Schools*. Reading, Mass.: Addison-Wesley.

Bertalanffy, Ludwig von. 1956. "General Systems Theory." In *General Systems: Yearbook of the Society for the Advancement of General Systems Theory*, vol. 1, edited by Ludwig von Bertalanffy and Anatol Rapoport. Ann Arbor, Mich.: Society for the Advancement of General Systems Theory.

Bidwell, Charles E. 1965. "The School as a Formal Organization." In *Handbook of Organizations*, edited by James G. March. Chicago: Rand McNally.

———. 1970. "Students and Schools: Some Observations on Client Trust in Client-Serving Organizations." In *Organizations and Clients: Essays in the Sociology of Service*, edited by William R. Rosengren and Mark Lefton. Columbus, Ohio: Charles E. Merrill.

———. 1972. "Schooling and Socialization for Moral Commitment." *Interchange* 3: 1–27.

———. 1999. "Sociology and the Study of Education: Continuity, Discontinuity, and the Individualist Turn." In *Issues in Education Research: Problems and Possibilities*, edited by Ellen Condliffe Lagemann and Lee S. Shulman. San Francisco: Jossey-Bass.

———. 2000. "School as Context and Construction: A Social Psychological Approach to the Study of Schooling." In *Handbook of the Sociology of Education*, edited by Maureen T. Hallinan. New York: Kluwer Academic/Plenum.

———. 2001. "Analyzing Schools as Organizations: Long-term Permanence and Short-term Change." *Sociology of Education* (extra issue): 100–14.

References

————. 2003. "The Problem of Classroom Goodwill." In *Stability and Change in American Education*, edited by Maureen T. Hallinan, Adam Gamoran, Warren Kubitschek, and Tom Loveless. Clinton Corners, N.Y.: Eliot Werner.

Bidwell, Charles E., Kenneth A. Frank, and Pamela Quiroz. 1997. "Teacher Types, Workplace Controls, and the Organization of Schools." *Sociology of Education* 70(4): 285–307.

Bidwell, Charles E., Kenneth A. Frank, Jeffrey Yasumoto, Pamela Quiroz, and Kazuaki Uekawa. In preparation. *The Organization of Teachers' Work*. Unpublished manuscript.

Bidwell, Charles E., and Noah E. Friedkin. 1988. "The Sociology of Education." In *The Handbook of Sociology*, edited by Neil Smelser. Beverly Hills, Calif.: Sage Publications.

Bidwell, Charles E., and John D. Kasarda. 1975. "School District Organization and Student Achievement." *American Sociological Review* 40(1): 55–70.

————. 1980. "Conceptualizing and Measuring the Effects of School and Schooling." *American Journal of Education* 88: 401–30.

————. 1985. *The Organization and Its Ecosystem: A Theory of Structuring in Organizations*. Vol. 2 of *Monographs in Organizational Behavior and Industrial Relations*, edited by Samuel B. Bacharach. Greenwich, Conn.: JAI Press.

————. 1987. *Structuring in Organizations: Ecosystem Theory Evaluated*. Vol. 7 of *Monographs in Organizational Behavior and Industrial Relations*, edited by Samuel B. Bacharach. Greenwich, Conn.: JAI Press.

Bidwell, Charles E., and Pamela A. Quiroz. 1991. "Organizational Control in the High School Workplace: A Theoretical Argument." *Journal of Research on Adolescence* 1(3): 211–29.

Bidwell, Charles E., and Jeffrey Yasumoto. 1999. "The Collegial Focus: Teaching Fields, Collegial Relationships, and Instructional Practice in American High Schools." *Sociology of Education* 72(4): 234–56.

Biraimah, Karen. 1989. "The Process and Outcomes of Gender Bias in Elementary Schools: A Nigerian Case." *Journal of Negro Education* 58(1): 50.

Blau, Judith R. 1984. *Architects and Firms: A Sociological Perspective on Architectural Practice*. Cambridge, Mass.: MIT Press.

Blau, Peter M. 1963. *The Dynamics of Bureaucracy*. Chicago: University of Chicago Press.

————. 1967. *Exchange and Power in Social Life*. New York: Wiley.

————. 1977. *Inequality and Heterogeneity*. New York: Macmillan.

Blau, Peter M., and Richard A. Schoenherr. 1971. *The Structure of Organizations*. New York: Basic Books.

Bollen, Kenneth A. 1989. *Structural Equations with Latent Variables*. New York: Wiley.

Bolman, Lee G., and Rafael Heller. 1995. "School Administrators as Leaders." In *Images of Schools*, edited by Samuel B. Bacharach and Bryan Mundell. Thousand Oaks, Calif.: Corwin Press.

Borgatta, Edgar, and Robert Bales. 1953a. "Task and Accumulation of Experience as Factors in the Interaction of Small Groups." *Sociometry* 16(3): 239–52.

————. 1953b. "The Consistency of Subject Behavior and the Reliability of Scoring in Interaction Process Analysis." *American Sociological Review* 18(5): 566–69.

Borgatti, Stephen, Martin Everett, and Linton C. Freeman. 1999. UCINET 5.0 for Windows: Software for Social Network Analysis. Columbia: Analytic Technologies.

Borton, John M., and James C. Brancheau. 1994. "Does an Effective Information Technology

Implementation Process Guarantee Success?" *Diffusion, Transfer, and Implementation of Information Technology, Elsevier Science B.V.* (A-45): 159–78.

Boser, Ulrich. 2000. "A Picture of the Teacher Pipeline: Baccalaureate and Beyond." In *Quality Counts 2000*. Washington, D.C.: Education Week.

Boserup, Ester. 1970. *Woman's Role in Economic Development*. New York: Allen and Unwin.

Bosk, Charles L. 1979. *Forgive and Remember: Managing Medical Failure*. Chicago: University of Chicago Press.

———. 1992. *All God's Mistakes: Genetic Counseling in a Pediatric Hospital*. Chicago: University of Chicago Press.

Bossert, Steven T. 1979. *Tasks and Social Relationships in Classrooms: A Study of Instructional Organization and Its Consequences*. Cambridge: Cambridge University Press.

Boulding, Kenneth E. 1956. "General Systems Theory: The Skeleton of Science." *Management Science* 2: 197–208.

Bourdieu, Pierre. 1986. "The Forms of Capital." In *Handbook of Theory and Research for the Sociology of Education*, edited by John G. Richardson. New York: Greenwood Press.

———. 1996. *The State Nobility: Elite Schools in the Field of Power*. Translated by Lauretta C. Clough. Palo Alto, Calif.: Stanford University Press.

Bourdieu, Pierre, and Jean-Claude Passeron. 1977. *Reproduction in Education, Society, and Culture*. Translated by Richard Nice. Beverly Hills, Calif.: Sage.

Bourdieu, Pierre, Jean-Claude Passeron, and Monique de Saint Martin. 1994. *Academic Discourse*. Translated by Richard Teese. Palo Alto, Calif.: Stanford University Press.

Bowles, Samuel, and Herbert Gintis. 1976. *Schooling in Capitalist America: Educational Reform and the Contradictions of Economic Life*. New York: Basic Books.

Brancheau, James C., and James C. Wetherbe. 1990. "The Adoption of Spreadsheet Software: Testing Innovation Diffusion Theory in the Context of End User Computing." *Information Systems Research* 1(2): 115–43.

Braverman, Harry. 1974. *Labor and Monopoly Capitalism: The Degradation of Work in the Twentieth Century*. New York: Monthly Review Press.

Briggs, Martin S. 1927. *The Architect in History*. Oxford: Clarendon Press.

Brinton, Mary C. 1993. *Women and the Economic Miracle: Gender and Work in Postwar Japan*. Berkeley: University of California Press.

Brookover, Wilbur, Charles Beady, Patricia Flood, John Schweitzer, and Joe Wisenbaker. 1979. *School Social Systems and Student Achievement: Schools Can Make a Difference*. New York: Praeger.

Brown, Bradford. 1986. "The Importance of Peer Group ('Crowd') Affiliation in Adolescence." *Journal of Adolescence* 9(1): 73–96.

———. 1989. "The Role of Peer Groups in Adolescents' Adjustment to Secondary School." In *Peer Relationships in Child Development*, edited by Thomas J. Berndt and Gary W. Ladd. New York: Wiley.

Bryk, Anthony, David Kerbow, and Sharon Rollow. 1997. "Chicago School Reform." In *New Schools for a New Century: The Redesign of Urban Education*, edited by Diane Ravitch and Joseph P. Viteritti. New Haven, Conn.: Yale University Press.

Bryk, Anthony S., Valerie E. Lee, and Peter B. Holland. 1993. *Catholic Schools and the Common Good*. Cambridge, Mass.: Harvard University Press.

Bryk, Anthony, Valerie E. Lee, and Julia Smith. 1990. "High School Organization and Its Effects on Teachers and Students: An Interpretive Summary of the Research." In *Choice and Control in American Education*, vol. 1, edited by William H. Clune and John F. Witte. Philadelphia: Falmer Press.

Bryk, Anthony, and Stephen W. Raudenbush. 1992. *Hierarchical Linear Models: Applications and Data Analysis Methods*. Newbury Park, Calif.: Sage Publications.

———. 2002. *Hierarchical Linear Models: Applications and Data Analysis Methods*, 2nd ed. Chicago: Scientific Software.

Bryk, Anthony, Stephen W. Raudenbush, and R. Congdon. 1996. *HLM: Hierarchical Linear and Nonlinear Modeling with the HLM/2L and HLM/3L Programs*. Chicago: Scientific Software International.

———. 2002. *Hierarchical Linear Models*. Chicago: Scientific Software.

Bryk, Anthony, and Barbara Schneider. 2000. *Trust in Schools*. Chicago: University of Chicago Press.

Buckley, Walter. 1967. *Sociology and Modern Systems Theory*. Englewood Cliffs, N.J.: Prentice-Hall.

Budin, Howard. 1999. "The Computer Enters the Classroom." *Teachers College Record* 100(3): 656–69.

Burawoy, Michael. 1979. *Manufacturing Consent: Changes in the Labor Process Under Monopoly Capitalism*. Chicago: University of Chicago Press.

Burkam, David T., Valerie E. Lee, and Becky A. Smerdon. 1997. "Gender and Science Learning in Early High School: Subject Matter and Laboratory Experiences." *American Educational Research Journal* 34: 297–331.

Burke, Peter J. 1967. "The Development of Task and Social-Emotional Role Differentiation." *Sociometry* 30(4): 379–92.

———. 1971. "Task and Social-Emotional Leadership Role Performance." *Sociometry* 34(1): 22–40.

Burt, Ronald S. 1982. *Toward a Structural Theory of Action*. New York: Academic.

———. 1987. "Social Contagion and Innovation: Cohesion Versus Structural Equivalence." *American Journal of Sociology* 92: 1287–335.

———. 1992. *Structural Holes: The Social Structure of Competition*. Cambridge, Mass.: Harvard University Press.

———. 2004. "Structural Holes and Good Ideas." *American Journal of Sociology* 110: 349–99.

Calhoun, Daniel. 1960. *The American Civil Engineer: Origins and Conflict*. Cambridge, Mass.: MIT Press.

———. 1965. *Professional Lives in America: Structure and Aspirations, 1750–1850*. Cambridge, Mass.: Harvard University Press.

Callahan, Raymond E. 1962. *Education and the Cult of Efficiency*. Chicago: University of Chicago Press.

Calvert, Monte A. 1967. *The Mechanical Engineer in America: 1830–1910: Professional Cultures in Conflict*. Baltimore: Johns Hopkins University Press.

Campbell, Ernest Q., and C. Norman Alexander. 1965. "Structural Effects and Interpersonal Relationships." *American Journal of Sociology* 71(3): 284–89.

Canaan, Joyce. 1987. "A Comparative Analysis of American Suburban, Middle-Class, Middle School, and High School Teenage Cliques." In *Interpretive Ethnography of Education: At Home and Abroad*, edited by George and Louise Spindler. London: LEA.

Caplow, Theodore. 1954. *The Sociology of Work*. Minneapolis: University of Minnesota Press.

Carbonaro, William J. 1998. "A Little Help from My Friend's Parents: Intergenerational Closure and Educational Outcomes." *Sociology of Education* 71(4): 295–313.

Carlin, Jerome. 1962. *Lawyers on Their Own: A Study of Individual Practitioners in Chicago.* New Brunswick, N.J.: Rutgers University Press.

———. 1964. *The Wall Street Lawyer: Professional Organization Man?* New York: Free Press of Glencoe.

Carlson, Richard O. 1964. "Environmental Constraints and Organizational Consequences: The Public School and Its Clients." In *Behavioral Science and Education Administration Year Book,* part 2, *National Society for the Study of Education,* edited by Daniel E. Griffiths. Chicago: University of Chicago Press.

Carnegie Forum on Education and the Economy. 1986. *A Nation Prepared: Teachers for the Twenty-first Century.* New York: Carnegie Forum on Education and the Economy.

Carr-Saunders, Alexander M., and Paul A. Wilson. 1933. *The Professions.* Oxford: Oxford University Press.

Catsambis, Sophia. 1994. "The Path to Math: Gender and Racial-Ethnic Differences in Mathematics Participation from Middle School to High School." *Sociology of Education* 67(3): 199.

Catterall, James S. 1989. "Standards and School Dropouts: A National Study of Tests Required for High School Graduation." *American Journal of Education* 98(1): 1–34.

———. 1998. "Risk and Resilience in Student Transitions to High School." *American Journal of Education* 106(2): 302–33.

Chabbott, Colette, and Francisco Ramirez. 2000. "Development and Education." In *Handbook of the Sociology of Education,* edited by Maureen Hallinan. New York: Kluwer Academic/Plenum Publishers.

Chafetz, Janet S. 1984. *Sex and Advantage: A Comparative, Macro-structural Theory of Sex Stratification.* Totowa, N.J.: Rowman and Allanheld.

Chang, Mariko. 2000. "The Evolution of Sex Segregation Regimes." *American Journal of Sociology* 105(6): 1658–1701.

Charles, Maria. 1992. "Cross-National Variation in Occupational Sex Segregation." *American Sociological Review* 57: 483–502.

Chinoy, Ely. 1955. *Automobile Workers and the American Dream.* Garden City, N.Y.: Doubleday.

Chiu, Ming Ming. 2000. "Effects of Status on Solutions, Leadership, and Evaluations During Group Problem Solving." *Sociology of Education* 73(3): 175–95.

Chubb, John E., and Terry M. Moe. 1990. *Politics, Markets, and America's Schools: The Impact of Communities.* Washington, D.C.: Brookings Institution Press.

Cicourel, Aaron V., and John I. Kitsuse. 1963. *The Educational Decisionmakers.* Indianapolis, Ind.: Bobbs-Merril.

Clark, Burton R. 1983. *The Higher Education System: Academic Organization in Cross-National Perspective.* Berkeley: University of California Press.

Cohen, David K., and Heather C. Hill. 2001. *Learning Policy: When State Education Reform Works.* New Haven, Conn.: Yale University Press.

Cohen, Elizabeth G., and Rachel A. Lotan. 1997a. *Working for Equity in Heterogeneous Classrooms.* New York: Teachers College Press.

———. 1997b. "Operational Status in the Middle Grades: Recent Complication." In *Status, Network, and Structure: Theory Development in Group Processes,* edited by Jacek Szmatka, John Skvoretz, and Joseph Berger. Palo Alto, Calif.: Stanford University Press.

References

Cohen, Michael, James March, and Johan Olsen. 1972. "A Garbage Can Theory of Organizational Choice." *Administrative Science Quarterly* 17: 1–25.

Coleman, James S. 1961a. *The Adolescent Society*. New York: Free Press.

———. 1961b. "Relational Analysis: The Study of Social Organizations." In *Complex Organizations*, edited by Amitai Etzioni. New York: Holt, Rinehart and Winston.

———. 1988. "Social Capital in the Creation of Human Capital." *American Journal of Sociology* 94(supp.): S95–120.

———. 1994. *Foundations of Social Theory*. Cambridge, Mass.: Belknap Press of Harvard University Press.

———. 1997. "Output-Driven Schools: Principles of Design." In *Redesigning American Education*, edited by James S. Coleman, Barbara Schneider, Stephen Plank, Kathryn S. Schiller, Roger Shouse, Huayin Wang, and Seh-Ahn Lee. Boulder, Colo.: Westview.

Coleman, James S., Ernest Q. Campbell, Carol J. Hobson, James McPartland, Alexander M. Mood, Frederic D. Weinfeld, and Robert L. York. 1966. *Equality of Educational Opportunity*. Washington: U.S. Government Printing Office.

Coleman, James S., and Thomas L. Hoffer. 1987. *Public and Private High Schools: The Impact of Communities*. New York: Basic Books.

Coleman, James S., Kathryn S. Schiller, and Barbara Schneider. 1993. "Parent Choice and Inequality." In *Parents, Their Children, and Schools*, edited by Barbara Schneider and James S. Coleman. Boulder, Colo.: Westview.

Coleman, James S., Barbara Schneider, Stephen Plank, Kathryn S. Schiller, Roger Shouse, Huayin Wang, and Seh-Ahn Lee. 1997. *Redesigning American Education*. Boulder, Colo.: Westview.

Collins, Randall. 1975. *Conflict Sociology: Toward an Explanatory Science*. New York: Academic Press.

———. 1979. *The Credential Society: A Historical Sociology of Education and Stratification*. New York: Academic Press.

———. 2000. "Comparative and Historical Patterns of Education." In *Handbook of the Sociology of Education*, edited by Maureen Hallinan. New York: Kluwer Academic/Plenum Publishers.

Condron, Dennis J., and Vincent J. Roscigno. 2003. "Disparities Within: Unequal Spending and Achievement in an Urban School District." *Sociology of Education* 76(1): 18–36.

Connell, James P., and James G. Wellborn. 1991. "Competence, Autonomy, and Relatedness: A Motivational Analysis of Self-System Processes." In *Minnesota Symposium on Child Psychology*, vol. 23, edited by Megan R. Gunnar, and L. Alan Sroufe. Hillsdale, N.J.: Erlbaum Associates.

Connelly, Rachel, Deborah DeGraff, and Deborah Levinson. 1996. "Women's Employment and Child Care in Brazil." *Economic Development and Cultural Change* 44: 619.

Conover, Ted. 2000. *Newjack: Guarding Sing Sing*. New York: Random House.

Cook, Karen S., and Joseph M. Whitmeyer. 1992. "Two Approaches to Social Structure: Exchange Theory and Network Analysis." *Annual Review of Sociology* 18: 109–27.

Cookson, Peter W., Jr. 1992. *The Choice Controversy*. Newbury Park, Calif.: Corwin Press.

Cooper, Randolph B., and Robert W. Zmud. 1990. "Information Technology Implementation Research: A Technological Diffusion." *Management Science* 36(2): 123–39.

Corcoran, Thomas, and Barbara Matson. 1998. "A Case Study of Kentucky's SSI (PRISM), 1992–1997." In *SSI Case Studies*, cohort 2, *California, Kentucky, Maine, Michigan, Vermont, and Virginia*, edited by Patrick M. Shields and Andrew A. Zucker. Menlo Park, Calif.: SRI International.

Corsaro, William A. 1994. "Discussion, Debate, and Friendship Processes: Peer Dispute in U.S. and Italian Nursery Schools." *Sociology of Education* 67(1): 1–26.

Corsaro, William A., and T. A. Rizzo. 1988. "Discussionne and Friendship: Socialization Processes in the Peer Culture of Italian Nursery School Children." *American Sociological Review* 53(6): 879–94.

Corwin, Ronald G., and Robert E. Herriott. 1988. "Occupational Disputes in Mechanical and Organic Social Systems: An Empirical Study of Elementary and Secondary Schools." *Sociology of Education* 53(4): 528–43.

Council of Chief State School Officers. 1995. *State Curriculum Frameworks in Mathematics and Science: How Are They Changing Across the States?* Washington, D.C.: Council of Chief State School Officers.

———. 1996a. *Key State Education Policies on K–12 Education*. Washington, D.C.: Council of Chief State School Officers.

———. 1996b. *Annual Survey of State Student Assessment Programs, Fall 1996*. Washington, D.C.: Council of Chief State School Officers.

———. 1997. *Mathematics and Science Content Standards and Curriculum Frameworks: State Progress on Development and Implementation*. Washington, D.C.: Council of Chief State School Officers.

Craig, John E. 1981. "The Expansion of Education." *Review of Research in Education* 91: 151–213.

Crawford, Alan. 1980. *Thunder on the Right*. New York: Pantheon Books.

Cremin, Lawrence A. 1970. *American Education: The Colonial Experience, 1607–1783*. New York: Harper & Row.

Cronbach, Lee J., ed. 2002. *Remaking the Concept of Aptitude: Extending the Legacy of Richard E. Snow*. Mahwah, N.J.: Erlbaum Associates.

Cronbach, Lee J., and Noreen Webb. 1975. "Between-Class and Within-Class Effects in a Reported Aptitude x Treatment Interaction: A Reanalysis of a Study by G. L. Anderson." *Journal of Educational Psychology* 67(6): 717–24.

Crozier, Michel. 1964. *The Bureaucratic Phenomenon*. Chicago: University of Chicago Press.

Csikszentmihalyi, Mihaly, and Barbara Schneider. 2000. *Becoming Adult: How Teenagers Prepare for the World of Work*. New York: Basic Books.

Cuban, Larry. 1999. "The Technology Puzzle: Why Is Greater Access Not Translating into Better Classroom Use?" *Education Week* (August): 47, 68.

Cunningham, Mick. 2001. "Parental Influences on the Gendered Division of Housework." *American Sociological Review* 66(2): 184–203.

Cusick, Philip A. 1973. *Inside High School: The Student's World*. New York: Holt, Rinehart and Winston.

———. 1983. *The Egalitarian Ideal and the American High School*. New York: Longman.

Cyert, Richard, and James March. 1963. *A Behavioral Theory of the Firm*. Englewood Cliffs, N.J.: Prentice-Hall.

Czarniawska, Barbara. 1997. *Narrating the Organization: Dramas of Institutional Identity*. Chicago: University of Chicago Press.

Darling-Hammond, Linda. 2001. "Standard Setting in Teaching: Changes in Licensing, Cer-

References

tification, and Assessment." In *Handbook of Research on Teaching*, edited by Virginia Richardson. Washington: American Educational Research Association.

Darling-Hammond, Linda, Arthur E. Wise, and Stephen P. Klein. 1999. *A License to Teach*. San Francisco: Jossey-Bass.

Davis, James A. 1965. *Undergraduate Career Decisions*. Chicago: Aldine.

———. 1967. "Clustering and Structural Balance in Graphs." *Human Relations* 20: 181–87.

DeGroot, Morris H. 1974. "Reaching a Consensus." *Journal of the American Statistical Association* 69: 118–21.

DeLany, Brian. 1991. "Allocation, Choice, and Stratification Within High Schools: How the Sorting Machine Copes." *American Journal of Education* 99(2): 181–207.

Devine, John. 2000. "Schools or 'Schools'? Competing Discourses on Violence." In *The Structure of Schooling: Readings in the Sociology of Education*, edited by Richard Arum and Irene R. Beattie. Mountain View, Calif.: Mayfield.

Dewey, John. 1934. *A Common Faith*. New Haven, Conn.: Yale University Press.

———. 1902/1974. *The Child and the Curriculum*. Chicago: University of Chicago Press.

Diani, Mario. 1996. "Linking Mobilization Frames and Political Opportunities in Italy." *American Sociological Review* 61(6): 1053–69.

DiMaggio, Paul. 1992. "Nadel's Paradox Revisited: Relational and Cultural Aspects of Organizational Structure." In *Networks and Organizations: Structure, Form, and Action*, edited by Nitin Nohria and Robert G. Eccles. Boston: Harvard Business School Press.

DiMaggio, Paul J., and Walter W. Powell. 1983. "The Iron Cage Revisited: Institutional Isomorphism and Collective Rationality in Organizational Fields." *American Sociological Review* 48(2): 147–60.

Dornbusch, Sanford M., and Philip L. Ritter. 1988. "Parents of High School Students: A Neglected Resource." *Educational Horizons* 66(2): 75–77.

Doyle, Walter. 1986. "Classroom Organization and Management." In *Handbook of Research on Teaching*, 3rd ed., edited by Merlin C. Wittrock. New York: Macmillan.

Draper, Joan. 1977. "The Ecole des Beaux-Arts and the Architectural Profession in the United States: The Case of John Galen Howard." In *The Architect: Chapters in the History of the Profession*, edited by Spiro K. Kostof. New York: Oxford University Press.

Dreeben, Robert. 1968. *On What Is Learned in School*. Reading, Mass.: Addison-Wesley.

———. 1970. *The Nature of Teaching: Schools and The Work of Teachers*. Glenview, Ill.: Scott Foresman.

———. 1971. "American Schooling: Patterns and Processes of Stability and Change." In *Stability and Social Change* 105(6): 1658–1701.

———. 1973. "The School as a Workplace." In *Second Handbook of Research on Teaching*, edited by Robert M. W. Travers. Chicago: Rand McNally.

———. 1994. "The Sociology of Education: Its Development in the United States." In *Research in Sociology of Education and Socialization*, vol. 10, edited by Aaron M. Pallas. Greenwich, Conn.: JAI Press.

———. 1996. "The Occupation of Teaching and Educational Reform." *Advances in Educational Policy* 2: 93–124.

———. 2000. "Structural Effects in Education: A History of an Idea." In *Handbook of the Sociology of Education*, edited by Maureen Hallinan. New York: Kluwer Academic/Plenum Publishers.

———. 2001. "Classrooms and Politics." In *Stability and Change in American Education*, edited by Maureen T. Hallinan, Adam Gamoran, Warren Kubitschek, and Tom Loveless. Clinton Corners, N.Y.: Eliot Werner Publications.

Dreeben, Robert, and Rebecca Barr. 1988. "Classroom Composition and the Design of Instruction." *Sociology of Education* 61(3): 129–42.

Dreeben, Robert, and Adam Gamoran. 1986. "Race, Instruction, and Learning." *American Sociological Review* 51(5): 660–69.

Duncan, Otis Dudley. 1964. "Social Organization and the Ecosystem." In *Handbook of Modern Sociology*, edited by Robert E. L. Faris. Chicago: Rand McNally.

Duncan, Otis Dudley, and Leo Schnore. 1959. "Cultural, Behavioral, and Ecological Perspectives in the Study of Social Organization." *American Journal of Sociology* 65(2): 132–46.

Durkheim, Émile. 1933. *The Division of Labor in Society*. New York: Macmillan.

———. 1925/1961. *Moral Education: A Study in the Theory and Application of the Sociology of Education*. Translated by Everett K. Wilson and Herman Schnurer. New York: Free Press.

———. 1973. *Moral Education: A Study in the Theory and Application of the Sociology of Education*. Translated by Everett K. Wilson and Herman Schnurer. New York: Free Press.

——— 1938/1977. *The Evolution of Educational Thought: Lectures on the Formation and Development of Secondary Education in France*. Translated by Peter Collins. London: Routledge and Kegan Paul.

Durlauf, Steven N. 2002. "On the Empirics of Social Capital." *Economic Journal* 112(127): 459–79.

Eccles, Jacquelynne. 1987. "Gender Roles and Women's Achievement-Related Decisions." *Psychology of Women Quarterly* 11(2): 135.

Eccles, Jacquelynne, Bonnie Barber, and Debra Jozefowicz. 1999. "Linking Gender to Educational, Occupational, and Recreational Choices: Applying the Eccles et al. Model of Achievement-Related Choices." In *Sexism and Stereotypes in Modern Society: The Gender Science of Janet Taylor Spence*, edited by William B. Swann Jr., Judith H. Langlois, and Lucia Albino Gilbert. Washington: American Psychological Association.

Eckert, Penelope. 1989. *Jocks and Burnouts: Social Categories and Identity in the High School*. New York: Teachers College Press.

Edelsky, Carole. 1981. "Who's Got the Floor?" *Language in Society* 10(3): 383–421.

Eder, Donna. 1988. "Building Cohesion Through Collaborative Narration." *Social Psychology Quarterly* 51(3): 225–35.

———. 1991. "The Role of Teasing in Adolescent Peer Culture." In *Sociological Studies of Child Development*, vol. 4, edited by Spencer Cahill. Greenwich, Conn.: JAI Press.

Eder, Donna, and Janet Enke. 1991. "The Structure of Gossip: Opportunities and Constraints on Collective Expression Among Adolescents." *American Sociological Review* 56(August): 495–508.

Eder, Donna, with Catherine Colleen Evans and Stephen Parker. 1995. *School Talk: Gender and Adolescent Culture*. New Brunswick, N.J.: Rutgers University Press.

Eder, Donna, and Stephen Parker. 1987. "The Cultural Production and Reproduction of Gender: The Effect Of Extracurricular Activities on Peer-Group Culture." *Sociology of Education* 60(3): 200–13.

Education Week, eds. 2000. "The High Cost of Teaching." In *Quality Counts*. Washington, D.C.: *Education Week*.

References

Edwards, Richard. 1979. *Contested Terrain: The Transformation of the Workplace in the Twentieth Century*. New York: Basic Books.

Eisenstadt, Shmuel N. 1956. *From Generation to Generation: Age Groups and Social Structure*. New York: Free Press of Glencoe.

Elam, Stanley. 1995. *How America Views Its Schools: The PDK/Gallup Polls, 1969–1994*. Bloomington, Ind.: Phi Delta Kappa Press Educational Foundation.

Elliott, Marta. 1998. "School Finance and Opportunities to Learn: Does Money Well Spent Enhance Students' Achievement?" *Sociology of Education* 71(3): 223–45.

Elmore, Richard. 2000. *Building a New Structure for School Leadership*. New York: Albert Shanker Institute.

Elmore, Richard F., and Consortium for Policy Research in Education. 1996. *Investing in Teacher Learning: Staff Development and Instructional Improvement in Community School District #2, New York City*. New York: National Commission on Teaching and America's Future.

Elmore, Richard F., Charles Abelman, and Susan Fuhrman. 1996. "The New Accountability in State Education Reform: From Process to Performance." In *Holding Schools Accountable: Performance-Based Reform in Education*, edited by Helen F. Ladd. Washington, D.C.: Brookings Institution Press.

Elmore, Richard F., Penelope L. Peterson, and Sarah J. McCarthey. 1996. *Restructuring in the Classroom: Teaching, Learning, and School Organization*. San Francisco: Jossey-Bass.

Embretson, Susan E., and Steven P. Reise. 2000. *Item Response Theory for Psychologists*. Mahwah, N.J.: Erlbaum Associates.

Emerson, Richard. 1972. "Exchange Theory, Part II: Exchange Relations and Networks." In *Sociological Theories in Progress*, edited by Joseph Berger, Morris Zelditch Jr., and Bo Anderson. Boston: Houghton Mifflin.

Emery, Fred E. 1959. *Characteristics of Socio-Technical Systems*. Tavistock Document 517. London: Tavistock.

Emirbayer, Mustafa. 1997. "Manifesto for a Relational Sociology." *American Journal of Sociology* 103(2): 218–317.

Etzioni, Amitai. 1961. *Complex Organizations: A Sociological Reader*. New York: Holt, Rinehart and Winston.

Evans, Robert. 1996. *The Human Side of School Change: Reform, Resistance, and the Real-Life Problems of Innovation*. San Francisco: Jossey-Bass.

Eveland, John D., and Louis Tornatzky. 1990. *The Deployment of Technology*. Lexington, Mass.: Lexington Books.

Farkas, Steve, Jean Johnson, and Ann Duffett. 1997. *Different Drummers: How Teachers of Teachers View Public Education*. New York: Public Agenda Foundation.

Farkas, Steve, Jean Johnson, and Tony Foleno. 2000. *A Sense of Calling: Who Teaches and Why*. New York: Public Agenda Foundation.

Feistritzer, C. Emily. 1999. *The Making of a Teacher: A Report on Teacher Preparation in the U.S.* Washington, D.C.: Center for Education Information.

Felner, Robert D., Melanie Ginter, and Judith Primavera. 1982. "Primary Prevention During School Transitions: Social Support and Environmental Structure." *American Journal of Community Psychology* 10(3): 277–91.

Felner, Robert D., Judith Primavera, and Ana M. Cauce. 1981. "The Impact of School Transitions: A Focus for Preventive Efforts." *American Journal of Community Psychology* 9(2): 449–59.

Fine, Gary Alan. 1987. *With the Boys: Little League Baseball and Preadolescent Culture*. Chicago: University of Chicago Press.

Finley, Merrilee K. 1984. "Teachers and Tracking in a Comprehensive School." *Sociology of Education* 57(4): 233–43.

Firestone, William A. 1985. "The Study of Loose Coupling: Problems, Progress, and Prospects." In *Research in Sociology of Education and Socialization*, vol. 5, edited by Alan C. Kerckhoff. Greenwich, Conn.: JAI Press.

Firestone, William, Margaret E. Goertz, and Gary Natriello. 1997. *From Cashbox to Classroom: The Struggle for Fiscal Reform and Educational Change in New Jersey*. New York: Teachers College Press.

Firestone, William, David Mayrowetz, and Janet Fairman. 1998. "Performance-Based Assessment and Instructional Change: The Effects of Testing in Maine and Maryland." *Educational Evaluation and Policy Analysis* 20(2): 95–113.

Fischer, Claude S. 1977. *To Dwell Among Friends: Personal Networks in Town and City*. Chicago: University of Chicago Press.

Fligstein, Neil. 1990. *The Transformation of Corporate Control*. Cambridge, Mass.: Harvard University Press.

Foster-Fishman, Pennie G., Deborah A. Salem, Nicole A. Allen, and Kyle Fahrbach. 2001. "Facilitating Interorganizational Exchanges: The Contributions of Interorganizational Alliances." *American Journal of Community Psychology* 29(6): 875–905.

Fourcade-Gourinchas, Marion, and Sarah L. Babb. 2002. "The Rebirth of the Liberal Creed: Paths to Neoliberalism in Four Countries." *American Journal of Sociology* 108(3): 533–79.

Fox, Renée C. 1959. *Experiment Perilous: Physicians and Patients Facing the Unknown*. New York: Free Press.

Frank, Kenneth A. 1993. "Identifying Cohesive Subgroups." Ph.D. diss., University of Chicago.

———. 1995. "Identifying Cohesive Subgroups." *Social Networks* 17(1): 27–56.

———. 1996. "Mapping Interactions Within and Between Cohesive Subgroups." *Social Networks* 18(2): 93–119.

———. 1998. "Quantitative Methods for Studying Social Context in Multilevels and Through Interpersonal Relations." *Review of Research in Education* (American Educational Research Association) 23: 171–216.

———. 2002. "The Dynamics of Social Capital." Paper presented to the annual meeting of the International Social Networks Association. New Orleans (August).

Frank, Kenneth A., and Kyle Fahrbach. 1999. "Organization Culture as a Complex System: Balance and Information in Models of Influence and Selection." *Organization Science* 10(3): 253–77.

Frank, Kenneth A., Andrew Topper, and Yong Zhao. 2000. "Diffusion of Innovations, Social Capital, and Sense of Community." Paper presented to the annual meeting of the American Sociological Association. Washington, D.C. (August).

Frank, Kenneth A., and Jeffrey Yasumoto. 1996. "Embedding Subgroups in the Sociogram: Linking Theory and Image." *Connections* 19(1): 43–57.

———. 1998. "Linking Action to Social Structure Within a System: Social Capital Within and Between Subgroups." *American Journal of Sociology* 104(3): 642–86.

Frank, Kenneth A., Yong Zhao, and Kathryn Borman 2004. "Social Capital and the Diffusion of Innovations Within Organizations: The Case of Computer Technology in Schools." *Sociology of Education* 77(2): 148–71.

Freeman, Linton C. 1979. "Centrality in Social Networks: Conceptual Clarification." *Social Networks* 1: 215–39.

———. 1992. "The Sociological Concept of 'Group': An Empirical Test of Two Models." *American Journal of Sociology* 98(1): 152–66.

Freidson, Eliot. 1973. *The Professions and Their Prospects*. Beverly Hills, Calif.: Sage Publications.

———. 1986. *Professional Powers: A Study of the Institutionalization of Formal Knowledge*. Chicago: University of Chicago Press.

———. 1994. *Professionalism Reborn: Theory, Prophesy, and Policy*. Chicago and Cambridge: University of Chicago Press and Polity Press.

———. 2001. *Professionalism: The Third Logic*. Chicago: University of Chicago Press.

Freund, James C. 1979. *Lawyering: A Realistic Approach to Legal Practice*. New York: Law Journal Seminars Press.

Friedkin, Noah E. 1998. *A Structural Theory of Social Influence*. Cambridge: Cambridge University Press.

Friedkin, Noah, and Scott L. Thomas. 1997. "Social Positions in Schooling." *Sociology of Education* 70(4): 239–55.

Fuhrman, Susan, William Clune, and Richard Elmore. 1988. "Research on Education Reform: Lessons on the Implementation of Policy." *Teachers College Record* 90(2): 237–57.

Furman, Gail C. 1998. "Postmodernism and Community in Schools: Unraveling the Paradox." *Educational Administration Quarterly* 34(3): 298–328.

Gallagher, James J., Perry Lanier, and Charles Kerchner. 1993. "Toledo and Poway: Practicing Peer Review." In *A Union of Professionals: Labor Relations and Educational Reform*, edited by Charles Taylor Kerchner and Julia E. Koppich. New York: Teachers College Press.

Gamoran, Adam. 1987. "The Stratification of High School Learning Opportunities." *Sociology of Education* 60(3): 135–55

———. 1989. "Measuring Curriculum Differentiation." *American Journal of Education* 97: 129–43.

———. 1992a. "Access to Excellence: Assignment to Honors English Classes in the Transition from Middle to High School." *Educational Evaluation and Policy Analysis* 14: 185–204.

———. 1992b. "The Variable Effects of High School Tracking." *American Sociological Review* 57(6): 812–28.

Gamoran, Adam, Charles W. Anderson, Pamela Anne Quiroz, Walter G. Secada, Tona Williams, and Scott Ashmann. 2003. *Transforming Teaching in Math and Science: How Schools and Districts Can Support Change*. New York: Teachers College Press.

Gamoran, Adam, and Mark Berends. 1988. "The Effects of Stratification in Secondary Schools: Synthesis of Survey and Ethnographic Research." *Review of Educational Research* 57: 415–35.

Gamoran, Adam, and Robert Dreeben. 1986. "Coupling and Control in Educational Organizations." *Administrative Science Quarterly* 31: 612–32.

Gamoran, Adam, and Sean Kelly. 2003. "Tracking, Instruction, and Unequal Literacy in Secondary School English." In *Stability and Change in American Education*, edited by Maureen T. Hallinan, Adam Gamoran, Warren Kubitschek, and Tom Loveless. Clinton Corners, N.Y.: Eliot Werner Publications, Inc.

Gamoran, Adam, Walter G. Secada, and Cora B. Marrett. 2000. "The Organizational Context of

Teaching and Learning: Changing Theoretical Perspectives." In *Handbook of the Sociology of Education*, edited by Maureen T. Hallinan. New York: Kluwer Academic/Plenum Publishers.

Garet, Michael S., and Brian DeLany. 1988. "Students, Courses, and Stratification." *Sociology of Education* 61(2): 61–77.

Garvey, Catherine. 1990. *Play*. Cambridge, Mass.: Harvard University Press.

Gaventa, John. 1980. *Power and Powerlessness: Quiescence and Rebellion in an Appalachian Valley*. Urbana: University of Illinois Press.

Giddens, Anthony. 1979. *Central Problems in Social Theory*. Berkeley: University of California Press.

———. 1984. *The Constitution of Society*. Berkeley: University of California Press.

Giordano, Peggy. 1995. "The Wider Circle of Friends in Adolescence." *American Journal of Sociology* 101(3): 661–97.

Giroux, Henry A. 1981. *Ideology, Culture, and the Process of Schooling*. Philadelphia: Temple University Press.

Goertz, Margaret, Robert Floden, and Jennifer O'Day. 1996. *Systemic Reform*. Washington: U.S. Department of Education, Office of Educational Research and Improvement.

Goffman, Erving. 1961. *Asylums*. New York: Anchor Books.

———. 1981. *Forms of Talk*. Philadelphia: University of Pennsylvania Press.

Good, Thomas L. 1983. "Research on Classroom Teaching." In *Handbook of Teaching and Policy*, edited by Lee S. Shulman and Gary Sykes. New York: Longman.

Goodson, Ivor F. 1992. "On Curricular Form: Notes Toward a Theory of Curriculum." *Sociology of Education* 65(1): 66–75.

Goodwin, Marjorie. 1980. "He-Said-She-Said: Formal Cultural Procedures for the Construction of a Gossip Dispute Activity." *American Ethnologist* 7(4): 674–95.

Gordon, C. Wayne. 1957. *The Social System of the High School: A Study in the Sociology of Adolescence*. Glencoe, Ill.: Free Press.

Gouldner, Alvin W. 1954. *Patterns of Industrial Bureaucracy*. Glencoe, Ill.: Free Press.

———. 1960. "The Norm of Reciprocity: A Preliminary Statement." *American Sociological Review* 25(2): 161–78.

Granovetter, Mark. 1973. "The Strength of Weak Ties: Network Theory Revisited." *American Journal of Sociology* 18(4): 279–88.

Grant, Gerald. 1988. *The World We Created at Hamilton High*. Cambridge, Mass.: Harvard University Press.

Grant, Gerald, and Christine E. Murray. 1999. *Teaching in America: The Slow Revolution*. Cambridge, Mass.: Harvard University Press.

Greenfield, Thomas B. 1975. "Theory About Organization: A New Perspective and Its Implications for Schools." In *Administrative Behavior in Education*, edited by Roald Campbell and Russell T. Gregg. London: Athlone.

Greenwald, Rob, Larry V. Hedges, and Richard D. Lane. 1996a. "The Effect of School Resources on Student Achievement." *Review of Educational Research* 66: 361–96.

———. 1996b. "Interpreting Research on School Resources and Student Achievement: A Rejoinder to Hanushek." *Review of Educational Research* 66: 411–16.

Grossman, Pamela L. 2001. "Research on the Teaching of Literature: Finding a Place." In *Handbook of Research on Teaching*, edited by Virginia Richardson. Washington: American Educational Research Association.

References

Hadley, Martha, and Karen Sheingold. 1993. "Commonalities and Distinctive Patterns in Teachers' Integration of Computers." *American Journal of Education* 101(May): 261–315.

Hage, Jerald T. 1999. "Organizational Innovation and Organizational Change." *Annual Review of Sociology* 25: 597–622.

Halliday, Terence C. 1987. *Beyond Monopoly: Lawyers, State Crises, and Professional Empowerment.* Chicago: University of Chicago Press.

Hallinan, Maureen T. 1991. "School Differences in Tracking Structures and Track Assignments." *Journal of Research on Adolescence* 1(3): 251–75.

———. 1992. "The Organization of Students for Instruction in the Middle School." *Sociology of Education* 65(2): 114–27.

———. 1994. "Tracking: From Theory to Practice." *Sociology of Education* 67(2): 79–84.

Hallinan, Maureen T., and Aage B. Sørensen. 1983. "The Formation and Stability of Instructional Groups." *American Sociological Review* 48(6): 838–51.

Hannan, Michael T., and John Freeman. 1977. "The Population Ecology of Organizations." *American Journal of Sociology* 82(5): 929–64.

———. 1989. *Organizational Ecology.* Cambridge, Mass.: Harvard University Press.

Hannaway, Jane, and Martin Carnoy. 1993. *Decentralization and School Improvement.* San Francisco: Jossey-Bass.

Hanushek, Eric A. 1996. "School Resources and School Performance." In *Does Money Matter?: The Effect of School Resources on Student Achievement and Adult Success,* edited by Gary Burtless. Washington, D.C.: Brookings Institution Press.

Hargreaves, Andy, and Ivor F. Goodson. 1996. "Teachers' Professional Lives: Aspirations and Actualities." In *Teachers' Professional Lives,* edited by Ivor F. Goodson and Andy Hargreaves. Bristol, Penn.: Falmer Press.

Harnisch, Delwyn. 1984. "Females and Mathematics: A Cross-National Perspective." In *Advances in Motivation and Achievement,* vol. 2, edited by Martin Maehr. Greenwich, Conn.: JAI Press.

Hartmann, Heidi. 1981. "The Family as the Locus of Gender, Class, and Political Struggle: The Example of Housework." *Signs* 6: 366.

Hawley, Amos. 1950. *Human Ecology.* New York: Ronald Press.

Hedström, Peter, and Richard Swedberg. 1998. "Social Mechanisms: An Introductory Essay." In *Social Mechanisms: An Analytical Approach to Social Theory,* edited by Peter Hedström and Richard Swedberg. New York: Cambridge University Press.

Heider, Fritz. 1958. *The Psychology of Interpersonal Relations.* New York: Wiley.

Heinz, John P., and Edward O. Laumann. 1994. *Chicago Lawyers: The Social Structure of the Bar.* Rev. ed. Evanston, Ill.: Northwestern University Press.

Henry, Jules. 1965. *Culture Against Man.* New York: Vintage.

Herbst, Jurgen. 1989a. "Teacher Preparation in the Nineteenth Century." In *American Teachers: Histories of a Profession at Work,* edited by Donald Warren. New York: Macmillan.

———. 1989b. *And Sadly Teach: Teacher Education and Professionalization in American Culture.* Madison: University of Wisconsin Press.

Heyns, Barbara. 1974. "Social Selection and Stratification Within Schools." *American Journal of Sociology* 79: 1434–51.

Hill, Lori Diane. 1997. "Quality Education 'By Any Means Necessary' Mobilizing Community Resources to Reform Failing Schools." John D. and Catherine T. MacArthur Foundation Report.

———. 2001. "Conceptualizing Educational Attainment Opportunities of Urban Youth: The Effects of School Capacity, Community Context, and Social Capital." Ph.D. diss., University of Chicago.

Hinings, Christopher R., David J. Hickson, Johannes M. Pennings, and Rodney E. Schneck. 1974. "Structural Conditions of Intraorganizational Power." *Administrative Science Quarterly* 19: 22–44.

Hoffman, Nancy. 1981. *Women's "True" Profession: Voices from the History of Teaching*. Old Westbury, N.Y.: Feminist Press.

Holland, Paul W., and Samuel Leinhardt. 1981. "An Exponential Family of Probability Distributions for Directed Graphs." *Journal of American Statistical Association* 76(373): 33–49.

Holmes Group. 1986. *Tomorrow's Teachers*. East Lansing, Mich.: Holmes Group.

———. 1990. *Tomorrow's Schools: Principles for the Design of Professional Development Schools.* East Lansing, Mich.: Holmes Group.

———. 1995. *Tomorrow's Schools of Education*. East Lansing, Mich.: Holmes Group.

Homans, George Caspar. 1950. *The Human Group*. New York: Harcourt Brace.

Honaker, James, Anne Joseph, Gary King, Kenneth Scheve, and Naunihal Singh. 1999. Amelia: A Program for Missing Data (Windows version). Cambridge, Mass.: Harvard University. Available at: http://Gking.Harvard.edu (accessed January 21, 2005).

Hu, Li-Tze, and Peter M. Bentler. 1995. "Evaluating Model Fit." In *Structural Equation Modeling: Concepts, Issues, and Applications*, edited by Rich H. Hoyle. Thousand Oaks, Calif.: Sage.

Hughes, Everett C. 1958. *Men and Their Work*. Glencoe, Ill.: Free Press.

Huizinga, Johan. 1950. *Homo Ludens: A Study of the Play-Element in Culture*. New York: Roy Publishers.

Ibarra, Hermina. 1992. "Structural Alignments, Individual Strategies, and Managerial Action: Elements Toward a Network Theory of Getting Things Done." In *Networks and Organizations: Structure, Form and Action*, edited by Nitin Nohria and Roberta G. Eccles. Boston: Harvard Business School Press.

———. 1993. "Network Centrality, Power, and Innovation Involvement." *Academy of Management Journal* 36(3): 471–501.

Igbaria, Magid, and Juhani Iivari. 1995. "The Effects of Self-Efficacy on Computer Usage." *Omega: International Journal of Management Science* 23(6): 587–605.

Ingels, Steven J., Leslie Scott, Judith Lindmark, Martin R. Frankel, and Sharon Myers. 1992. *National Education Longitudinal Study of 1988—First Follow-up: Student Component Data File User's Manual*. Washington: U.S. Department of Education, Office of Educational Research and Improvement.

Ingersoll, Richard. 1993. "Loosely Coupled Organizations Revisited." *Research in the Sociology of Organizations* 11: 81–112.

———. 1994. "Organizational Control in Secondary Schools." *Harvard Educational Review* 64: 150–72.

———. 1996. "Teachers' Decisionmaking Power and School Conflict." *Sociology of Education* 69(2): 159–76.

———. 1997. "Teacher Professionalization and Teacher Commitment: A Multilevel Analysis." Washington: U.S. Department of Education.

References

———. 2003. *Who Controls Teachers' Work? Power and Accountability in America's Schools.* Cambridge, Mass.: Harvard University Press.

Jackson, Philip W. 1968. *Life in Classrooms.* New York: Holt, Rinehart, and Winston.

Jacobs, James B. 1977. *Stateville: The Penitentiary in Mass Society.* Chicago: University of Chicago Press.

Jacobs, Janis, Laura Finken, Nancy Griffin, and Janet Wright. 1998. "The Career Plans of Science-Talented Rural Adolescent Girls." *American Educational Research Journal* 35(4): 681–704.

James, Deborah, and Janice Drakich. 1993. "Understanding Gender Differences in Amount of Talk: A Critical Review of Research." In *Gender and Conversational Interaction*, edited by Deborah Tannen. New York: Oxford University Press.

Jarausch, Konrad H. 1990. *The Unfree Professions: German Lawyers, Teachers, and Engineers, 1900–1950.* New York: Oxford University Press.

Jarrett, Robin L. 1995. "Growing Up Poor: The Family Experiences of Socially Mobile Youth in Low-Income African American Neighborhoods." *Journal of Adolescent Research* 10: 111–35.

Jensen, Michael, and William Meckling. 1976. "Theory of the Firm: Managerial Behavior, Agency Costs, and Ownership Structure." *Journal of Financial Economics* 3: 305–60.

Johnson, Susan Moore. 1989. "Bargaining for Better Schools: Reshaping Education in the Cincinnati Public Schools." In *Allies in Educational Reform: How Teachers, Unions, and Administrators Can Join Forces for Better Schools*, edited by Jerome M. Rosow and Robert Zager. San Francisco: Jossey-Bass.

———. 1990. *Teachers at Work: Achieving Success in Our Schools.* New York: Basic Books.

———. 2001. "Can Professional Certification for Teachers Reshape Teaching as a Career?" *Phi Delta Kappa* 82(5): 393–99.

Johnson, Susan Moore, and Sarah E. Birkeland. 2003. "'Pursuing a Sense of Success': New Teachers Explain Their Career Decisions." *American Educational Research Journal* 40(3): 581–617.

Johnson, Susan Moore, and Susan M. Kardos. 2000. "Reform Bargaining and Its Promise for School Improvement." In *Conflicting Missions? Teachers Unions and Educational Reform*, edited by Tom Loveless. Washington, D.C.: Brookings Institution Press.

Johnson, Susan Moore, and the Project on the Next Generation of Teachers. 2004. *Finders and Keepers: Helping New Teachers Survive and Thrive in Our Schools.* San Francisco: Jossey-Bass.

Johnson, Terence J. 1972. *Professions and Power.* London: Macmillan.

Johnstone, Quintin, and Dan Hopson Jr. 1967. *Lawyers and Their Work: An Analysis of the Legal Profession in the United States and England.* Indianapolis, Ind.: Bobbs-Merrill.

Jøreskog, Karl. 1969. "A General Approach to Confirmatory Maximum Likelihood Factor Analysis." *Psychometrika* 34(2): 183–202.

Jovanovic, Jasna, and Sally Steinback King. 1998. "Boys and Girls in the Performance-Based Science Classroom: Who's Doing the Performing?" *American Educational Research Journal* 35: 477–96.

Kadushin, Charles. 1995. "Friendship Among the French Financial Elite." *American Sociological Review* 60(April): 202–21.

Kanter, Rosabeth Moss. 1977. *Men and Women of the Corporation.* New York: Basic Books.

———. 1983. *The Change Masters.* New York: Simon & Schuster.

Kantor, Harvey, and Barbara Brenzel. 1992. "Urban Education and the 'Truly Disadvantaged': The Historical Roots of the Contemporary Crisis, 1945–1990." *Teachers College Record* 14: 278–313.

Katz, Daniel, and Robert L. Kahn. 1966. *The Social Psychology of Organizations*. New York: Wiley.

Katz, Michael B. 1968. *The Irony of Early School Reform: Educational Innovation in Mid-Nineteenth-Century Massachusetts*. Cambridge, Mass.: Harvard University Press.

Katznelson, Ira, and Margaret Weir. 1985. *Schooling for All: Class, Race, and the Decline of the Democratic Ideal*. New York: Basic Books.

Kelley, Harold H. 1947. "Two Functions of Reference Groups." In *Readings in Social Psychology*, edited by Guy E. Swanson, Theodore M. Newcomb, and Eugene L. Hartley. New York: Holt, Rinehart and Winston.

Kellman, S. 1982. *What in God's Name Is Going on in Schools?* Sydney: New Age Publishers.

Kerbow, David. 1996. "Patterns of Urban Student Mobility and Local School Reform." *Journal of Education for Students Placed at Risk* 1(2): 147–69.

Kerchner, Charles Taylor, and Julia E. Koppich.1993. *A Union of Professionals: Labor Relations and Educational Reform*. New York: Teachers College Press.

Kerckhoff, Alan C. 1993. *Diverging Pathways: Social Structure and Career Deflections*. Cambridge: Cambridge University Press.

Kett, Joseph F. 1968. *The Formation of the American Medical Profession: The Role of Institutions, 1780–1860*. New Haven, Conn.: Yale University Press.

Kilgore, Sally B. 1991. "The Organizational Context of Tracking in Schools." *American Journal of Sociology* 56(2): 189–203.

Kilgore, Sally B., and William W. Pendleton. 1993. "The Organizational Context of Learning: A Framework for Understanding the Acquisition of Knowledge." *Sociology of Education* 66(1): 63–87.

King, Byron. 1993. "Cincinnati: Betting on an Unfinished Season." In *A Union of Professionals: Labor Relations and Educational Reform*, edited by Charles Taylor Kerchner and Julia E. Koppich. New York: Teachers College Press.

King, Gary, James Honaker, Anne Joseph, and Kenneth Scheve. 2001. "Analyzing Incomplete Political Science Data: An Alternative Algorithm for Multiple Imputation." *American Political Science Review* 95(March): 49–69.

Kinney, David A. 1993. "From Nerds to Normals: The Recovery of Identity Among Adolescents from Middle School to High School." *Sociology of Education* 66(1): 21–40.

Kirst, Michael W. 1985. *Who Controls Our Schools? American Values in Conflict*. New York: W. H. Freeman.

Kleinbaum, David, Lawrence Kupper, and Keith Muller. 1988. *Applied Regression Analysis and Other Multivariable Methods*. Belmont, Calif.: Duxberry Press.

Kohn, Melvin L., and Carmi Schooler. 1983. *Work and Personality*. Norwood, N.J.: Ablex.

Koppich, Julia E. 1993. "Rochester: The Rocky Road to Reform." In *A Union of Professionals: Labor Relations and Educational Reform*, edited by Charles Taylor Kerchner and Julia E. Koppich. New York: Teachers College Press.

Krackhardt, David. 1992. "The Strength of Strong Ties: The Importance of Philos in Organizations." In *Networks and Organizations: Structure, Form, and Action*, edited by Nitin Nohria and Robert G Eccles. Boston: Harvard Business School Press.

———. 1993. "Informal Networks: The Company Behind the Chart." *Harvard Business Review* (July): 105–11.

References

Krause, Ann E., Kenneth A. Frank, Doran M. Mason, Robert E. Ulanowicz, and William W. Taylor. 2003. "Compartments Exposed in Food-Web Structure." *Nature*. 426(6964): 282–85.

Kwon, T. H., and R. W. Zmud. 1987. "Unifying the Fragmented Models of Information Systems Implementation." In *Critical Issues in Information Systems Research*, edited by R. Boland Jr. and R. A. Hirscheim. Chichester: Wiley.

Larson, Magali Sarfatti. 1977. *The Rise of Professionalism: A Sociological Analysis*. Berkeley: University of California Press.

———. 1993. *Behind the Postmodern Facade: Architectural Change in Late-Twentieth-Century America*. Berkeley: University of California Press.

Lawrence, Paul R., and Jay W. Lorsch. 1967. *Organization and Environment: Managing Differentiation and Integration*. Boston: Harvard University, Graduate School of Business Administration.

Lawrence, Paul R., and John A. Seiler. 1965. *Organizational Behavior and Administration*. Homewood, Ill.: Irwin Dorsey.

Layton, Edwin T., Jr. 1971. *The Revolt of the Engineers: Social Responsibility and the American Engineering Profession*. Cleveland: Press of Case Western Reserve University.

Lazega, Emmanuel, and Maritjte Van Duijn. 1997. "Position in Formal Structure, Personal Characteristics, and Choices of Advisers in a Law Firm: A Logistic Regression Model for Dyadic Network Data." *Social Networks* 19(4): 375–97.

Lee, Jae Kyung. 1997. "State Activism in Education Reform: Applying the Rasch Model to Measure Trends and Examine Policy Coherence." *Educational Evaluation and Policy Analysis* 19(1): 29–44.

Lee, Valerie E., and Anthony S. Bryk. 1989. "A Multilevel Model of the School Distribution of High School Achievement." *Sociology of Education* 62(3): 172–92.

Lee, Valerie E., and Julia B. Smith. 1995. "Effects of High School Restructuring and Size on Early Gains in Achievement and Engagement." *Sociology of Education* 68(4): 241–70.

———. 1997. "High School Size: What Works Best for Whom?" *Educational Evaluation and Policy Analysis* 19: 205–28.

———. 1999. "Social Support and Achievement for Young Adolescents in Chicago: The Role of School Academic Press." *American Educational Research Journal* 36: 907–46.

Lee, Valerie E., Julia B. Smith, and Robert G. Croninger. 1997. "How High School Organization Influences the Equitable Distribution of Learning in Math and Science." *Sociology of Education* 70(2): 128–50.

Legum, Stanley, Nancy Caldwell, Huseyin Goksel, Jacqueline Haynes, Charles Hynson, Keith Rust, and Nina Blecher. 1993. *The 1990 High School Transcript Study Tabulations: Comparative Data on Credits Earned by Demographics for 1990, 1987, and 1982 High School Graduates*. Washington: U.S. Department of Education, Office of Educational Research and Improvement, National Center for Education Statistics.

Leloudis, James L. 1996. *Schooling the New South: Pedagogy, Self, and Society in North Carolina, 1880–1920*. Chapel Hill: University of North Carolina Press.

Levine, Roger, and David L. Stevenson. 1997. *Changes in America's High Schools, 1980–1993: The National Longitudinal Study of Schools*. Washington: U.S. Department of Education.

Lewis, Anne. 1989. *Restructuring America's Schools*. Arlington, Va.: American Association of School Administrators.

Lin, Nan. 2001. *Social Capital: A Theory of Social Structure and Action*. New York: Cambridge University Press.

Linacre, John Michael, and B. Wright. 2000. *A User's Guide to WINSTEPS Rasch-Model Computer Program*. Chicago: MESA Press.

Linn, Robert. 1993. "Educational Assessment: Expanded Expectations and Challenges." *Educational Evaluation and Policy Analysis* 15(1): 1–16.

Littell, Ramon, George Milliken, Walter Stroup, and Russell Wolfinger. 1996. *SAS System for Mixed Models*. Cary, N.C.: SAS Institute.

Little, Roderick J. A., and Donald B. Rubin. 1987. *Statistical Analysis with Missing Data*. New York: Wiley.

Liu, Edward, and Susan M. Kardos. 2002. "Hiring and Professional Culture in New Jersey Schools." Working paper 25. Cambridge, Mass.: Harvard Graduate School of Education, Project on the Next Generation of Teachers.

Lloyd, Paulette, and Elizabeth Cohen. 1999. "Peer Status in the Middle School: A Natural Treatment for Unequal Participation." *Social Psychology of Education* 3: 193–216.

Lockheed, Malaine, Abigail Harris, and W. Nemceff. 1983. "Sex and Social Influence: Does Sex Function as a Status Characteristic in Mixed-Sex Groups of Children?" *Journal of Educational Psychology* 75: 877–86.

Lortie, Dan C. 1969. "The Balance of Control and Autonomy in Elementary School Teaching." In *The Semi-Professions and Their Organization: Teachers, Nurses, and Social Workers*, edited by Amitai Etzioni. New York: Free Press.

———. 1973. "Observations on Teaching as Work." In *Second Handbook of Research on Teaching*, edited by Robert M. W. Travers. Chicago: Rand McNally.

———. 1975. *Schoolteacher: A Sociological Study*. Chicago: University of Chicago Press.

———. 1977. "Two Anomalies and Three Perspectives: Some Observations on School Organization." In *Perspectives on Organizations*, edited by Ronald G. Corwin and Roy Edelfelt. Washington: American Association of Colleges for Teacher Education.

Louis, Karen S., and Helen M. Marks. 1998. "Does Professional Community Affect the Classroom? Teachers' Work and Student Experiences in Restructuring Schools." *American Journal of Education* 106(4): 532–75.

Loveless, Tom. 1996. "Why Aren't Computers Used More in Schools?" *Education Policy* 10(4): 448–67.

———, ed. 2001. *The Great Curriculum Debate: How Should We Teach Reading and Math?* Washington, D.C.: Brookings Institution Press.

———. 2003. "The Regulation of Teaching and Learning." In *Stability and Change in American Education*, edited by Maureen T. Hallinan, Adam Gamoran, Warren Kubitschek, and Tom Loveless. Clinton Corners, N.Y.: Eliot Werner Publications.

Lucas, Samuel R. 1999. *Tracking Inequality: Stratification and Mobility in American High Schools*. New York: Teachers College Press.

Lynch, Kristine D., W. W. Taylor, and K. Frank. 2001. "Factors Influencing Interorganizational Collaboration: An Analysis of Watershed-Based Fisheries Stakeholder Organizational Networks." Paper presented to the 131st annual meeting of the American Fisheries Society. Phoenix (August 19–23).

Mac Iver, Douglas J., and Joyce L. Epstein. 1991. "Responsive Practices in the Middle

Grades: Teacher Teams, Advisory Groups, Remedial Instruction, and School Transition Programs." *American Journal of Education* 99(4): 587–622.

March, James G. 1965. *Handbook of Organizations*. Chicago: Rand McNally.

———. 1991. "Exploration and Exploitation in Organizational Learning." *Organization Science* 2: 71–87.

March, James G., and Johan Olsen. 1976. *Ambiguity and Choice in Organizations*. Bergen, Norway: Universitetsforlaget.

March, James G., and Herbert A. Simon. 1958. *Organizations*. New York: Wiley.

Marini, Margaret M., and Mary Brinton. 1984. "Sex-Typing in Occupational Socialization." In *Sex Segregation in the Workplace: Trends, Explanations, Remedies*, edited by Barbara F. Reskin. Washington: National Academy Press.

Marsden, Peter V., and Noah E. Friedkin. 1994. "Network Studies of Social Influence." In *Advances in Social Network Analysis*, edited by Stanley Wasserman and Joseph Galaskiewicz. Thousand Oaks, Calif.: Sage Publications.

Maslow, Abraham H. 1943. "A Theory of Human Motivation." *Psychological Review* 50: 370–96.

Masters, G. N. 1982. "A Rasch Model for Partial Credit Scoring." *Psychometrika* 47(2): 149–74.

Maynard, Douglas. 1985. "On the Functions of Social Conflict Among Children." *American Sociological Review* 50(2): 207–23.

Mayo, Elton. 1945. *The Social Problems of an Industrial Civilization*. Boston: Harvard University, Graduate School of Business Administration.

McDill, Edward L., and Leo C. Rigsby. 1973. *Structure and Process in Secondary Schools: The Academic Impact of School Climates*. Baltimore: Johns Hopkins University Press.

McDonnell, Lorraine. 1994. "Assessment Policy as Persuasion and Regulation." *American Journal of Education* 102(4): 394–420.

McFarland, Daniel A. 1999. "Organized Behavior in Social Systems: A Study of Student Engagement and Resistance in High Schools." Ph.D. diss., University of Chicago.

———. 2001. "Student Resistance: How the Formal and Informal Organization of Classrooms Facilitates Everyday Forms of Student Defiance." *American Journal of Sociology* 107(3): 612–78.

———. 2003. "When Tensions Mount: Conceptualizing Classroom Situations and the Conditions of Student-Teacher Conflict." In *Stability and Change in American Education: Structure, Process, and Outcomes*, edited by Maureen T. Hallinan, Adam Gamoran, Warren Kubitschek, and Tom Loveless. New York: Elliot Werner Publications.

———. 2004. "Resistance as a Social Drama: A Study of Change-Oriented Encounters." *American Journal of Sociology* 109(6): 1249–1318.

McGinn, Noel F. 1980. *Education and Development in Korea*. Cambridge, Mass.: Harvard University Press.

McLaren, Peter. 1986. *Schooling as a Ritual Performance: Towards a Political Economy of Educational Symbols and Gestures*. Boston: Routledge & Kegan Paul.

McLaughlin, Milbrey W., and L. Shepard. 1995. *Improving Education Through Standards-Based Reform*. Stanford, Calif.: National Academy of Education.

McLaughlin, Milbrey W., and Joan E. Talbert. 2001. *Professional Communities and the Work of High School Teaching*. Chicago: University of Chicago Press.

McNeal, Ralph B., Jr. 1995. "Extracurricular Activities and High School Dropouts." *Sociology of Education* 68(1): 62–81.

McNeil, Linda M. 2000. *Contradictions of School Reform: Educational Costs of Standardized Testing*. New York: Routledge.

McPherson, Gertrude H. 1972. *Small Town Teacher*. Cambridge, Mass.: Harvard University Press.

Mead, George Herbert. 1934. *Mind, Self, and Society*. Edited by Charles W. Morris. Chicago: University of Chicago Press.

Mehan, Hugh. 1979. *Learning Lessons: Social Organization in the Classroom*. Cambridge, Mass.: Harvard University Press.

———. 1980. "The Competent Student." *Anthropology and Education* 11(3): 131–52.

Mehan, Hugh, Alma Hertweck, and J. Lee Meihls. 1986. *Handicapping the Handicapped: Decision Making in Students' Educational Careers*. Palo Alto, Calif.: Stanford University Press.

Meng, Xiao-Li. 1994. "Multiple Imputation with Uncongenial Sources of Input (with Comment)." *Statistical Science* 9: 538–73.

Merritt, Raymond H. 1969. *Engineering in American Society, 1850–1875*. Lexington: University Press of Kentucky.

Merton, Robert K. 1957a. "The Role Set: Problems in Sociological Theory." *British Journal of Sociology* 8: 106–20.

———. 1957b. *Social Theory and Social Structure*. Glencoe, Ill.: Free Press.

Messerli, Jonathan. 1971. *Horace Mann: A Biography*. New York: Alfred A. Knopf.

Metz, Mary Haywood. 1978. *Classrooms and Corridors: The Crisis of Authority in Desegregated Schools*. Berkeley: University of California Press.

Metzger, Walter P. 1987. "A Specter Is Haunting American Scholars: The Specter of 'Professionalism.'" *Educational Researcher* 16(August–September): 10–21.

Meyer, Alan D., and James B. Goes. 1988. "Organizational Assimilation of Innovations: A Multilevel Contextual Analysis." *Academy of Management Journal* 31(4): 897–923.

Meyer, John W. 1977. "The Effects of Education as an Institution." *American Journal of Sociology* 85(3): 55–77.

———. 1994. "Rationalized Environments." In *Institutionalized Environments and Organizations: Structural Complexity and Individualism*, edited by W. Richard Scott and John W. Meyer. Thousand Oaks, Calif.: Sage Publications.

Meyer, John W., and Michael T. Hannan, eds. 1979. *National Development and the World System: Educational, Economic, and Political Change*. Chicago: University of Chicago Press.

Meyer, John W., D. Kamens, and A. Benavot. 1992. *School Knowledge for the Masses*. Bristol, Penn.: Falmer Press.

Meyer, John W., and Brian Rowan. 1977. "Institutionalized Organizations: Formal Structure as Myth and Ceremony." *American Journal of Sociology* 83(2): 340–63.

———. 1978. "The Structure of Educational Organizations." In *Environments and Organizations*, edited by Marshall W. Meyer et al. San Francisco: Jossey-Bass.

Meyer, John W., and W. Richard Scott. 1983. *Organizational Environments: Ritual and Rationality*. Beverly Hills, Calif.: Sage Publications.

Meyer, John W., W. Richard Scott, Sally Cole, and Joanne Intili. 1978. "Instructional Dissensus and Institutional Consensus in Schools." In *Environments and Organizations*, edited by Marshall W. Meyer et al. San Francisco: Jossey-Bass.

Miech, Richard Allen, and Glen H. Elder. 1996. "The Service Ethic and Teaching." *Sociology of Education* 69(3): 237–53.

References

Milkman, Ruth, and Eleanor Townsley. 1994. "Gender and the Economy." In *The Handbook of Economic Sociology*, edited by Neil Smelser and Richard Swedberg. New York: Russell Sage Foundation.

Morgan, Stephen L., and Aage B. Sørenson. 1999. "Parental Networks, Social Closure, and Mathematics Learning: A Test of Coleman's Social Capital Explanation of School Effects." *American Sociological Review* 64(5): 661–81.

Muller, Chandra, and Kathryn S. Schiller. 2000. "Leveling the Playing Field? Students' Educational Attainment and States' Performance Testing." *Sociology of Education* 73(3): 196–218.

Muraki, E. 1992. "A Generalized Partial Credit Model: Application of an EM Algorithm." *Applied Psychological Measurement* 16(2): 159–76.

Murphy, J. 1992. "Restructuring American Schools: An Overview." In *Education Reforms in the 90s*, edited by C. Finn and T. Rebarber. New York: Macmillan.

Murphy, Marjorie. 1990. *Blackboard Unions: The AFT and the NEA 1900–1980*. Ithaca, N.Y.: Cornell University Press.

Murray, Charles, and Richard Herrnstein. 1996. "What's Really Behind the SAT-Score Decline?" *The Public Interest* 106: 32–56.

Muthén, Bengt O. 1984. "A General Structural Equation Model with Dichotomous, Ordered Categorical, and Continuous Latent Variable Indicators." *Psychometrika* 49: 115–32.

———. 1989. "Dichotomous Factor Analysis of Symptom Data." *Sociological Methods and Research* 18(21): 19–65.

Muthén, Bengt O., and Anders Christoffersson. 1981. "Simultaneous Factor Analysis of Dichotomous Variables in Several Groups." *Psychometrika* 46(6): 407–19.

National Board for Professional Teaching Standards. 2002. "6,500 New National Board Certified Teachers; 16,035 Total National Board Certificates." *The Professional Standard* 21: 1, 4.

National Center for Education Statistics.1983. *The Condition of* Education. Washington: U.S. Department of Education, Office of Educational Research and Development.

———. 1998. *Digest of Education Statistics 1997*. Washington: U.S. Department of Education, Office of Educational Research and Improvement, National Center for Education Statistics.

———. 2001. *Digest of Education Statistics 2001*. Washington: U.S. Department of Education, Office of Educational Research and Improvement, National Center for Educational Statistics.

National Commission on Excellence in Education. 1983. *A Nation at Risk: The Imperative for Educational Reform: A Report to the Nation and the Secretary of Education*. Washington: U.S. Department of Education, National Commission on Excellence in Education.

National Commission on Teaching for America's Future. 1996. *What Matters Most: Teaching for America's Future*. New York: National Commission on Teaching for America's Future.

National Education Association. 1972, 1982, 1987, 1992, 1996. *Status of the American Public School Teacher*. Washington: National Education Association.

Nelson, Richard R., and Sidney G. Winter. 1982. *An Evolutionary Theory of Economic Change*. Cambridge, Mass.: Belknap Press of Harvard University Press.

Newcomb, Theodore M. 1961. *The Acquaintance Process*. New York: Holt, Rinehart and Winston.

Newmann, Fred M., and Associates. 1996. *Authentic Achievement: Restructuring Schools for Intellectual Quality*. San Francisco: Jossey-Bass.

Newmann, Fred M., M. Bruce King, and Mark Rigdon. 1997. "Accountability and School Performance: Implications for Restructuring Schools." *Harvard Educational Review* 67: 41–74.

Newmann, Fred M., Helen M. Marks, and Adam Gamoran. 1996. "Authentic Pedagogy and Student Performance." *American Journal of Education* 104(4): 280–312.

Norris, Cathleen, Jennifer Smolka, and Elliot Soloway. 1999. "Convergent Analysis: A Method for Extracting the Value from Research Studies on Technology in Education." Paper presented to the meeting of the U.S. Education Secretary's conference on education, "Evaluating the Effectiveness of Technology." Washington (July 12–13).

North, Douglass. 1990. *Institutions, Institutional Change, and Economic Performance*. Cambridge: Cambridge University Press.

Oakes, Jeannie. 1985. *Keeping Track: How Schools Structure Inequality*. New Haven, Conn.: Yale University Press.

———. 1990. "Opportunities, Achievement, and Choice: Women and Minority Students in Science and Mathematics." *Review of Research in Education* 16: 153–222.

———. 1994. "More Than Misapplied Technology: A Normative and Political Response to Hallinan on Tracking." *Sociology of Education* 67(2): 84–89, 91.

Oakes, Jeannie, Adam Gamoran, and Reba N. Page. 1992. "Curriculum Differentiation: Opportunities, Outcomes, and Meanings." In *Handbook of Research on Curriculum*, edited by Philip W. Jackson. New York: Macmillan.

Oakes, Jeannie, and Gretchen Guiton. 1995. "Matchmaking: The Dynamics of High School Tracking Decisions." *American Educational Research Journal* 32: 3–33.

O'Day, Jennifer, and Marshall Smith. 1993. "Systemic Reform and Educational Opportunity." In *Designing Coherent Education Policy: Improving the System*, edited by Susan H. Fuhrman. San Francisco: Jossey-Bass.

Odden, Allan, and Carolyn Kelley. 1997. *Paying Teachers for What They Know and Do: New and Smarter Compensation Strategies*. Thousand Oaks, Calif.: Corwin Press.

Ogawa, Rodney T., and Paula A. White. 1994. "School-Based Management: An Overview." In *School-Based Management: Organizing for High Performance*, edited by Susan Albers Mohrman and Priscilla Wohlstetter. San Francisco: Jossey-Bass.

Okin, Susan Moller 1995. "Inequalities Between the Sexes in Different Cultural Contexts." In *Women, Culture, and Development*, edited by Martha C. Nussbaum and Jonathan Glover. Oxford: Clarendon Press.

Orloff, Anna Shola. 1993. "Gender and the Social Rights of Citizenship: The Comparative Analysis of Gender Relations and Welfare States." *American Sociological Review* 58: 303–28.

Orr, Julian E. 1996. *Talking About Machines: An Ethnography of a Modern Job*. Ithaca, N.Y.: Cornell University Press/ILR Press.

Orr, Marion. 1996. "Urban Politics and School Reform: The Case of Baltimore." *Urban Affairs Review* 31(3): 314–45.

Orton, J. Douglas, and Karl Weick. 1990. "Loosely Coupled Systems: A Reconceptualization." *Academy of Management Review* 15(2): 203–33.

Ouchi, William. 1977. "The Relationship Between Organizational Structure and Organizational Control." *Administrative Science Quarterly* 22: 95–113.

Ouchi, William, and Alan L. Wilkins. 1985. "Organizational Culture." *Annual Review of Sociology* 11: 457–83.

Padilla, Christine, and Michael S. Knapp. 1995. "How the Policy Environment Shapes Instruction in High-Poverty Classrooms." In *Advances in Educational Productivity*, vol. 5. Greenwich, Conn.: JAI Press.

References

Pallas, Aaron M., Gary Natriello, and Carolyn Riehl. 1994. *Tweaking the Sorting Machine: The Dynamics of Students' Schedule Changes in High School*. Paper presented at the annual meeting of the American Sociological Association, Los Angeles (August).

Pampel, Fred, and Kazuko Taneka. 1986. "Economic Development and Female Labor Force Participation: A Reconsideration." *Social Forces* 4(3): 599.

Parsons, Talcott. 1939. "The Professions and Social Structure." *Social Forces* 17(3): 457–67.

———. 1959. "The School Class as a Social System: Some of Its Functions in American Society." *Harvard Educational Review* 29: 297–318.

———. 1960. *Structure and Process in Modern Societies*. Glencoe, Ill.: Free Press.

Parsons, Talcott, and Gerald M. Platt. 1973. *The American University*. Cambridge, Mass.: Harvard University Press.

Patzer, Gordon L. 1985. *The Physical Attractiveness Phenomena*. New York: Plenum Press.

Perlmann, Joel, and Robert A. Margo. 2001. *Women's Work: American Schoolteachers, 1650–1920*. Chicago: University of Chicago Press.

Perrow, Charles. 1967. "A Framework for the Comparative Analysis of Organizations." *American Sociological Review* 32: 194–208.

———. 1986. *Complex Organizations: A Critical Essay*. New York: Random House.

Peske, Heather, Edward Liu, Susan Moore Johnson, David Kauffman, and Susan Kardos. 2001. "The Next Generation of Teachers: Changing Conceptions of a Career in Teaching." *Phi Delta Kappan* 83(4): 304–11.

Peterson, Paul E. 1985. *The Politics of School Reform, 1870–1940*. Chicago: University of Chicago Press.

Petrin, Robert A. 2004. "Discourses and Resources: Instructional and Structural Effects in Secondary Education."

Pfeffer, Jeffrey. 1981. *Power in Organizations*. Marshfield, Mass.: Pitman.

———. 1982. *Organizations and Organization Theory*. Marshfield, Mass.: Pitman.

Pfeffer, Jeffrey, and Gerald R. Salancik. 1978. *The External Control of Organizations*. New York: Harper & Row.

Phillips, La Rae. 1993. "Miami: After the Hype." In *A Union of Professionals: Labor Relations and Educational Reform*, edited by Charles Taylor Kerchner and Julia E. Koppich. New York: Teachers College Press.

Phillips, Meredith. 1997. "What Makes Schools Effective? A Comparison of the Relationships of Communitarian Climate and Academic Climate to Mathematics Achievement and Attendance During Middle School." *American Educational Research Journal* 34: 633–62.

Plank, Stephen. 2000a. *Finding One's Place: Teaching Styles and Peer Relations in Diverse Classrooms*. New York: Teacher's College.

———. 2000b. "More on Peer Relations: Cohesive Subgroups." In *Finding One's Place: Teaching Styles and Peer Relations in Diverse Classrooms*, by Stephen Plank. New York: Teachers College Press.

Pondy, Louis, and Ian Mitroff. 1979. "Beyond Open System Models of Organization." In *Research in Organization Behavior*, vol. 1, edited by Barry M. Staw. Greenwich, Conn.: JAI Press.

Pong, Suet-ling. 1998. "The School Compositional Effect of Single Parenthood on Tenth-Grade Achievement." *Sociology of Education* 71(1): 23–42.

Portes, Alejandro. 1998. "Social Capital: Its Origins and Applications in Modern Sociology." *Annual Review of Sociology* 24: 1–24.

Powell, Arthur G., Eleanor Farrar, and David K. Cohen. 1985. *The Shopping Mall High School: Winners and Losers in the Educational Marketplace*. Boston: Houghton Mifflin.

Powell, Walter W. 1990. "Neither Market nor Hierarchy: Network Forms of Organization." *Research in Organizational Behavior* 12: 295–336.

Powell, Walter W., and Paul J. DiMaggio, eds. 1991. *The New Institutionalism in Organizational Analysis*. Chicago: University of Chicago Press.

President's Committee of Advisers on Science and Technology. 1997. *Report to the President on the Use of Technology to Strengthen K–12 Education in the United States*. Washington: President's Committee of Advisers on Science and Technology.

Pressman, Jeffrey L., and Aaron Wildavsky. 1984. *Implementation: How Great Expectations in Washington Are Dashed in Oakland*. 3rd ed. Berkeley: University of California Press.

Pugh, Derek Salman, and D. J. Hickson. 1976. *Organizational Structure in Its Context: The Aston Programme I*. Lexington, Mass.: Heath.

Pugh, Derek Salman, David J. Hickson, Christopher R. Hinings, and Christopher Turner. 1968. "Dimensions of Organization Structure." *Administrative Science Quarterly* 13: 65–91.

Quiroz, Pamela A., Nilda F. Gonzalez, and Kenneth A. Frank. 1996. "Carving a Niche in the High School Social Structure: Formal and Informal Constraints on Participation in the Extra Curriculum." In *Research in Sociology of Education and Socialization*, edited by Aaron Pallas. Greenwich, Conn.: JAI Press.

Raghunathan, Trivellore E., and James E. Grizzle. 1995. "A Split Questionnare Survey Design." *Journal of the American Statistical Association* 90: 54–63.

Ramamurthy, K., and G. Premkumar. 1995. "Determinants and Outcomes of Electronic Data Interchange Diffusion." *IEEE Transactions on Engineering Management* 42(4): 332–51.

Ramirez, Francisco O. 1997. "The Nation-State, Citizenship, and Educational Change: Institutionalization and Globalization." In *International Handbook of Education and Development*, edited by William K. Cummings and Noel F. McGinn. New York: Pergamon/Elsevier Science.

Ravitch, Diane. 1995. *National Standards in American Education: A Citizen's Guide*. Washington, D.C.: Brookings Institution Press.

Reader, William J. 1966. *Professional Men: The Rise of the Professional Classes in Nineteenth-Century Britain*. London: Weidenfeld and Nicolson.

Reynolds, David R. 1999. *There Goes the Neighborhood: Rural School Consolidation in Early-Twentieth-Century Iowa*. Iowa City: University of Iowa Press.

Ridgeway, Cecilia, and David Diekema. 1989. "Dominance and Collective Hierarchy Formation in Male and Female Task Groups." *American Sociological Review* 54(1): 79–93.

Ridgeway, Cecilia, and Cathryn Johnson. 1990. "What Is the Relationship Between Socioemotional Behavior and Status in Task Groups?" *American Journal of Sociology* 95(5): 1189–1212.

Riegle-Crumb, Catherine. 1996. "The Effects of Social Capital and Self-concept: Math and Science Achievement by Gender." M.A. thesis, University of Chicago.

Riehl, Carolyn, Aaron M. Pallas, and Gary Natriello. 1999. "Rites and Wrongs: Institutional Explanations for the Student Course-Scheduling Process in Urban High Schools." *American Journal of Education* 107: 116–54.

Ritti, Richard. 1971. *The Engineer in the Industrial Corporation*. New York: Columbia University Press.

References

Roderick, Melissa R. 1993. *The Path to Dropping Out: Evidence for Intervention*. Westport, Conn.: Auburn House.

Roethlisberger, F. J., and William J. Dickson. 1939. *Management and the Worker*. Cambridge, Mass.: Harvard University Press.

Rogers, Everett. 1995. *Diffusion of Innovations*. New York: Free Press.

Rosenbaum, James E. 1986. "Institutional Career Structures and the Social Construction of Ability." In *Handbook of Theory and Research for the Sociology of Education*, edited by John G. Richardson. New York: Greenwood Press.

Rosenberg, Morris. 1957. *Occupations and Values*. New York: Arno Press.

Rothstein, William G. 1972. *American Physicians in the Nineteenth Century: From Sects to Science*. Baltimore: Johns Hopkins University Press.

Rowan, Brian. 1990a. "Applying Conceptions of Teaching to Organizational Reform." In *Restructuring Schools: The Next Generation of Educational Reform*, edited by Richard Elmore. San Francisco: Jossey-Bass.

———. 1990b. "Commitment and Control: Alternative Strategies for Organizational Design in Schools." In *Review of Research in Education*, vol. 16, edited by Courtney Cazden. Washington: American Educational Research Association.

———. 1995. "The Organizational Design of Schools." In *Images of Schools*, edited by Samuel B. Bacharach and Bryan Mundell. Thousand Oaks, Calif.: Corwin Press.

Rowan, Brian, Richard Correnti, and Robert J. Miller. 2002. "What Large-Scale Survey Research Tells Us About Teacher Effects on Student Achievement: Insights from the *Prospects* Study of Elementary Schools." *Teachers College Record* 104: 1525–67.

Rubin, Donald B. 1987. *Multiple Imputation for Nonresponse in Surveys*. New York: Wiley.

———. 1996. "Multiple Imputation After 18+ Years." *Journal of the American Statistical Association* 91: 473–89.

Rury, John L. 1989. "Who Became Teachers? The Social Characteristics of Teachers in American History." In *American Teachers: Histories of a Profession at Work*, edited by Donald Warren. New York: Macmillan.

Rutter, Michael S., Barbara Maughan, Peter Mortimore, and Janet Ouston. 1979. *Fifteen Thousand Hours*. Cambridge, Mass.: Harvard University Press.

Ryan, Richard M. 1995. "Psychological Needs and the Facilitation of Integrative Processes." *Journal of Personality* 63(3): 397–427.

Sampson, Robert, Jeffrey Morenoff, and Felton Earls. 1999. "Beyond Social Capital: Spatial Dynamics of Collective Efficacy for Children." *American Sociological Review* 64(5): 633–60.

Sandefur, Rebecca L., and Edward O. Laumann. 1998. "A Paradigm for Social Capital." *Rationality and Society* 10: 481–501.

Sanford, Stephanie, and Donna Eder. 1984. "Adolescent Humor During Peer Interaction." *Social Psychology Quarterly* 47(3): 235–43.

Sassen, Saskia. 2001. *The Global City: New York, London, Tokyo*. 2nd ed. Princeton, N.J.: Princeton University Press.

Sayles, L. 1963. "Work Group Behavior and the Larger Organization." In *Organizations: Structure and Behavior*, edited by Joseph A. Litterer. New York: Wiley.

Schiller, Kathryn S. 1995. "Organizations, Individuals, and Uncertainty: The Transition to High School." Ph.D. diss., University of Chicago.

————. 1999. "Effects of Feeder Patterns on Students' Transition to High School." *Sociology of Education* 72(4): 216–33.

Schiller, Kathryn S., and Donald Hunt. 2001. *Leading Up or Out: Paths Through High School Mathematics*. Seattle: American Educational Research Association.

Schiller, Kathryn S., and Chandra Muller. 2000. "External Examinations and Accountability, Educational Expectations, and High School Graduation." *American Journal of Education* 108(2): 73–102.

Schneider, Barbara, and David L. Stevenson. 1999. *The Ambitious Generation: America's Teenagers, Motivated but Directionless*. New Haven, Conn.: Yale University Press.

Schneider, Barbara, Christopher B. Swanson, and Catherine Riegle-Crumb. 1998. "Opportunities for Learning: Course Sequences and Positional Advantages." *Social Psychology of Education* 2: 25–53.

Scott, W. Richard. 1987. *Organizations: Rational, Natural and Open Systems*. 2nd ed. Englewood Cliffs, N.J.: Prentice-Hall.

————. 1988. "The Adolescence of Institutional Theory." *Administrative Science Quarterly* 32: 493–511.

————. 2001a. *Institutions and Organizations*. 2nd ed. Thousand Oaks, Calif.: Sage Publications.

————. 2001b. "Organizations, Overview." In *International Encyclopedia of the Social and Behavioral Sciences*, vol. 16, edited by Neil J. Smelser and Paul B. Baltes. Amsterdam: Pergamon/Elsevier Science.

————. 2003. *Organizations: Rational, Natural, and Open Systems*. 5th ed. Upper Saddle River, N.J.: Prentice-Hall.

Scott, W. Richard, and Søren Christensen. 1995. "Crafting a Wider Lens." In *The Institutional Construction of Organizations: International and Longitudinal Studies*, edited by W. Richard Scott and Søren Christensen. Thousand Oaks, Calif.: Sage Publications.

Scott, W. Richard, and John W. Meyer, eds. 1994. *Institutional Environments and Organizations: Structural Complexity and Individualism*. Thousand Oaks, Calif.: Sage Publications.

Selznick, Philip. 1949. *TVA and the Grass Roots: A Study of Politics and Organization*. Berkeley: University of California Press.

————. 1957. *Leadership in Administration: A Sociological Interpretation*. Evanston, Ill.: Row, Peterson and Co.

————. 1961. "Foundations of the Theory of Organization." In *Complex Organizations*, edited by Amitai Etzioni. New York: Holt, Rinehart and Winston.

Sewell, William, Jr. 1992. "A Theory of Structure: Duality, Agency, and Transformation." *American Journal of Sociology* 98(1): 1–29.

Sexias, Peter. 2001. "Review of Research on Social Studies." In *Handbook of Research on Teaching*, edited by Virginia Richardson. Washington: American Educational Research Association.

Seybolt, Robert F. 1925. *The Evening School in Colonial America*. Bulletin 24. Urbana: University of Illinois, Bureau of Educational Research.

————. 1935. *The Private Schools of Colonial Boston*. Cambridge, Mass.: Harvard University Press.

Seymour, Elaine, and Nancy M. Hewitt. 1997. *Talking About Leaving: Why Undergraduates Leave the Sciences*. Boulder, Colo.: Westview.

References

Shedd, Joseph B., and Samuel B. Bacharach. 1991. *Tangled Hierarchies: Teachers as Professionals and the Management of Schools*. San Francisco: Jossey-Bass.

Shouse, Roger C. 1996. "Academic Press and Sense of Community: Conflict and Congruence in American High Schools." In *Research in Sociology of Education and Socialization*, vol. 11, edited by Aaron M. Pallas. Greenwich, Conn.: JAI Press.

Shryock, Richard H. 1947. *The Development of Modern Medicine: An Interpretation of the Social and Scientific Factors Involved*. New York: Alfred A. Knopf.

Shulman, Lee S. 1987. "Knowledge and Teaching: Foundations of the New Reform." *Harvard Educational Review* 57(1): 1–22.

Sieber, R. T. 1979. "Classmates as Workmates: Informal Peer Activity in the Elementary School." *Anthropology and Education* 10(4): 207–35.

Silverman, David. 1971. *The Theory of Organisations: A Sociological Framework*. New York: Basic Books.

Simmel, Georg. 1949. "The Sociology of Sociability." Translated by Everett C. Hughes. *American Journal of Sociology* 55(3): 254–61.

———. 1955. *Conflict and the Web of Group Affiliations*. Translated by Kurt Wolff. Glencoe, Ill.: Free Press.

Simon, Herb A. 1965. "The Architecture of Complexity." In *General Systems: Yearbook of the Society for General Systems*, vol. 10, edited by Ludwig von Bertalanffy and Anatol Rapoport. Ann Arbor, Mich.: Society for the Advancement of General Systems Theory.

Simpson, Richard. 1985. "Social Control of Occupations and Work." *Annual Review of Sociology* 11: 415–36.

Singer, Judith. 1998. "Using SAS PROC MIXED to Fit Multilevel Models, Hierarchical Models, and Individual Growth Models." *Journal of Educational and Behavioral Statistics* 23(4): 323–55.

Siskin, Leslie S. 1991. "Departments as Different Worlds: Subject Subcultures in Secondary Schools." *Educational Administration Quarterly* 2710 (2): 134–60.

———. 1994. *Realms of Knowledge: Academic Departments in Secondary Schools*. Washington, D.C.: Falmer Press.

Smigel, Erwin O. 1964. *The Wall Street Lawyer: Professional Organization Man?* New York: Free Press of Glencoe.

Smith, Julia B. 1997. "Effects of Eighth-Grade Transition Program on High School Retention Experiences." *Journal of Educational Research* 90: 144–52.

Smith, Marshall, and J. O'Day. 1991. "Systemic School Reform." In *The Politics of Curriculum and Testing*, edited by Susan H. Fuhrman and B. Malen. Philadelphia: Falmer Press.

Smith, Richard N. 1984. *An Uncommon Man: The Triumph of Herbert Hoover*. New York: Simon & Schuster.

Snow, David. 1986. "Frame Alignment Processes, Micro-mobilization, and Movement Participation." *American Sociological Review* 51: 464–81.

Sørenson, Aage B. 1970. "Organizational Differentiation of Students and Educational Opportunity." *Sociology of Education* 43(4): 355–76.

———. 1987. "The Organization and Differentiation of Students in Schools as an Opportunity Structure." In *The Social Organization of Schools*, edited by Maureen T. Hallinan. New York: Plenum Press.

Sørenson, Aage B., and Maureen T. Hallinan. 1977. "A Reconceptualization of School Effects: Theoretical and Methodological Issues." *Sociology of Education* 50(4): 522–35.

Sørenson, Aage B., and Arne L. Kalleberg. 1981. "An Outline of a Theory of the Matching of Persons to Jobs." In *Sociological Perspectives on Labor Markets*, edited by Ivor E. Berg. New York: Academic.

Spear, Allan H. 1967. *Black Chicago: The Making of a Negro Ghetto 1890–1920*. Chicago: University of Chicago Press.

Spencer, Dee Ann. 2001. "Teachers' Work in Historical and Social Context." In *Handbook of Research on Teaching*, edited by Virginia Richardson. Washington: American Educational Research Association.

Sperling, Melanie, and Sarah W. Freedman. 2001. "Research on Writing." In *Handbook of Research on Teaching*, edited by Virginia Richardson. Washington: American Educational Research Association.

Spilerman, Seymour. 1971. "Raising Academic Motivation in Lower-Class Adolescents: A Convergence of Two Research Traditions." *Sociology of Education* 44(1): 103–18.

Stage, F., and S. Maple. 1996. "Incompatible Goals: Narratives of Graduate Women in the Mathematics Pipeline." *American Educational Research Journal* 33: 23.

Stanton-Salazar, Ricardo D., and Sanford M. Dornbusch. 1995. "Social Capital and the Reproduction of Inequality: Information Networks Among Mexican-Origin High School Students." *Sociology of Education* 68(2): 116–35.

Starr, Paul. 1982. *The Social Transformation of American Medicine: The Rise of a Sovereign Profession and the Making of a Vast Industry*. New York: Basic Books.

Stein, Mary, Barbara Grover, and Marjorie Henningsen. 1996. "Building Student Capacity for Mathematical Thinking and Reasoning." *American Educational Research Journal* 33(2): 455–88.

Stevenson, David L., and Kathryn S. Schiller. 1999. "State Education Policies and Changing School Practices: Evidence from the National Longitudinal Study of School, 1980–1993." *American Journal of Education* 107: 261–88.

Stevenson, David L., Kathryn S. Schiller, and Barbara Schneider. 1994. "Sequences of Opportunities for Learning." *Sociology of Education* 67(3): 184–98.

Stinchcombe, Arthur. 1965. "Social Structure and Organizations." In *Handbook of Organizations*, edited by James G. March. Chicago: Rand McNally.

———. 1968. *Constructing Social Theories*. Chicago: University of Chicago Press.

———. 1990. *Information and Organizations*. Berkeley: University of California Press.

Stodolsky, Susan S. 1988. *The Subject Matters*. Chicago: University of Chicago Press.

Stodolsky, Susan S., and Pamela L. Grossman. 1995. "The Impact of Subject Matter on Curricular Activity: An Analysis of Five Academic Subjects." *American Educational Research Journal* 32: 227–49.

Streeck, Jürgen. 1984. "Embodied Contexts, Transcontextuals, and the Timing of Speech Acts." *Journal of Pragmatics* 8: 113–37.

Summers, Anita, and Barbara L. Wolfe. 1977. "Do Schools Make a Difference?" *American Economic Review* 67(4): 639–52.

Sumner, William Graham. 1906. *Folkways*. Boston: Ginn.

Swanson, Christopher B., Stephen B. Plank, and Gina M. Hewes. 2003. *From National Move-*

ment to Local Action: The Status of Standards-Based Science Instruction in Middle School Class-rooms. Baltimore, Md.: The Johns Hopkins University.

Swanson, Christopher B., and Catherine Riegle-Crumb. 1999. "Early Steps to College Success: High School Course Sequences and Postsecondary Matriculation." Paper presented to the annual meeting of the American Educational Research Association. Montreal (April).

Swanson, Christopher B., and Barbara Schneider. 1999. "Students on the Move: Residential and Educational Mobility in America's Schools." Sociology of Education 72(1): 54–67.

Swanson, Christopher B., and David L. Stevenson. 2002. "Standards-Based Reform in Practice: Evidence on State Policy and Classroom Instruction from the NAEP State Assessments." Educational Evaluation and Policy Analysis 24(1): 1–27.

Swidler, Ann, and Jorge Arditti. 1994. "The New Sociology of Knowledge." Annual Review of Sociology 20: 305–29.

Sykes, Gary. 1983. "Reckoning with the Specter." Educational Researcher 16: 19–21.

Sykes, Gresham M. 1958. The Society of Captives: A Study of a Maximum Security Prison. Princeton, N.J.: Princeton University Press.

Tabar, Keith S. 1992. "Science-Relatedness and Gender-Appropriateness of Careers: Some Pupil Perception." Research in Science and Technological Education 10: 105–15.

Taylor, Frederick W. 1947. Scientific Management. New York: Harper & Brothers.

Theobald, Paul. 1995. Call School: Rural Education in the Midwest to 1918. Carbondale: University of Southern Illinois Press.

Thomas, William I. 1923. The Unadjusted Girl. Montclair, N.J.: Patterson Smith.

Thompson, James D. 1967. Organizations in Action. New York: McGraw-Hill.

Tinto, Vincent. 1988. "Stages of Student Departure: Reflections on the Longitudinal Character of Student Leaving." Journal of Higher Education 59: 483–55.

Tornatzky, Louis G., J. D. Eveland, Myles G. Boyland, William A. Hetzner, Eimima C. Johnson, David Roitman, and Janet Schneider. 1983. Innovation Processes and Their Management: A Conceptual, Empirical, and Policy Review of Innovation Process Research. Washington: National Science Foundation.

Tornatzky, Louis G., and Mitchell Fleischer. 1990. The Process of Technological Innovation. New York: Lexington Books.

Trent, Stanley C. 1992. "Collaboration Between Special Educators and Regular Educators: A Cross-Case Analysis." Ph.D. diss., University of Virginia.

Tyack, David B. 1974. The One Best System: A History of American Urban Education. Cambridge, Mass.: Harvard University Press.

Tyler, William E. 1985. "Organizational Structure of the School." Annual Review of Sociology 11: 49–73.

———. 1988. School Organization. New York: Croom Helm.

U.S. Congress. 1994. Goals 2000: Educate America Act (H.R. 1804). Available at: www.ed .gov/legislation/GOALS2000/TheAct/index.html (accessed March 11, 2005).

U.S. Department of Education. 1984. The Nation Responds: Recent Efforts to Improve Education. Washington: U.S. Government Printing Office (May).

———. 1996. National Education Longitudinal Study: 1988 to 1994. CD-ROM. Washington: Office of Educational Research and Improvement.

Useem, Elizabeth L. 1991. "Student Selection into Course Sequences in Mathematics: The

Impact of Parental Involvement and School Policies." *Journal of Research on Adolescence* 1(3): 231–50.

Vogel, Morris J. 1980. *The Invention of the Modern Hospital: Boston, 1870–1930.* Chicago: University of Chicago Press.

Waller, Willard. 1932. *The Sociology of Teaching.* New York: Wiley.

Ware, Helen. 1988. "The Effects of Fertility, Family Organization, Sex Structure of the Labor Market, and Technology on the Position of Women." In *Women's Position and Demographic Change in the Course of Development.* Oslo: IUSSP Proceedings.

Wasserman, S., and P. Pattison. 1996. "Logit Models and Logistic Regressions for Univariate and Bivariate Social Networks: I. An Introduction to Markov Graphs." *Psychometrika* 61(3): 401–26.

Weber, Max. 1946. "Science as a Vocation." In *From Max Weber: Essays in Sociology,* edited by H. H. Gerth and C. Wright Mills. New York: Oxford University Press.

———. 1947. *The Theory of Economic and Social Organization,* edited by Talcott Parsons. New York: Oxford University Press.

———. 1921/1978. *Economy and Society: An Interpretive Sociology.* Vol. 1. Edited by G. Roth and C. Wittich. Berkeley: University of California Press.

Webster, Murray, Jr., and James Driskell, Jr. 1983. "Beauty as Status." *American Journal of Sociology* 89(1): 140–65.

Weick, Karl. 1969. *The Social Psychology of Organizing.* Reading, Mass.: Addison-Wesley.

———. 1976. "Educational Organizations as Loosely Coupled Systems." *Administrative Science Quarterly* 21(1): 1–19.

———. 1979. *The Social Psychology of Organizing.* 2nd ed. Reading, Mass.: Addison-Wesley.

———. 1984. "Management of Organizational Change Among Loosely Coupled Elements." In *Change in Organizations,* edited by Paul S. Goodman. San Francisco: Jossey-Bass.

———. 2001. *Making Sense of the Organization.* Malden, Mass.: Blackwell.

Weiner, Norbert. 1954. *The Human Use of Human Beings: Cybernetics and Society.* Garden City, N.Y.: Doubleday/Anchor.

Weiss, Christopher C. 2001. "Difficult Starts: Turbulence in the School Year and Its Impact on Urban Students' Achievement." *American Journal of Education* 109: 196–227.

Wellman, Barry A., and Kenneth A. Frank. 2001. "Network Capital in a Multilevel World: Getting Support from Personal Communities." In *Social Capital,* edited by Nan Lin, Ronald Burt, and Karen Cook. Chicago: Aldine De Gruyter.

Wells, John G., and Daniel K. Anderson. 1997. "Learners in a Telecommunications Course: Adoption, Diffusion, and Stages of Concern." *Journal of Research on Computing in Education* 30(1): 83–105.

Wenglinsky, Harold. 1997. "How Money Matters: The Effect of School District Spending on Academic Achievement." *Sociology of Education* 70: 221–37.

White, Richard. 2001. "The Revolution on Research in Science Teaching." In *Handbook of Research on Teaching,* edited by Virginia Richardson. Washington: American Educational Research Association.

Whyte, William Foote, and Burleigh Gardner. 1945. "The Man in the Middle." *Applied Anthropology* 4: 1–28.

Wilcox, Danielle D. 1999. "The National Board for Professional Teaching Standards: Can It Live Up to Its Promise?" In *Better Teachers, Better Schools,* edited by Marci Kanstoroom and

References

Chester E. Finn Jr. Washington: Thomas B. Fordham Foundation.

Wilensky, Harold. 1964. "The Professionalization of Everyone?" *American Journal of Sociology* 70(2): 137–58.

Williams, Trevor, Dan Levine, Leslie Jocelyn, Patricia Butler, Camilla Heid, and Jacqueline Haynes. 2000. *Mathematics and Science in Eighth Grade: Findings from the Third International Mathematics and Science Survey.* Washington: National Center for Education Statistics.

Williamson, Oliver. 1975. *Markets and Hierarchies: Analysis and Antitrust Implications.* New York: Free Press.

Willms, J. Douglas, and Stephen W. Raudenbush. 1989. "A Longitudinal Hierarchical Linear Model for Estimating School Effects and Their Stability." *Journal of Educational Measurement* 26(3): 209–32.

Wilson, Alan B. 1959. "Residential Segregation of Social Classes and Aspirations of High School Boys." *American Sociological Review* 24(6): 836–45.

Wilson, Suzanne M. 2001. "Research on History Teaching." In *Handbook of Research on Teaching,* edited by Virginia Richardson. Washington: American Educational Research Association.

Wilson, Suzanne M., and Deborah L. Ball. 1991. *Changing Visions and Changing Practices: Patchworks in Learning to Teach Mathematics for Understanding.* Research report 91-2. East Lansing: Michigan State University, National Center for Research on Teacher Learning.

Wilson, William Julius. 1996. *When Work Disappears: The World of the New Urban Poor.* New York: Alfred A. Knopf.

Woodham-Smith, Cecil. 1960. *The Reason Why.* New York: E. P. Dutton.

Woodward, Joan. 1958. *Management and Technology.* London: HMSO.

———. 1965. *Industrial Organization: Theory and Practice.* New York: Oxford University Press.

Wright, Benjamin, and Geoff Masters. 1982. *Rating Scale Analysis.* Chicago: MESA Press.

Yair, Gad. 2000. "Educational Battlefields in America: The Tug-of-War over Students' Engagement with Instruction." *Sociology of Education* 73(4): 247–69.

Yasumoto, Jeffrey, Kazuaki Uekawa, and Charles E. Bidwell. 2001. "The Collegial Focus and Student Achievement: Consequences of High School Faculty Social Organization for Students' Achievement in Mathematics and Science." *Sociology of Education* 74(3): 181–209.

Yetton, Philip, Rajeev Sharma, and Gray Southon. 1999. "Successful IS Innovation: The Contingent Contributions of Innovation Characteristics and Implementation Process." *Journal of Information Technology* 14: 53–68.

Yoshida, Makoto. 1999. "Lesson Study: A Case Study of a Japanese Approach to Improving Instruction Through School-Based Teacher Development." Ph.D. diss., University of Chicago.

Zeichner, Kenneth, and Jennifer Gore. 1989. *Teacher Socialization.* East Lansing: Michigan State University, College of Education, National Center for Research on Teacher Learning.

Zey-Ferrell, Mary, and Michael Aiken, eds. 1981. *Complex Organizations: Critical Perspectives.* Glenview, Ill.: Scott, Foresman.

Zhao, Yong, and Kenneth A. Frank. 2002. "Technology Uses in Michigan Schools: An Empirical Study." Unpublished manuscript, Michigan State University.

———. 2003. "An Ecological Analysis of Factors Affecting Technology Use in Schools." *American Educational Research Journal* 40(4): 807–40.

Zmud, Robert W. 1983. "The Effectiveness of External Information Channels in Facilitating Innovation." *MIS Quarterly* 7(2): 43–58.

Zmud, Robert W., and L. Eugene Apple. 1992. "Measuring Technology Incorporation/Infusion." *Journal of Product Innovation Management* 9: 148–55.

Zucker, Lynne. 1977. "The Role of Institutionalization in Cultural Persistence." *American Journal of Sociology* 42: 726–43.

———. 1987. "Institutional Theories of Organization." *Annual Review of Sociology* 13: 443–64.

Zussman, Robert. 1985. *Mechanics of the Middle Class: Work and Politics Among American Engineers.* Berkeley: University of California Press.

Index

Numbers in **boldface** refer to tables or figures.

Abbott, Andrew, 52, 54, 70
ability grouping. *See* tracking by ability
abortion availability, and women's opportunities in labor force, 232
Abu-Lughod, Janet, 18, 20
academia's role in educational reform, 62, 68, 69, 70–71*n*1, 249. *See also* research issues
academic environment: and curricular experience for students, 182, **190**, 192; status and student participation levels, 152–53, 157–58, 167, 170, 171. *See also* achievement, academic
academic high schools, 59, 133
academic vs. social learning, 100–104, 133–34. *See also* task and social participation
access to education. *See* equity, social-educational
accountability-based reforms: alignment with policy, **260**; and disadvantaged school environments, 301–2, 316; equity and achievement effects, 278–83; federal mandates, 270; and organizational control, 251–53, 268; overview, 10–11, **256–57**; personal vs. collective, 108; problems with, 88–89, **263**; public origins of teaching, 77; state role in, **266**, 267
achievement, academic: in accountability model, 252, **256**; challenges for poor schools, 302; and curricular differentiation, 17; and equal opportunity, 270–83; and gender gap in math-science, 234–35, **236**; motivation formation for, 27; and normative school cul-

ture, 130, 131, 132–33, 135–36, 137–38, 139; as primary focus of educational reform, 26, 68, 96; student focus of, 20, 68, 192; validity as competence measurement, 60
actors, school. *See* administrators; students; teaching and teachers
adaptation vs. selection processes, 40
administrators: control methods over teachers, 107; as local influences on school social context, 26; microsociological approach to relationships with teachers, 25; and teachers in technology diffusion, 210. *See also* principals
adolescence and school social systems, 135, 141, 288. *See also* psychological factors
The Adolescent Society (Coleman), 16
advanced placement (AP) programs, 311
African American students, 278, 306
AFT (American Federation of Teachers), 67–68
agency models of organizations, 178, 303–4, 315, 317–18
Aldrich, Howard, 39, 40, 95
aligned assessments, 251, 265
alternative certification programs, 88
altruistic motivations of teachers, 77, 97–98
American Federation of Teachers (AFT), 67–68
AP (advanced placement) programs, 311
aptitudes, student, and instructional effects, 179

Archer, Margaret, 17, 22
assessments: and academic vs. social learning, 101; and accountability-based reforms, 252, 253, **257**, **263**; aligned, 251, 265; equity and achievement effects, 274, 278; pressures of standardized tests, 89, 90; social stratification effects, 280; in standards-based reforms, **263**, 264–65, **265**; and technology use by teachers, 205–6. *See also* work activity assessments
assigned public schools and transition programs, 286, **293**, 294, **295**
associative forms of organization, ecological approach to, 39–40
Aston group, 41
attitudes about math and science, gender gap in, 236–37, **238**
authority, teachers' lack of professional, 84, 104, 108
autonomy: in academic vs. socialization roles of teachers, 104; decentralization of control and teacher, 106; and instructional practice, 93, 112; as key to better quality teaching, 78, 79; limitations on teacher, 4–5, 20, 29, 72, 77, 84, 90; vs. need for organizational control, 98–99; and standardized testing, 89; of states and localities in education control, 253, 254, 267, 301–19; and teacher-student relationship, 28–29, 132, 144–45

background effects on student participation, 161–62, **162–63**, background effects on student participation (*cont.*) 164, **164–65,** 166. *See also* demographic factors

Baker, David, 229

Barnard, Chester, 43

Barr, Rebecca, 201

Becker, Howard, 36*n*6

behavioral vs. structural focus on organizations, 42–43. *See also* socialization

Bidwell, Charles: on anomaly of school organization, 92–93; on collegial ties among teachers, 111; ecosystem approach to organizational structure, 37–46; on lack of research in classroom sociology, 129–30; loose coupling analysis contribution, 200; on normative culture effects, 139, 140, 144–45, 147; on organizational control of teachers, 109*n*1; on social psychological processes in schools, 201–3; structure and values in school context, 132; on student-teacher relationship, 179

Blau, Peter, 41, 42–43, 142

board certification of teachers, 82–83

Borman, Kathryn, 205

Bosk, Charles, 59

Boulding, Kenneth, 37–38

Bourdieu, Pierre, 19

Branscomb, Lewis, 78

Bryk, Anthony, 137–38, 203, 305

bureaucracy: entrenchment of, 34; and faculty social organization, 31–32, 74, 91–92; historical perspective, 16, 19; and organizational control, 91–94, 105–7, 109*n*2; and power relations in education, 56–57; and service to parents as educational clients, 98

Burt, Ronald, 31, 45, 221

Calvert, Monte, 62

career, teaching as: commitment to, 64–65, 72, 74–75, 86–87; mobility issue, 63, 71*n*3, 76, 83–84, 87–88

career planning as school mission focus, 137

Catholic schools and transition programs, 292, **293, 295,** 296

certification of teachers, advanced, 82–83. *See also* credentialing for teachers

Chabbot, Colette, 19

Chicago public school system, community-based reform program, 301–19

Chicago School Reform Act (1995), 302, 307

child care, teaching as, 72

Chiu, Ming Ming, 152

choice public schools and transition programs, 286, **293,** 294, **295**

civic participation, schools as training source for, 24, 27, 131–32, 133

civil engineering, development of profession, 62–63

class, socioeconomic. *See* socioeconomic status (SES)

classroom environment: academic and social status in, 157–58; and curricular experience for students, 183, **190,** 193; and microsociology of education, 2–3; normative culture of, 142; policymakers' neglect of, 307; reform challenges for instruction, 312, 314; research neglect of, 59–60, 129–30. *See also* participation, student

closed vs. open organizational systems, 37–41, 42, 44, 46–47*n*1, 201

cognitive effects of normative culture for students, 140–44, 145–46

cognitive frameworks and institutional theory, 39, 47*n*4

Cohen, Elizabeth G., 152

Coleman, James, 16, 100, 101, 135, 141, 148, 303–4

collaboration among teachers. *See* collegial environment

colleague interactions. *See* collegial environment

collective actors and substantialist conceptions, 44

collective bargaining and teachers, 77, 84

colleges, changes in entrance criteria, 283

collegial environment: and collective social power, 28–29, 30; and credentialing reforms, 83; inner city school challenges in, 308; limitations on teachers', 29, 32, 55, 61, 69; and professional development of teachers,

30–31, 111–26; work effects of, 20. *See also* subgroups

Collins, Randall, 19, 282

commitment to teaching as career, 64–65, 72, 74–75, 86–87

communities: community collaborative reform program, 301–19; functional community in education, 101; and microsociological approach, 25; organizational populations as, 40; professionalization of school staff, 5–6, 30–31, 111–26, 249, 250

community college as goal for school mission, 137

compensatory models of organizational change, 248

comprehensive vs. academic high school cultures, 133

conscription vs. recruitment of students, 286, 294

content standards in school reform models, 252, **256, 263,** 264. *See also* curricula

content vs. form of classroom discourse, 149

contingency theory, 38, 44

control, organizational: behavioral vs. structural focus, 42; and bureaucracy, 91–94, 105–7, 109*n*2; and faculty social organization, 30–31; and normative culture, 130; and promotion of collegial relations, 118, 123; state and local powers, 253, 254, 267, 301–19; and teachers' dependence on student goodwill, 17; through professional faculty community, 30–31, 112–14. *See also* coupling, organizational; public control over education

coordination approach to school transition, 287–88, **289,** 290–91, 294, **295,** 296–98

copier repair technicians, 54–56

counselors, school, school transition role, 287, 288, 290–91

coupling, organizational: data and methods, 254–58; internal coupling of reforms, 262, **263,** 264–65, **266,** 267; introduction, 244–46; national reform vs. state policies, 261–62; policy issue summary, 267–69; professional standards effects, 259, **260,** 261; regulatory vs. process organizational models, 246–48; research issues, 254; standards- vs. accountability-based reforms, 249–54. *See also* loose coupling perspective

course requirements in accountability reforms, **256**. *See also* curricula

Cousin, Victor, 71*n*4

credentialing for teachers, 23, 75–76, 81–83, 88, 89

cross-curricular position variation in student experience, 179–81

cross-national comparisons, 17, 23–25, 227–41

cultural factors in global diffusion of education, 23

cumulative skill acquisition, teaching vs. engineering, 63

curricula: and accountability-based reforms, 252; in community-based school reform initiative, 310–11; course placement, 278–79, 287, 299, 311; ease of reforms in, 267; and local variation in global diffusion of education, 23, 24–25; in microsociological approach, 26; and occupational opportunity differentiation, 271–72; and school transition coordination, 287; socialization, 100; socialized differentiation in, 17, 26, 230, 271–72; and standards-based reforms, 249–51. *See also* math and science subjects

cybernetic model of control, 42

Cyert, Richard, 38

Czarniawska, Barbara, 45

D. L. Vernon High School, Chicago, 12, 302–19

Darling-Hammond, Linda, 75, 81

data and methods: case study value for educational research, 22; community-based school reform initiative, 305–6; curricula and instructional effects, 181–84, 197–99*n*2–18; equity and achievement study, 272–77, **281–82**; math-science gender gap study, 230–32, 234–35, 236–37, 240–41, 241–43*n*1–11; and nonrandom shock response research, 35; organizational coupling and reform, 254–58; school transition study, 288–89, 292, 293–94, 300*n*1; study design proposal, 32–35; subgroup analysis, 203–4, 207–8, 213–15, 222–23*n*5–14; task and social participation study, 153–60, 172*n*1–4, 172–73*n*7–12

decentralized governance: and community-based school reform initiative, 302, 308; and functions of bureaucracy, 106; for schools, 84, 85, 254. *See also* state and local governments

decisionmaking and organizational change, 42

Del Vista High School, 137

demographic factors: adjustment to student population changes, 114; and curricular experience for students, 183; and inner city school failures, 306; and normative culture changes, 136; and student experience of instruction, 188, **189–90**; of teaching, 86–88

density of social networks, 159, 167, 169–70, 208, **209**

Devine, John, 138

Dewey, John, 100

diffuse status characteristics and student participation, 161–62, **163**, 164, **165**, 166

diffusion of education and globalization, 18–25, 21, 22–25

DiMaggio, Paul, 38

dimensional vs. interdimensional aspects of task-social participation, 151–53, 168, 169

disadvantaged communities. *See* socioeconomic status (SES)

discipline, student, research neglect of, 102–3

diversity of teaching environment and practice, 55

division of labor: and limitations on collegiality among teachers, 29, 32; sexual, 228–29; theoretical considerations, 41

domination, social. *See* status, student; status of teaching

Dornbusch, Sanford, 304

Dreeben, Robert, 17, 34, 201

drop outs and reform stratification effects, 279

dual captivity of teachers and students, 96

Duncan, Otis Dudley, 41, 42–43

Durkheim, Émile, 15, 100, 102, 130, 131–32

dynamic vs. static approach, 21, 22, 43–46, 114, 246–51. *See also* relational approach

ecological approach, 3, 37–46, 46–47*n*1, 177

economic factors: and future teacher populations, 88; and gender stratification, 229, 231, 232–34, 235, **236**, 237, **238**; poverty levels and curricular experience for students, 192. *See also* socioeconomic status (SES)

economic-production model of organization, 101

Economy and Society (Weber), 15–16

ecosystems approach, 3, 37–46, 46–47*n*1, 177

education, sociology of, overview of themes, 1–12

elementary schools and faculty social organization, 29

elites, power: and cross-national variations in educational focus, 24–25; curricular concerns of, 23; and emergence of educational institutions, 17; and global diffusion of education, 22–23; influence on formal school organizations, 34–35; and socialization power of education, 21–22

Emery, Fred, 38

Emirbayer, Mustafa, 21, 43

emotional life of students, 140–44, 145–46, 149. *See also* psychological factors

engagement with curriculum, student, 184, **189**, 194, 195

engineering vs. other professions, 61–67, 71*n*3

enrollment levels as change factor, 36*n*5, 286

entities vs. processes approach, 21, 22, 43–46

environmental factors: and accountability-based reforms, 301–2, 316; and catalysts for school cultural changes, 134,

Index

environmental factors (*cont.*)
136; challenges of teaching
environment, 55, 69–70,
100–104; ecosystems ap-
proach to organizations, 3,
37–46, 46–47*n*1, 177; enrollment levels, 36*n*5, 286; and
inner city school reform
challenges, 307–8; and pay
for teachers, 85–86; and
power elites' education
agendas, 21–22; and school
transition issues, 286–87. *See
also* academic environment;
classroom environment; collegial environment; demo-
graphic factors; urban school
systems
environmental selection, 23, 28
Epstein, Joyce, 288
equality of opportunity. *See* equity, social-educational
equity, social-educational: and
achievement levels, 270–83;
development of policy concern, 16, 26; and gender gap
in math and science, 227–41;
and social capital role in
inequality, 303, 304; and
social stratification, 23;
and standards-based re-
forms, 249; and student-
centered instruction, 175;
and teacher career development, 83
ethic of community involvement in schools, 312, 313. *See
also* moral behavior
evolutionary perspective on organizational change, 40
expertise- vs. seniority-based
faculty social organization,
31–32, 76
exploitation vs. exploration of
accepted teaching methods,
28, 31–32
external vs. internal organizational environments, 40–41
extracurricular activities, 133,
139, 172*n*6
extrinsic vs. intrinsic rewards
of teaching, 77, 97–98. *See
also* pay for teachers

faculty social organization. *See*
teaching and teachers
family and school socialization
responsibilities, 102
federal-level educational reforms, 249–52, 253–54,

261–62, 270–83. *See also* government
feeder middle schools and high
school recruitment, 286
Feistritzer, Emily, 87
fertility rates and economic development, 232
financial resources of schools.
See resources, schooling
Finley, Merrilee, 178–79
fixed attendance zones and
transition issues, 286–87
Fligstein, Neil, 45
formal vs. informal social organization: and diffusion of
technology information,
206–8, **209**, 210, **211**, 212–13;
dimensional cross-over of
participation in, 151–52; and
microsociological approach,
26; and nature of school institutions, 16; oppositional
relationship, 148; research directions for, 34–35, 195; and
teaching, 20, 92; unidirectional porosity in classrooms,
171. *See also* participation,
student; subgroups
form vs. content of classroom
discourse, 149
Fox, Renée, 59
Frank, Kenneth, 202, 203, 205
Fred Newmann and Associ-
ates, 112
Freeman, John, 39, 40
Freidson, Eliot, 73–74
Friedkin, Noah, 202, 221
friendship networks, student,
150–51, 159, 167, 168,
169–70
functional community in education, 101
Furman, Gail, 143

Gamoran, Adam, 113, 114
"garbage can" decisionmaking,
16
Gardner, Burleigh, 108
gender issues: and experience
of instruction, 188; and itinerant nature of teaching careers, 72, 74–75; overview, 9;
and social status of professions, 62, 64; sociological factors in math-science gap,
227–41, 241–43*n*1–11; and
student task participation,
166; and teacher population
trends, 86–87
Giddens, Anthony, 44–45

globalization and diffusion of
institutions, 18–25
Good, Thomas L., 75
Goodson, Ivor, 74
Gouldner, Alvin, 141–42
government: federal-level educational reforms, 249, 252;
and gender stratification,
231, 232–33, 235, **236**, 239;
and limitations on decentralizing of school governance,
84; national reform vs. state
policies, 252, 253–54, 261–62,
268, 270–83; student achievement focus, 68; teacher competence reforms, 78; and
teacher training responsibility, 65. *See also* public control
over education; state and
local governments
grade level as definer of collegial relationships among
teachers, 208, 210, 216,
220–21
grades vs. test scores for
achievement analysis, 274
graduation requirements in accountability reforms, **256, 263**

habit patterns and student participation, 159–60
Hallinan, Maureen T., 20
Hannan, Michael T., 39, 40
Hargreaves, Andy, 74
Hawley, Amos, 39
Herbst, Jurgen, 71*n*4
hierarchical linear modeling
(HLM), 270, 275–76
hierarchies, theoretical considerations, 41, 93
high schools: community collaborative reforms in, 12,
302–19; and faculty social organization, 29; transition
programs, 284–99. *See also*
normative culture
HLM (hierarchical linear modeling), 270, 275–76
Hoffer, Thomas, 100, 101
Holland, Peter, 137–38
Holmes Group, 80
home and family domain, and
gender stratification, 231,
236, 237, **238**, 239
Hopson, Dan, 57
Hopwood v. University of Texas,
283
Hughes, Everett, 68
human capital, 101, 178–79
human relations and occupa-

tional competence analysis,
54, 58
human services occupations,
93, 95, 97. *See also* teaching
and teachers

inequality. *See* equity, social-educational
inertia, institutional, 272
influence vs. selection in collegial development, 121–24
informal social organizations.
See formal vs. informal social
organization
information transfer in school
transition, 287–88, 290–91,
294, **295**, 296–97
Ingersoll, Richard: on administrative structural influence on
teachers, 20, 29, 84; on credentialing in professions, 76;
on knowledge-based nature
of professions, 75; on loose
coupling perspective, 195; on
public view of teacher professionalization, 73; on salaries
for teachers, 86
institution, variations in definition of, 110n7
institutional theory, 16–18,
21–22, 38–39, 47n4, 109–10n3
institutions, schools as social, 5,
16–18
instructional practice: and
aligned assessments method,
251; and autonomy of teachers, 93, 112; challenges of
documenting, 57, 58–61,
65–66; exploitation of accepted teaching methods, 28,
31–32; and institutions as
creators of value, 30–31; lesson teaching in Japan, 69–70;
nebulous nature of, 63;
overview, 7–8; reform challenges, 312, 314; and student
participation, 158–59, 168;
and technology use by
teachers, 206. *See also* science
curriculum
instrumental communities, 40
INTASC (interstate teacher licensing consortium), 81–82
integration of students into
new schools, 288, **289,**
291–92, 294, **295,** 296–98
interaction models: loose coupling perspective, 201, 221;
and open system model,
46–47n1; symbolic interac-

tionism, 142–43; and teaching, 97; types of, 44. *See also*
subgroups
interdimensional vs. dimensional aspects of participation, 151–53, 168, 169
interest groups, lack of reform
connection with teaching, 68
intergenerational transmission
of gender stratification, 228,
229, 239
internal vs. external organizational environments, 40–41
international issues: cross-national comparisons, 17,
23–25, 227–41; globalization
and diffusion of institutions,
18–25
interpersonal systems, organizations as, 40. *See also* relational approach
interstate teacher licensing consortium (INTASC), 81–82
intrinsic vs. extrinsic rewards
of teaching, 77, 97–98. *See
also* pay for teachers
IRT (item response theory),
255, 258, 259
isolation of teachers: and competence measurement, 61;
and lack of career mobility,
76; from peers, 20, 28, 116–17;
and reliance on students for
support, 17; and self-training
environment, 67
item response theory (IRT),
255, 258, 259

Jensen, Michael, 45
Johnson, Cathryn, 149
Johnstone, Quinton, 57
Jones, Deborah, 229

Kasarda, John D., 37–46, 200
Kentucky, standards activism
in, 265
Kerckhoff, Alan, 272
KliqueFinder software, 203
"Knowledge and Teaching:
Foundations of the New Reform" (Shulman), 79
knowledge base, professional:
assumption of, 74; collegiality and shared vocabulary,
116; importance in professions, 62; vs. occupational
competence, 51–53; peda-
gogy as teaching's, 70, 73, 75;
reforms in teaching, 79–80,
112; setting of standards by,

81; teaching's lack of, 58, 65,
72–73

labor force participation and
gender stratification, 229,
231, 232–34
lateral differentiation in organizations, 29, 32, 41
Lawrence, Paul, 38
law vs. teaching, 56–58
leadership: community-based
school reform program, 314,
315–16; opportunities for
teacher, 79, 82–84; and
prospects for school cultural
change, 134
Lee, Valerie, 137–38
legal structures as basis for institutional theory, 39
Leloudis, James, 65–66
lesson teaching method in
Japan, 69–70
licensing of teachers, 76, 81–83.
See also credentialing for
teachers
local educational level: administrators' social role, 26; and
community-based reform
program, 301–19; curricular
variation at, 23, 24–25; formal organizational changes,
34–35; and globalization of
institutions, 18, 19–20, 22, 23;
and teacher professionalism,
6. *See also* microsociology of
education; state and local
governments
local school councils (LSCs) in
Chicago, 308, 309
loose coupling perspective: and
accountability reforms,
251–53; Bidwell-Kasarda
analysis contribution, 200;
critique of, 244–45, 268–69;
and interaction structuring
in schools, 201, 221; limitations for schooling analysis,
195; and organizational control measurement, 104–8,
110n5; overview, 16, 91–93,
108–9; and reform models,
258–61; and school transition
issues, 287; and technology
diffusion in schools, 212; theoretical context, 94–96; and
unusual organizational characteristics of schools, 96–99;
vs. weak structural relationships, 245–46; and work of
teachers definition, 100–104

Lorsch, Jay, 38
Lortie, Dan: academic bias of teachers, 59; dual captivity of teachers and students, 96; on isolation of teachers, 20, 28; on itinerant nature of teaching careers, 74; on knowledge-based nature of professions, 75; on pay and promotion of teachers, 77, 106; and personal orientation of teaching, 93; and school as faculty workplace, 17, 53; on social status of teaching, 72
loyalty to organizations and standardization of control, 106
LSCs (local school councils) in Chicago, 308, 309

Mac Iver, Douglas, 288
macro theories of organizational structure, 42–43
magnet schools and transition programs, 11–12, 286, 289–90, 292, 294, 297
mandatory nature of school attendance, 96
Mann, Horace, 64
Maple Wood High School, 137
March, James, 16, 28, 38, 43–44
Marrett, Cora, 114
Marxist interactional models, 44
Maryland, standards activism in, 265
Maslow, Abraham, 143
material resource environment. See resources, schooling
math and science subjects: and faculty professional community, 114–23; gender stratification in, 229–41, 241–43n1–11; policy difficulties in reforms of, 264; state reforms and equity issues, 277–79. See also science curriculum
McFarland, Daniel, 28, 202
McWalters, Peter, 83
Mead, George Herbert, 160
mechanical engineering, development as profession, 61–62
Meckling, William, 45
Meriwether Lewis High School, 135
methodology, research. See data and methods
Metzger, Walter, 72
Meyer, John, 18, 19, 35, 38, 95, 104, 201

MGCA (multigroup confirmatory factor analysis), 181
MGSEM (multigroup structural equation model), 181
microsociology of education: overview of, 2–3, 6–9; and professional staff community in school, 5–6, 111–26; research issues, 25–35. See also curricula; formal vs. informal social organization; normative culture
midcareer teacher entrants, 87–88
middle, men and women in organizational, 107–8
Middle Brook High School, 137
middle schools, transition programs to high schools, 284–99
missions of schools and normative culture, 132–33
Mitroff, Ian, 46–47n1
mobility, career, 63, 71n3, 76, 83–84, 87–88
moral behavior: importance to public, 103; and normative school culture, 130–32, 133, 134–36, 138; school's role in passing on, 100
motivations of students and experience of instruction, 188, **189**
motivations of teachers, altruistic nature of, 77, 97–98
multicultural schools, advantages for student attitudes, 145
multigroup confirmatory factor analysis (MGCA), 181
multigroup structural equation model (MGSEM), 181

National Board for Professional Teaching Standards, 82–83, 84–85, 89
National Commission on Teaching and America's Future, 80
National Council for Accreditation of Teacher Education (NCATE), 81
National Education Association (NEA), 66, 67–68
national reform vs. state policies, 252, 253–54, 261–62, 268, 270–83
A Nation at Risk, 73, 78, 251–52
A Nation Prepared: Teachers for the Twenty-first Century, 78–79

NCATE (National Council for Accreditation of Teacher Education), 81
NCLB (No Child Left Behind) Act (2001), 270–71
NEA (National Education Association), 66, 67–68
Nelson, Richard, 40
neo-institutional theories of organizational form, 16, 17–18, 21
networking approach to organizations, 6, 45. See also social networks
nexus of contracts model, 45
No Child Left Behind (NCLB) Act (2001), 270–71
non-academic activities, 133, 139, 172n6
nonrandom shocks to institutions, importance of research on, 34–35
nonroutine changes in school structure, 28, 34–35
normal school training, 64–65
normative basis for institutional theories, 39
normative culture: dimensions and variations in, 130–40; introduction, 129–30; and organizational control, 105; overview, 6–7, 145–46; psychological effects on students, 140–44, 145–46; student responses to, 144–45. See also socialization
normative reference group theory, 141

occupational competence in teaching: concepts, 53–54; introduction, 51–53; overview, 3–4; and practice of teaching, 58–61, 71n4; and professionalism, 67–70, 70–71n1; and reform efforts, 85; teaching vs. other occupations, 54–58, 61–67, 71n3; and training reforms, 80
occupational structure and diffusion of education, 23–24
Ogawa, Rodney, 84
Olsen, Johan, 16
open system approach: vs. closed organizational models, 37–41, 42, 44, 46–47n1, 201; and diffusion of technology, 204
operators (workers) vs. regulators (managers), 42

Opportunity to Learn (OTL) paradigm, 20, 176–77
organizational control. *See* control, organizational
The Organization and Its Ecosystems: A Theory of Structuring in Organizations (Bidwell), 37
organizing vs. organization, 45
orientation programs for transitioning students, 291, 292
Orr, Julian, 54
OTL (Opportunity to Learn) paradigm, 20, 176–77
Ouchi, William, 95
outcomes, student, need for expansion of measured, 26–27. *See also* achievement, academic; socialization

parenting, school socialization as, 101
parents: as clients of educational services, 98; education level and student experience of instruction, 188, 192; as local influences on school social context, 26; occupational status and student participation levels, 166
Parsons, Talcott, 39, 51
participation, student, microsociological approach, 27. *See also* normative culture; science curriculum; subgroups; task and social participation
pay for teachers, 72, 76–77, 85–86, 88, 90, 106
pedagogy: historical lack of teacher training in, 71n4; as knowledge base for teaching, 70, 73, 75; need for student-instructional fit, 177; and reform of teaching, 79–80. *See also* instructional practice
peer relationships: students, 141, 150–51, 159, 167, 168, 169–70, 171; teachers, 83–84, 89. *See also* collegial environment; social networks
performance standards, 81, 250–51, **256, 263,** 264. *See also* occupational competence in teaching
Perrow, Charles, 38, 105
personal loyalty form of organizational control, 105
personal vs. hierarchical orientation of teaching, 93
physical attractiveness and stu-

dent status-participation, 166, 170, 172n5
placement, course, 278–79, 287, 299, 311
play vs. work forms of conduct. *See* task and social participation
POET (population, organization, environment, technology) framework, 42
policy issues: and accountability vs. standards-based reforms, **260, 263;** engagement of faculty in development, 32; and equity issues, 16, 26, 231, 239–40; and microsociological approach, 25, 26; neglect of classroom environment, 307; and open systems model, 201; and organizational control of teaching, 104–5; and organizational coupling, 267–69; and social psychological processes, 220; and student experience of instruction, 194–96; and student participation study, 171. *See also* reforms, educational
political context: and aligned assessments, 265; and authority-responsibility for teacher training, 65; for Chicago's decentralized governance system, 308; and climate of classrooms, 150–51, 158; and community engagement models, 317; elites' influence on formal school organizations, 34–35; historical perspective, 15–16; and lack of consensus on social outcomes of education, 97; and professionalization of teaching, 74; and reform effects on social equity, 282–83; and social context of schooling, 15–18; and social learning goals, 103; for standards-based reforms, 250. *See also* elites, power
political interactional models, 44
Pondy, Louis, 46–47n1
populations: ecological theory focus on, 40, 42; students, 58–59, 114; teacher trends, 86–89
poverty. *See* socioeconomic status (SES)
Powell, Walter, 38
power relations: and authority

vs. responsibility for teachers, 108; and bureaucracy, 56–57; and collegial collective influence, 28–29, 30; and student socialization, 21–22, 28; in student social organization, 33–34; subduing of school's power, 221; and violation of regulations, 107. *See also* control, organizational; elites, power
practices of teaching. *See* instructional practice
preparation of teachers. *See* training, teacher
Pressman, Jeffrey, 244
principals: influence on school culture, 134; influence over teachers, 36n6; as key leaders in school reform, 314, 315–16; school transition role, 288, 290, 291
private schools: enrollment uncertainties for, 286; and history of schooling, 63–64; moral instruction emphasis in, 134, 135–36; and normative school culture, 137–38, 139; and school transition challenges, 11, 289–90, 292, **293, 294, 295,** 296, 297–98
private vs. public spheres, gender stratification in, 228
processes approach, 21, 22, 43–46, 246–51
professionalism: and accountability reforms, **257;** authority issues for teachers, 84, 104, 108; and curricular experience for students, 181–82, **190,** 192; development of, 5–6; lack of common criteria for, 73–74; and standards-based reforms, 249, 250, 251, 259, **260,** 261; teaching's lack of legitimacy, 4–5, 17, 20–21. *See also* collegial environment; occupational competence in teaching; status of teaching
psychological factors: normative culture effects on students, 140–44, 145–46; and school transition programs, 284, 285, 288, **289,** 291–92; social psychological processes focus, 201–3, 220; and student participation, 149. *See also* relational approach; socialization

public control over education: and anomalous nature of school organization, 96; and board certification controversy, 82–83; and occupational competence measurement, 58; and pay limitations for teachers, 72, 88, 90; and public service mentality of teachers, 97–98; reforms oversight, 73; and social status of teachers, 56, 64, 67–68, 70, 76–77; and work practice assessments, 66. *See also* government

public schools: community-based reform program, 301–19; and decline of private schools, 63–64; and school transition issues, 11, 286, **293**, 294, **295**, 297

public vs. private spheres, gender stratification in, 228

quality of teachers, declining trend in, 90

Quiroz, Pamela, 202

Ramirez, Francisco, 19

rationalized bureaucracy, 92–93, 94, 105–7, 109n2

Ravitch, Diane, 280

reconstitution program in Chicago schools, 302, 305, 314, 315–16, 318

recruitment for high schools, 286–87, 289–90, 291, 294, **295**

reforms, educational: community-based, 301–19; equity and achievement issues, 270–83; gender gap in math and science, 227–41; and importance of competence, 68; and loose-coupling perspective, 95–96; and professionalization efforts, 78–86; public oversight of, 73; and social learning goals, 103; theoretical vs. practical bases for, 60; transition programs, 284–99. *See also* coupling, organizational

regulation of organizations: challenges of applying, 98–99; and constraints on teachers, 20, 29; ineffectiveness of, 78; institutional resistance to change from, 34; and loyalty, 106; and models of organizational control,

246–48, 251–53; as source of centralized power, 107

regulators (managers) vs. operators (workers), 42

relational approach: and ecological theory, 41; importance of, 32; and microsociological approach, 26; overview, 3; and processes approach, 21, 22, 43–46, 246–51; and social context of schooling, 16–17; and trust issue for local school reform, 303–5, 312–14. *See also* collegial environment; formal vs. informal social organization

relationships, student-teacher: and autonomy of teachers, 28–29, 132, 144–45; inner city school challenges, 305, 308, 313–14, 316; and microsociological approach, 25; overview, 7–8; research neglect of, 20; and student resistance, 27, 28–32; teacher expectations for students, 272. *See also* formal vs. informal social organization; science curriculum

religious belief systems and normative culture of private schools, 137–38

research issues: and anomaly of school organization, 92; collegiality analysis for SAMM, 115, 117–18, 124–26; costs of specialization, 18–21; ecological approach, 3, 37–46, 46–47n1, 177; formal vs. informal social organization, 34–35, 195; for gender stratification in learning, 239; historical perspective, 15–18; instructional practices, 57, 59–60, 75, 177, 180–81; interaction structuring in schools, 201–4; microsociology of education, 25–35; neglect of classroom environment, 59–60, 129–30; neglect of student discipline issue, 102–3; on nonrandom shocks to institutions, 34–35; organizational coupling, 254; overview, 2–3; and pedagogical development, 79–80; student focus, 33–34, 66, 195–96; theory of institutionalization, 21–32. *See also* data and methods

resistance, student, 27, 28–32, 144–45

resource-dependence interaction models, 44

resources, schooling: and curricular experience for students, 182–83; in ecological theory, 39, 47n4; inner city school reform challenges, 310, 314, 315; resource allocation and teacher change, 112; social inequality of, 303

responsibility vs. authority problem for teachers, 108

reward structures and normative culture, 131, 139, 142

Ridgeway, Cecilia, 149

Ritti, Richard, 56

Rowan, Brian, 17, 29, 35

rules systems as basis for institutional theory, 39

rural school systems and transition issues, 292, **293**, **295**, 296, 297, 298

St. Aloysius High School, 135–36

salaries, teacher. *See* pay for teachers

SAMM (Science and Mathematics Modeling), 114–23

Sassen, Saskia, 18, 19, 20

SBM (school-based management), 84, 85

Schneider, Barbara, 136–37, 305

Schoenherr, Richard, 142

school-based governance schemes, 84, 85

school-based management (SBM), 84, 85

school choice movement, 286

school-site councils, 84

Schoolteacher (Lortie), 53

Science and Mathematics Modeling (SAMM), 114–23

science curriculum: analytical strategy for, 180–81; data and methods, 181–84, 197–99n2–18; intraorganizational contexts, 176–79; introduction, 175–76; policy issues, 194–96; student experience results, 185, **186–87**, 188, **189–91**, 192–93; student subject engagement, 194

scientific knowledge and professions, 53, 69

Scott, W. Richard, 95, 104

Secada, Walter, 114

security, school, 311
selection vs. adaptation processes, 40
selection vs. influence in collegial development, 121–24
self-action models, 43–44
Selznick, Philip, 22, 52
seniority-based faculty system, 31–32, 76
serial career trend and future teacher cohorts, 87
shared-agentic instruction, 185, **186–87, 189–91,** 192–93, 194
shortage of teachers and shifts in teacher population, 88
Shulman, Lee, 79
Silverman, David, 45
Simon, Herbert, 38, 43–44
size of schools and curricular experience for students, 181, 192
Smigel, Erwin, 57
social capital, 28–29, 101, 111–26, 302–4
social cognitive perspective and normative culture effects, 143
social context of schooling: and globalization of education, 18–20; and need for relational approach, 16–17; overview of themes, 1–12; and political perspective, 15–18. *See also* microsociology of education; research issues; teaching and teachers
socialization: and civic participation training, 24, 27, 131–32, 133; classroom as source for, 15; and defining of teachers' work, 100–104; importance to public, 103; overview, 2; as responsibility of schools, 96–97; and social power relations, 21–22, 28. *See also* moral behavior; normative culture
social networks: density of, 159, 167, 169–70, 208, **209;** and faculty social organization, 30–32; importance of studying school, 201, 219–20; and student family-neighborhood influences, 36*n*7; student friendships, 150–51, 159, 167, 168, 169–70; theoretical perspective, 6, 45. *See also* collegial environment; formal vs. informal social organization

social participation. *See* task and social participation
social psychological processes, 201–3, 220. *See also* psychological factors
social vs. academic learning, 100–104, 133–34. *See also* task and social participation
society as client of educational services, 96
socioeconomic status (SES): equity and achievement reforms, 274, 278, 280; inner-city community-based program, 301–19; and school transition issues, 286, 299; and student participation levels, 166. *See also* stratification, social
The Sociology of Teaching (Waller), 16
sociotechnical theory, 38
Sørenson, Aage, 20, 176
specialization in sociological research, costs of, 18–21
specialized knowledge base, professional. *See* knowledge base, professional
Spilerman, Seymour, 141
standards-based reforms: elements and policies summary, **256;** and organizational control, 249–51, 252, 268; overview, 9–10; policy alignment, **260;** policy difficulty levels, **263;** professional standards focus, 259, 261; and reform effects on equity and achievement, 280–83; state vs. national focus, 262, 264; student focus of, 88–89
Stanton-Salazar, Ricardo, 304
state and local governments: and adoption of educational reforms, 254, 259, 261–62, 264–65, **266,** 267, 268, 270–83; and inconsistent credentialing of teachers, 76, 81–82; organizational control by, 253, 254, 267, 301–19
static vs. dynamic approach, 21, 22, 43–46, 114, 246–51. *See also* relational approach
status, student: and adolescent subculture influence, 141; diffuse vs. specific school-classroom, 157, 173*n*13–14; and participation outcomes, 152–55, 157–58, 161–67, 170–71, 172*n*5; and school

transitions, 285. *See also* socioeconomic status (SES)
status characteristics theory, 149, 152, 171, 174*n*16
status of teaching: and changes in teacher population, 86–89; historical origins of, 73–77; introduction, 72–73; vs. other occupations, 62, 64; overview, 3–5; and professionalization, 89–90; and public control over education, 56, 64, 67–68, 70, 76–77; recent efforts to raise, 78–86
Stevenson, David, 136–37
Stinchcombe, Arthur, 21, 67, 148
stratification, social: and access to schools, 23–24; and curricular differentiation, 271–72; education's role in, 19–20, 101; gender, 229–41, 241–43*n*1–11; and reform effects on equity and achievement, 278–80; vs. social psychology approach to schools, 201–2; and student outcomes, 176; and tracking by ability, 101, 102
structural analysis approach: and collegial ties in schools, 213–19; and controls in organizations, 105–7, 112, 118, 123; and ecosystems perspective, 41–43; for instructional practice, 176, 178–79, 185, 195, 196; loose coupling vs. weak structural relationships, 245–46; and technology use by teachers, 206
Structuring in Organizations: Ecosystem Theory Evaluated (Bidwell and Kasarda), 37
student-centered instruction, 158–59, 168, 175, 178, 183–94
students: as clients of educational system, 96; family-neighborhood influences, 36*n*7; and mandatory obligation of learning, 97; population issues, 58–59, 114; reform focus on, 88–89; relating of learning to real life, 309, 310–11; research focus on, 33–34, 66, 195–96; resistance behavior, 27, 28–32, 144–45; school social organization, 16–27, 33–34; as social support for isolated teachers, 17, 28–29, 30; teaching for understanding focus, 113, 115–16;

students (*cont.*)
  transition programs for
  new high school, 11–12, 284–
  99. *See also* formal vs. informal social organization;
  relationships, student-
  teacher; socialization; status,
  student
subgroups: cohesiveness of,
  206–7, 212–13; data and
  methods, 203–4, 207–8,
  213–15, 222–23n5–14; interaction structuring in schools,
  201–4, 219–22, 222n2; introduction, 200; need for research on, 33–34; and technological innovations, 8–9,
  204–19
subject matter, instructional.
  See curricula
substantialist conceptions,
  43–44, 46
suburban school systems and
  school transition issues, 286,
  292, **293, 295,** 296, 297
Summer Institute program at
  Vernon High School, 311–12,
  314
summer student integration
  programs, 291, 297
Sumner, William Graham,
  21–22
Sykes, Gary, 72, 78
symbolic expression by students, 132
symbolic interactionism,
  142–43

task and social participation:
  contexts for, 150–52; data and
  methods, 153–60, 172n1–4,
  172–73n7–12; introduction,
  147–48; overview, 27; qualities of task vs. social, 148–49;
  results of study on task vs.
  social, 156–71; and social status, 152–53
Task Force on Teaching as a
  Profession, 78–79
teacher-centered instruction, 8,
  158–59, 168, 178, 183–94
teaching and teachers: and accountability vs. standards-
  based reforms, 251, 252;
  building of social capital for,
  111–26; and curricular experience for students, 178–79,
  190–91, 193; differing expectations for students, 272; historical perspective, 16–17;

and normative school cul-
  ture, 134–35, 136, 140, 142,
  144; overview of issues, 3–6;
  population shifts, 36n5; and
  reconstitution program in
  Chicago schools, 302; research approach to, 20–21;
  resistance to reform, 312;
  school transition role,
  287–88, 291–92; socializing
  influences on, 201; social organization of, 27–32; and
  technology information diffusion, 205–8, **209,** 210, **211,**
  212–13. *See also* autonomy;
  professionalism; relationships, student-teacher
teaching for understanding approach, 113–23
technicians and teachers as
  professionals, 54–56
technology, 8–9, 176–77, 222n1.
  See also subgroups
testing. *See* assessments
Texas, state university entrance
  criterion, 283
theoretical considerations. *See*
  research issues
Thompson, James, 38
tracking by ability: and normative culture, 142; and
  school social organization,
  17; and school transition issues, 287; and social stratification, 101, 102; and student
  classroom participation,
  172n6; and student-instructional fit, 177
training, teacher: credentialing
  issues, 23, 75–76, 81–83, 88,
  89; vs. engineering, 62; historical neglect of, 60–61, 64,
  72; nebulous nature of, 66;
  reform efforts, 79, 80–81
transaction cost interaction
  models, 44
transition programs for high
  school, 11–12, 284–99
trust, relational, 303–5, 312–14
turnover: student, 284–99;
  teacher, 74–75

Uekawa, Kazuaki, 202
understanding, teaching for,
  113–23
union approach to teaching
  profession, 21, 67–68, 70,
  76–77, 83
universities, changes in entrance criteria, 283

University of Texas, Hopwood v.,
  283
urban school systems: community-based reform program,
  301–19; and school transition
  issues, 286, 292–93, **293, 295,**
  296, 297, 298
Urbanski, Adam, 83
Useem, Elizabeth, 287

Vallas, Paul, 310
valorization of institutions, 22,
  24
value, institutions as creators
  of, 22, 24–25, 30–31, 39
Vernon High School Collaborative, 12, 302, 306–19
vertical differentiation in organizations, 41, 93
violence as normative school
  culture, 138
vocational-technical schools
  and transition programs, **293,**
  294, **295,** 297

Waller, Willard, 16, 29, 66, 97,
  148
weak structural relationships
  vs. loose coupling, 245–46
Weber, Max, 15–16, 25, 43, 94,
  105, 106
Weick, Karl, 16, 45, 244–45
White, Paula A., 84
Whyte, William Foote, 108
Wildavsky, Aaron, 244
Williamson, Oliver, 38
Winter, Sidney, 40
women: and current vs. future
  trends in teacher population,
  86–87; and gender gap in
  math and science, 227–41;
  and ideal of teaching as domestic calling, 64; and itinerant nature of teaching careers, 72, 74–75. *See also*
  gender issues
Woodward, Joan, 38
work activity assessments:
  challenges in teaching environment, 69–70, 100–104; collegiality as space to display
  work practices, 116–17;
  teaching's lack of, 77; teaching vs. engineering, 63, 66;
  and training reforms, 80

Yair, Gad, 198n11
Yasumoto, Jeffrey, 202, 203

Zhao, Yong, 205